Quantitative Decision Aiding Techniques
for
Research and Development Management

Quantitative Decision Aiding Techniques
for
Research and Development Management

Edited by

MARVIN J. CETRON
HAROLD DAVIDSON
ALBERT H. RUBENSTEIN

GORDON AND BREACH

New York   London   Paris

Contents

Preface

Why This Book?

The papers reprinted herein were all presented at the Military Operations Research Society (MORS) Working Group on Research Management. They were presented at three sessions, the first of which was held at Fort Bragg, N.C., October 19-21, 1966; the second at the Navy Post Graduate School, Monterey, Calif., December 1968; and the third at the Navy Electronics Laboratory Center, San Diego, Calif., in November 1969. These meetings of the Working Group, which were concerned primarily with quantitative approaches to R&D planning and management relevance of research, were thought to have such wide interest that we have taken the opportunity, with the approval of MORS and of the IEEE (since the great bulk of these papers were first published in the March 1967 and the November 1969 issues of the IEEE Transactions on Engineering Management) of presenting a selected group of the un-classified papers in this volume. We felt, since the IEEE Transactions were out of print and were not originally readily available to the general community, that it would be appropriate to collect these papers and bring together the latest R&D management thinking in the military-industrial complex for possible utiliza-tion in other sections of the economy.

Purpose and Objectives of the Working Group on Research Management

A major objective of MORS is to foster the develop-ment and application of operations research and sys-tems analysis to military problems by providing a forum for the survey and interchange of information, primarily of a classified nature, on all aspects of mili-tary operations research. The Working Group on Re-search Management was established to encompass the areas of research approaches, concepts, techniques, and problems in R&D management. Its guiding question is: 'How may operations research lead to improved R&D management?'

Objectives of the Working Group are to define R&D management requirements, to illustrate ways in which operations research is contributing to the meeting of such requirements, and to suggest high-priority re-search and development opportunities in this field.

This Working Group was also concerned with means by which military requirements are utilized by R&D managers to select, budget for, guide, and evaluate R&D programs. The group was concerned also with the process by which the results of R&D programs are applied to military operations. Their interest was in the systems of interaction among the producers and users of military R&D, and the overall theme of the sessions was R&D Management in a Military Environ-ment.

Working Group meetings during October 1966 were held over a three-day period; the general chairman was M. J. Cetron of Headquarters, Naval Material Command. The three working quarters were: I. Quan-titative Approaches to R&D Planning; II. Mission Rele-vance of Research; III. Research Needs in R&D Manage-ment. These were chaired by Louis Roepcke, Joseph Martino, and Edward Roberts, respectively.

Twelve papers were given at the sessions. However, due to security restrictions, only nine unclassified abstracts appear here.

The first paper by Cetron, Martino, and Roepcke sur-veys the quantitative techniques that are now being utilized and the criteria that are considered in these techniques.

The second paper, by Wells, discusses an approach to storing, tracking, and properly relating judgments con-cerning systems, and shows the impact of these judg-ments on the assessment and selection of system can-didates for development.

The third paper, by Roman and Johnson, presents a methodology for allocating resources among multiple R&D projects in a time continuum. This methodology can assist management in the planning of projects by simulating the capability of resources to perform the tasks required.

The fourth paper, by Dean and Hauser, is a report con-cerned with the development of mathematical models, computer programs, and data requirements to conduct development system planning in large R&D organiza-. tions. Dean also develops cost-effectiveness relation-ships in a manual presented for use in the training of planners.

In the fifth paper, Dean develops a mathematical model for use in measuring and evaluating the performance of a research laboratory in meeting the needs to develop items to satisfy stated operational requirements.

In the sixth paper, Smith presents the structure of a procedure for the development of long-range R&D planning which is particularly aimed at the logical, objective determination of the requirements imposed by the Navy mission on new ship procurement. This methodology, when completed and validated, will pro-vide a means for determining future requirements and a standardized format for Naval Ship System Formula-tion.

Cetron, in the seventh paper, describes one method (QUEST) of determining the relevance of research and exploratory development to missions and the develop-ment of guides for the allocation of dollars and man-power thereto.

The eighth paper, by Martino, discusses the thesis that a research activity can contribute much more to a mission-oriented organization than would be indicated by a simple count of military systems to which the research has contributed. In particular, it deals with the nature and type of activities of a mission-oriented research organization which are not hardware related, but which are still essential to the accomplishment of the military mission.

In the ninth paper, Clarke discusses how the Office of Research Analysis attempts to assist the Office of Aerospace Research in insuring that Air Force Re-search programs are relevant to future military missions and that systems planning agencies are aware of the operational implications of research results. Also described are current research efforts to expand, extend, and improve research analysis methodology.

The next nine abstracts represent papers presented at the Working Group on Research Management at the 22nd Military Operations Research Society (MORS) Symposium, late in 1968, held at the Naval Post-Graduate School, Monterey, Calif.

Like the 1966 sessions, Working Group meetings were held over a three-day period; the General Chairman was Harold Davidson of the Army Research Office. The three working sessions were 1) Coupling Research to Development, 2) Technological Forecasting and Planning, and 3) Resource Allocation. These were chaired by Albert Rubenstein, Bodo Bartocha, and Lewis Roepcke, respectively.

Nine papers were given at the 1968 sessions and they appear here. The first paper by Rubenstein and Douds describes the process concerned with the transmission and application of results at one stage of the process to other stages, including final utilization. Specifically, a number of behavioral aspects of the phenomena appear to be crucial. Among them are factors influencing the decision of a participant in the process to ask for and/or give information; factors facilitating or inhibiting communication between groups; and the characteristics and behaviors of the people occupying coupling, interface, or liaison roles.

The second paper by Bieber states that management is beginning to recognize that technology is primarily transferred by people, not by organization charts or formal reports. Optimum technology transfer or 'coupling' can therefore be aided 1) by putting researchers in close proximity to technologists with real problems to solve; 2) by motivating either the initiator or recipient of key relevant information to catalyze its transfer and innovation utilization; or 3) by setting up specific liaison groups to bridge the gap between invention in the laboratory and innovation in the marketplace.

The third paper by Schoman, Dick, and McKnight discusses a simple and logical method for using Navy exploratory development goals (EDG) and the Navy technological forecast (NTF) for the allocation of resources to technology to meet future requirements. First, the military worth of the various EDG to meeting Navy objectives is determined. Second, the technological utilization of the various technologies to the EDG is determined by systems design and scientific/engineering offices. The military worth and technology utilization values are then combined into an Index of Worth value indicating the worth of the various technologies to meeting Navy objectives. A mathematical model is suggested as a future refinement.

The fourth paper by Cetron and Dick explains some of the problems and pitfalls encountered in the planning and production of the NTF. These problems grow from the basic considerations facing an individual (or group of individuals) who must plan or prepare a forecast. This paper covers the areas of technology to be forecast, the forecast content, and the types of forecasts. Permeating these considerations are the concepts of utilization, goals, and functional structuring. The interrelationship of these items and how they were handled is discussed.

The fifth paper by Walker and Phillips presents some case studies from World War II through the Vietnamese War that illustrate the prevalence of the problem of allocating resources based on combat-effectiveness measurements. This covers the total system life from initial R&D to obsolescence. The basic rationale shown is that from a lack of minor detailed information, incorrect conclusions have been reached in operations analysis reports, leading to unnecessarily costly operations.

The sixth paper by Dean, Mantel, and Roepcke, discusses project/task cost distribution and budget forecasting. The primary purpose of this study is to determine the nature of Army research-project costs, the probability distributions, and the corresponding parameter values so that long-range budget forecasts and variances can be provided. The distribution and parameters of the research-project costs for the years 1963-1967 have been developed and are discussed.

The seventh paper by Cetron and Johnson on technological resource allocation describes many of the general resource-allocation approaches that are used in government and industry. The system-analysis approach, which focuses on military goals or corporate goals, is presented to interrelate technological forecasting and resource allocation. Methodology of assessing technology together with the important consideration in making technology assessments are covered from a theoretical standpoint, as well as relating them to real world problems. Emphasis is placed throughout the article on the intention of using quantitative techniques to yield information on which to base decisions.

The eighth paper by Dean and Roepcke discusses cost effectiveness in R&D laboratory resource allocation. Specifically, it describes a method of resource allocation to a multilaboratory, multitask research and exploratory development program. The basic elements of the underlying model are 1) tasks, projects, and laboratories, 2) contributing sciences and technologies, 3) criticality of such field to achieving organizational objectives, 4) relative values of objectives, and 5) costs of performing tasks. Structural models for interrelating these elements are developed in this paper.

The ninth paper by Nutt discusses the Air Force experiment in testing the resource-allocation model called Technology or Research Quantitative Utility Estimate (TORQUE). This model, which was developed by an interservice team for DOD, provides for a closer coupling between future desired military capabilities and laboratory efforts. Specifically, it addresses the area of exploratory development projects and tasks and attempts to provide a balanced allocation of resources within the laboratory. This paper gives the background of TORQUE, the methodology used, and some of the findings. A complete appraisal of TORQUE has not yet been made by the Air Force and, therefore, the final evaluation of the technique has not yet been determined.

The last three papers, abstracts of which follow, were presented at the 1969 meeting of the Working Group and are presented here to provide data from some of the latest papers on research and development managers.

The first of the 1969 papers by Harold Linstone, currently teaching part-time at the University of Southern

California and employed by Lockheed, examines the world environment of the 1970-85 period noting that the defense community, government and industry have entered a period of flux not encountered since World War II. As part of the background for his forecast, Linstone gives a 'traditional' look into the future including the roles of the superpowers, the challenging powers, and the 'poor' world. A 'view' look into the future is also provided with the effects of technology; over-population; and the socio-economic, ecological, and organizational imbalance of the world examined in detail. The author views as a challenge the 'new' kind of planning necessary and discusses the relationship between forecasting and planning with the caveat that any analysis of the future must take into full account the shortcomings of the present planning approach and the hurdles which impede rational creative planning.

Forward planning—by J. F. Langston of General Dynamics notes that events in the future can best be met by responding to a plan of action rather than by reacting to a situation as it develops. The author examines his company's Strategic Plan covering a ten-year period and using an environmental forecast, a technology forecast, departmental plans, and budget plans as major inputs. Resource allocation as a contributor to long range planning is also discussed. Since the planning cycle is an interative process, the author correctly points out that continued use is expected to point out the need for changes, particularly in the transition from intuitive planning to utilization of more analytical techniques for forecasting and resource allocation.

The paper by Hoshofsky discusses the coupling of science to technology and begins with a definition of coupling as a flow of information which serves to bring problems and goals into productive association with the potential of science and technology. The numerous elements of coupling are pointed out as are lessons from experienced knowledge about the adequacies and deficiencies of existing coupling processes as well as barriers to effective coupling. The importance of enlightened management in encouraging and enhancing coupling is clearly pointed out and coupling incentives, machinery, resources, visibility and accountability are examined. Several basic references are also offered.

MARVIN J. CETRON
HAROLD DAVIDSON
ALBERT H. RUBENSTEIN

The Selection of R&D Program Content—Survey of Quantitative Methods

MARVIN J. CETRON, JOSEPH MARTINO, SENIOR MEMBER, IEEE, AND LEWIS ROEPCKE

Abstract—This paper presents a summary of methods of evaluating and selecting R&D projects. Approximately thirty methods, which have appeared in scattered places in the literature, are described briefly, and a bibliography is provided for further information. The various methods are compared and contrasted with each other relative to a standard set of features which they may possess, to a standard set of characteristics relating to ease of use, and to scientific or technological area of applicability.

I. INTRODUCTION

THIS PAPER provides a summary of a number of known techniques for quantitative evaluation of R&D projects. Successful application of quantitative methods to problems such as inventories, queueing, transportation, and other problems requiring decisions on resource allocation or scheduling, has at least made it conceivable to raise the question of whether comparable quantitative evaluation methods could also be applied to research and development projects. The advent of the computer has made such applications appear feasible, where the R&D efforts are large in number. The desired outputs from such quantitative methods would be an evaluation of a prescribed selection of projects, or better yet, a procedure for scheduling projects or allocating resources among competing projects.

Interest in such quantitative methods, especially within the Department of Defense, has become quite high within the past few years. As a result of this interest, the authors have conducted a survey of methods, both completed and on-going, which have been devised in industry and in the government, and have evaluated those methods against a fixed set of factors. While the original purpose of this survey and evaluation was to form a basis for recommending a system for application within one of the military services, the results of the survey may well be of interest to others, and are therefore presented here.

Manuscript received January 11, 1967. This paper was presented at the 18th Military Operations Research Symposium (MORS), Fort Bragg, N. C., October 1966. The views expressed in this paper are those of the authors and do not necessarily represent those of the Department of Defense.
M. J. Cetron is with the Advanced Concepts Branch, HQ. Naval Material Command, Washington, D. C.
J. Martino is with the Office of Scientific Research, Office of Aerospace Research, Washington, D. C.
L. Roepcke is with the Directorate of Developments, U. S. Army Materiel Command, Washington, D. C.

II. FEATURES OF THE METHODS

The various methods uncovered in our survey took into account various items of information about the R&D projects to be evaluated, and provide various items of information as output from the evaluation. A total of 15 different features were found which could describe the items of input and output of the various methods. No single method possessed all the features. The various features are described in some detail below.

1) *Utility Measure:* Does the method take into account some measure of the utility or value of success of a particular R&D project? This measure may be share of a market, profitability, some measure of military worth, etc.

2) *Probability of Success:* Does the method explicitly take into account an estimate of the probability of success of each individual R&D project?

3) *Orthogonality of Criteria:* Are the criteria used by the method mutually exclusive (orthogonal), rather than being highly correlated or having a high degree of overlap?

4) *Sensitivity:* Has the sensitivity of the output to small changes in the input been checked? A high degree of sensitivity to small variations in input is undesirable, since the output then becomes unstable in the presence of minor perturbations in the input.

5) *Rejected Alternatives Retention:* When a project is rejected for funding, is it retained for later consideration in the event of a budget increase or other adjustment, rather than being rejected completely?

6) *Classification Structure:* Does the method provide a structural relationship between the R&D project and a hierarchy of higher-level goals of the organization?

7) *Time:* Does the method take into account scheduling requirements, or provide scheduling information as an output?

8) *Strategies:* Does the method permit the user to take into account several possible scenarios, world environments, market situations, etc.?

9) *System Cross Support:* Does the method give a system development credit for support which it provides to another system development?

10) *Technology Cross Support:* Does the method give a project for advancement of technology credit for support which it provides to the advancement of other technologies?

11) *Graphical Display:* Is the output amenable to presentation in some graphical form which gives the user a condensed picture of the evaluation of various projects?

12) *Flagging:* Does the method flag problem areas, to bring them to the attention of the responsible management?

13) *Optimization Criteria:* What criterion for optimization does the method use, and what constraints are considered? All methods used either a composite score from a number of factors, to obtain a ranking, or used some form of maximum (discounted) net value.

14) *Constraints:* Constraints considered by the methods were: budget, skills available, facilities available, competitor efforts, and raw materials available.

15) *Computerized:* Is the method implemented in a computer program, and is it a linear program or a dynamic program? Those marked as computerized are known to the authors to have been programmed for some machine. It should be noted that most of the techniques could be computerized if desired.

III. Ease of Use

Each method was evaluated according to several criteria bearing on ease of use. The criteria considered are described below.

1) *Data Requirements:* While in general the more data a method uses as input, the more information it provides as output, nevertheless, the ease of use is affected by the amount of data required. Two factors enter into the amount of data required: the level of organization at which data is obtained, i.e., individual work unit, subsystem, system, etc.; and the amount of data required on each effort on which data is gathered.

2) *Manual:* Is manual operation of the method possible or reasonable to consider?

3) *Computer Program:* If a computer is required, has the method been programmed for some computer?

4) *Running Time:* If the method has been programmed, what is the running time for one cycle of evaluation or allocation?

5) *Updating:* What is the ease of updating the system to take into account new information, whether the new information is developed periodically or new items come in on an unscheduled basis?

6) *Proficiency Level:* What level of proficiency is required of the operator (not the manager who is using the output)? Can it be handled by a clerk? Does it require a skilled technician? Does it require a degreed professional?

7) *Outside Help:* Is help or information required from persons outside the R&D organization, in evaluating goals set by others, environments not under control of the R&D organization, etc.?

IV. Area of Applicability

Few of the systems appeared to be applicable throughout the entire R&D spectrum. Some were more applicable to one portion of the spectrum than to others. The methods are rated as being applicable to research, to exploratory development, to advanced development, or to engineering development.

V. Description of Methods

Each method surveyed is described briefly below. The methods are identified with the name or names of the originators, unless some acronym or title has been used to designate the method. Methods 1 through 10 and their descriptions are from the Baker–Pound article "R&D Project Selection: Where We Stand," printed in IEEE Transactions on Engineering Management, vol. EM-11, no. 4, December 1964.

1) *Mottley–Newton, 1959:* "A decision theory approach. Project proposals are rated with respect to a number of evaluation criteria. An overall score is computed and used to rank the alternatives. Selection criteria are considered with respect to constraints including research budget, risk, and overall program balance."

2) *Gargiulo et al., 1961:* "A decision theory approach. Project proposals are rated with respect to a number of evaluation criteria. An overall score is computed and used to rank the alternatives. Constraints such as research budget, skills available, facilities available, and competitor efforts in the area are considered."

3) *Pound, 1964:* "A decision theory approach. Project proposals are rated with respect to a number of weighted selection objectives. An overall score is computed and used to rank the alternatives. The budget constraint is considered."

4) *Sobelman, 1958:* "An operations research approach. For each alternative project, estimates are made of average value per year, economic life, average development cost per year and development time. Selection is accomplished by maximizing discounted net value, perhaps subject to constraints."

5) *Freeman, 1960:* "An operations research approach. For each alternative project, an estimate is made of the probability distribution of net value. Selection is accomplished by maximizing expected discounted net value subject to constraints on the total budget, facilities, and personnel. A linear programming formulation is used."

6) *Asher, 1962:* "An operations research approach. For each alternative project, estimates are made of the discounted net value of the project and probability of success. Selection is accomplished by maximizing expected discounted net value subject to constraints on the man hours available and on the raw materials available. The optimal manpower allocation is indicated by the result. A linear programming formulation is used."

7) *Hess, 1962:* "An operations research approach. For each alternative project, estimates are made of the discounted gross value as of several points in time. Probabilities of success are also estimated. Selection is accomplished by maximizing expected discounted net value subject to a budget constraint for the first period. The optimal allocation to each project is indicated for each period. A dynamic programming formulation is used."

8) *Dean–Sengupto, 1962:* "An economic analysis and operations research approach. The optimal research budget is first determined. Then for each alternative project, estimates are made of the discounted net value and the probability of technical and commercial success. Selection is accomplished by maximizing expected discounted net value subject to a budget constraint. A linear programming formulation is suggested."

9) *Disman, 1962:* "An economic analysis approach. For each alternative project, an estimate is made of the discounted net value (not including R&D costs). This estimate, perhaps modified by a probability of technical and/or commercial success is considered to be the maximum expenditure justified. The ratio of the maximum expenditure justified to estimated project cost is an index of the desirability of the project."

10) *Cramer–Smith, 1964:* "An economic analysis and operations research approach. An application of portfolio selection and utility theory to the problem of research project selection. For each alternative project, estimates are made of net values and probabilities of occurrence. Utility curves are also obtained. Projects may be ranked on the basis of expected value or expected utility. Lack of project independence is also mentioned."

11) *Esch, "PATTERN," 1963:* Combination decision theory approach and operations research approach. Project PATTERN is a continuing, large-scale, corporate effort to assign quantitative, relative values to the importance of conducting R&D on the various technology deficiencies which now stand in the way of the achievement of the national security objectives for the decade from 1968 to 1978. The model considers national survival, threat force structure, capability, prestige, cost effectiveness, requirements, scientific implications, feasibility, effort, risk, capability improvement, and operational advantages. This technique is the first full-scale application of the heuristic "relevance tree" concept development in 1958 by H. Wells in his Ohio State University Master's thesis.

12) *Blum, 1963:* A mathematical treatment leading to a methodology of ranking R&D events in the project by their cost, risk, time, and value. The methodology sequences the efforts by a version of the DOD and NASA PERT-cost technique.

13) *Bakanas, 1964:* A model to aid in the selection of applied research and development tasks for inclusion in a long-range R&D program. The model consists of a structure relating the conceptional elements of the R&D program; formats for delineating the characteristics of the conceptional elements; mathematical relations between the expected program value and military priority, probability of task success, task cost, and program cost; and a rank-ordering procedure to select a program of maximum expected value. A computer program aids in formulating the R&D program.

14) *Dean, 1964:* An operations research approach. Mathematical models consider the relevant resource variables, noncontrollable variables, parameters, and constraints that are responsive to corporate goals and yield solutions for allocating technical resources to projects. The scoring model permits determination of important factors in a profitability model.

15) *Hill–Roepcke, 1964:* An operations research approach. A mathematical model considering the military value of the objective for technology, the technical probability of success, the expected value of the individual efforts, and a method to select the optimum program from many such efforts.

16) *Nutt, 1965:* An operations research approach. A deterministic model which quantifies the value or technical payoff of each research task. The model developed considers the world environment; the Air Force missions; future weapons systems configurations; laboratory technical objectives; and the timeliness, complexity, and scope of each research effort. The result consists of recommended funding levels of efficient tasks along with suggested tasks for close scrutiny or possible elimination. A modified linear program.

17) *Cetron, "PROFILE," 1965:* Decision theory of approach designed to aid in exploring (a) the total structure of project selection decision problems in the context of the R&D manager, and (b) R&D processes which are relevant to the design and implementation of management systems for planning, appraising, and controlling resource allocation among various projects. PROFILE's nine quantified criteria (value to warfare, task responsiveness, timeliness, long range plan, probability of success, technological transfer, manpower facilities, and funding) are used in developing a task "Profile" as well as in determining the military utility, the technical feasibility, and the application of resources for each project.

18) *Rosen & Saunder, 1965:* An operations research approach. A modification of Hess' dynamic programming approach by discussing it in the context of different optimization criteria for obtaining optimum expenditure patterns. The optimization criteria are: expected profit; total expected output; life expected output; and a minimum fixed percent return on nondiscounted expenditure.

19) *Sacco, 1965:* An operations research approach. A refinement to the Hill–Roepcke model that permitted dynamic programming to be used and thus achieving a more nearly optimum R&D program.

20) *Albertini, 1965:* An operations research approach.

A methodology for the evaluation and selection of research and development tasks directed toward the determination of materiel development objectives. A mathematical choice model to assist management in the synthesis of pertinent information for the purpose of selection, within applicable constraints, of a maximum expected value program of research and development effort. Specifications, in the form of flow charts, are included for the computerization of the model.

21) *Berman, 1965:* An economic analysis and decision tree approach. The approach considers the incremental cost of the project in R&D resources; the incremental production and operating and manning costs of introducing the new technology, and the incremental military value of the technology.

22) *Sobin–Gordon, 1965:* A comparative method which will analyze alternative applications of resource allocation techniques and attempt to evaluate the value of these techniques against various frames of reference. The analytical method thus developed (basically using ordinal values converted to relative value made up of interdependence of different proposals, definiteness of applications, capability values, probability of success, and military utility) will be used to optimize the selected principles of resource allocation in the dynamic multiple project environment. Linear programming will be used. Principal application to laboratory selection of efforts.

23) *Albertini, 1965:* An operations research approach to synthesize information pertinent to the planning process for the purpose of determining which long-range technical plan tasks to recommend for funding. This technique begins with given major barrier problem areas (MBPA's), operations on these MBPA's using the following criteria: expected technical value, annual cost of a configuration, annual monetary quota cost of a configuration. A computer program helps formulate the recommended R&D program.

24) *Wells, 1966:* A decision theory approach to store, track, and properly relate judgments concerning systems; to show the impact of these judgments; to permit real-time iterations of planning problems to facilitate the assessment and selection of system candidates for development. Criteria are: threat, types of war, policy objectives, functions, systems contributions, force structure, technical feasibility, schedule & cost, and budget.

25) *Cetron, "QUEST," 1966:* An operations research approach. QUEST utilizes a double set of matrices, consisting of the sciences, technologies, and missions, developed with the "technology" parameter common to both. By having "figures of utility" assigned to each mission and by determining the value of the contribution of each technological area to each mission, a cumulative quantified value for each technological area is then related to each scientific area and the relevant impact of each of the scientific disciplines is identified with each technological area.

26) *Dean–Hauser, 1966:* An economic analysis and operations research approach. An application of project selection under constrained resource conditions. By using mathematical models, computer programs, and available information concerning costs, uncertainties, and military values, it is possible to obtain optimum solutions. The Case study has developed a mathematical model for handling the large number of alternatives through the use of a series of simpler computerized methods, where the results of one stage are used in the succeeding stage. A dynamic programming formulation is used.

27) *Belt, 1966:* A decision theory approach based on quantified subjective judgments on the predicted value of a successful laboratory project outcome, the likelihood of success of the project in terms of its technological achievability, the specific plan of attack and the suitability of the proposed performers of the work, and the predicted cost. This technique stops short of producing a single numerical rating of project value, but gives the decision maker the opportunity to select from a group of alternative projects.

28) *De L'Estoile, 1966:* A decision theory approach. This refined rating scheme uses a formula including four factors: military utility, probability of technical success, possibility of realization in France, and direct and indirect economic impact (including the cross support to the civilian sector of the economy). This total system, because of the large number of projects involved, will be computerized in 1967.

29) *Martino et al., 1967:* An operations research approach. Factors taken into account are importance of military missions, criticality of technological effort to mission, and level of technology required. Funds are allocated among technical projects on the basis of maximum marginal payoff per dollar, within a budget total.

30) *Caulfield–Freshman, 1967:* A decision theory approach. Development project proposals are rated with respect to a number of weighted selection categories. These six categories consist of progress of program, military utility, technical risk, resources, management environment, and technological transfer; an overall score is computed and used to rank the alternatives. This technique is used to develop a task "Profile" which serves as an aid in the allocation of resources.

VI. COMPARISON OF METHODS

The various methods are compared as to features, ease of use criteria, and area of applicability in Figs. 1, 2, and 3, respectively. The various methods and features, criteria, or areas are displayed in matrix form. An entry of X in the matrix indicates that the method has the feature, satisfies the criterion, or is applicable to that area. For level of information or data required, the methods are coded L for little or none, M for moderate amount, and C for considerable amount. These evaluations are subjective, of course, but will provide some guidance as to the ease of use.

	Utility Measure	Prob. of Success	Orthog. Criteria	Sensitivity	Retain Rej. Alt.	Class Struc.	Time Strategies	Sys. Cross Support	Tech. Cross Support	Graph. Displ.	Flag.	Optimize* Criteria	Constraints**	Computerized
1. Mottley–Newton, 1959	X	X	X	X			X	X	X			1	1, 6, 7	X
2. Gargiulo et al., 1961	X	X	X				X	X				1	1, 2, 3, 4	
3. Pound, 1964	X	X				X	X					7	1	
4. Sobelman, 1958	X	X	X				X					7		
5. Freeman, 1960	X	X	X									7		X
6. Asher, 1962	X	X										7	1, 2, 3	X
7. Hess, 1962	X	X					X					7	2, 5	X
8. Dean–Sengupta, 1962	X	X	x	X	X	X						7	1	
9. Disman, 1962	X	X		X	X							7		
10. Cramer–Smith, 1964	X	X		X	X	X						7	1	
11. Esch, "PATTERN," 1963	X	X	X	X	X	X	X	X				1, 2		X
12. Blum, 1963	X	X	X	X	X	X						6	6	
13. Bakanas, 1964	X	X	X	X	X	X						3	1, 6	X
14. Dean, 1964	X	X	X	X	X	X						4		
15. Hill–Roepcke, 1964	X	X	X	X	X	X	X		X	X		2	1, 6, 7	X
16. Nutt, 1965	X	X	X	X	X	X	X		X	X	X	1, 2, 3	1, 2, 3	X
17. Cetron, "PROFILE," 1965	X	X		X	X	X			X			1, 2	1, 2	
18. Rosen–Saunder, 1965	X	X			X							3, 4, 7	1	X
19. Sacco, 1965	X	X	X		X	X		X	X			3		
20. Albertini, 1965	X	X			X	X	X	X	X			2	1, 6, 7	X
21. Berman, 1965	X	X		X								5		
22. Sobin–Gordon, 1965	X	X	X		X	X	X		X		X	1		X
23. Albertini, 1965	X	X	X	X	X	X	X				X	2	1, 2, 3, 7	X
24. Wells, 1966	X	X	X		X	X	X			X	X		1, 6, 7	X
25. Cetron, "QUEST", 1966	X	X		X	X	X	X		X			1, 2	1, 7	X
26. Dean–Hauser, 1966	X	X	X	X	X	X			X			2, 3	1, 7	
27. Belt, 1966	X	X		X	X	X			X				1, 6	X
28. De l'Estoile, 1966	X	X		X	X	X	X		X			3		X
29. Martino et al., 1967	X	X	X	X	X	X	X	X	X	X	X	3	1, 7	X
30. Caulfield–Freshman, 1967	X			X	X	X						1, 2, 3	1, 7	

* Optimization Criteria
1. Ordinal Ranking
2. Expected Value
3. Cost-Benefit
4. Profitability
5. Incremental Costs
6. Composite Score
7. Discounted Net Value

** Constraints
1. Budget
2. Skills Available
3. Facilities Available
4. Competitor Efforts
5. Raw Materials Available
6. Risk
7. Program Balance

Fig. 1. Features of the methods.

Fig. 3 (R&D areas of applicability)

	Rsch.	Expl. Devel.	Adv. Devel.	Engr. Devel.
1. Mottley–Newton, 1959	X	X	X	X
2. Gargiulo et al., 1961		X	X	X
3. Pound, 1964		X	X	X
4. Sobelman, 1958				X
5. Freeman, 1960			X	X
6. Asher, 1962				X
7. Hess, 1962				X
8. Dean–Sengupta, 1962		X	X	X
9. Disman, 1962				
10. Cramer–Smith, 1964	X	X	X	X
11. Esch, "PATTERN," 1963		X	X	X
12. Blum, 1963		X	X	X
13. Bakanas, 1964		X	X	X
14. Dean, 1964		X	X	X
15. Hill, Roepcke, 1964		X	X	X
16. Nutt, 1965		X	X	X
17. Cetron, "PROFILE," 1965		X	X	
18. Rosen–Saunder, 1965		X	X	X
19. Sacco, 1965		X	X	
20. Albertini, 1965		X	X	
21. Berman, 1965		X	X	X
22. Sobin–Gordon, 1965	X	X	X	
23. Albertini, 1965	X	X	X	
24. Wells, 1966		X	X	X
25. Cetron, "QUEST," 1966	X	X	X	
26. Dean–Hauser, 1966		X	X	X
27. Belt, 1966		X	X	X
28. De l'Estoile, 1966		X	X	
29. Martino et al., 1967	X	X	X	
30. Caulfield–Freshman, 1967		X	X	

Fig. 3. R&D areas of applicability.

Fig. 2 (Ease of use)

	Data Req'ts	Manual Oper'n Poss.	Comp. Prog. Avail.	Comp. Run Time	Diffic. of Updating	Operator Profic. Level	Need for Outside Help
1. Mottley–Newton, 1959	L	X	X		L		L
2. Gargiulo et al., 1961	M	X				T	L
3. Pound, 1964	C	X				T	L
4. Sobelman, 1958	M	X	X				
5. Freeman, 1960	C		X			T	
6. Asher, 1962	C		X			T	
7. Hess, 1962	C					T	
8. Dean–Sengupta, 1962	M		X				
9. Disman, 1962	C	X					M
10. Cramer–Smith, 1964	M		X	C	C	P	M
11. Esch, "PATTERN," 1963	C	X			L	T	C
12. Blum, 1963	M		X	M	L	P	
13. Bakanas, 1964	C				L	T	L
14. Dean, 1964	C	X	X	M	L	P	L
15. Hill, Roepcke, 1964	C			L	L	T	C
16. Nutt, 1965	L	X	X		L	P	M
17. Cetron, "PROFILE," 1965	C					P	
18. Rosen–Saunder, 1965	C	X	X	L	L	T	L
19. Sacco, 1965	C			M	L	T	
20. Albertini, 1965	M	X	X	C	L	T	L
21. Berman, 1965	C			M	L	P	L
22. Sobin–Gordon, 1965	M	X	X	L	L	P	C
23. Albertini, 1965	M	X	X		M	P	C
24. Wells, 1966	C			L	M	P	L
25. Cetron, "QUEST," 1966	M	X	X		L	P	L
26. Dean–Hauser, 1966	C				M	P	C
27. Belt, 1966	M	X	X	C	C	P	C
28. De l'Estoile, 1966	C				M	P	C
29. Martino et al., 1967	C	X	X		M	P	C
30. Caulfield–Freshman, 1967	C	X			M	P	C

Symbol Keys

Computer Running Time
L—little
M—moderate
C—considerable

Difficulty of Updating
L—low
M—moderate
C—considerable

Need for outside help
L—little or none
M—moderate
C—considerable

Operator Proficiency
C—clerk
T—technician
P—degreed professional

Fig. 2. Ease of use.

VII. Summary

Several methods for appraisal of R&D programs have been evaluated against a set of criteria. The capabilities and limitations of each of the methods have been indicated. Each method, within its capabilities and limitations, can provide assistance to the management of an R&D enterprise in appraising the worth of its R&D effort. In particular, the use of quantitative methods tends to eliminate bias, provide a degree of consistency, and force managers to render their judgments more explicit in evaluating R&D programs. While some of the techniques described lack certain features, these usually can be added with some modification, if desired.

The value of any of the appraisal methods is further limited by two factors:

a) the validity of input information supplied by the laboratory workers and management staff;

b) the effective support and use of the system by higher management. If management supports a method, and makes proper use of it, and furthermore insures that the input information is as valid as humanly possible, the methods can provide a very valuable tool for improving the management of an R&D organization.

Considering the limitations of the methods described, there is clearly much room for further refinement and improvement of quantitative methods for appraisal of R&D programs. However, even in the absence of these refined methods, the spectrum of existing methods can provide the R&D manager with considerable assistance in appraising his program.

Bibliography

Ackoff, R. L., *Scientific Method: Optimizing Applied Research Decisions.* New York: Wiley, 1962.

——, Ed., *Progress in Operations Research,* vol. 1. New York: Wiley, 1961.

——, "Specialized versus generalized models in research budgeting," presented at the 2nd Conf. on Research Program Effectiveness, Washington, D. C., July 1965.

Ackoff, R. L., E. L. Arnoff, and C. W. Churchman, *Introduction to Operations Research.* New York: Wiley, 1957.

Adams, J. G., and H. R. E. Nellums, "Engineering evaluation—tool for research management," *Indust. Engrg. Chem.,* vol. 49, p. 40A, May 1957.

Albertini, J., "The QMDO planning process as it relates to the U. S. Army Materiel Command," Cornell Aeronautical Lab. Rept. VQ-2044-H-1, USAMC Contract DA-49-185 AMC-237(X), August 31, 1965.

——, "The LRTP planning process as it relates to the U. S. Army Materiel Command," Cornell Aeronautical Lab. Rept. VQ-2044-H-2, USAMC Contract DA-49-186 AMC-237(X), October 30, 1965.

——, "LRTP mathematical model brochure," Cornell Aeronautical Lab. Rept. VQ-2044-H-3, USAMC Contract DA-49-186 AMC-237(X), October 30, 1965.

Amey, L. R., "The allocation and utilization of resources," *Operations Research Quart.,* vol. 15, June 1964.

Andersen, S. L., "Venture analysis, a flexible planning tool," *Chem. Engrg. Prog.,* vol. 57, pp. 80–83, March 1961.

——, "A 2×2 risk decision problem," *Chem. Engrg. Prog.,* vol. 57, pp. 70–73, May 1961.

Anderson, C. A., "Notes on the evaluation of research planning," presented at the 2nd Conf. on Research Program Effectiveness, Washington, D. C., July 1964.

Ansoff, H. I., "Evaluation of applied research in a business firm," in *Technological Planning on the Corporate Level,* (Proc. Conf. at Harvard Business School), J. R. Bright, Ed. Cambridge, Mass.: Harvard University Press, 1962, pp. 209–224.

Andrew, G. H. L., "Assessing priorities for technical effort," *Operations Research Quart.,* vol. 5, pp. 67–80, September 1954.

Anthony, R. N., and J. S. Day, *Management Controls in Industrial Research Organizations.* Cambridge, Mass.: Harvard University Press, 1952.

Asher, D. T., "A linear programming model for the allocation of R&D efforts," *IRE Trans. on Engineering Management,* vol. EM-9, pp. 154–157, December 1962.

Aumann, R. J., and J. B. Kruskal, "Assigning quantitative values to qualitative factors in the naval electronics program," *Naval Research Logistics Quart.,* vol. 4, p. 15, March 1959.

Asher, D. I., and S. Disman, "Operations research in R&D," *Chem. Engrg. Prog.,* vol. 59, pp. 41–45, January 1963.

Bakanas, V., "An analytical method to aid in the choice of long range study tasks," Cornell Aeronautical Lab. Rept. VQ-1887-H-1, USAMC Contract DA-49-186 AMC-97(X), May 19, 1964.

Baker, N. R., and W. H. Pound, "R and D project selection: Where we stand," *IEEE Trans. on Engineering Management,* vol. EM-11, pp. 124–134, December 1964.

Barmby, J. G., "The applicability of PERT as a management tool," *IRE Trans. on Engineering Management,* vol. EM-9, pp. 130–131, September 1962.

Battersby, A., *Network Analysis for Planning and Scheduling.* New York: St. Martins Press, 1964.

Baumgartner, J. S., *Project Management.* Homewood, Ill.: Richard Irwin Press, 1963.

Beckwith, R. E., "A cost control extension of the PERT system," *IRE Trans. on Engineering Management,* vol. EM-9, pp. 147–149, December 1962.

Belt, J. R., "Military applied R&D project evaluation," Master's thesis, U. S. Navy Marine Engineering Lab., Annapolis, Md., June 1966 (unpublished).

Bensley, D. E., "Planning and controlling a research and development program: A case study." Master's thesis, Mass. Inst. Tech., Cambridge, Mass., 1955.

Berman, E. R., "Research allocation in a PERT network under continuous activity time-cost functions," *Management Science,* vol. 10, 1964.

——, Draft: "Theoretical structure of a methodology for R&D resource allocation," Research Analysis Corp., May 26, 1965.

Bernstein, A., and I. de Sola Pool, "Development and testing of an evaluation model for research organization substructures," presented at the 2nd Conf. on Research Program Effectiveness, Washington, D. C., July 1964.

Blinoff, V., and C. Pacifico, *Chem. Processing,* vol. 20, pp. 34–35, November 1957.

Blood, J. W., Ed., *The Management of Scientific Talent.* New York: American Management Association, 1963.

Blum, S., "Time, cost, and risk analysis in project planning," U. S. Army Frankford Arsenal Rept., August 22, 1963.

Bock, R. H., and W. K. Holstein, *Production Planning and Control.* Columbus, Ohio: Merrill Books, 1963.

Bonini, C. P., R. K. Jaedicke, and H. M. Wagner, *Management Controls: New Directions in Basic Research.* New York: McGraw-Hill, 1964.

Boothe, N. et al., *From Concept to Commercialization, A Study of the R&D Budget Allocation Process.* Stanford, Calif.: Stanford University, 1962.

Brandenburg, R. G., *A Descriptive Analysis of Project Selection.* Pittsburgh, Pa.: Carnegie Inst. Tech., July 1964.

——, "Toward a multi-space information conversion model of the research and development process," Carnegie Inst. Tech., Pittsburgh, Pa., Management Sciences Research Rept. 48, August 1965.

Bright, J. R., Ed., *Technological Planning on the Corporate Level* (Proc. Conf. at Harvard Business School). Cambridge, Mass.: Harvard University Press, 1962.

Busacker, R. G., and T. L. Saaty, *Finite Graphs and Networks: An Introduction With Applications.* New York: McGraw-Hill, 1965.

Bush, G. P., *Bibliography on Research Administration, Annotated.* Washington, D. C.: University Press, 1964.

Carroll, P., *Profit Control—How to Plug Profit Leaks.* New York: McGraw-Hill, 1962.

Caulfield, P., and R. Freshman, "Technology evaluation workbook," HQ Research and Technology Div., AFSC, Bolling AFB, Washington, D. C., January 1967.

Cetron, M. J., "Programmed functional indicies for laboratory evaluation, 'PROFILE,'" presented at the 16th Military Operations Research Symp. (MORS), Seattle, Wash., October 1965.

Cetron, M. J., "Quantitative utility estimates for science & technology 'Quest,'" presented at the 18th Military Operations Research Society, Fort Bragg, N. C., October 1966.

Cetron, M. J., and R. Freshman, "Some results of 'PROFILE,'" presented at the 17th MORS, Monterey, Calif., May 1966.

Charnes, A., "Conditional chance-constrained approaches to organizational control," presented at the 2nd Conf. on Research Program Effectiveness, Washington, D. C., July 1964.

Charnes, A., and A. C. Stedry, "Optimal real-time control of research funding," presented at the 2nd Conf. on Research Program Effectiveness, Washington, D. C., July 1965.

Churchman, C. W., *Prediction and Optimal Control.* Englewood Cliffs, N. J.: Prentice-Hall, 1960.

Churchman, C. W., C. Kruytbosch, and P. Ratoosh, "The role of the research administrator," presented at the 2nd Conf. on Research Program Effectiveness, Washington, D. C., July 1965.

Clark, W., *The Gantt Chart.* London: Pitman and Sons, 1938.

Clarke, R. W., "Activity costing—key to progress in critical path analysis," *IRE Trans. on Engineering Management,* vol. EM-9, pp. 132–136, September 1962.

Combs, C. E., "Decision theory and engineering management," *IRE Trans. on Engineering Management,* vol. EM-9, pp. 149–154, December 1962.

Cook, E. F., "A better yardstick for project evaluation," *Armed Forces Management,* pp. 20–23, April 1958.

Cramer, R. H., and B. E. Smith, "Decision models for the selection of research projects," *The Engineering Economist,* vol. 9, pp. 1–20, January–February 1964.

Crisp, R. D., "Product planning for future projects," *Dun's Review and Modern Industry,* March 1958.

Dantzig, G. B., *Linear Programming and Extensions.* Princeton, N. J.: Princeton University Press, 1963.

Daubin, S. C., "The allocation of development funds: An analytic approach," *Naval Research Logistics Quart.,* vol. 3, pp. 263–276, September 1958.

Davidson, H. F., "Surveys as tools for acquisition of research management information," presented at the 2nd Conf. on Research Program Effectiveness, Washington, D. C., July 1964.

Davis, K., "The role of project management in scientific manufacturing," *IRE Trans. on Engineering Management,* vol. EM-9, pp. 109–113, September 1962.

Dean, B. V., Ed., *Operations Research in Research and Development* (Proc. Conf. at Case Inst. Tech.). New York: Wiley, 1963.

——, "Allocation of technical resources in a firm," presented at the 1st Conf. on Research Program Effectiveness, Washington, D. C., July 1964.

——, "Stochastic networks in research planning," presented at the 2nd Conf. on Research Program Effectiveness, Washington, D. C., July 1965.

——, "Scoring and profitability models for evaluating and selecting engineering projects," Case Inst. Tech., Operation Research Group, 1964.

Dean, B. V., and Glogowski, "On the planning of research," ONR-AMC Project NOOR1141(19), July 1965.

——, and L. E. Hauser, "Advanced materiel systems planning," Case Inst. Tech., Cleveland, Ohio, Operations Research Group Tech. Memo. 65, ONR-AMC Project Nonr-1141(19) September 15, 1966.

Dean, B. V., and S. Sengupta, "On a method for determining corporate research development budgets," *Management Sciences, Models, and Techniques,* vol. 2, C. W. Churchman and M. Verhulst, Eds. New York: Pergamon Press, 1960.

Dean, J., *Managerial Economics.* Englewood Cliffs, N. J.: Prentice-Hall, 1951, pp. 249–610.

——, "Measuring the productivity of capital," *Harvard Business Review,* vol. 32, January–February, 1954.

De L'Estoile, "Resource allocation model," French Ministere Des Armees, Paris, France.

DeVries, M. G., *A Dynamic Model for Product Strategy Selection.* Ann Arbor, Mich.: The University of Michigan, 1963.

——, "The dynamic effects of planning horizons on the selection of optimal product strategies," *Management Science,* vol. 10, pp. 524–544, April 1964.

Disman, S., "Selecting R&D projects for profit," *Chem. Engrg.,* vol. 69, pp. 87–90, December 1962.

Dooley, A. R., "Interpretations of PERT," *Harvard Business Review,* vol. 42, pp. 160–171, March–April, 1964.

Drucker, P. F., "Twelve fables of research management," *Harvard Business Review,* vol. 41, January–February, 1963.

——, *Managing for Results.* New York: Harper & Row, 1964, pp. 25–50.

Easton, D., *A Systems Analysis of Political Life.* New York: Wiley, 1965.

Eisner, H., "Generalized network approach to the planning and scheduling of a research program," *Operations Research,* vol. 10, pp. 115–125, 1962.

——, "The application of information theory to the planning of research," presented at the TIMS American Internat'l Meeting, September 1963.

Elmaghraby, S. E., "An algebra for the analysis of generalized activity networks," *Management Sciences,* vol. 10, pp. 494–514, April 1964.

Emlet, H. E., "Methodological approach to planning and programming Air Force operational requirements," Research and Development (MAPORD), Analytic Services Rept. 65-4, October 1965.

Esch, M. E., "Planning assistance through technical evaluation 'pattern'" presented at the 17th Nat'l Aerospace Electronics Conf., Dayton, Ohio, May 1965.

Ewing, D. W., Ed., *Long-Range Planning of Management.* New York: Harper & Brothers, 1958.

Flood, M. W., "Research project evaluation," in *Coordination, Control, and Financing of Industrial Research,* A. R. Rubenstein, Ed. New York: Columbia University and King's Crown Press, 1955.

Fong, L. B. C., "A visual method of program balance and evaluation," *IRE Trans. on Engineering Management,* vol. EM-8, pp. 160–163, September 1961.

Ford, L. R., Jr., and D. R. Fulkerson, *Flows in Networks.* Princeton, N. J.: Princeton University Press, 1962.

Freeman, J. R., "A survey of the current status of accounting in the control of R&D," *IRE Trans. on Engineering Management,* vol. EM-9, pp. 179–181, December 1962.

Freeman, R. J., "A generalized network approach to project activity sequencing," *IRE Trans. on Engineering Management,* vol. EM-7, pp. 103–107, September 1960.

——, "An operational analysis of industrial research," Ph.D. dissertation, Department of Economics, Mass. Inst. Tech., Cambridge, Mass., 1957.

——, "A stochastic model for determining the size and allocation of the research budget," *IRE Trans. on Engineering Management,* vol. EM-7, pp. 2–7, March 1960.

——, "Quantitative methods in R&D management," *California Management Review,* vol. 11, pp. 36–44, 1960.

Fry, B. L., "SCANS—system description and comparison with PERT," *IRE Trans. on Engineering Management,* vol. EM-9, pp. 122–129, September 1962.

Galbraith, J. K., *The Affluent Society.* New York: Mentor Books, 1958.

Gargiulo, G. R., J. Hannoch, D. B. Hertz, and T. Zang, "Developing systematic procedures for directing research programs," *IRE Trans. on Engineering Management,* vol. EM-8, pp. 24–29, March 1961.

Gloskey, C. R., "Research on a research department: An analysis of economic decisions on projects," *IRE Trans. on Engineering Management,* vol. EM-7, pp. 166–172, December 1960.

——, M.A. thesis, Mass. Inst. Tech., Cambridge, Mass., 1959.

Goldberg, L. C., "Dimensions in the evaluation of technical ideas in an industrial research laboratory," M.S. thesis, Northwestern University, Evanston, Ill., 1963.

Guy, K., *Laboratory Organization and Administration.* London: Macmillan, and New York: St. Martin's Press, 1962.

Hackney, J. W., "How to appraise capital investments," *Chem. Engrg.,* vol. 68, pp. 146–167, May 1961.

Hahn, W. A., and H. D. Pickering, "Program planning in a science-based service organization," presented at the 2nd Conf. on Research Program Effectiveness, Washington, D. C., July 1965.

Hansen, B. J., *Practical PERT Including Critical Path Method.* Washington, D. C.: American House, 1964.

Harrel, C. G., "Selecting projects for research," in *Research in Industry: Its Organization and Management,* C. C. Furnas, Ed. New York: Van Nostrand, 1948, ch. 7, pp. 104–144.

Heckert, J. E., and J. B. Willson, *Business Budgeting and Control.* New York: Ronald Press, 1955.

Henke, R., *Effective Research & Development for the Smaller Company.* Houston: Gulf Publ. Co., 1963.

Hertz, D. B., *The Theory and Practice of Industrial Research.* New York: McGraw-Hill, 1950.

Hertz, D. B., and P. G. Carlson, "Selection, evaluation, and control of research and development projects," in *Operations Research in Research and Development,* B. V. Dean, Ed. New York: Wiley, 1963, pp. 170–188.

Hertz, D. B., and A. H. Rubenstein, *Costs, Budgeting and Economics of Industrial Research* (Proc. 1st Ann. Conf. of Industrial Research). New York: Columbia University Press, 1951.

Hertz, D. B., and A. H. Rubenstein, Eds., *Proc. 3rd Ann. Conf. on Industrial Research: Research Operations in Industry.* New York: Columbia University Press, 1953, esp. pp. 55, 153.

Hess, S. W., "A dynamic programming approach to R&D budgeting and project selection," *IRE Trans. on Engineering Management,* vol. EM-9, pp. 170–179, December 1962.

——, "On research and development budgeting and project selection," Ph.D. dissertation, Case Inst. Tech., Cleveland, Ohio, 1960.

Heyel, C., Ed., *Handbook of Industrial Research Management.* New York: Reinhold, 1959.

Hickey, A. E., Jr., "The systems approach: Can engineers use the scientific method?" *IRE Trans. on Engineering Management,* vol. EM-7, pp. 72–80, June 1960.

Hildenbrand, W., "Application of graph theory to stochastic scheduling," presented at the 2nd Conf. on Research Program Effectiveness, Washington, D. C., July 1965.

Hill, F. I., and L. A. Roepcke, "An analytical method to aid in the choice of long range study tasks," presented at the U. S. Army Operations Research Symp. at Rock Island Arsenal, May 1964.

Hill, L. S., "Toward an improved basis of estimating and controlling R&D tasks," presented at the 10th Nat'l Meeting of the American Association of Cost Engineers, Philadelphia, Pa., June 1966.

Hitchcock, L. B., "Selection and evaluation of R&D projects," *Research Management,* vol. 6, pp. 231–244, May 1963.

Hodge, M. H., Jr., et al., "Basic research as a corporate function," Stanford, Calif.: Stanford University, 1961.

Honig, J. G., "An evaluation of research and development problems," presented at the 1st Conf. on Research Program Effectiveness, Washington, D. C., July 1964.

Horowitz, I., "The economics of industrial research," Ph.D. dissertation, Mass. Inst. Tech., Cambridge, Mass., 1959.

Janofsky, L., and S. Sobelman, "Balancing equations to project feasibility studies," presented at Operations Research Society of America, Detroit, Mich., October 1960.

Johnson, E. A., and H. S. Milton, "A proposed cost-of-research index," *IRE Trans. on Engineering Management,* vol. EM-8, pp. 172–176, December 1961.

Johnson, R. A., F. E. Kast, and J. E. Rosenzweig, *The Theory and Management of Systems.* New York: McGraw-Hill, 1963.

Karger, D. C., and R. G. Murkick, *Managing Engineering and Research.* New York: Industrial Press, 1963, pp. 193–253.

Kelley, J. E., Jr. and M. R. Walker, "Critical-path planning and scheduling," *Proc. of the Eastern Joint Computer Conf.,* 1959; see also, *Operations Research,* vol. 9, pp. 296–320, 1961.

Kiefer, D. M., "Winds of change in industrial chemical research," *Chemical Engineering News,* vol. 42, pp. 88–109, March 1964.

Klein, B., and W. Meckling, "Applications of operations research to development decisions," *Operations Research,* vol. 6, pp. 352–363, May–June 1958.

——, "The decision-making problem in development," in *The Rate and Direction of Inventive Activity.* Princeton, N. J.: Princeton University Press, 1962, pp. 477–508.

Kliever, W. R. and R. Z. Bancroft, "Choosing and evaluating research projects," *Product Engrg.,* June 1953.

Koontz, H., *Toward A Unified Theory of Management.* New York: McGraw-Hill, 1963.

Landi, D. M., *A Model of Investment Planning for Research and Development.* Evanston, Ill.: Northwestern University, 1964.

Leermakers, J. A., "The selection and screening of projects," in *Getting the Most from Product Research and Development.* New York: American Management Association, 1955, pp. 81–94.

Levy, F. K., G. L. Thompson, and J. E. Wiest, "Multiship, multi-shop, workload-smoothing program," *Naval Research Logistics Quart.,* vol. 11, March 1962.

Lipetz, B.-A., *Measurement of Effectiveness of Science Research.* Carlisle, Mass.: Intermedia, 1965.

Lytle, A. A., "The yardsticks for research success," *Product Engrg.,* vol. 30, pp. 34–37, October 1959.

Magee, J. F., "How to use decision trees in capital investment," *Harvard Business Review,* vol. 42, pp. 79–96, September–October 1964.

Manning, P. D., "Long range planning of product research," in *R&D Series #4.* New York: American Management Association, 1957.

Marples, D. L., "The decisions of engineering design," *IRE Trans. on Engineering Management,* vol. EM-8, pp. 55–71, June 1961.

Marquis, D. G., "Organization and management of R&D," presented at the 1st Conf. on Research Program Effectiveness, Washington, D. C., July 1964.

Marschak, T. A., "Models, rules of thumb, and development decisions," in *Operations Research in Research and Development,* B. V. Dean, Ed., New York: Wiley, 1963, pp. 247–263.

——, "Strategy and organization in a system development project," in *The Rate and Direction of Inventive Activity.* Princeton, N. J.: Princeton University Press, 1962, pp. 509–548.

Marshall, A. W., and W. H. Meckling," Predictability of the costs, time and success of development," in *The Rate and Di-*

rection of Inventive Activity. Princeton, N. J.: Princeton University Press, 1962, pp. 461–475.

Martino, J. P., Caulfield, M. Cetron, H. Davidson, H. Liebowitz, and L. Roepcke, "A method for balanced allocation of resources among R&D projects," USAF Office of Scientific Research, Tech. Rept., February 1967.

Massey, R. J., "A new publication: Department of the Navy RDT&E management guide," presented at the 1st Conf. on Research Program Effectiveness, Washington, D. C., July 1964.

McMaster, S. B., "Study of project selection techniques in an R&D organization," Master's thesis, Northwestern University, Evanston, Ill., 1964, (unpublished).

McMillian, C., and R. F. Ganzalez, *Systems Analysis: A Computer Approach to Decision Models.* Homewood, Ill.: Richard D. Irwin, 1965.

Mees, C. E. K., and J. A. Leermakers, *The Organization of Industrial Scientific Research,* 2nd ed. New York: McGraw-Hill, 1950, esp. ch. 11.

Mellon, W. G., *An Approach to a General Theory of Priorities: An Outline of Problems and Methods,* Princeton University Econometric Research Program, Memo. 42. Princeton, N. J.: Princeton University Press, 1962.

Miller, D. W., and M. K. Starr, *Executive Decisions and Operations Research.* Englewood Cliffs, N. J.: Prentice-Hall, 1960.

Miller, R. W., *Schedule, Cost and Profit Control with PERT.* New York: McGraw-Hill, 1963.

Miller, T. T., "Projecting the profitability of new products," American Management Association, New York, N. Y., Special Rept. 20, pp. 20–33, 1957.

Morgenstern, O., R. W. Shephard, and H. G. Grabowski, "Adaption of graph theory and an input-output model to research description and evaluation," presented at the 2nd Conf. on Research Program Effectiveness, Washington, D. C., July 1965.

Moshman, J., J. Johnson, and M. Larson, "RAMPS—A technique for resource allocation and multi-project scheduling," *Proc. of the Spring Joint Computer Conf.* Baltimore, Md.: Spartan Books, 1963, pp. 17–27.

Mottley, C. M., and R. D. Newton, "The selection of projects for industrial research," *Operations Research,* vol. 7, pp. 740–751, November–December 1959.

National Science Foundation, Washington, D. C., "Science and Engineering in American Industry," Final Rept. on 1953–1954 Survey, October 1956.

Norden, P. V., "Curve fitting for a model of applied research and development scheduling," *IBM J. Research and Devel.,* vol. 2, pp. 232–248, July 1958.

——, "Some properties of R&D project recovery limits," presented at the 2nd Conf. on Research Program Effectiveness, Washington, D. C., July 1965.

——, "The study committee for research, development and engineering (SCARDE): A progress report and an invitation to participate," *IRE Trans. on Engineering Management,* vol. EM-8, pp. 3–10, March 1961.

Norton, J. H., "The role of subjective probability in evaluating new product ventures," *Chem. Engrg. Prog. Symp.,* Ser. 42, vol. 59, pp. 49–54, 1963.

Nutt, A. B., "An approach to research and development effectiveness," *IEEE Trans. on Engineering Management,* pp. 103–112, September 1965.

Nyland, H. V., and G. R. Towle, "How we evaluate return from research," *Nat'l Association of Cost Accountants Bull.,* May 1956.

Olsen, F., "The control of research funds," in *Coordination, Control and Financing of Industrial Research,* A. H. Rubenstein, Ed. New York: King Crown Press and Columbia University, 1955, pp. 99–108.

Pacifico, C., "Is it worth the risk?," *Chem. Engrg. Prog.,* vol. 60, pp. 19–21, May 1964.

Pappas, G. F., and D. D. MacLaren, "An approach to research planning," *Chem. Eng. Prog.,* vol. 57, pp. 65–69, May 1961.

Pound, W. H., "Research project selection: Testing a model in the field," *IEEE Trans. on Engineering Management,* vol. EM-11, pp. 16–22, March 1964.

Quinn, J. B., *Yardsticks for Industrial Research: The Evaluation of Research and Development Output.* New York: Ronald Press, 1959.

Quinn, J. B., and J. A. Mueller, "Transferring research results to operations" *Harvard Business Review,* vol. 41, January–February 1963.

Rae, R. H., and Synnott, "Project RDE, a framework for the comprehension and analysis of research and development effectiveness," USAF Flight Dynamics Lab., Dayton, Ohio, TM 63-22, October 1961.

——, "A systems development planning structure," ABT Associates, Inc., November 1965.

——, "An Automated Scenario Generator," ABT Associates, Inc., January 1966.

Raiffa, H., and R. Schlaifer, *Applied Statistical Decision Theory.* Boston, Mass.: Harvard University Press, 1957.

Roberts, E. D., *The Dynamics of Research and Development.* New York: Harper & Row, 1964.

Roberts, C. S., "Product selection—witchcraft or wisdom," *IRE Trans. on Engineering Management,* vol. EM-6, pp. 68–71, September 1959.

Roman, D. D. "Organization for control," *J. Academy of Management* (Proc. of the Annual Meeting, Pittsburgh, December 1962).

——, "The PERT system: An appraisal of program evaluation review technique," *J. Academy of Management,* vol. 5, April 1962.

——, "Project management recognizes R&D performance," *J. Academy of Management,* vol. 7, pp. 7–20, March 1964.

Roman, D. D., and J. Johnson, "On the allocation of common physical resources to multiple development tasks," presented at the 18th Military Operations Research Society, Fort Bragg, N. C., October 1966.

Roseboom, J. H., C. E. Clark, and W. Fazer, "Application of a technique for research and development program evaluation," *Operations Research,* vol. 7, pp. 651–653, September–October 1959.

Rosen, E. M., and W. E. Souder, "A method for allocating R&D expenditures," *IEEE Trans. on Engineering Management,* vol. EM-12, pp. 87–93, September 1965.

Rubenstein, A. H., Ed., *Coordination, Control, and Financing of Industrial Research.* New York: King's Crown Press and Columbia University, 1955.

——, "Evaluation of the possibilities of research effort in a new field of technology, Sweden," vol. 6, pp. 239–251, 1965.

——, "Setting criteria for R&D," *Harvard Business Review,* pp. 95–104, January–February 1957.

Rubenstein, A. H., and I. Horowitz, "Project selection in new technical fields," *Proc. Nat'l Electronics Conf.,* vol. 15, 1959.

——, "Studies of project selection behavior in industry," in *Operations Research in Research and Development,* B. V. Dean, Ed. New York: Wiley, 1963, pp. 189–205.

Rubenstein, A. H., and C. W. Maberstroh, Eds., *Some Theories of Organization.* Homewood, Ill.: Richard D. Irwin, 1960.

——, "Some common concepts and tentative findings from a ten-project program of research on R&D management," presented at the 2nd Conf. on Research Program Effectiveness, Washington, D. C., July 1965.

Saaty, T. L., *Mathematical Methods of Operations Research.* New York: McGraw-Hill, 1959.

Sacco, W. J., "On the choice of long range study tasks," Ballistic Research Lab. Memo Rept. 1693, August 1965.

Savage, J. J., *The Foundation of Statistics.* New York: Wiley, 1954.

Scherer, F. M., "Time-cost tradeoffs in uncertain empirical research projects," *Naval Research Logistics Quart. ONR,* vol. 13, March 1966.

Schweyer, H. E., "Graphs can reveal project feasibility," *Chem. Engrg.* pp. 175–178, September 1961.

Seiler, R. E., *Improving the Effectiveness of Research and Development.* New York: McGraw-Hill, 1965.

Shank, R. J., "Planning to meet goals," in *Optimum Use of Engineering Talent, AMA Rept. 58.* Cambridge, Mass.: Riverside Press, 1961.

Shaller, H. I., "An exploratory study in research planning methodology," Dept. of the Navy, Washington, D. C., ONR Tech. Rept. ACR/NAR-27, September 1963.

Sher, I. H., and E. Garfield, "New tools for improving and evaluating the effectiveness of research," presented at the 2nd Conf. on Research Program Effectiveness, Washington, D. C., July 1965.

Silk, L. S., "An optimal method for selection of product development projects," presented at the 15th Nat'l Meeting of the Operations Research Society of America, Washington, D. C., May 1959.

S. Herbert, *The New Science of Management Decisions.* New York: Harper & Row, 1960.

S. Herbert, *The Research Revolution.* New York: McGraw-Hill, 1960.

Sobelman, S. A., "Modern dynamic approach to product development," Picatinny Arsenal, Dover, N. J., December 1958.

——, "An optimal method for selection of product development projects," presented at the 15th Nat'l Meeting of the Operations Research Society of America, Washington, D. C., May 1959.

Sobin, B., and A. Proschan, "Search and evaluation methods in research and exploratory development," presented at the 2nd Conf. on Research Program Effectiveness, Washington, D. C., July 1965.

——, "Proposal generation and evaluation methods in research and exploratory developments," Research Analysis Corp., Paper RAC-P-11, November 1965.

Special Projects Office, *PERT Summary Report I.* Washington, D. C.: Bureau of Naval Weapons, 1959.

Spencer, M. H., and L. Siegelman, *Managerial Economics.* Homewood, Ill.: Richard D. Irwin, 1964, pp. 461–567.

Stanley, A. O., and K. K. White, *Organizing the R&D Function.* AMA Research Study No. 72. New York: American Management Association, 1963.

Steiner, G. A., *Managerial Long-Range Planning.* New York: McGraw-Hill, 1963.

Stilian, C. N. et al., *PERT—A New Management Planning and Control Technique.* New York: American Management Association, 1962.

Stoessl, L., "Linear programming techniques applied to research planning," Master's thesis, U. S. Naval Post-Graduate School, 1964.

Stoodley, F. H., "A Study of methods which could improve the relevance of naval applied research and exploratory development," Office Naval Research Rept., June 1, 1966.

Sullivan, C. I., "CPI management looks at R&D project evaluation," *Indus. Engrg. Chem.,* vol. 53, pp. 42A–46A, September 1961.

Taylor, F. W., *Scientific Management.* New York: Harper & Brothers, 1947.

Theil, H., "On the optimal management of research; a mathematical approach," presented at the Conf. of the Internat'l Federation of Operations Research Societies, Oslo, Norway, July 1963.

Thompson, R. E., "PERT—Tool for R&D project decisionmaking," *IRE Trans. on Engineering Management,* vol. EM-9, pp. 116–121, September 1962.

University of California, Berkeley, "A system engineering approach to corporate long-range planning," Department of Engineering, Rept. EEP-62-1. June 1962.

Walters, J. E., *Research Management: Principles and Practice.* Washington, D. C.: Spartan Books, 1965.

Wasson, C. R., *The Economics of Managerial Decision.* New York: Appleton-Century-Crofts, 1965, pp. 147–218.

Wells, H. A., "Systems planners guide," presented at the 18th Military Operations Research Society Meeting, Fort Bragg, N. C., October 1966.

——, "The allocation of research and development resources," Wright Air Development Center, August 1958 (unpublished).

Wachold, G. R., "An investigation of the technical effectiveness of a government research and development test and evaluation organization," Navy Missile Center, Pt. Mugu, Calif., July 1965 (unpublished).

Weapon System Planner's Guide

HOWARD A. WELLS

Abstract—This paper describes a model that stores, tracks and properly relates judgments concerning systems; shows the impact of these judgments; permits real-time iteration of planning problems to facilitate the assessment and selection of system candidates for development. Criteria are threat, types of war, policy objectives, functions, systems contributions, force structure, technical feasibility, schedule and cost, and budget.

A GREAT DEAL of publicity has been given to the concept of cost/effectiveness, or cost/benefit analysis as an approach to the problem of evaluation and selection of new weapon systems. In spite of this, there is no generally available guide to assist the systems planner in his day-to-day use of the concept.

The system planner's guide was developed to meet this need.

The weapon system planner is faced with a myriad of factors to be considered before he is able to make a recommendation concerning a particular system that he thinks should be acquired for the operational inventory. Many of these factors such as salability at high levels or political and economic acceptability are so vague that they cannot be easily described, even in qualitative terms. However, many of the factors are quantifiable, even though few of them are actually measurable. Most factors depend exclusively on judgment. The planning process discussed in this paper requires that the systems planner express his judgments in quantitative terms. Some planners argue that the judgments involved in the problem cannot be reduced to numbers, but it should be remembered that the annual budget is expressed in terms of nine significant figures. Since these quantities are influenced by systems planning, it would seem reasonable to require that the output of systems planning be reliable to at least one or two significant figures. Therefore, at several points in the model, the planner is asked to select a figure that represents his best estimate concerning the relative value of an item in a particular situation. This decision aid is not offered as a substitute for the planner's judgment, but, rather, as a device to assist him in making judgments and in the assessment of their impact.

The purpose of using a computer-based decision aid is to assist the planner by having the computer do what it does best, that is, to remember information. The computer can store, track, and relate judgments better than an individual can, once someone has thought out what

these relationships should be and has properly instructed the computer. Second, the impact of a judgment in any area of the problem can be shown immediately through computer calculations and outputs. The real-time iterations of the planning problem permit the person making the judgment to adjust his thinking if the answer is more sensitive to that judgment than expected. This will help to prevent over-reaction to dramatic pieces of information or to emotional elements of the problem.

The relative desirability of any system, whether it is a current system or a new system candidate still in the planning phase, depends almost entirely on three overall factors: military worth, feasibility, and cost. Most previous cost-effectiveness studies have merely divided the military worth of a system by its cost to determine a figure of merit. The system candidate is normally assumed to be available in the planning period under consideration. However, this model provides for uncertainty as to the availability of the system candidate through the expression of technical feasibility, which is multiplied by the cost-effectiveness figure. The estimate of system desirability would be very simple if these parameters were single-valued quantities. Of course, this is not the case. Each of the parameters varies with time, with the threat, and with changes in national policy.

The end result of the system planner's efforts is a recommendation concerning which of the alternative systems candidates should be acquired for the force structure. His problem is how to consider all the various factors involved in the decision and how to express their relative importance. In this model, the approach has been to segment the problem into portions which are handled by people with different backgrounds, or areas of competence. First, the entire problem of system planning must be based on a solid and accepted assessment of the threat within which we must operate our military forces in the future planning period under consideration.

Significant changes in the force structures of the U. S. or of potentially hostile nations will change the threat and will make it necessary for the planner to reassess his estimates.

Second, the military worth of a system should be treated as a derived value. This value is best assessed through the use of a hierarchy of objectives. Since the importance of these objectives is sensitive to the intensity of conflict, a decision must be made concerning the relative emphasis to be placed on preparations for various types of war. The relative importance of each policy objective can then be assessed for each war type. This permits an assessment of the relative importance of mil-

Manuscript received January 11, 1967. This paper was presented at the 18th Military Operations Research Symposium (MORS), Fort Bragg, N. C., October 1966.

The author is with Bell Aerosystems, Buffalo, N. Y. He was formerly with Hdq. AF Systems Command, Washington, D. C.

itary functions, such as logistics, intelligence, firepower, command and control, and in carrying out each of the policy objectives in each war type. An estimate of the contributions of each to the system ability of the force structure to carry out these military functions provides a means for arriving at a final estimate of the total system value.

There are an infinite number of war types. However, for convenience in using the model, we have defined only three kinds that are sufficiently distinct that the general characteristics of weapon systems must be different. These three kinds are nuclear war, possibly ending in mutual annihilation, cold war and counterinsurgency, and conventional, limited war. The judgment concerning emphasis to be placed on each type of war is probably more intricate than it first appears. In order to make this judgment, a force structure must be assumed, both for the U. S. and for any potential enemies. This force structure is necessary in order to calculate the probability of occurrence of each type of war. This probability of occurrence is then multiplied by the consequences of the occurrence of that particular type of war. The resulting figure is interpreted as emphasis to be placed on the types of war. This emphasis is entered into the computer as a number from 0 to 1 for convenience, although any other numbers could be used just as easily. When a force structure is recommended based on the output of this model, that new force structure should be considered for a new assessment of the probability of each type of war. This will complete the loop in this iterative planning process.

When the planner has made a decision regarding the relative importance of each war type under consideration, the military policy objectives which are based upon national policy goals are evaluated one at a time with respect to each type of war. The planner is asked to assign a number between one and ten to the objective, depending on how important he feels it is in that situation. After completion of this process, the value of any single policy objective can be calculated by multiplying its value in each type of war by the emphasis on that type of war, and summing these products over all war types. The resulting figures, which represent the value of each policy objectives, are used as the basis for determining the value of each of the military functions.

These functions must be performed by a weapon system in order to achieve the military policy objectives. For the purpose of the model, four functions have been defined, but others may be used if the planner wishes. The four are intelligence, firepower, command and control, and logistics. Their relative importance is evaluated by assessing the importance of each of them in carrying out each policy objective under each type of war. Thus, the relative value of each function can be calculated by summing the products of its importance to the objective times the values of that objective. It should be noted that a function such as intelligence has a different value under general war than its value under limited war or cold war. Instead of attempting to calculate an overall value for each function, the planner carries these separate values throughout the model. This is important because the systems developed to carry out these functions must perform differently in each kind of war.

At this point it should be recognized that very few systems can completely carry out any function such as intelligence or firepower alone. Therefore, the system must be evaluated in the context of the total force structure in which it is expected to operate. However, each system may make some contribution to each function in each war type. It is this contribution that determines the value of that system in the year under consideration. The question that the system planner should ask himself at this point is "What percent of each function can a given system carry out at its stage of development in the year under consideration, in the expected operational environment?" This percent should be entered in the computer for each function and for each system. Of course, many of these contributions will be zero. It should be stressed that this contribution is judged only for one year at a time. The value of any system can now be calculated by summing the products of its contribution to each function in each war type times the value of that function, as previously calculated.

The technical feasibility of each system candidate is expressed as the probability that a system can be acquired by a specified date. However, a specific initial operational capability (IOC) date must be selected in order to prepare system milestones and cost projections. The system's value obviously varies with the life cycle of the system. The year that a system attains its IOC, its value is obviously not as great as the year in which it obtains complete operational capability (COC). To simplify the value profile, the growth in value between IOC and COC is assumed to be proportional to the increase in the number of units of that system in the inventory. After the COC date, however, obsolescence diminishes the system's value until the phase-out date. This obsolescence rate is represented in this model by a straight line whose slope is determined by the residual value in the year in which it is phased out. This residual value judgment is expressed in terms of a percentage of the maximum system value (at COC). The total system value can now be calculated through the use of a simplified value profile and the system value for any one year as calculated from the contribution table. The computer can handle these calculations if the following data are provided: the IOC date, the COC date, the phase-out date, the number of units at IOC and COC, and the residual value at phase-out, expressed as a percentage of the maximum value at COC date.

In the case of those systems that are not yet operational, provisions are made for estimating the time from the current year to the IOC date. The time required for the concept formulation phase is defined as the longest time required to solve any technical problems that must be solved to satisfy the prerequisites to the initiation of contract definition. The time required to complete contract definition and acquisition is defined as the total time for acquisition of the system. Provisions are made for handling uncertainty in these time estimates by asking the planner to estimate the longest time, the shortest time, and the most likely time required to solve each of the technical problems and to complete the acquisition phase. The computer then calculates the mean time from the current year to the IOC date and indicates the variance in this estimate.

The individual system value profiles can now be combined to estimate the value profiles for total force structures. It is obvious that more than one contribution table must be prepared in order to cover all future planning periods. Experience to date with the model has indicated that only two complete tables are required: one for an early period and one for a late period in order to calculate at least one point on the curve for each system.

Because the planner must operate within the limits of a budget, he must consider the cost of developing, acquiring, and operating the system he selects. In spite of its military worth, it will be of little value if economic constraints prevent its acquisition. Provisions are made in the model for the planner to record his estimates of the year-by-year cost of each system in two categories: 1) research and development, and 2) investment and operation.

In summary, the "system value for a specific year"

is the sum of the products of the system contribution to a function in each war type, times the value of the function for each war type, summed over all functions and war types. The "total system value" is the area under the curve of a system value profile plotted from the current date through the phase-out date of the system. The "expected total system value" is the total system value times the probability of achieving the designated IOC date. This expected total system value divided by the total system cost results in the relative system "desirability."

This is the end of the planner's problem, if he wishes to select systems and plan a force structure manually. However, when budget constraints are entered into the computer model, an "optimum" buy list can be constructed. This buy list will indicate the relative desirability and marginal value of all system candidates.

In this model, "marginal value" is defined as the amount by which the value of an optimum force structure is decreased, if a recommended system candidate is withdrawn from it and the released funds are applied to the next most desirable systems.

The computer will then indicate to the planner the value of his force structure for all the years in his planning period. The resulting figure can be compared with similar figures for alternative force structures to determine which is the most desirable among the alternatives considered.

On the Allocation of Common Physical Resources to Multiple Developmental Tasks

DANIEL D. ROMAN AND JACOB N. JOHNSON

Abstract—This article discusses the allocation of common physical resources among multiple development tasks. The contribution of this research will be the evolution of a quantitative model for performing the resource allocation. The model differs from others in that it allocates commonly used resources to multiple tasks over time; available resources are constraints and the allocation process is based upon network relationships, time considerations, and management objectives. Previous models have taken into account one or more of these factors, but none has considered them all.

The scope of the article is limited to a definition of the general

Manuscript received January 11, 1967. This paper was presented at the 18th Military Operations Research Symposium (MORS), Fort Bragg, N. C., October 1966.
The authors are with the American University, Washington, D. C.

environment for the model and its broad characteristics. Much of the information presented is derived from interviews with over 70 laboratory managers and others actively engaged in resource allocation for research and development (R&D) activities. A later article will present details of the model structure and the results of tests to be performed in actual management situations.

PROBLEM STATEMENT AND DEFINITION

THE PROBLEM IS the allocation of common physical resources to multiple tasks over time. Additional discussion of this problem will be accomplished by definition of the terms used and thus the evolution of the problem considered. The managerial importance and setting will be discussed later.

Multiple Tasks Over Time

A development task has two basic characteristics: it has some goal, and the intermediate stages and efforts required to reach that goal are definable. Therefore, the fundamental tool for this model is a network (or work flow plan) to represent the work of each task (project). The network depicts a series of related events and activities; the events reflect significant accomplishments, and the activities are the time-consuming elements.[1]

Because several tasks must be performed simultaneously,[2] several networks are required to represent these tasks in a time continuum (see Fig. 1). Each task will have independent starting and ending times and technical objectives.

Common Physical Resources

Resources to be utilized by the projects can be broadly divided into the following three classes:

1) resources utilized exclusively by one project,
2) resources used by only a few projects, and
3) resources utilized by all or most projects.

The resources in class 3) will be called "common" resources; the environment in which they are consumed is illustrated in Fig. 2. Because this resource allocation problem is complex[3] and for ease of discussion, not all of the common resources are considered. The common resources to be considered will be those directly coordinated or required by the task managers, for example, the test equipment and technicians. Other common resources may not be as directly coordinated into the task performance, for example, the computer programming and operation, administrative support or specialized consultation. Numerous types of resources and their normal utilization for development tasks are shown in Fig. 3.

The Allocation Process

The problem of coordinating the allocation of common resources to numerous development tasks (projects) is one of assigning the available resources in such a way so that all tasks progress as planned. Because the basic planning of task (project) selection has been performed, the total resources required for the multiple tasks can be determined by summing over time. Total resource requirements for resources A and B for tasks I, II, and III are shown in Fig. 4. It is often difficult for managers to predict the increased demand for a resource such as the demand for six units of resource A in time period 5 as shown in Fig. 4. If the manager has only three units of resource A, a decision must be made concerning the scheduling of the tasks. Such managerial decisions are the center of this problem. Decision criteria need to be established and methods for application of the criteria require development for the allocation of these common resources.

Several decisions could be proposed for the solution of the problem posed for resource A in Fig. 4 as:

1) delay task III,
2) obtain more units of resource A in time period 5 through time period 7 by hiring, over time or subcontracting,
3) change task schedules by starting task III in time period 1 or by changing task I to start in time period 1 and task III to start in time period 4, or
4) accelerate the first activities in task I through the application of additional resources to the activities.

Other Assumptions

A basic assumption for the environment is that task selection has been performed and that task priorities have been established. The anticipated start time, objective completion time, and task objectives are also considered as known factors for this analysis. Activities will be represented to reflect only the common resources considered. Task delays that may occur due to the lack of other resources would be reflected by a time shift for an activity.

IMPORTANCE OF THE PROBLEM

The importance of the problem has been evident in all interviews conducted. The importance is highlighted by pertinent aspects as:

1) development task leaders do not have direct access to all resources required for task performance,
2) the common resources are a vital source of accelerating or delaying task accomplishment, and
3) the coordination of the common resources is often too complex for undertaking by manual analysis or too important to be arbitrarily resolved.

The organization of development work is an entire area of study in itself but also the organization has a significant bearing on the resource allocation process and the importance of this problem.

At one extreme, the task leader may have all required resources under his control. At the other extreme, the task leader has control of no resources and is principally

---

[1] For information on network computations see D. C. Malcolm, J. H. Roseboom, C. E. Clark, and W. Fazar "Application of a technique for research and development program evaluation," *Operations Research*, vol. 7, pp. 651–652, September–October 1959.

For an overview of PERT and networks as a management tool see Daniel D. Roman, "The PERT system: An appraisal of program evaluation review technique," *J. Acad. Management*, vol. 5, April 1962.

[2] Interviews with managers of development effort have all indicated that numerous tasks must be worked on simultaneously. These tasks may originate by outside contract, as an internal service function (support) or as an internal subcontract.

[3] P. E. Holden, L. S. Fish, and H. L. Smith, *Top-Management Organization and Control* (New York: McGraw-Hill Book Company, Inc., 1951), pt. B, sect. 3; discuss this problem and indicate that typically the lower level managers in a production setting make these decisions and tend to be arbitrary in the allocation process. The author finds that the decisions for allocating these common resources in development work have a significant impact on tasks accomplishment.

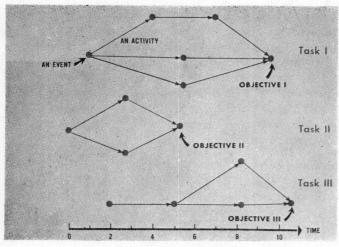

Fig. 1. Multiple projects over time.

RESOURCE TYPES CONSIDERED

Broad Resource Type	Examples of Resource Use	Normal Use of Resource PROJECTS			Considered in This Research
		ONE	FEW	MOST	
FINANCIAL	Funding			X	NO
TOP MGMT	Long Range Planning			X	NO
ADMIN	Purchasing			X	NO
	Computing			X	NO
SENIOR TECH TALENT	Task Leaders	X			NO
	Tech Specialties	X	X		NO
JUNIOR TECH TALENT	Specialists	X	X		NO
	Supporting			X	YES
TECHNICAL SUPT TALENT	Specialists	X	X		NO
	General			X	YES
TECHNICAL EQUIPMENT	Special	X	X		NO
	General			X	YES

Fig. 3. Resource types considered.

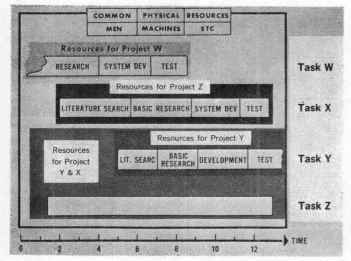

Fig. 2. Resources: common, individual task, few tasks.

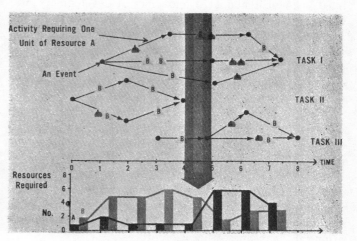

Fig. 4. Resources required by multiple tasks.

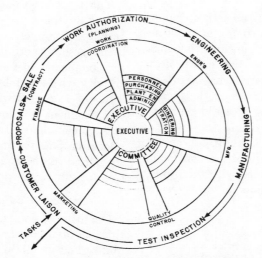

Fig. 5. Organization structure with operational flow.

a coordinator.[4] A more typical situation is that the task leader assumes prime responsibility for the entire project. This is unrealistic since many functions make significant contributions to the task but the task leader has no authority for these functions.[5] A circular organizational structure, resembling a wheel and emphasizing contribution and coordination, is shown in Fig. 5. Each prime function in the operational cycle is a spoke leading to the hub which is the executive. The flow of numerous tasks places a significant burden of resource allocation on the hub of the organization because coordination is required between task leaders and functional areas.

The use of common resources to accelerate tasks is recognized as an important method of altering schedules. It has been found that the requirement for assignment or reassignment of these common resources occurs as often as weekly and usually at least monthly.

APPROACH TO PROBLEM SOLUTION

The method being employed to solve the problem outlined is to visit about 70 managers of development activity or persons closely associated with this problem. A general model will then be constructed and the model will be altered and adopted to an actual managerial situation. Testing of the validity of the model will be conducted. Emphasis will be placed on the usefulness of the model in assisting management decision making.

GENERAL MODEL DESIGN

To provide a brief indication of the factors and complexity of the model, some of the considerations are presented. The design of the model will be expanded and improved after additional contact with the industry. The interviews conducted, historical developments, and logical backgrounds are used as the basis for these considerations of the resource allocation process.

Project Value Function

Associated with each project is an objective completion time which will be used for the computation of activity slack. In addition, a project value function must be given to provide a relative worth between projects and a value of time. The value function may represent the return for completing a project, such as the present worth of the chain of annual profits. It could represent the contractual penalty to be incurred in the event of project slippages. (Examples are given in Fig. 6.)

Activity scheduling flexibility in the time continuum is represented by slack. When combined with the project value function, slack provides a guide for decisions on resource allocations.

Activity Amount of Work

The amount of work for an activity is derived by multiplying the number of unit time periods required to complete an activity under normal conditions by the number of units of resource applied per time period. The unit time period may be an hour, day, month, or any unit of time that defines the smallest period within which work will be scheduled and resources allocated. The amount of time required for any activity can be determined by dividing the resources assigned into the amount of work as shown in Fig. 7.

Alternate Resource Levels

To provide for the possibility of doing the job faster or slower than normal, alternate levels of resource application can be provided. The first may be a resource level under accelerated work conditions ("speed-up"); the second may be a resource level under relaxed or extended work conditions ("slow-down"). The work efficiency at other than the normal rate is introduced to account for the absence of precise linear relationships. (Figure 7 shows examples of alternate resource levels.)

Levels of resource utilization provide great flexibility in manipulating time and resource requirements of each activity to meet resource availability levels. The same flexibility extends from activity concept to project concept where the speed-up, normal, and slow-down rates allow the system to adjust work accomplishment rates to meet project completion deadlines.

In Fig. 8, task I could be completed in as few as 9 time periods at the speed-up rate, or as many as 32 time periods at the slow-down rate. At the normal rate, the project could be completed in 16 time periods. Note that each rate requires a different peak work force. The total work force required reaches peaks of 20 men during period 5 at speed-up, 10 men during period 8 at normal, and 6 men during period 15 at slow-down rates.

Combinations of Resource Levels

The time required to complete an activity is determined by the level of resource allocation made to the activity. Examination of possible combinations for allocating resources in an extremely limited situation shows the complexity of the overall problem. In Fig. 9, a single activity with an amount of work equal to 6 and resource levels of 1, 2, or 3 with 6 time periods available for accomplishment is shown. The amount of work must be exactly completed. In this simple example, there are 71 allocation possibilities. This illustrates the complexity of the overall problem and the helplessness of human intuition for solving the problem.

Common Resource Pool

Quantity of common resources available and time periods of availability must be specified. Normal availability and premium or overtime availability should also be provided. Corresponding costs of resources are required.

---

[4] A recent study has shown that the authority of project managers varies but few have authority over all required resources. M. C. Yovits et al., Eds., *Research Program Effectiveness.* New York: Gordon and Breach, 1966, pp. 441–458.

[5] This discussion is aptly covered by D. D. Roman in his forthcoming book on R&D management.

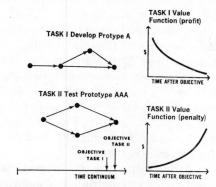

Fig. 6. Multiple task concept with task value functions.

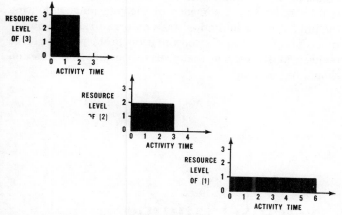

ACTIVITY AMOUNT OF WORK = 6 (CONTINUOUS RESOURCE ALLOCATION.)

Fig. 7. Alternate activity times by allocation of varying resource levels.

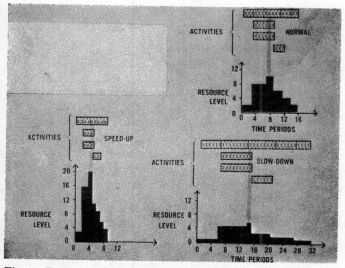

Fig. 8. Possible task completion and resource requirements at various homogenous resource levels.

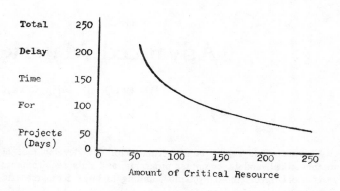

ACTIVITY AMOUNT OF WORK = 6, MUST BE EXACTLY COMPLETED; TIME FOR ACCOMPLISHMENT IS 6 TIME PERIODS

Fig. 9. Resource allocation combinations for one activity.

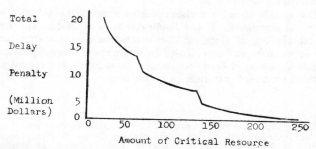

Fig. 10. Functions determined by parametric resource allocation.

Use of Model by Decision Maker

These procedures would give the decision maker the allocation of resources which would "optimize" his objectives, for example, the allocation of resources required (while observing availability of resources) to perform all projects "on time." One of the most valuable contributions to management is the flexibility of testing various policies, such as resource availabilities, and obtaining results of the policy in terms of output such as work slippage or overtime expense prior to implementing a policy.

Alternative management strategies may be inaccurately evaluated if resource constraints and costs are not observed. For example, some strategies may require more resources than are available or may use premium resources extensively without proper consideration of the costs involved. Inaccuracies in allocations are prone to occur in complex situations, because human intuition is inadequate for simultaneous consideration of the multidimensional interactions involved.

For example, parametric availability of a resource could be performed. The most critical resource may be selected for parametric study. The available amount of this resource could be variable while the availability of all other resources is constant. Resource allocation may be performed for each variation in critical resource availability, and the resultant total periods of project delay recorded together with the total penalty.

Figure 10 shows these figures and related incremental increases in penalty cost to incremental changes in resource availability. By the same procedure, the functions may be determined for other resources and for sets of resources changed simultaneously. The function for costs could also be found by accumulating normal and premium costs for resources consumed.

A tool is provided for use by managemnt which would objectively compare multiple tasks during the resource allocation process. Therefore, it should minimize any tendency of task leaders to employ devious approaches to obtaining the resources for his tasks. The tool should provide a means of viewing and evaluating the impact of an individual task on organizational objectives. The task leaders coordination problems should be reduced and a central managerial coordination function should be possible.

Advanced Materiel Systems Planning

BURTON V. DEAN AND LAWRENCE E. HAUSER

Abstract—This report is concerned with the development of mathematical models, computer programs, and data requirements to conduct development systems planning in large Research and Development organizations.

The specific planning decision problems are 1) the selection of technical alternatives, 2) the funding of system components, and 3) the funding of systems. Cost-effectiveness relationships are developed. A manual is presented for use in the training of planners in the utilization of computer results. Tests have been conducted utilizing simulated cost, risk, and value data.

Manuscript received January 11, 1967. This paper was presented at the 18th Military Operations Research Symposium (MORS), Fort Bragg, N. C., October 1966. Technical Memorandum 65, a study performed for the Office of Naval Research (ONR) and the Army Materiel Command (AMC), Department of Defense, Washington, D. C., was partially supported under Contract Nonr-1141(19).

B. Dean is with the Case Institute of Technology, Cleveland, Ohio.

L. E. Hauser is with General Dynamics—Convair, San Diego, Calif.

I. Introduction and Summary

Large Scale R&D Program Management under Uncertainty

A STUDY OF large-scale Research and Development (R&D) planning and decision making is being conducted by Case Institute of Technology. The complex problems of R&D planning and decision making require the use of quantitative methods. The principle uses of these methods are to consider the effects of different decisions on organizational objectives and to determine the optimal courses of action under constrained resource conditions.

The Case study has been involved in the development of mathematical models for use in R&D resource allocation problems. The problems are concerned with technical approach selection, component funding, and system planning.

By using mathematical models, computer programs, and available information concerning costs, uncertainties, and values, it is possible to obtain optimal solutions to decision problems. The mathematical model is the basic tool used to translate organizational objectives, technical approaches, and resource constraint statements into computer programs and analyses.

Since R&D planning requires the evaluation of future alternative courses of action, uncertainty is an important aspect of R&D planning. Removal of this uncertainty would result in a considerable loss in the potential for future system development. The Case study utilizes the available information on uncertainty in achieving technical alternatives or approaches, and develops a procedure for dealing with this uncertainty.

R&D planning requires the investigation of a large number of approaches. For example, there are 2^n possible courses of action on funding (or subsets of decisions) in the case of go–no go decisions involving n technical alternatives. The Case study has developed a mathematical model for handling the large number of alternatives through the use of a series of simple computerized methods, where the results of one stage are used in the succeeding stage.

It is expected that any systematic quantitative procedure ought to be *adaptable* to considering different organizational objectives and to be *capable* of investigating different decision criteria. The Case study methods are capable of being applied to different objectives and criteria, where the output solutions are optimal for each objective and can be analyzed by R&D planners.

R&D Decision Problems

The Case study has been primarily concerned with some of the specific decisions that are made in organizations where there are 1) a large number of technical alternatives; 2) uncertainties in ultimate system values, costs, and likelihood of success; 3) major restrictions on resources; and 4) the need to investigate a number of organizational objectives. The R&D decision problems of concern in this study are as follows:

1) *Technical Approach Selection:* What technical approaches ought to be followed for different amounts of funds, and what is the effect of different funding levels on the probability of achieving a system component concept?

2) *System Component Funding:* For a range of potentially available funds for system development, how should the system components be funded, so as to maximize the probability of achieving the system?

3) *System Planning:* For a range of potential budgets to be allocated to a set of systems, how should the systems be funded, so as to maximize the total expected value (or other decision criteria)?

The Structure of the Decision Models

As a basic part of the Case study, the underlying structure for decision making must be carefully developed. In each of the following statements the structure of the decision problem is briefly described.

1) *Technical Approach Selection:* A set of alternative technical approaches may be funded, where it is assumed that a forecast of the chance of success and the estimated cost are known. The purpose of a member of this set of approaches is to achieve a component concept, where any one of the parallel approaches, if successful, will satisfy the requirements for the component concept. A number of parallel approaches may be funded. The problem is to select the optimal set of technical approaches that maximize the probability of achieving the component concept, for a range of possible funding levels.

2) *System Component Funding:* For a specified system and associated set of system components, the problem is to determine the optimal funding levels for each system component so that the probability of achieving the system is maximized. This is to be answered for a range of available budgets.

3) *System Planning:* Consider that a large number of systems are to be funded, where the systems have corresponding values or priorities. In each case the systems have associated components and technical approaches. The problem is to determine the optimal allocation of funds to the systems so as to maximize a stated organizational criteria of effectiveness, such as total value or probability of achieving all systems. The satisfaction of minimum laboratory resource funding is to be included as one decision criteria. A range of total available funds is to be investigated.

4) *Cost–Effectiveness Analysis:* In each of the basic problems described in 1) to 3), the outputs (effectiveness) are related to inputs (cost). In each case the planner is able to relate the cost of system or component funding to value of probability of success. The cost–effectiveness relationship may be used to determine the proper organizational budget.

Optimization Criteria

To develop a mathematic model and corresponding computer programs, it is necessary to consider specific organizational criteria. The Case study has not been concerned with the development of these criteria, but rather with the formulation of the models and programs that make use of the criteria. Our concern has not been with a critique of these criteria, but rather with the development of methods that enable the planner to synthesize the large amount of available information so that alternative criteria may be examined. In each of the cases, a cost–effectiveness relationship has been developed for the specific criteria.

The criteria that have been used in the Case study are:

1) Minimize expected cost to achieve a technical approach.
2) Maximize the probability of achieving a system component for a specified cost.
3) Maximize the probability of achieving a system for a specified cost.
4) Maximize total expected value for a specified cost, with

   i) no priority on systems,
   ii) priority on certain systems to be funded at maximum effort, or
   iii) all systems to be funded.

5) Maximize probability of achieving all systems with

   i) no priorities on systems, or
   ii) priority on certain systems to be funded at maximum effort.

6) Provide all laboratories with at least minimum funding, with maximum total expected value.

We consider the three problems:

1) How should technical alternatives be selected so as to maximize the probability of achieving a component concept?
2) How should component concepts be funded so as to maximize the probability of achieving a system?
3) How should funds be allocated across systems so as to maximize total value?

Problems 1) to 3) may be solved sequentially, where the results in the form of relationships between cost and probability of success for one model may be used as inputs to a succeeding model.

Methods

The application of operations research is to develop decision models and solutions to the above problems that are parameterized by the dollar amounts to be made available. In this way it is possible to construct a cost–effectiveness approach to research planning which presents a relationship between the amount allocated to R&D and the maximum expected value to be achieved.

The basic method that is proposed for use in research planning is dynamic programming. Dynamic programming is a mathematical method for determining the optimal allocation of resources to activities so as to best achieve an organizational objective. For example, if an organization is engaged in a number of tasks, and can estimate the expected costs and benefits of each task, then dynamic programming may be used to find the optimal amount to allocate to each task so as to maximize the performance of the organization. In nontechnical terms, this is accomplished by solving a number of one-dimensional decision problems, instead of the many-dimensional allocation problem as originally formulated.

Since planning involves the allocation of resources to activities, it may be observed that dynamic programming is a useful planning tool. In particular, the measures of performance of alternate plans that correspond to different budget levels are obtained as a direct result of the dynamic programming solution. Because dynamic programming is an iterative method it is capable of being easily converted into a computer program. The use of dynamic programming is illustrated in the solutions of the decision problems 1) to 3).

Conclusions

This paper presents the basic methodology to be used in the solution of decision problems in large R&D organizations where uncertainties in outcomes and values are major factors.

The essential element of a management science is the use of scientific methods and models. Through the use of mathematical models of R&D management decision problems, it is possible to plan and control R&D programs efficiently. Because the models are probabilistic in nature, the parameters are subject to errors of estimation. However, computer programs utilizing the mathematical models permit the R&D manager to analyze the impact of technical, economic, and social changes on plans and to provide for the effective use of scientists and engineers to meet goals.

This report presents a theoretical model for solving three decision problems involved in research planning.

1) selection of technical alternatives (Model T),
2) funding of materiel concepts (Model M),
3) cost allocation across systems (Model S).

The models are *sequential* in that the results of each decision problem are used in the subsequent decision problem. The solutions are *parameterized* in that all results are presented in cost–effectiveness form so that the decision maker can select the minimal cost level to achieve effectiveness objectives. The solutions are *adaptive* to changes in the values of the model parameters.

To implement and make effective use of the models, data and information on parameter values are required as inputs to the models. However, only limited amounts of data are required for the initial decision problems. Problems 1) and 2) require estimates of the probability of success and costs. However, in addition, payoff value is required in the case of problem 3). It may be observed that an estimate of payoff value is not required in order to solve problems 1) and 2).

Computer programs have been developed and applied to the analysis of Army Materiel Command (AMC) problems. A small number of simulations have indicated that decisions are not sensitive to variations of parameter values within a range of 2 to 1 to each parameter. A manual is presented in the Appendix, which describes the procedures to be used by the planner.

II. System Planning Elements

The Army Materiel Command Application

The specific area of application of interest to AMC concerns the Army's QMDO (Qualitative Materiel Development Objective) planning. A QMDO is, in Army Materiel Command terms, "A statement of a Department of the Army military need for developing new materiel, the feasibility or specific definition of which cannot be determined sufficiently to permit establishing a qualitative materiel requirement." In the applications considered thus far, QMDO's include advanced materiel systems, such as advanced weapons systems desired by military planners. The time from the initiation of the QMDO stage to actual hardware production of these systems is expected to be between five and ten years.

Army requirements stipulate that a QMDO plan will contain at least the following aspects:

1) alternative technical approaches and a definition of the anticipated barriers to success in each case,
2) a summary of existing research projects and tasks, as well as an estimate of the additional research projects and tasks required to reduce the barrier, and an estimate of the research risks involved in each approach,
3) a task network for each approach considered feasible,
4) priorities for approaches and tasks,
5) an estimate of the time required to fulfill the objective for the level of funding recommended as appropriate, and
6) a cost estimate for each approach.

Also the Army has *three* priority classes for use in classifying QMDO's which are used to indicate their relative importance. These classes are

I) items of materiel essential to the security of the nation or mandatory for the successful accomplishment of assigned missions,
II) items of materiel which will increase, substantially, the combat effectiveness of the future Army or which will provide such a marked improvement over existing items that complete or extensive replacement would be justified, and
III) additional items of materiel required to complement higher priority items and improve the overall effectiveness of the future Army.

In "Stochastic Networks and Research Planning,"[1] mathematical models were developed for use in R&D budget allocation problems. This paper describes current progress in attempts to modify, extend, and implement these models for use by the Army Materiel Command (AMC).

[1] B. V. Dean, "Stochastic networks and research planning," Case Institute of Technology, Cleveland, Ohio, Tech. Memo. 40, September 1965.

The AMC Decision Problems

For analytic purposes, a QMDO can be represented as the end result in a network of tasks leading to higher-level elements.

We say that a QMDO is composed of several "materiel concepts." In order for a QMDO to be achieved, all necessary materiel concepts must be achieved. Consider, for example, a QMDO which represents a new anti-ICBM missile. In this case, the essential components for this missile system would be a guidance system, a warhead, including fuzing, a propulsion system, and a structure for the missile (Fig. 1). If the system is to have a new or extended capability, perhaps all of several of the components must develop new capability over existing components. At any rate, it is clear that all components are essential to the development of the anti-ICBM missile system.

In this example, suppose that there are requirements for a new guidance system, and that there are several possible technical approaches which may be followed in order to achieve the required guidance capability (see Fig. 2). Clearly, even if only one of these several technical approaches is successful, then the materiel component capability has been achieved. In other words, at least one of the several possible approaches must succeed.

The AMC can provide subjective estimates of the probability of success and probable cost of all technical approaches, assuming that each approach is followed. Since there are severe budget constraints, it may not be possible to fund all possible technical approaches for a given materiel concept. However, *at least one* approach must be funded in order to have any chance of achieving the materiel concept. Furthermore, *all* materiel concepts must be funded to have any chance of achieving a QMDO.

AMC's decision problem is *how to plan to fund the technical areas that need support.* AMC must select for funding a "most effective" menu of technical approaches which will lead to the development of all QMDO's.

This budget allocation problem decomposes into the three interrelated problems that have been formulated.

1) For a fixed budget, and many possible QMDO's to fund, AMC must decide how to best *allocate* funds among the various QMDO's.
2) Once the amount to allocate to a particular QMDO has been determined, AMC must decide how best to *allocate* this amount among the necessary materiel concepts.
3) Similarly, for each materiel concept allocation, an optimal *selection* of technical approaches must be made. The end result of the allocation of the original budget is a *list* of all technical approaches which are to be funded, an *amount* to be expended on each materiel concept, and an *amount* to be expended on each QMDO. Finally, a *cost–effectiveness* relationship is determined which relates the total cost to the maximum expected military

value or a suitable alternate criteria, so that a planner can select a desired total budget level.

Data Requirements

It will be seen that the models require specific data. These requirements are

i) complete network structures of each QMDO, that is, the QMDO–materiel concept–technical approach descriptions,

ii) estimates of probability of success for each potential technical approach, and

iii) estimates of expected cost during the planning period for each technical approach.

If a decision criterion specifies additional constraints, for example,

iv) assignments of military value to the QMDO's, or minimum funding levels for laboratories which perform applied research and development for AMC,

then these additional data must be provided.

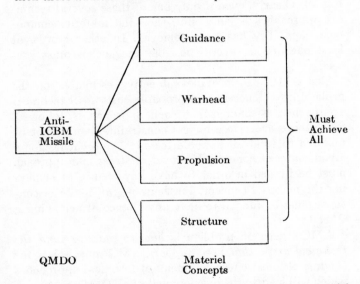

QMDO   **Materiel Concepts**

Fig. 1. The relationship between the QMDO and its materiel concepts.

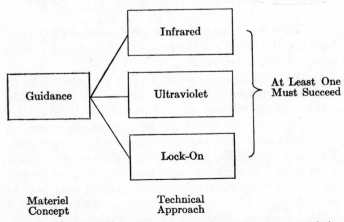

Materiel Concept   **Technical Approach**

Fig. 2. The relationship between a materiel concept and its alternative technical approaches.

The Military Value Concept

Although all QMDO's are assigned a priority level which describes their military importance, it is necessary to derive a *numerical* value for this rating in order to maximize total expected military value. In this case, all QMDO's are assigned a relative military value, with the range of the scale of values and the actual values to be determined by the military planner. A decision criterion might be to "maximize the expected military value" attainable for a given budget level. As will be demonstrated subsequently, it is possible to vary the numerical military values, in order to *test* for the sensitivity of decisions to estimates of military values.

The AMC Data

In order to test the efficiency of methods and sensitivity of solutions developed by the Case mathematical models, AMC provided input data.

Specifically, 18 materiel systems (of a total of 157 which AMC must consider for budgeting) were selected, and for each of the 18 systems, a QMDO plan was simulated which consisted of the following:

i) planning networks including the technical approach level,

ii) estimated annual R&D cost for each technical approach and the laboratory where the work would be performed,

iii) estimated probability of success for each technical approach,

iv) three sets of military values; each set of values being arrived at by means of a different order-ranking technique based on estimates of future strategic needs.

The order-ranking values given by AMC are displayed in Table I.

TABLE I
ORDER-RANKING VALUES ASSIGNED BY AMC

QMDO	Code	First Technique*	Second Technique*	Third Technique*	Priority Class (CDC)†
1	A	10.00	9.65	1.90	1
2	B	9.00	8.20	10.00	1
3	C	9.75	6.40	9.00	1
4	D	8.95	4.60	5.30	1
5	E	8.65	2.80	3.35	1
6	F	8.35	2.60	5.90	1
7	GAC	7.25	8.00	7.75	2
8	GA	6.95	7.50	7.35	2
9	GB	6.95	7.50	7.35	2
10	GC	6.95	7.50	7.35	2
11	H	4.45	6.40	9.75	2
12	I	5.85	10.00	8.60	2
13	J	5.85	9.85	1.00	2
14	K	3.95	2.05	2.65	2
15	M	3.10	6.60	8.20	3
16	N	2.55	4.80	9.35	3
17	O	1.70	4.05	4.70	3
18	P	1.00	1.00	4.10	3

* Estimated by AMC
† CDC (Combat Development Command)

III. Mathematical Modelling and Dynamic Programming

The Need for a Mathematical Model

QMDO planning requires the investigation of a very large number of courses of action. In the data for the QMDO's provided by AMC, there were 198 technical approaches to be considered for funding, or $2^{198} \approx 10^{60}$ possible decisions to consider. Although many of these could be eliminated at very low overall budget values, it is clear that it is not feasible to consider a manual approach and expect to obtain approximately optimal funding. Thus, a mathematical model is required to aid in the optimization. The mathematical model is merely a tool to increase the planner's capacity to search for and evaluate different policies for the allocation of funds.

Dynamic Programming as an Optimization Method

One necessary feature of any quantitative procedure is that it be flexible enough to handle different decision (or optimization) criteria. Dynamic programming was chosen primarily because it lends itself to the development of algorithms for use on electronic digital computers. However, the dynamic programming technique possesses many other characteristics which are noteworthy:

1) *flexibility* in choice of optimization criteria,
2) *rapidity* of achieving optimal solutions on computers,
3) solutions are given not only for the budget level under consideration, but for *all* feasible budget levels.
4) the solutions lend themselves to *cost–effectiveness* analysis, and
5) the models permit a *decomposition* into three submodels, each of which can be solved using dynamic programming.

IV. The Mathematical Models

Optimal Selection of Technical Approaches (Model T)

For a specified materiel concept we define

P_i as the *probability* that the ith technical approach is successful, if it is selected for funding,

C_i as the estimated *cost* of funding the ith technical approach, if it is selected for funding, and

$f_i(C)$ as the *maximum* probability of accomplishing the materiel concept, choosing an optimal set of the first i technical approaches, with C dollars available to allocate across the technical approaches in a materiel concept.

The underlying assumption is that *only one* of several parallel technical approaches need be successful for attainment of the materiel concept.

Then

$$f_1(C) = \begin{cases} P_1, & \text{if } C_1 \leq C \\ 0, & \text{if } C_1 > C \end{cases}$$

$$f_2(C) = \begin{cases} \text{MAX } \{1 - (1 - P_2)[1 - f_1(C - C_2)], f_1(C)\}, \\ \qquad\qquad\qquad\qquad \text{if } C_2 \leq C \\ f_1(C), \quad \text{if } C_2 > C \end{cases}$$

and, in general,

$$f_N(C) = \begin{cases} \text{MAX } \{1 - (1 - P_N)[1 - f_{N-1}(C - C_N)], f_{N-1}(C)\}, \\ \qquad\qquad\qquad\qquad \text{if } C_N \leq C \\ f_{N-1}(C), \quad \text{if } C_N > C \end{cases}$$

Optimal Funding of Materiel Concepts (Model M)

For a specified QMDO comprised of j materiel concepts, the solution of Model T yields probabilities $P_j(C)$, the maximum probability of achieving the jth materiel concept if C dollars are allocated to it. Furthermore, this optimal solution for all increments of C dollars is derived by noting the choice (yes or no) in the maximizing criteria at each step. Considering an amount to be allocated to a QMDO, the decision problem is to find how much to allocate to each materiel concept within the given QMDO.

Define

$F_i(C)$ as the maximum probability of achieving materiel concepts $1, 2, \ldots, i$.

The underlying assumption is that *each* materiel concept must be successful before the QMDO is achieved.

Then

$$F_1(C) = P_1(C).$$

$$F_2(C) = \underset{0 \leq x \leq C}{\text{MAX}} [P_2(x) F_1(C - x)],$$

and in general,

$$F_M(C) = \underset{0 \leq x \leq C}{\text{MAX}} [P_M(x) F_{M-1}(C - x)].$$

Optimal System Funding (Model S)

Now suppose there are W distinct QMDO's to which funds must be allocated. Each QMDO has a military value, or priority, V_i, assigned to it which describes its importance relative to the other QMDO's.

The decision problem is to determine how to allocate the total budget B so as to maximize the total expected military value, $\sum_{K=1}^{W} V_K G_K(C_K)$, subject to $\sum_{K=1}^{W} C_K \leq B$, where

$G_K(Y)$ is the maximum probability of attaining QMDO K, with Y dollars to allocate to it. The G_K functions are determined, of course, by Model M.

Let

$H_i(B) = $ the maximum attainable expected military values with QMDO's $1, 2, \cdots, i$.

Then

$$H_1(B) = V_1 G_1(B),$$

$$H_2(B) = \underset{0 \leq x \leq B}{\text{MAX}} [V_2 G_2(x) + H_1(B - x)], \text{ and}$$

in general

$$H_w(B) = \underset{0 \leq x \leq B}{\text{MAX}} [V_w G_w(x) + H_{w-1}(B - x)].$$

V. Additional Objectives and Model Extensions

i) The optimal solution to Model S may allocate no funds to one or more QMDO's. However, it may be desirable to stipulate that each QMDO must be funded at some minimum threshold level, which provides each QMDO with a positive probability of being attained. It is not difficult to add this criterion to Model S, and the "loss" involved in using this constraint in the example to be described is negligible. At the other extreme, it may be desirable to fund a certain (priority) class of QMDO's at a maximum level, and then use Model S to allocate any excess funds across the remaining QMDO's. This can be accomplished, but again, the expected military value will in general be somewhat less than that attainable without using this constraint.

ii) Suppose that, instead of each QMDO being assigned a priority or military value, it is determined to be essential that *all* QMDO's be achieved, and it is desired to maximize the *probability* of achieving all QMDO's. Then, if $M(C)$ is the maximum probability of attaining the first i QMDO's, we have (in analogy to Model M)

$$M_1(B) = G_1(B)$$

$$M_2(B) = \underset{0 \leq x \leq B}{\text{MAX}} [G_2(x) M_1(B - x)]$$

and in general

$$M_w(B) = \underset{0 \leq x \leq B}{\text{MAX}} [G_w(x) M_{w-1}(B - x)].$$

Note that the specifications of maximizing the probability of attaining all QMDO's insures that each QMDO K will be funded at a level C_k such that $G_k(C_k) > 0$. That is, a threshold funding level of positive probability is assured in most cases.

VI. The Computer Programs

Models T, M, and S (with its modifications) have been incorporated into computer programs. The programs are written in ALGOL, and runs have been made on Case Institute of Technology's UNIVAC 1107 computer, utilizing the AMC data.

In its present form, the program includes some "oversolving" of the problem—that is, more calculations than necessary are made to provide programming simplicity. If the program were to be used on a large scale, some detailed reprogramming would probably be worthwhile; however, on the basis of present usage, the program is reasonably efficient (manual operations are not difficult) and very fast (the total running time is less than five minutes per run).

The nature of the program—three optimal search models in sequence—are such that the number of calculations increase exponentially with the number of QMDO's. Originally, it was planned to supply AMC with optimal solutions for increments of $10 000 in the QMDO funding, from $0 to $22.5 million (the cost to fund all technical approaches given). However, computer run times were very high using such a fine grid. For example, models T and M alone took about 15 minutes. It is estimated that model S would require about eight hours of running time to solve one optimization problem in $10 000 increments.

As a result, it was necessary to choose a less fine grid. Model T was solved as before in $10 000 increments, because of the extreme sensitivity of technical approaches to larger intervals. However, Models M and S were solved in intervals of $100 000. Analysis of outputs indicates that solutions (expected military values) are not too sensitive to even these rather large increments, that is, the rise in expected military value is modest under the $100 000 search. Since computer time is quite expensive, and computer-time increases are of the order of the square of the number of points evaluated, and because solutions do not seem sensitive to the $100 000 interval, it appears that the larger search grid is quite well justified. To solve in $10 000 increments would require roughly 100 times the present computer running times.

Under these modifications, run times are about five minutes for each optimization criterion with the AMC data. Runs using only 12 of the 18 QMDO's were less than two minutes each. The figure below shows the increases in computer time that have been experienced for increases in the number of QMDO's.

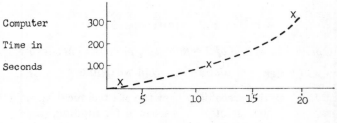

Number of QMDO's

For reference purposes, sample printouts of the computer solution to each of the three basic models are included in this paper. Figure A shows optimal funding to QMDO 1 at various budget levels; Fig. B displays optimal funding to the materiel concept of QMDO 5; while Fig. C is a sample of the computer solution to allocation among technical approaches.

A manual has been written explaining, in detail, what the different sheets display and how solutions are extracted from them. It is included as the Appendix.

TIMAL FUNDING FOR QMDO 11

Fig. A.

DATA FOR QNOO   3   MAXIMUM ATTAINABLE PROBABILITIES FOR ACHIEVING ALL MATERIEL

QNOO						
0	0	.000	0	.000	0	.000
10000	10000	.000	10000	.000	0	.000
20000	20000	.400	20000	.000	0	.000
30000	30000	.400	30000	.000	0	.000
40000	40000	.400	30000	.200	0	.000
50000	50000	.400	30000	.200	0	.000
60000	60000	.580	30000	.200	0	.000
70000	70000	.580	30000	.200	0	.000
80000	80000	.580	30000	.200	0	.000
90000	90000	.580	30000	.290	0	.000
100000	100000	.580	30000	.290	0	.000
110000	110000	.580	30000	.290	0	.000
120000	120000	.580	30000	.290	0	.000
130000	130000	.706	30000	.290	100000	.120
140000	140000	.706	30000	.290	100000	.120
150000	150000	.706	30000	.290	100000	.120
160000	160000	.706	30000	.353	100000	.120
170000	170000	.706	30000	.353	100000	.120
180000	180000	.706	30000	.353	100000	.120
190000	190000	.706	30000	.353	100000	.174
200000	200000	.794	30000	.353	100000	.174
210000	210000	.794	30000	.353	100000	.174
220000	220000	.794	30000	.353	100000	.174
230000	230000	.794	130000	.397	100000	.174
240000	240000	.794	130000	.397	100000	.174
250000	250000	.794	130000	.423	100000	.211
260000	260000	.794	130000	.423	100000	.211
270000	270000	.794	130000	.423	100000	.211
280000	280000	.794	130000	.423	100000	.211
290000	290000	.794	130000	.423	100000	.211
300000	300000	.794	130000	.423	100000	.211
310000	310000	.794	130000	.423	100000	.211
320000	320000	.794	130000	.423	100000	.211
330000	330000	.794	130000	.476	100000	.211
340000	340000	.794	130000	.476	100000	.238
350000	350000	.794	130000	.476	100000	.238
360000	360000	.794	130000	.476	100000	.254
370000	370000	.794	130000	.476	100000	.254
380000	380000	.794	130000	.476	100000	.254
390000	390000	.794	130000	.476	100000	.254
400000	400000	.794	130000	.476	100000	.254
410000	410000	.794	130000	.476	100000	.254
420000	420000	.794	130000	.476	100000	.254
430000	430000	.794	130000	.476	100000	.254
440000	440000	.794	230000	.508	100000	.266
450000	450000	.794	230000	.508	100000	.286
460000	460000	.794	230000	.508	100000	.286
470000	470000	.794	230000	.508	100000	.286
480000	480000	.794	230000	.508	100000	.286
490000	490000	.794	230000	.508	100000	.286

Fig. B.

OMDO 3

DATA FOR MATERIEL CONCEPT 1

TECHNICAL ALTERNATIVE	COST OF PERFORMING ALTERNATIVE	PROBABILITY OF SUCCESS
1	30000	.500
2	20000	.600
3	70000	.100
4	30000	.100
5	40000	.200

CALCULATIONS OF MAXIMUM ATTAINABLE PROBABILITIES FOR MATERIEL CONCEPT 1 WITH BASIC ALTERNATIVES LISTED

									ALTERNATIVES LISTED	
0	0	.000	0	.000	0	.000	0	.000		
10000	0	.000	0	.000	0	.000	0	.000		
20000	1	.000	1	.600	0	.600	0	.600	2	
30000	1	.500	1	.600	0	.600	0	.600	2	
40000	1	.500	1	.600	0	.600	0	.600	2	
50000	1	.500	1	.600	0	.600	0	.600	1 2	
60000	1	.500	1	.800	0	.800	0	.800	1 2	
70000	1	.500	1	.800	0	.800	0	.800	1 2	
80000	1	.500	1	.800	1	.820	1	.820	1 2 4	
90000	1	.500	1	.800	1	.820	1	.840	1 2 4 5	
100000	1	.500	1	.800	1	.820	1	.840	1 2 4 5	
110000	1	.500	1	.800	1	.820	1	.840	1 2 4 5	
120000	1	.500	1	.820	1	.820	1	.856	1 2 4 5	TIE
130000	1	.500	1	.820	1	.820	1	.856	1 2 4 5	TIE
140000	1	.500	1	.820	1	.820	1	.856	1 2 4 5	TIE
150000	1	.500	1	.820	1	.838	1	.856	1 2 4 5	
160000	1	.500	1	.820	1	.838	1	.856	1 2 4 5	
170000	1	.500	1	.820	1	.838	1	.856	1 2 4 5	
180000	1	.500	1	.820	1	.838	1	.856	1 2 4 5	
190000	1	.500	1	.820	1	.838	1	.870	1 2 3 4 5	

Fig. C.

TABLE II

DESCRIPTION OF OPTIMIZATION CRITERIA

Run I	Maximize expected military value using first-order-ranking technique
Run II	Maximize expected military value using second-order-ranking technique
Run III	Fund all priority class 1 QMDO's at maximum level; maximize expected military value of remaining QMDO's using first-order-ranking technique
Run IV	Fund all priority class 1 QMDO's at maximum level; maximize expected military value of remaining QMDO's using second-order-ranking technique
Run V	Maximize expected military value using first-order-ranking technique, under constraint that all QMDO's must be funded at a level to give them a positive (nonzero) probability of attainment
Run VI	Maximize expected military value using second-order-ranking technique, under constraint that all QMDO's must be funded at a level to give them a positive (nonzero) probability of attainment
Run VII	Fund all priority class 1 QMDO's at maximum level; find allocation across remaining QMDO's which maximize the probability of achieving all of them
Run VIII	Maximize the probability of achieving all QMDO's
Run IX	Maximize expected military value using third-order-ranking technique.

VII. OPTIMIZATION CRITERIA

At the outset, AMC asked for optimal solutions to the problem "maximize expected military value," and provided two order-rankings for the eighteen QMDO's. When the solutions were developed, there were some unexpected results—under both order-ranking techniques, there were several QMDO's which were not funded in the optimal solutions for the budgets rated high, average, and low by AMC.

When these results were presented, the reaction was quite typical of operations research work: the decision makers decided that perhaps the decision criterion used was not entirely suitable, and began to suggest new constraints which should be satisfied by any "optimal" solution. One comment was that all QMDO's should have some funding, in order to satisfy user requirement, so that all QMDO's receive emphasis to some degree. Another comment pointed out that by allowing "no funding" solutions, continuity in research programs could be lost, as an on-going project one year could be dropped the next year, then possibly reinstated later.

Also, it was pointed out that perhaps all priority class I) systems should be funded at their maximum level, in order to provide such QMDO's with the best chance of success. In this case, any remaining funds would be allocated across QMDO's in priority classes II) and III) according to some optimization criterion.

These new decision criteria were programmed and more test runs were made. In all, nine different computer runs have been made for AMC. Descriptions of each of these runs are given in Table II.

AMC also hoped to impose funding constraints on the solution to insure that each research laboratory would receive some minimum amount of support. AMC provided Case with data showing the cost relationship between laboratories and technical approaches. Section IX is devoted entirely to the laboratory constraint problem.

VIII. ANALYSIS OF SOME RESULTS

In Table III, some actual solutions derived for AMC are given.

It should be noted that the use of $100 000 increments builds an inherent bias into the budget values. Specifically, technical approaches can be allocated funds only in increments of $100 000, and this tends to build slack into the budget levels in the final solutions. For example, in Run I, a budget level of $14 million from the QMDO 18 sheet reduces, when the slack is removed, to $12.34 million. Because this effect is uniform, optimality is not affected—the optimal solutions are correct as listed at the $12.34 million level. To the military planner, this bias means only that to find an optimal solution for a given budget of about 12 percent (for the present data) greater than he desires, in which case the actual budget as determined will be approximately correct. The actual solutions are optimal at the actual budget level.

Detailed Solution for Run I, $12.34 Million Budget

In Table III, the complete solution to Run I is given for an initial budget of $14 million, and an actual budget of $12.34 million. Funding of QMDO's in Run I seems to be of two types—near maximum funding or no funding at all. This characteristic is caused by the high initial dollar input required to achieve a nonzero probability of success for a QMDO, which is in the form of a "set-up" cost.

TABLE III
OPTIMAL SYSTEM FUNDING, MATERIEL CONCEPT FUNDING, AND TECHNICAL APPROACH SELECTION

Run I
Initial Budget = $14 million   Actual Budget = $12.34 million   Value = 36.607

QMDO	Initial Allocation*	Actual Allocation*
18	300	110
17	0	0
16	0	0
15	800	800
14	400	280
13	1100	1030
12	0	0
11	1300	1130
10	800	660
9	500	360
8	600	560
7	900	730
6	600	510
5	1500	1420
4	1100	1030
3	1300	1200
2	1200	940
1	1600	1580
	14 000	12 340

* Thousands of dollars

QMDO 18—$110,000—Probability = 0.940

Materiel Concepts	Technical Alternatives
3—$10,000—1.0†	3
2—$30,000—1.0	2
1—$70,000—0.94	1, 2

QMDO 17—None

QMDO 16—None

QMDO 15—$800,000—Probability = 0.361

Materiel Concepts	Technical Alternatives
4—$170,000—0.520†	1, 2
3—$320,000—0.880	1, 3
2—$110,000—0.940	1, 2
1—$200,000—0.840	2, 3

QMDO 14—$280,000—Probability = 0.393

Materiel Concepts	Technical Alternatives
3—$150,000—0.900†	1
2—$ 60,000—0.840	1, 2
1—$ 70,000—0.520	1, 2

QMDO 13—$1,030,000—Probability = 0.112

Materiel Concepts	Technical Alternatives
4—$170,000—0.608	1, 2, 3
3—$230,000—0.664	1, 2, 3
2—$390,000—0.533	1, 2, 3, 4, 5
1—$240,000—0.568	1, 2, 3

QMDO 12—None

QMDO 11—$1,130,000—Probability = 0.192

Materiel Concepts	Technical Alternatives
4—$340,000—0.706†	1, 2, 3
3—$390,000—0.764	1, 2, 3, 4
2—$240,000—0.300	1, 2
1—$160,000—0.697	1, 2, 3, 4

QMDO 10—$660,000—Probability = 0.448

Materiel Concepts	Technical Alternatives
3—$100,000—0.969†	1, 2, 3, 4, 5, 6
2—$140,000—0.680	1, 2, 3
1—$120,000—0.680	1, 2, 3

QMDO 9—$360,000—Probability = 0.744

Materiel Concepts	Technical Alternatives
2—$130,000—0.846†	1, 2, 3, 4
1—$230,000—0.879	1, 2, 3, 4, 5

QMDO 8—$560,000—Probability = 0.486

Materiel Concepts	Technical Alternatives
3—$350,000—0.984†	1, 2, 3, 4, 5, 6
2—$100,000—0.744	1, 2, 3
1—$110,000—0.664	1, 2, 3

QMDO 7—$730,000—Probability = 0.488

Materiel Concepts	Technical Alternatives
3—$460,000—0.949†	1, 2, 3, 4, 5, 6
2—$140,000—0.680	1, 2, 3
1—$130,000—0.680	1, 3, 2

QMDO 6—$510,000—Probability = 0.071

Materiel Concepts	Technical Alternatives
3—$150,000—0.280†	1, 2
2—$160,000—0.440	1, 2
1—$200,000—0.580	2, 3

QMDO 5—$1,420,000—Probability = 0.116

Materiel Concepts	Technical Alternatives
3—$250,000—0.600†	1, 2
2—$500,000—0.440	1, 2
1—$670,000—0.440	2, 3 or 1, 3 (tie)

QMDO 4—$1,030,000—Probability = 0.620

Materiel Concepts	Technical Alternatives
3—$600,000—0.880†	1, 2
2—$150,000—0.860	1, 2
1—$280,000—0.820	1, 2, 3

QMDO 3—$1,200,000—Probability = 0.270

Materiel Concepts	Technical Alternatives
5—$110,000—0.996†	2, 3, 5
4—$370,000—0.937	1, 2, 3
3—$270,000—0.904	1, 2, 3
2—$250,000—0.400	1
1—$200,000—0.800	1, 2

QMDO 2—$940,000—Probability = 0.309

Materiel Concepts	Technical Alternatives
4—$250,000—0.952	1, 2, 3
3—$250,000—0.640	1, 2
2—$230,000—0.640	1, 2, 3
1—$210,000—0.794	1, 2, 3, 4

QMDO 1—$1,580,000—Probability = 0.282

Materiel Concepts	Technical Alternatives
4—$190,000—0.720†	1, 2, 3
3—$190,000—0.748	1, 2, 3, 4
2—$600,000—0.808	1, 2, 3, 4
1—$600,000—0.650	1, 3

† Maximum probability of achieving the materiel concept

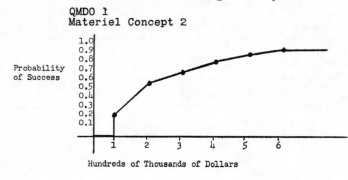

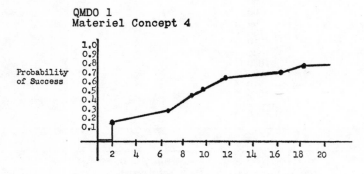

Fig. 3. Example of cost–effectiveness analysis at the materiel concept level.

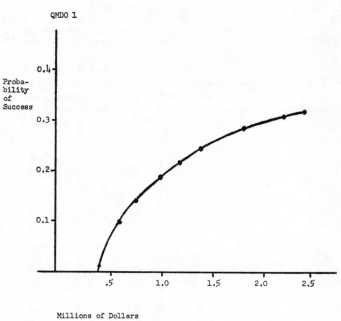

Fig. 4. Example of cost–effectiveness analysis at the QMDO level.

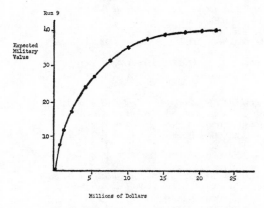

Fig. 5. Example of cost–effectiveness analysis at the total system level.

Cost–Effectiveness Analysis

One particularly appealing aspect of the Case dynamic programming solution is that cost–effectiveness relations can be derived and analyzed at all levels of QMDO planning.

In Figs. 3 to 5, sample graphs showing illustrative cost–effectiveness relationships are presented.

Figure 3 gives examples of cost–probability of success relations for the materiel concept level (Model T).

Figure 4 shows cost–probability of success curves for the QMDO level (Model M). Note that the curve tends to smooth out at this level, and that the threshold of non-zero effectiveness tends to increase.

Figure 5 depicts the relationship between cost and expected military value (Model S). The very rapid growth under optimal funding is typical of results obtained from the AMC data. A general type of result for runs to date seems to be that about 40 percent of the budget needed for total funding will, under optimum funding, yield about 85 percent, of the maximum attainable expected military value.

Comparisons of Solutions Generated by Different Optimization Criteria

Table IV compares the solutions for optimal $14 million allocations for the nine runs made to date. ($14.8 was required to provide minimum funding in Run VII).

Runs I, II, and IX are identical except for the military

values assigned. Comparison of the optimum allocations given with the military values listed with the AMC data reveals that significant discrepancies usually occur only when there is at least a threefold difference in the military value weightings given a QMDO!

Runs III to VIII are all constrained solutions; however, the Case method permits direct analysis of budgets and values, providing a cost–effectiveness relation to be developed. For example, Run V is identical to Run I, except that Run V does not permit any QMDO to be omitted in funding. The tradeoff for this benefit (funding all systems) is seen to be a drop in expected military value from 35.6 to 33.5, or about a 5.8-percent loss. The important fact is that the analyst can determine what must be lost in relative military effectiveness for additional organizational constraints that are to be imposed on the solution.

TABLE IV
COMPARISON OF SOLUTIONS GENERATED BY DIFFERENT OPTIMIZATION CRITERIA IN MILLIONS OF DOLLARS*

QMDO	I	II	III	IV	V	VI	VII	VIII	IX
1	1.6	2.4	2.4	2.4	1.6	1.6	2.4	1.0	—
2	1.2	1.2	1.2	1.2	1.0	1.0	1.2	0.7	1.2
3	1.3	1.3	1.5	1.5	1.3	1.0	1.5	1.0	1.3
4	1.1	0.9	1.1	1.1	0.9	0.9	1.1	0.5	1.1
5	1.5	—	2.3	2.3	0.4	0.4	2.3	0.7	0.4
6	0.6	—	0.8	0.8	0.6	0.3	0.8	0.6	0.8
7	0.9	0.9	0.9	0.8	0.8	0.8	0.3	0.6	0.9
8	0.6	0.6	0.6	0.6	0.6	0.6	0.3	0.5	0.6
9	0.5	0.5	0.5	0.5	0.5	0.5	0.2	0.5	0.5
10	0.8	0.8	0.8	0.8	0.8	0.7	0.3	0.6	0.8
11	1.3	1.3	—	—	1.0	0.9	0.5	1.1	1.3
12	—	—	—	—	1.5	1.5	1.3	1.9	—
13	1.1	1.2	—	—	0.4	0.9	0.4	1.0	—
14	0.4	0.4	0.6	0.4	0.4	0.4	0.4	0.4	0.6
15	0.8	1.3	1.0	1.3	0.8	0.8	0.4	0.8	1.3
16	—	—	—	—	0.7	0.7	0.7	1.3	1.8
17	—	0.9	—	—	0.4	0.7	0.4	0.7	1.1
18	0.3	0.3	0.3	0.3	0.3	0.3	0.3	0.3	0.3
Expected Military Value	35.607	34.112	34.059	30.767	33.469	31.992	(32.3)†	(33.1)†	37.991

* Budget: $14 million except in VII, where $14.8 million was required.
† Approximate expected military value, using first-order-ranking technique, listed for purposes of comparison.

IX. THE LABORATORY CONSTRAINT PROBLEM

As was previously mentioned, AMC was interested in the effect of the proposed mathematical model's allocations on the various laboratories which perform research for AMC. AMC hoped to be able to insure that each laboratory would be funded at a specified minimum level in order to provide continuity in R&D programs.

Hypothetical AMC laboratory data is included in this section. The Case team evaluated the allocations to the various laboratories under the computer-given optimal solution in Run I (Tables III and IV) and found that severe violations occurred only at a low funding budget level.

Case believes that a computer-programmed solution to the constraint problem would be both difficult to develop and costly to use in terms of computer time. A manual computer-aided "approximation" method is suggested by the Case team.

The approach is predicated on the experience gained from the AMC QMDO problem, where at budget levels considered likely or reasonably by AMC, there do not seem to be severe laboratory constraint violations.

The computer can be programmed to list the funding by QMDO and by laboratory, under a specified budget. Tables present worksheets which show the type of data required from the computer.

Example

We now give an example, in some detail, of the manual method proposed for handling laboratory constraints.

Table V displays the funding to the laboratories under the normal ($12.5 million) budget. Table VI summarizes data provided by AMC which identified each technical approach with one of the nine laboratories. Under complete funding each laboratory would receive funds as shown in the "total" of Table VI. AMC required, arbitrarily, that each laboratory receive minimum funding of 40 percent of this potential total funding.

The results of the analysis are shown in Table VII. The results of a similar analysis for the reduced ($10 million) budget problem are shown in Table VIII.

Table V indicates that there are two constraint violations at the normal budget level. Laboratory F required $2170 thousand, but received only $1700 thousand. Laboratory H was supposed to receive at least $1045 thousand, but was allocated only $945 thousand.

The violation in Laboratory F was handled as follows: comparison of potential allocation in Table VI with actual allocation in Table VII showed that Laboratory F could obtain "extra" funds from only two sources. QMDO 1 had a possible $1700 thousand allocation, and was using only $1100 thousand of it under the present solution. And QMDO 12, with a possible allocation of $3150 thousand to Laboratory F, was not funded under the present solution.

It was decided to bring Laboratory F up to its minimum level by adding funds to QMDO 1, since QMDO 12 would have to be at least $1300 thousand before QMDO 12 would have any probability of being achieved.

From other AMC data (not presented here) it was found that materiel concept 1 of QMDO 1 was the location of the potential funds to Laboratory F. The data were

Technical Approach	Cost	Probability
1	$400 000	0.3
2	600 000	0.2
3	200 000	0.5

The present solution was to fund approaches 1 and 3. Approach 2 could be brought in as well, and funding for Laboratory F would increase to $2300 thousand. Other variations exist, at the discretion of the analyst.

This example shows how the Case team proposes laboratory constraints be satisfied. The results of analyzing AMC data indicate that if the problem is solved at a slightly reduced budget (5 to 10 percent below that desired), then research dollars can be added in the appropriate areas to fulfill AMC constraints. This will result in a nearly, but not exactly, optimal solution.

There is considerable flexibility in the manner in which the analyst may modify the basic solution in order to remedy constraint violations. Although such modifi-

cations will, in general, cause the solution to deviate from optimality, results to date indicate that the loss in expected military value is very small. And, in fact, a planner can evaluate his modified solution in terms of expected military value to see, quantitatively, exactly what he is giving up in expected military value in order to satisfy constraints.

TABLE V
SUMMARY OF LABORATORY CONSTRAINTS†

Lab	Allocated‡	Minimum‡	Violations
A	$1345	$ 535	
B	$1255	$ 794	
C	$1130	$ 684	
D	$1850	$ 764	
E	$2240	$1578	
F	$1700	$2170	*
G	$1820	$1210	
H	$ 945	$1045	*
I	$ 200	$ 80	

† Normal Budget ($12.5 Million)
‡ in thousands of dollars

TABLE VI
(HYPOTHETICAL) LABORATORY FUNDING DATA

QMDO	A	B	C	D	E	F	G	H	I	Total
1	300				200	1700	200			2400
2	150				75	450	145	130		950
3			370		20		240	525	200	1355
4			600		200		230			1030
5		1250			900		250			2400
6		670								670
7	275			110	50		140			575
8			80	140		150				370
9	300			150	50		170			670
10	320			150	50		220			740
11				1145						1145
12					350	3150	650			4150
13			1050							1050
14		75			700		60			835
15				400			450	290		1140
16								1680		1680
17			590		225		100			915
18						205				205
Total	1345	1995	1720	1920	3965	5450	3060	2625	200	22 280
Total Minimum Funding	535	794	684	764	1578	2170	1210	1045	80	8860

TABLE VII
SAMPLE WORKSHEET FOR USE IN ANALYZING THE LAB CONSTRAINT PROBLEM

LAB / QMDO		Normal Budget									
		A	B	C	D	E	F	G	H	I	Total
1.	1						600				600
	2	100					500				600
	3							200			200
	4	200									200
2.	1	50				75		95			220
	2	100							130		230
	3						250				250
	4						200	50			250
3.	1									200	200
	2							250			250
	3							275			275
	4				370						370
	5					20		90			110
4.	1					200		80			280
	2							150			150
	3				600						600
5.	1	670									670
	2					500					500
	3							250			250
6.	1		200								200
	2		160								160
	3		150								150

(*Table VII continued on next page*)

TABLE VII (*cont'd*)
SAMPLE WORKSHEET FOR USE IN ANALYZING THE LAB CONSTRAINT PROBLEM

LAB / QMDO		Normal Budget									Total
		A	B	C	D	E	F	G	H	I	
7.	1	130									
	2				150						
	3	190				50		220			460
8.	1	115									115
	2				110						110
	3	160				50		140			350
9.	1		80				150				230
	2				140						140
10.	1	120									120
	2				150						150
	3	180				50		170			400
11.	1					165					165
	2					250					250
	3					390					390
	4					340					340
12.											
13.	1			250							250
	2			400							400
	3			230							230
	4			170							170
14.	1		75								75
	2							60			60
	3					150					150
15.	1							200			200
	2								115		115
	3				330						330
	4								175		175
16.											
17.											
18.	1							75			75
	2							30			30
	3							10			10
Total Allocated		1345	1255	1130	1850	2240	1700	1820	945	200	12485

TABLE VIII
SUMMARY OF LABORATORY CONSTRAINTS†

Lab	Allocated‡	Minimum‡	Violations
A	$1345	$ 535	
B	$ 685	$ 794	*
C	$ 80	$ 684	*
D	$1850	$ 764	
E	$ 545	$1578	*
F	$1700	$2170	*
G	$1620	$1210	
H	$ 945	$1045	*
I	$ 200	$ 80	

† Reduced Budget ($8.97 Million)
‡ in thousands of dollars

X. Sensitivity of Solutions

Probably the most important question that can be raised about the validity of the quantitative models described in this paper concerns the sensitivity of the optimum solutions to errors in the (subjective) data inputs from the user.

It is not possible to investigate the problem of sensitivity analysis by analytical methods, and thus there are severe limitations placed on the methods available for attacking the problem, and on the reliability of any results which might come forth. This is due to the fact that the models are not expressed in closed analytic form and solutions are obtained by means of computer programs.

One method of analyzing sensitivity is through computer simulation. In this procedure, the parameters under consideration could be assigned, instead of a fixed numerical value, a probability distribution about this value. The characteristics of this probability distribution would be determined by the organization. Then, several computer runs would be made, using, instead of the original input data, the parameter values as sampled from the distribution. Comparison of runs would provide some insight into the sensitivity of the solution to errors in the input data.

An important effect that could be examined by such simulation is the result obtained by using the solution generated by the original data in the case where different parameter values "actually were true" (as determined by the simulated data). The loss in expected military value—the penalty for using the original solution under conditions of error in the input data—could be readily computed. At the present time, only a few such experimental simulations have been performed. Results to date indicate, quite encouragingly, that using the original solution under conditions of errors in the data will not result in severe penalties, providing the errors are within a range of 2 to 1 in parameter values.

Nevertheless, more extensive analysis should be performed in this area, and it is planned that additional research will be conducted along these lines in the near future.

XI. Further Research

This paper would not be complete without a brief indication of the potential and actual limitations in the methods developed to date and the need for further research:

1) The model is dependent on the ability to obtain probability/cost estimates that are sufficient, accurate, and consistent.
2) The solution is sensitive to major differences in opinion as to future values of proposed systems, and is also sensitive to the total range of possible values.
3) Although, the discretization of cost estimates is somewhat unrealistic, more complex cost–probability functions could be handled if it were possible to obtain such functions from performers of the technical activities.
4) Computational times increase exponentially with the number of QMDO's. However, approximations in costing would reduce computational time.
5) As a result of 4), and since it is quite expensive to perform simulations to estimate the sensitivity of solutions generated, further research is needed to provide analytic forms of solutions.
6) The consideration of "time to completion" of various technical approaches is not considered in the models. Scheduling problems will be investigated.
7) Finally, it requires understanding of the model, and some training, for analysts to be able to extract the solutions from the computer print-out sheets. The Appendix presents a manual for specific instructional purposes. However, further study on reducing the manual effort by more extensive computer print-outs of solutions, will be investigated.

Appendix

Extracting Solutions From Computer Runs: A Manual

The following manual is intended to serve as a guide to the system planner who must extract optimum solutions from the computer print-out sheets which are generated by the present program.

Phase 1. The Budget Selection

In order to inaugurate the process, some specific desired budget must be selected. That is, the system planner must know what dollar-value optimal solution he wants to develop, be it $8 million, $14 million, or whatever.

This budget value may not be within the authority of the planner to determine. Nevertheless, the planner should first draw up a cost–effectiveness curve relating dollar expenditure to expected military value. Figure 5 displays an example of this curve. The curve is developed by plotting dollar expenditure versus expected military value using the data from the last (highest numbered QMDO) system funding tableau in the computer print-out sheets. This step is important in understanding where the budget chosen lies in the dollar/military value tradeoff situation, to insure favorable location.

Because of slack built into the solution budgets by the use of $100 000 increments, it is necessary to begin with a budget about 12 percent higher than actually desired. This effect, and its causes, are explained in Section VIII.

Phase 2. Finding the Proper Allocation of Funds to Each QMDO

The procedure for finding the optimal allocation to each particular QMDO is begun by turning to the last (the sheet corresponding to the highest numbered QMDO) page of the run.

Suppose, for example, we have a system comprised of 12 QMDO's to consider. We turn to the last page, which is labeled Optimal Funding for QMDO 12 (Figure 6 presents hypothetical data for such a situation). Note that we would use this page to derive a cost–effectiveness curve, similar to Fig. 5, for our system.

Further, suppose we have decided to spend a $9 million budget. We correct this to a budget on the computer sheet of about $10.1 million (about 12 percent higher), because of the slack previously mentioned.

The box drawn in Fig. 6 draws attention to the important data on the sheet. With a budget of $10.1 million to allocate, location of the $10.1 million value displays

10 100 000: 300 000 24.076.

This tells us that, with an initial budget of $10.1 million, we allocate $300 000 to QMDO 12. And further, with an optimal $10.1 million allocation, we "buy" an expected military value of 24.076. The value 24.076 refers to the sum, for all 12 QMDO's under consideration, of the product of the probability of attaining the system, at the funding level given in the solution, and the military value assigned by the military planners. We know that 24.076 is the maximum military value that $10.1 million will buy, and by looking at Fig. 6, we can find that total funding of the system, which requires $12.9 million, would yield an expected military value of 25.228.

To aid in deriving the proper allocation, a table similar to Table IX is suggested.

Table IX is calculated, as we have seen, by threading through the QMDO print-out results, working from the higher numbered QMDO to the lowest.

Thus, from Fig. 6, we find we are to allocate $300 000 to QMDO 12. That allocation leaves us $10 100 000–$300 000 = $9 800 000 to distribute optimally among the remaining 11 QMDO's. To derive the next allocation, i.e., the next entry in Table IX, we turn to the sheet for QMDO 11 (Fig. 7) and find how much of the remaining $9 800 000 we are to allocate to QMDO 11. Note that we do *not* read the allocation for $10 100 000 for QMDO 11, because we no longer have that amount of funds remaining. The entry (the rectangular box in Fig. 7) tells us to allocate $1 000 000 to QMDO 11.

It might be worthwhile to explain the expected military value listed, 23.499. That figure means that an optimal allocation of $9.8 million across QMDO's 1 to 11 will yield an expected military value of 23.499. Of course, QMDO 12 is not considered in this value. We can easily develop the contribution of QMDO 12 (in military value) to our optimum allocation by calculating 24.076–23.499 = 0.577.

And of course, we would then have $9 800 000 − $1 000 000 = $8 800 000 to allocate among the remaining 10 QMDO's. As such, we would continue in like fashion, **reading** the allocation to QMDO 10 at the $8 800 000

level, subtracting this allocation from $8 800 000 and proceeding to QMDO 9, and so forth, until we reach QMDO 1.

As a check, the sum of the dollars allocated to each QMDO must be equal to the original military budget.

Phase 3. Finding the Proper Allocation of Funds to Materiel Concepts within a Given QMDO

Following the procedure described in Phase 2 will yield the proper dollar allocations to each QMDO under consideration. The next step is to develop the optimum allocation of funds to each materiel concept within each QMDO. For this step, the analyst works with one QMDO at a time, sequentially, through the tables labelled Fig. 8.

A brief description of what is displayed in Fig. 8 would be in order. The circled numbers at the bottom of the figure refer to the possible dollar allocations, in increments of $10 000, from no funding to total funding for the QMDO under consideration.

Now, the analyst should note that the remaining data are grouped in pairs. The number of such pairs corresponds exactly to the number of materiel concepts in the QMDO being considered. In the example of Fig. 8, there are three pairs, viz., { (2), (3) }, { (4), (5) }, and { (6), (7) }. Hence the QMDO 3 of this example has three materiel concepts.

The data above the pair on the extreme right corresponds to the highest numbered materiel concept. Then, moving toward the left, each pair presents data to the remaining materiel concepts numbered in descending order.

For clarification, let us assume we are to allocate $400 000 to QMDO 3. Rectangles drawn in Fig. 8 show the $400 000 level and the data for the data pair, { (2), (3) }, which of course is materiel concept 3. The results printed in column (3) at the $400 000 level tell us to allocate $100 000 to materiel concept 3. The results in column (2) at the $400 000 level indicate that the probability for attaining all materiel concepts at the $400 000 level is 0.254.

Now, as before, we subtract the amount allocated to materiel concept 3 from our original budget, and find we have $400 000 − $100 000 = $300 000 to allocate among the remaining two materiel concepts.

To find the proper amount to allocate to materiel concept 2, we read column (5) at the $300 000 level. (See arrow, Fig. 8.) We are told to allocate $130 000 to materiel concept 2, which leaves us $300 000 − $130 000 = $170 000 to allocate to materiel concept 1.

Corresponding to this $130 000 allocation is a value 0.423 in column (4). That figure refers to the probability of attaining both materiel concepts 1 and 2 with an optimal allocation of $300 000 across them.

Now we will see the effect of using $100 000 increments in solving the problem: there is slack in the budget, since the result is the same for allocating $140 000 and $170 000

OPTIMAL FUNDING FOR QMDO 12

100000:	0	.000	200000:	0	3.648	300000:	0	4.838	400000:	0	5.245	500000:		
600000:	0	7.103	700000:	0	7.841	800000:	0	9.391	900000:	0	8.226	1000000:	[illegible]	
1100000:	0	9.809	1200000:	0	10.519	1300000:	0	11.068	1400000:	0	11.563	1500000:	[illegible]	
1600000:	0	12.416	1700000:	0	13.064	1800000:	0	13.614	1900000:	0	14.049	2000000:	[illegible]	
2100000:	0	14.745	2200000:	0	15.078	2300000:	300000	15.344	2400000:	300000	15.557	2500000:	[illegible]	
2600000:	300000	15.986	2700000:	300000	16.343	2800000:	300000	16.682	2900000:	0	17.041	3000000:		
3100000:	300000	17.620	3200000:	300000	17.834	3300000:	300000	18.025	3400000:	300000	18.198	3500000:	[illegible]	
3600000:	300000	18.639	3700000:	300000	18.851	3800000:	300000	19.005	3900000:	300000	19.150	4000000:	[illegible]	
4100000:	300000	19.323	4200000:	300000	19.398	4300000:	300000	19.435	4400000:	300000	19.510	4500000:	[illegible]	
4600000:	300000	19.780	4700000:	300000	19.875	4800000:	300000	20.019	4900000:	300000	20.145	5000000:	[illegible]	
5100000:	300000	20.354	5200000:	300000	20.429	5300000:	300000	20.528	5400000:	300000	20.602	5500000:	[illegible]	
5600000:	300000	20.776	5700000:	300000	20.883	5800000:	300000	20.985	5900000:	300000	21.066	6000000:	[illegible]	
6100000:	300000	21.263	6200000:	300000	21.375	6300000:	300000	21.462	6400000:	300000	21.584	6500000:	[illegible]	
6600000:	300000	21.757	6700000:	300000	21.832	6800000:	300000	21.893	6900000:	300000	22.005	7000000:	[illegible]	
7100000:	300000	22.214	7200000:	300000	22.295	7300000:	300000	22.368	7400000:	300000	22.409	7500000:	[illegible]	
7600000:	300000	22.622	7700000:	300000	22.671	7800000:	300000	22.734	7900000:	300000	22.808	8000000:	[illegible]	
8100000:	300000	22.898	8200000:	300000	22.935	8300000:	300000	22.961	8400000:	300000	22.998	8500000:	[illegible]	
8600000:	300000	22.992	8700000:	300000	23.058	8800000:	300000	23.136	8900000:	300000	23.211	9000000:	[illegible]	
9100000:	300000	23.331	9200000:	300000	23.432	9300000:	300000	23.513	9400000:	300000	23.606	9500000:	[illegible]	
9600000:	300000	23.765	9700000:	300000	23.840	9800000:	300000	23.690	9900000:	300000	23.952	10000000:	[illegible]	
10100000:	300000	24.076	10200000:	300000	24.116	10300000:	300000	24.169	10400000:	300000	24.250	10500000:	[illegible]	
10600000:	300000	24.316	10700000:	300000	24.341	10800000:	300000	24.379	10900000:	300000	24.379	11000000:	[illegible]	
11100000:	300000	24.479	11200000:	300000	24.541	11300000:	300000	24.616	11400000:	300000	24.666	11500000:	[illegible]	
11600000:	300000	24.778	11700000:	300000	24.828	11800000:	300000	24.863	11900000:	300000	24.941	12000000:	[illegible]	
12100000:	300000	25.031	12200000:	300000	25.072	12300000:	300000	25.112	12400000:	300000	25.149	12500000:	[illegible]	
12600000:	300000	25.212	12700000:	300000	25.212	12800000:	300000	25.212	12900000:	300000	25.228	13000000:	[illegible]	
13100000:	300000	25.228	13200000:	300000	25.228	13300000:	300000	25.228	13400000:	300000	25.228	13500000:	[illegible]	
13600000:	300000	25.228	13700000:	300000	25.228	13800000:	300000	25.228	13900000:	300000	25.228	14000000:	[illegible]	

Fig. 6.

TABLE IX

WORKSHEET FOR DEVELOPING PROPER ALLOCATION OF FUNDS TO EACH QMDO

Initial Budget Value $10.1 Million
Expected Military Value 24,076

QMDO	Dollars Available For Allocation	Dollars To Be Allocated At This Level	New Amount Available
12	10 100 000	300 000	9 800 000
11	9 800 000	1 000 000	8 800 000
10	8 800 000		
9			
8			
7			
6			
5			
4			
3			
2			
1			

OPTIMAL FUNDING FOR QMDO 11

Fig. 7.

DATA FOR QMDO 3 MAXIMUM ATTAINABLE PROBABILITIES FOR ACHIEVING ALL MATERIEL

(1)	(2)	(3)	(4)	(5)	(6)	(7)
0	.000	0	.000	0	.000	0
10000	.000	0	.000	0	.000	10000
20000	.000	0	.000	0	.400	20000
30000	.000	0	.000	0	.400	30000
40000	.000	0	.200	30000	.400	40000
50000	.000	0	.200	30000	.400	50000
60000	.000	0	.200	30000	.580	60000
70000	.000	0	.200	30000	.580	70000
80000	.000	0	.290	30000	.580	80000
90000	.000	0	.290	30000	.580	90000
100000	.000	0	.290	30000	.706	100000
110000	.000	0	.290	30000	.706	110000
120000	.000	0	.290	30000	.706	120000
130000	.000	0	.290	30000	.706	130000
140000	.000	0	.290	30000	.706	140000
150000	.120	100000	.290	30000	.706	150000
160000	.120	100000	.353	30000	.794	160000
170000	.120	100000	.353	30000	.794	170000
180000	.120	100000	.353	30000	.794	180000
190000	.120	100000	.353	30000	.794	190000
200000	.174	100000	.353	30000	.794	200000
210000	.174	100000	.353	30000	.794	210000
220000	.174	100000	.397	30000	.794	220000
230000	.174	100000	.397	130000	.794	230000
240000	.174	100000	.423	130000	.794	240000
250000	.174	100000	.423	130000	.794	250000
260000	.211	100000	.423	130000	.794	260000
270000	.211	100000	.423	130000	.794	270000
280000	.211	100000	.423	130000	.794	280000
290000	.211	100000	.423	130000	.794	290000
300000	.211	100000	.423	130000	.794	300000
310000	.211	100000	.423	130000	.794	310000
320000	.211	100000	.423	130000	.794	320000
330000	.238	100000	.476	130000	.794	330000
340000	.238	100000	.476	130000	.794	340000
350000	.254	100000	.476	130000	.794	350000
360000	.254	100000	.476	130000	.794	360000
370000	.254	100000	.476	130000	.794	370000
380000	.254	100000	.476	130000	.794	380000
390000	.254	100000	.476	130000	.794	390000
400000	**.254**	**100000**	.476	130000	.794	400000
410000	.254	100000	.476	130000	.794	410000
420000	.254	100000	.476	130000	.794	420000
430000	.254	100000	.476	130000	.794	430000
440000	.254	100000	.476	130000	.794	440000
450000	.286	100000	.506	230000	.794	450000
460000	.286	100000	.506	230000	.794	460000
470000	.286	100000	.506	230000	.794	470000
480000	.286	100000	.506	230000	.794	480000
490000	.286	100000	.506	230000	.794	490000

Fig. 8.

TABLE X

WORKSHEET FOR INDIVIDUAL QMDO FUNDING

QMDO 3
Amount to Allocate $400 000 (from previous work)

Probability of Achieving All Materiel Concepts 0.254

Materiel Concept	Dollars Available For Allocation	Dollars To Be Allocated At This Level	New Amount Available
3	400 000	100 000	300 000
2	300 000	130 000	170 000
1	170 000	140 000	30 000

Slack = 30 000

QMDO 3

DATA FOR MATERIEL CONCEPT 1

TECHNICAL ALTERNATIVE	COST OF PERFORMING ALTERNATIVE	PROBABILITY OF SUCCESS
1	30000	.500
2	20000	.600
3	70000	.100
4	30000	.100
5	40000	.200

CALCULATIONS OF MAXIMUM ATTAINABLE PROBABILITIES FOR MATERIEL CONCEPT 1 WITH BASIC ALTERNATIVES LISTED

0	0	.000	0	.000	0	.000	0	.000	0	.000		
10000	0	.000	0	.000	0	.000	0	.000	0	.000		
20000	0	.000	1	.600	0	.600	0	.600	0	.600	2	
30000	1	.500	1	.600	0	.600	0	.600	0	.600	2	
40000	1	.500	1	.600	0	.600	0	.600	0	.600	2	
50000	1	.500	1	.600	0	.800	0	.600	0	.800	1 2	
60000	1	.500	1	.600	0	.800	0	.600	0	.800	1 2	
70000	1	.500	1	.600	0	.800	0	.600	0	.800	1 2	
80000	1	.500	1	.600	0	.800	1	.820	0	.820	1 2 4	
90000	1	.500	1	.600	0	.800	1	.820	1	.840	1 2 5	
100000	1	.500	1	.600	0	.800	1	.820	1	.840	1 2 5	
110000	1	.500	1	.600	0	.800	1	.820	1	.840	1 2 5	
120000	1	.500	1	.600	1	.820	1	.820	1	.856	1 2 5	TIE
130000	1	.500	1	.600	1	.820	1	.820	1	.856	1 2 5	TIE
140000	1	.500	1	.600	1	.820	1	.820	1	.856	1 2 5	TIE
150000	1	.500	1	.600	1	.820	1	.838	1	.856	1 2 5	
160000	1	.500	1	.600	1	.820	1	.838	1	.856	1 2 4 5	
170000	1	.500	1	.600	1	.820	1	.838	1	.856	1 2 4 5	
180000	1	.500	1	.600	1	.820	1	.838	1	.856	1 2 4 5	
190000	1	.500	1	.600	1	.820	1	.838	1	.870	1 2 3 4 5	
		(1)		(2)								

Fig. 9.

to materiel concept 1. This is observed by reviewing the probabilities shown at the $140 000–$210 000 level in column (6) which corresponds to materiel concept 1.

This slack need only be considered in the allocation to materiel concept 1, and the analyst need not worry about further exceptions. The rule is, simply, allocate the minimum amount to materiel concept 1 *which yields the same probability of success.* Thus the proper allocations at the $400 000 level are

$$MC\ 3 = \$100\ 000$$

$$MC\ 2 = \$130\ 000$$

$$MC\ 1 = \$140\ 000$$

$$Slack = \$\ 30\ 000.$$

Table X presents a worksheet summarizing these results. Another worksheet is given below to aid the analyst in developing the correct solution.

A final note on the probability value 0.254, the maximum attainable probability of attaining the hypothetical QMDO 3 with a $400 000 allocation. In Phase 4 it will be shown how to develop the menu of technical approaches from the results in Phase 3. The allocation of $140 000 to materiel concept 1 will yield a probability of success, say, P_1. Similarly, if P_2 and P_3 are the probabilities of success corresponding to allocations of $130 000 in materiel concept 2 and $100 000 in materiel concept 3, it will turn out that the product $P_1 P_2 P_3 = 0.254$.

Phase 4. Developing Proper Allocations to Individual Materiel Concepts

Figure 9 displays the individual materiel concept print-out sheet. The sheets are labeled

QMDO _____

Data for Materiel Concept_____.

These sheets list, for quick references, the original cost and probability of success data provided by the technical and program analysis.

The results are developed quite straightforwardly.

Previoius analysis (Phases 2 and 3) have yielded the proper allocation to each QMDO. Suppose, in the example of Fig. 9, we are told to allocate $80 000 to materiel concept 1 of QMDO 3. The rectangles drawn show the pertinent data, at the $80 000 level, the probability of succeeding in materiel concept 1 is 0.820, and alternatives 1, 2, 4 are printed out to show that they are the proper alternatives to select. Note that with $90 000 one would choose alternatives 1, 2, 5 and have a success probability of 0.840, and so forth.

It is not necessary for the analyst to consider the remaining data in Fig. 9. For completeness, it should be noted that the values 0 and 1 in some intermediate columns refer to whether a particular technical approach is used or not in some solution at the particular funding level. The remaining intermediate columns list sequential probabilities of success considering the first technical approach (column 1), and first and second technical approaches (column 2), and so forth.

The solution print-out eliminates the need of concern about this intermediate data. However, one could develop the solution, as printed, by proceeding in a fashion directly analogous to that of Phase 3.

Attention should be called to the word TIE which is sometimes printed alongside the listing of basic alternatives. It means that, somewhere at the level, there are two or more ways to achieve the same probability of success at that level of funding. The TIE can occur without relating to the basis printed out, that is, a tie may evolve among the first few alternatives which is no longer in effect when the basis is printed. The TIE calls the analyst's attention to potentially unusual situations.

BIBLIOGRAPHY

R. E. Bellman and S. E. Dreyfus, *Applied Dynamic Programming*. Princeton, N. J.: Princeton University Press, 1962.

B. V. Dean and S. S. Sengupta "Research budgeting and project selection," *IEEE Trans. on Engineering Management*, vol. EM-9, pp. 158–169, December 1962.

C. J. Hitch, "An appreciation of systems analysis," *Operations Research*, vol. 3, pp. 466–481, 1955.

C. J. Hitch, "Sub-optimization in operations research problems," *Operations Research*, vol. 1, pp. 87–99, 1953.

R. B. Foster and F. P. Hoeber, "Cost-effectiveness analysis for strategic decisions," *Operations Research*, vol. 3, pp. 482–492, 1955.

G. H. Fisher, "The role of cost-utility analysis in program budgeting," RAND Corp., RM-4279-RC, September 1964.

A Research Laboratory Performance Model

BURTON V. DEAN

Abstract—A mathematical model is developed for use in measuring and evaluating the performance of a research laboratory in meeting the needs to develop items to satisfy stated Army operational requirements.

Three submodels are developed, where the overall laboratory model is obtained by means of matrix multiplication. Illustrative examples have been developed using Army research laboratory data.

The model may be modified to include stochastic variables and data on the relative importance of projects and sciences.

I. Introduction

THIS STUDY IS concerned with the development of a mathematical model for use in measuring and evaluating the performance of a research laboratory in meeting the needs to develop items to satisfy stated Army operational requirements. This study is an outgrowth of research being conducted by the Concept Analysis Branch, R&D Division, U. S. Army Materiel Command.

The development of the overall model is based on the construction and integration of three submodels.

1) A *project-science* submodel that describes the relationships between project effort in a research laboratory and contributions to science (and technology).

2) A *science-requirement* submodel that describes the relationship between science (and technology) contributions and the satisfaction of user requirements needs for operational items.

3) A *requirement-value* submodel that establishes the relative values of operational requirements.

The overall model provides the means for integrating the submodels by means of matrix multiplication. The Army Materiel Command has performed illustrative calculations using a number of R&D projects being performed at several Army research laboratories.

II. Structure

Figure 1 illustrates the underlying structure of the submodels.

Consider a laboratory *l*. Let P_i represent the set of projects that are being performed by laboratory *l*. This list of projects can be tabulated and represent the work-in-progress being conducted in the laboratory.

Associated with each project P_i there are groups of

Manuscript received January 11, 1967. This paper was presented at the 18th Military Operations Research Symposium (MORS), Fort Bragg, N. C., October 1966. This study, Technical Memorandum 70, was partially supported by the Office of Naval Research and the Army Material Command under Contract Nonr-1141(19).

The author is with the Case Western Reserve University, Cleveland, Ohio.

sciences and technologies S_j which are expected to benefit from the effort being expended in project P_i. The identification of the groups can be made at each stage of the project.

For each operational requirement there is a number of groups of sciences and technologies from which contributions are expected to support operational requirements. Accordingly, with each science and technology there corresponds a number of operational requirements R_k which are dependent on it.

Associated with each requirement R_k there is a numerical value V_k which expresses the relative value or importance of the corresponding requirement on a numerical scale.

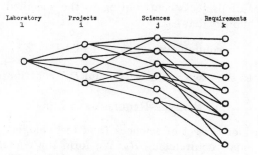

Fig. 1. Structure of the laboratory submodels.

III. Project-Science Model

Consider the set of laboratory projects P_i and the set of sciences (and technologies) S_j. We form the *transfer* matrix

$$A = (a_{ij})$$

which is composed of zeroes and ones defined as follows:

$$a_{ij} = \begin{cases} 1, & \text{if project } P_i \text{ contributes to science } S_j; \\ 0, & \text{if project } P_i \text{ does not contribute to science } S_j. \end{cases}$$

Example

Suppose the laboratory is engaged in the projects P_1, P_2, and P_3 which contribute to four sciences S_1, S_2, S_3, and S_4 in the following way:

$$P_1 \to S_1, S_2$$

$$P_2 \to S_2, S_3, S_4$$

$$P_3 \to S_1, S_3.$$

The transfer matrix A is given as follows. Each row corresponds to a project and each column corresponds to a science. An entry a_{ij} in the ith row and jth column denotes the contribution of project P_i to science S_j. In this example the entries in the transfer matrix are given as

	To S_1	S_2	S_3	S_4
From				
P_1	1	1	0	0
P_2	0	1	1	1
P_3	1	0	1	0

and the matrix A is thus given by

$$A = \begin{bmatrix} 1 & 1 & 0 & 0 \\ 0 & 1 & 1 & 1 \\ 1 & 0 & 1 & 0 \end{bmatrix}.$$

We note the row sum indicates the number of sciences (and technologies) that the project contributes to, as e.g.,

$$\text{row sum of } P_1 = 1+1+0+0 = 2$$

indicating that P_1 contributes to two sciences (and technologies). Similarly, the column sums indicate the number of projects contributing to the specified science (or technology), as e.g.,

$$\text{column sum of } S_1 = 1+0+1 = 2$$

indicates that two projects (P_1 and P_3) contribute to S_1.

IV. Science-Requirement Model

Consider the set of sciences (and technologies) S_j and operational requirements R_k. We form the *transfer* matrix

$$B = (b_{jk})$$

which is composed of zeroes and ones defined as follows:

$$b_{jk} = \begin{cases} 1, & \text{if a development in science } S_j \\ & \text{is required to satisfy a requirement} \\ & R_k; \\ 0, & \text{otherwise.} \end{cases}$$

Example

Suppose the laboratory is engaged in work in the four sciences (in the previous example, S_1, S_2, S_3, and S_4), by means of the projects P_1, P_2, and P_3, which are contributing to satisfying the operational requirements R_1, R_2, and R_3, in the following way:

$$S_1 \rightarrow R_1$$

$$S_2 \rightarrow R_2, R_3$$

$$S_3 \rightarrow R_1, R_3$$

$$S_4 \rightarrow R_1, R_2, R_3.$$

In the same way as the previous example, we have the transfer matrix B given by

$$B = \begin{bmatrix} 1 & 0 & 0 \\ 0 & 1 & 1 \\ 1 & 0 & 1 \\ 1 & 1 & 1 \end{bmatrix}.$$

Similarly, the row sum for a science indicates the number of requirements that it is contributing to, and the column sum for a requirement indicates the number of contributions in sciences (and technologies) that are required.

V. Project-Requirement Calculation: Amalgamation of Models

We are now in a position to calculate the relationship between projects and operational requirements. Suppose that a project P_i, which is contributing to a science (or technology) S_j, is expected to contribute to a requirement R_k. Thus we have a complete link of project P_i to R_k given by

$$P_i \rightarrow S_j \rightarrow R_k$$

and this can be calculated as

$$a_{ij}b_{jk} = 1.$$

However, if P_i is not related to S_j, or S_j is not related to R_k, then we have

$$a_{ij}b_{jk} = 0.$$

Thus the number of complete linkages from project P_i to requirement R_k, or the number of ways in which project P_i is contributing to satisfying requirement R_k, can be found by summing the values of $a_{ij}b_{jk}$ over all values of j,

$$\sum_j a_{ij}b_{jk}.$$

If we let

$$c_{ik} = \sum_j a_{ij}b_{jk},$$

then c_{ik} is the number of ways in which project P_i is contributing to satisfying requirement R_k.

If we let C be the matrix of c_{ik},

$$C = (c_{ik})$$

we have that C can be determined by means of the *matrix multiplication* of the matrices A and B, so that

$$C = AB.$$

The matrix C amalgamates the number of contributions made to and by the sciences (and technologies) given by the two basic submodels.

Example

Consider the laboratory in the previous examples with projects (P_1, P_2, P_3), sciences (S_1, S_2, S_3, S_4)

and requirements (R_1, R_2, R_3), where A and B have been given in the previous example.

We have that

$$C = AB$$

$$= \begin{bmatrix} 1 & 1 & 0 & 0 \\ 0 & 1 & 1 & 1 \\ 1 & 0 & 1 & 0 \end{bmatrix} \begin{bmatrix} 1 & 0 & 0 \\ 0 & 1 & 1 \\ 1 & 1 & 1 \end{bmatrix}$$

$$= \begin{bmatrix} 1 & 1 & 1 \\ 2 & 2 & 3 \\ 2 & 0 & 1 \end{bmatrix}.$$

We can interpret the matrix C as follows:

P_1 contributes to each requirement in one way,

P_2 contributes to requirements R_1 and R_2 in two ways each, and to requirement R_3 in three ways, and

P_3 contributes to R_1 in two ways, it does not contribute to R_2, and it contributes to R_3 in one way.

VI. Requirement-Value Model

To complete the laboratory performance model, it is necessary to have a measure of the expected value of satisfying an operational requirement.

We suppose that it is possible to attach a numerical value expressing the relative importance to each requirement V_k, where V_k is a non-negative number associated with the requirement R_k,

$$R_k \rightarrow V_k.$$

We will suppose that the values are normalized so that

$$\sum_k V_k = 1,$$

where each V_k represents the relative importance of requirement R_k among the set (R_k). We write the values of the requirements as the column matrix

$$V = (V_k).$$

VII. Construction of the Laboratory Performance Model

Consider a project P_i that contributes to a requirement R_k in c_{ik} ways. We have that the value of project P_i relative to requirement R_k is given by

$$c_{ik}V_k.$$

The total value of project P_i is given by the weighted sum

$$e_i = \sum_k c_{ik} V_k$$

and the column matrix $E = (e_i)$ exhibits the set of values of the laboratory projects.

A measure of performance of the laboratory E^* is given by summing the project values, over all projects in the laboratory,

$$E^* = \sum_i e_i.$$

We can calculate the laboratory performance by means of matrix multiplication as follows,

$$E^* = \sum_i e_i = JE,$$

where J is a row matrix consisting of ones, and therefore

$$E^* = JE$$
$$= JCV$$
$$E^* = JABV.$$

Thus E^* can be found by multiplying the four matrices J, A, B, and V.

Example

Consider the laboratory in the previous example, where the requirements are valued as

$$V = \begin{bmatrix} \frac{1}{2} \\ \frac{1}{3} \\ \frac{1}{6} \end{bmatrix}.$$

It is possible to measure the performance of the laboratory E^*, where

$$C = \begin{bmatrix} 1 & 1 & 1 \\ 2 & 2 & 3 \\ 2 & 0 & 1 \end{bmatrix}.$$

We have that

$$E = \begin{bmatrix} 1 & 1 & 1 \\ 2 & 2 & 3 \\ 2 & 0 & 1 \end{bmatrix} \begin{bmatrix} \frac{1}{2} \\ \frac{1}{3} \\ \frac{1}{6} \end{bmatrix}$$

$$= \begin{bmatrix} 1 \\ 2\frac{1}{6} \\ 1\frac{1}{6} \end{bmatrix}, \quad \text{and}$$

$$E^* = (1 \quad 1 \quad 1) \begin{bmatrix} 1 \\ 2\frac{1}{6} \\ 1\frac{1}{6} \end{bmatrix}$$

$$E^* = 4\frac{1}{3}.$$

VIII. Conclusions

This model develops a means for evaluating the expected contribution of a set of research projects for achieving operational requirements. The model utilizes data that is readily available in laboratories and in reports. The model may be modified to include stochastic variables and additional data on the relative importance of projects and sciences.

Long-Range R&D Planning

DONALD F. SMITH

Abstract—The Marine Engineering Laboratory (MEL), the Annapolis Division, Naval Ship R&D Center, has developed a procedure for the development of long-range R&D planning particularly aimed at the logical objective determination of the requirements imposed on new ship procurement by the Navy mission.

Starting from a broad concept suggested by Naval Ship Systems Command (NAVSHIPSYSCOM), MEL has developed the structure of a procedure which, when completed and validated, will provide a logical, objective determination of future requirements and a standardized format for Ship System Formulation.

The structure consists of mission objectives, vehicle types, specific techniques and components, as well as forecasts of the functional capabilities techniques and components.

THE LONG-RANGE R&D planning procedure described here is being developed by the Marine Engineering Laboratory (MEL) for NAVSHIPS, to provide:

1) a logical objective determination of future requirements and to indicate R&D necessary to meet these requirements, and

2) a standardized approach to Ship System Formulation.

This procedure, being mission-oriented, and displaying future technical capabilities in mission-usable form, will assist operational planners in better expressing their desires in terms to which technical types can respond.

This flow diagram shows the steps of the procedure and is merely a representation of what should be done in any R&D activity. This represents no breakthrough. The aim was to organize, not invent. The procedure has two basic parts—the developing and satisfying of requirements, shown down the center of Fig. 1, and technological forecasting, shown on the left. The development of requirements encompasses that portion of Ship System Formulation termed "requirements definition" for those familiar with that effort. While this diagram shows the procedure starting with National Goals, at MEL we have not, as yet, gone back that far, and our starting point has been at the strategic mission requirements, where primary (or design) tasks and contingent tasks are assumed to be designated.

It is not intended here to go into a lengthy description of the steps involved in this procedure. This procedure is described in considerable detail in reference [1]. Rather, it is intended to expand on certain facets of the procedure which we feel make the procedure workable.

At present there is no *standard* mathematical approach to a generalized mission-to-vehicle analysis similar to linear programming or other popular mathematical models. Obviously there are specialists who must, and do perform analyses of this type for specific projects, but these are primarily based on their accumulated experience. There have been mathematical attempts aimed at specific problems, but again these are isolated cases drawing primarily on the judgment of experienced men. The mission analysis portion of the procedure has no magic formula to substitute numbers for experience and thereby make every engineer an expert. Rather we think we have found a way to make it easier for the experienced man to communicate by providing the framework for such a standardized approach.

The major problem encountered in the development of a usable mission analysis technique was to find a way to include all possible missions, both current and future, without developing matrices of incomprehensible complexity. A solution has been found[2] the key to which lies in the recognition that missions are made up of phases and it is these phases that spell out vehicle and subsystem performance requirements. An example may clarify my meaning: let us assume that we have a mission task stated broadly as "map subsurface ocean currents." Regardless of the vehicle to be used for this mission, each vehicle would have to be made ready to leave its base— thus the phase "ready." It would have to cruise on the surface for some distance upon leaving port—thus the phase "cruise (surface)," and to further refine such a phase we could add "in friendly waters." At least one vehicle to be considered for such a mission is the submersible; therefore another phase would be "cruise (subsurface)," and again we could add "in friendly waters," etc. From this, one can envision how the breakdown of such a completely different mission task as "destroy enemy shipping" would start off with the same three phases.

Phases, as used, are order-free, unique, vehicle activities which impose performance requirements upon the vehicle and its subsystems. Further, it appears that if all conceivable mission profiles are considered, and broken down into phases, the total number of phases is quite small. Thus, using this technique, it is possible to handle all missions for a particular vehicle type, and the hor-

Manuscript received January 11, 1967. This paper was presented at the 18th Military Operations Research Symposium (MORS) Fort Bragg, N. C., October 1966.

The author is with the U. S. Navy Marine Engineering Laboratory, Annapolis, Md.

[2] Certain facets of this solution have appeared previously; see especially the 16th MORS presentations by H. E. Emlet, Jr., Analytic Services, Inc., and R. F. Poppe of the Boeing Company, and to the Spring 1966 ORSA Conference at which J. Redman of Lockheed presented an impact matrix of similar nature.

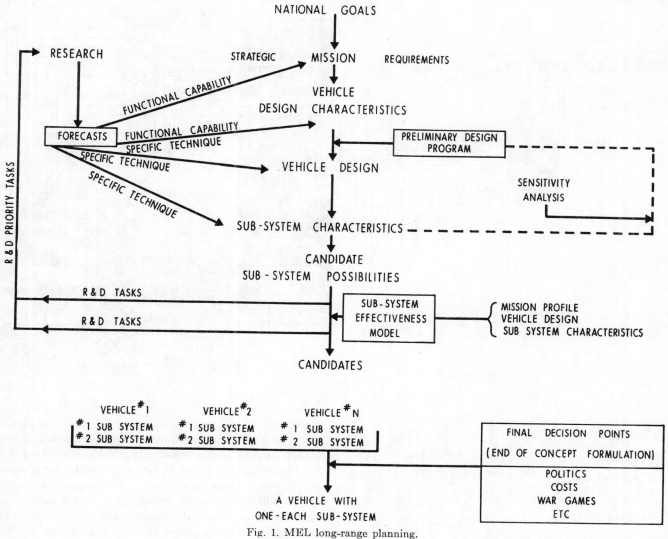

Fig. 1. MEL long-range planning.

rendous number of possible mission profiles, by delineating those vehicle capabilities required to perform a relatively few phases.

To illustrate how such an approach would be implemented, and because no OR presentation would be complete without at least one unreadable matrix, we have prepared an "impact matrix" (Fig. 2) for the first mission mentioned—that of mapping subsurface ocean currents. The first categories involve the Mission Tasks and Environment indicating possible vehicle types. Here we have indicated, for the sake of simplicity, that each vehicle type would have its own further impact matrix. (For multipurpose vehicles this would not necessarily be so.) From vehicle types we proceed to the Mission Phases—the step we consider the crux of this procedure. Obviously, the phases listed here do not cover every possible vehicle activity, but it would not require too many more phases to make this list complete for any conceivable mission employing a submersible. To follow the

rationale of this matrix, one must only recognize that when two items of adjacent categories are related, that is, when changes in one require or result in perturbations in the other, an impact is indicated and the appropriate matrix intersection marked with an "X." Going *up* around the matrix we can see that subsurface cruise, for example, requires and influences among other primary subsystems, the propulsion subsystem, which in turn has an impact on all of the support subsystems. Going *down* around the matrix, those Vehicle Characteristics impacting with Mission Phases are marked, and then the subsystems producing these characteristics noted. Blank spaces indicate possible impacts, depending on the particular mission task under consideration (blocked-in spaces indicate no impact between categories); the hull structure, for instance, has no effect on navigational accuracy.

What is presented here is in reality a super checkoff list identifying those parameters and equipments which

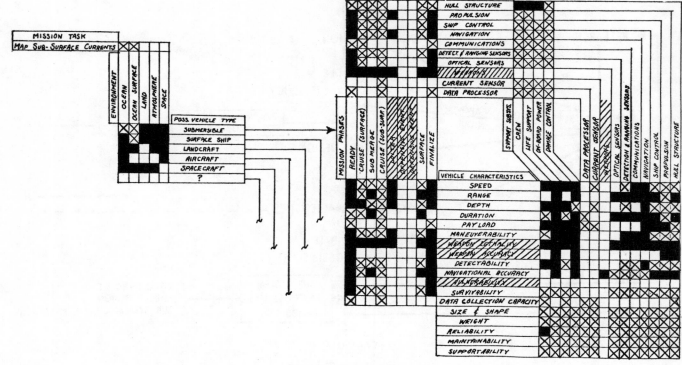

Fig. 2. Impact matrix.

U—Up
D—Down
S—Stand-by

MISSION PHASES	Sensors	Propulsion	Control	Navigation	Communication	Armament	Auxiliary	Life Support	Special
Ready	D	S	U	D	U	D	U	U	
On-Load (Friendly Waters)	D	D	U	D	U	D	U	U	
Cruise	D	U	U	U	U	D	U	U	
Loiter (Friendly Waters)	U	S	U	U	U	D	U	U	
Media Change (Friendly Waters)	U	U	U	U	U	D	U	U	
Off-Load (Friendly Waters)	U	D	U	D	U	D	U	U	
On-Load (Enemy Waters)	U	S	U	D	U	S	U	U	
Cruise (Enemy Waters)	U	U	U	U	U	S	U	U	
Loiter (Enemy Waters)	U	S	U	U	U	S	U	U	
Media Change (Enemy Waters)	U	U	U	U	U	S	U	U	
Off-Load (Enemy Waters)	U	S	U	D	U	S	U	U	
Attack	U	U	U	U	U	U	U	U	
Defend	U	U	U	U	U	U	U	U	
Finalize	D	D	U	D	U	D	U	U	

Fig. 3. Mission phases: activities defined in sufficient detail to define subsystem Up, Down, or Stand-by condition.

contribute to the performance and effectiveness of each phase of a mission, and those items which would be perturbed in performing sensitivity analyses, *without* having to design the tactics to be employed in carrying out the mission. Those who have a background in systems design will, undoubtedly, recognize this as a definite advantage in dealing with operational types, who traditionally hold tactics design to be their exclusive prerogative. In performing the mission analysis, the magnitude of impacts would be determined by development of appropriate transfer functions, using modeling or simulation techniques with inputs from technological forecasting.

Figure 3 further clarifies the discussion of Mission Phases, and shows how the first step in developing transfer functions can be taken.

Technological forecasting has been referred to several times, as it is an integral part of the planning procedure. Much has been written and discussed regarding this subject in recent months, and it appears that at least all Department of Defense agencies will be required to produce technological forecasts of one type or another very shortly. The MEL technique is described in the report mentioned at the beginning of this paper and there is no point in describing it in detail here. The technique is based on the work reported by Ralph Lenz[2] of the U. S. Air Force and Colonel Isensen,[3] that is, functional technology advances in an exponential fashion. The format and methods are in accordance with instructions and guidance given in Lenz.[2] If we follow the stated assumption, and plot the historical development, not as revealed by one-of-a-kind laboratory experimental equipments, but as the best operational results at any given point in time, it is believed that a conservative, realistic picture will be presented of what the straight-line projection (on a semilog plot) of that functional technology will be in the real world. Here we begin to run into comments. One of the first is: "Great! Then the Navy doesn't have to spend money to develop some advance in state-of-the-art—just sit back and wait." To some degree this could be true if the field of interest lies primarily outside the Navy, and the Navy's contribution in the past has been negligible. The functional advances in the past have been made because of many factors, but two prime factors must have been present:

1) a general need or desire by the whole technical community, and
2) an interest in satisfying that need which has been reflected by support from that technical community.

If the Navy has been part of that technical community, then it cannot withdraw and expect development to continue as before.

At MEL we apply to the functional capability forecasts the results of a study of the theoretical maximums so that we have a feel for the potential improvement in each function of interest. This so-called "gap analysis" is popular in industry (it is used at the Dupont Company to guide their in-house R&D programs).

We recognize that, historically speaking, functional capability forecasts are based on maxima of all the applicable specific technique capabilities. However, for examination of the future, the functional capability projections serve as goals against which to measure the potential of new specific techniques.

When forecasting in the specific technique areas, it is tempting to simply extrapolate the historical curve at its most recent slope; however, this is obviously hazardous without substantiating evidence. To improve the confidence level of the forecast and to determine how the curve should be approaching natural or physical limits, the components and subparameters of the specific techniques were investigated and forecasts of these generated from both operational and experimental data. A typical set of forecast curves is represented by these curves showing the specific weight and supporting data

for a gas turbine power plant. For this particular type of power plant, it was determined that turbine inlet temperature has had the greatest single effect on the shaft horsepower per pound of gas turbines. Accordingly, the turbine inlet temperature was correlated to the parameter of interest, namely, specific weight. In addition to portraying the theoretical limit as an indicator of growth potential, the specific technique curve for a closely associated application—the aircraft power plant—is plotted. With these data, the original forecast of interest now has assumed a much more valid appearance.

One more question may arise: are all parameters of importance predictable? Our experience at MEL has been limited to ship machinery. However, it is felt that this is one of the toughest fields to tackle because of its variety and complexity. To date MEL has forecasts on five types of marine energy converters and two types of transmission systems, covering four parameters (i.e., specific weight, specific volume, efficiency, noise). Forecasts of ease of automation are being made, and we will forecast reliability within the next year. In our judgment, these five parameters can be forecast, and, once completed, will provide valid data to use in the planning procedure under development.

The procedure, once the required vehicle characteristics have been developed, concentrates on an iterative process of sensitivity analyses and optimization routines. This portion of the procedure has been computerized to produce optimum candidate vehicles and subsystems once appropriate optimization criteria are inputed. The final output of this whole procedure, and, in fact, the initial reason behind this entire project effort, is a listing of those R&D tasks necessary if the optimized candidate systems are to be possible at the desired date in the future. This listing, containing an indicated priority for each task, is obtained by a rather involved process which basically compares the forecasted capabilities to the vehicle and subsystem required characteristics for that point in the future dictated by the mission.

REFERENCES

[1] "Long-range R&D planning," U. S. Navy Marine Engineering Laboratory, Annapolis, Md., MEL Rept. 395/66, August 1966.
[2] R. C. Lenz, Jr., "Technological forecasting," 2nd ed., ASTIA Doc. 408 085.
[3] R. S. Isenson, Colonel, General Staff, "Technological forecasting: a manning tool."
[4] "Proposed Naval technological forecast," Final Report of the Navy Technological Forecasting Group to the Chief of Naval Development, NAVMAT P-3920, April 1966 (Confidential).

QUEST Status Report

MARVIN J. CETRON

Abstract—Recently, DOD has had more emphasis placed on it by Congress to develop a logical method of allocating its resources to the sciences and technologies. QUEST (Quantitative Utility Estimates for Science and Technology) describes one method of determining the relevance of research and exploratory development to missions and thereby aid in efficient allocation of dollars and manpower thereto.

A double set of matrices consisting of the sciences, technologies, and missions are developed with the "technology" parameter common to both. By having "figures of utility" assigned to each mission and by determining the value of the contribution of each technological area to each mission, a cumulative quantified value for each technological area is then related to each scientific area and the relevant impact of each of the scientific disciplines is identified with each technological area. Having previously developed the quantified values for each technology area and its relative impact, one can determine each discipline's significance. The resultant summation for each line of the matrix would then make available "mission relevance" numbers for each scientific area.

Technological forecasts for each scientific and technological area (under given resource levels) must be generated in order to determine the probability of success (risk) of each project.

By combining the military utility and the probability of success, an expected value is determined which could provide the Department of Defense with quantitative data to aid in allocating resources to both research as well as exploratory development.

INTRODUCTION TO QUANTITATIVE TECHNIQUES

THE USE OF "relevance numbers," "figures of merit," and other numerical techniques for evaluating action alternatives are traditional procedures in operations research and management science.

There are differences of opinions, however, as to the applications of these techniques. Seiler says, for instance, "The use of scientific management processes, which include formulas and models, has infiltrated all areas of management endeavor. The research activity is no exception, although the use of formulas and models is more difficult in this area."[1] On the other hand, Anthony states these techniques are, in essence, game theory, and the difference between the complexity of real life and the relative simplicity that is essential in applying game theory probably accounts for the fact that there are few published reports of the application of the theory of games to actual business problems. Even if it is assumed

that illustrations in texts and articles on the subject are taken from real life, which is not usually the case, most of the reported applications turn out to deal with operating problems.[2] Possibly the best statement on the subject has come from an operator, or potential user of this appraisal information, Capt. Mahinske, USN, when he stated in a Management Memo: "A Planning Appraisal System which operates on task area proposals . . . is a crucial necessity to our attempts to derive our program on a basis of relatively unimpeachable logic. . . . An appraisal system is the crux of our problem and *must* be solved. . . . Remember our goal is to *improve* our management of the program *not* to perpetuate the 'control' we now exercise."[3]

Miller and Starr comment: "Operations research and decision-theory framework are part of a current, worldwide management science movement. They provide one important avenue for increasing the executive's ability to generalize. As such, they are a logical development in the evolutionary process of the managerial function. . . . Management science is essentially quantitative; however, important problems that cannot be quantified are handled qualitatively. Whether quantitative methods are applied, operations research is used to produce rational decisions and logical plans of action."[4]

In a paper entitled "R&D" project selection,"[5] the statement was made that the general reception of project selection techniques has been favorable. However, the developers of these techniques have been greatly concerned over the apparent resistance to implementing these techniques.

From what I have been studying recently (conferences, articles, and implementing instructions), I am now of the opinion that this is changing and that we are in the transition period toward applying these techniques to R&D management.

DEFINITIONS AND CONCEPTS

There is a need to define the terms and relationships between the military research and development concepts

Manuscript received January 11, 1967. This paper was presented at the 18th Military Operations Research Symposium (MORS), Fort Bragg, N. C., October 1966. Any views expressed in this report are those of the author. They should not be interpreted as reflecting the views of the Navy or the official opinion or position of the Navy; nor do they necessarily represent the opinions of the Exploratory Development Division of which he is a member.

The author is with the Headquarters Naval Material Command, Washington, D. C. 20360.

[1] R. E. Seller, *Improving the Effectiveness of Research and Development*. New York: McGraw-Hill, 1965, p. 172.

[2] R. N. Anthony, "Planning and control systems—a framework for the analysis," Division of Research, Harvard Business School, Boston, Mass., 1965, pp. 56–57.

[3] E. B. Mahinske, "HQ Naval Material Command memorandum on exploratory development planning appraisal system," November 22, 1966.

[4] D. W. Miller and M. K. Starr, *Executive Decisions and Operations Research*. Englewood Cliffs, N. J.: Prentice Hall, 1960, pp. 9–10.

[5] N. R. Baker and W. H. Pound, "R&D project selection: where we stand," *IEEE Trans. on Engineering Management*, vol. EM-11, pp. 124–134, December 1964.

and the economic world at this point, for this paper draws on both.

Under conditions of certainty, the decision process considers the maximization of known objectives (such as military utility or profits) subject to known constraints (such as costs). Under conditions of uncertainty, the functions, and/or constraints are not known and therefore the decision maker, or his experts, must make subjective estimates of the important criteria.

"In the recently developed Bayesian probability approach, a procedure followed by the decision maker consists of listing the set of values of outcomes that the particular parameter may take and the corresponding subjective probability of each outcome or occurrence. These subjectively "weighted" outcomes are then summed to obtain what is known as the "expected value of the parameter."[6]

Utility may be defined as something which serves a purpose or helps in accomplishing an end.

Some economists seem to have been much concerned with the measurability of utility. They adopted the same idea that experimental psychology did when it began measuring aspects of sensation. If a subject reacts to changes in a physical stimulus and the pattern of his reactions is known, then a functional relationship can be set between the stimulus and the response. Since the physical stimulus can be measured, measures of the response from the functional relationship can be derived.

"To see how this might work out for utility measurements, suppose we want to compare a person's preference for various commodities (apples, beer, pigs, TV sets, and so on). Suppose we could find a physically measurable commodity of this nature: When we present a subject with x units of this "standard" commodity and y units of apples, he feels that he is indifferent as to which he received. That is, he feels he prefers equally x units of the standard commodity and y units of apples. Then why not say that his degree of "pleasure" associated with y apples is measured by the x standard units? If this could be done for all quantities of every commodity, then we would apparently have a general "pleasure" scale (sometimes called a preference scale and sometimes a utility scale)".[7]

Value is defined by Webster as that which renders anything desirable or useful, and worth, in the classic sense, refers to price. However, Churchman says, "values are a basis of predicting choice when the probabilities are known."[8]

Risk and Uncertainty: A distinction must be made between risk and uncertainty. *Risk* refers to relatively ob-

jective probabilities which can be computed on the basis of past experience or some "a priori" principle. Examples of the use of past experience are the actuarial probabilities in the insurance business that certain proportions of fires of various magnitudes will take place or that certain numbers of people of various ages will die. Examples of the "a priori" types are the odds that a coin will turn up heads or that an ace will be drawn from a deck of cards. In any of these cases the probability of the outcomes can be computed with considerable precision. In risk situations, experience is repetitive and provides a frequency distribution about which inferences can be drawn by objective statistical procedures. *Uncertainty*, on the other hand, is relatively subjective, there being insufficient past information of insufficient stability in the structure of the variables to permit exact prediction. Most business decisions take place under conditions of uncertainty, for each decision is made in a somewhat different environment. Sometimes the term objective probability is used in connection with risk, and subjective probability in connection with uncertainty.[9]

A *technological forecast* may be defined as the "prediction, with a level of confidence, of a technical achievement in a given time frame with a specific level or support."[10]

I have considered technological forecasting as objective probability and the future environment as part of subjective probability.

Expected value, as mentioned before, is future value under conditions of uncertainty.

Development includes all efforts directed toward the solution of problems which may range from fairly fundamental multipurpose exploratory development to quite sophisticated experimental models or prototypes. To put it simply, *science* generates a blank of knowledge, and *technology* applies to that knowledge in a useful manner.

A *mission* may be defined as a task or function assigned or undertaken.

"*Operations research* is a scientific method of providing executive departments with a quantitative basis for decisions regarding the operations under their control."[11]

Balance: Although Webster defines balance as to make equal, or to bring into equilibrium, I have intended in the context of this paper for a "balanced program" to mean one in which due consideration has been given to aspects such as the following: What the customer has expressed as his needs (operational capability requirements), operational utility, timeliness, success expectancy, credibility and performance of performing or-

[6] M. H. Spencer and L. Siegelman, *Managerial Economics.* Homewood, Ill.: Richard D. Irwin, 1964, p. 29.
[7] C. W. Churchman, *Prediction and Optimal Decision.* Englewood Cliffs, N. J.: Prentice-Hall, 1961, pp. 42–43.
[8] ——, op. cit., p. 217.

[9] W. W. Haynes, *Managerial Economics.* Homewood, Ill.: Dorsey Press, 1963, p. 556.
[10] R. C. Lenz, Jr., "Technological forecasting," Aeronautical Systems Division, AFSC, Wright-Patterson Air Force Base, Dayton, Ohio, June 1966.
[11] P. M. Morse and G. E. Kimball, *Methods of Operations Research.* New York: Wiley, 1951, p. 1.

ganizations, technological opportunities, technological forecasts, adequacy of funding (specific) an availability of funds (total). The results of these trade-offs should give a "balanced program."

The key word, according to McNamara, in discussing allocation of exploratory development funds is "balance." In some sense or other, the funds allocated to various technological areas must be properly balanced with respect to each other and the goals of the entire program. The problem of balance arises only because the total resources available are insufficient to do all that might be desired. If unlimited resources were available, all the desired technological programs could be pursued, and the remaining money returned to the Treasury.

In practice, however, choices must be made. In general, each avenue of technological advance will be pursued at something less than the maximum rate which might be possible. The problem of balance, then, is one of deciding at what rate each area of technology should be advanced, recognizing that advances in one area are obtained at the cost of slower advance in some other area.

The Concept of R&D Planning: The funds available to the formal DOD program should be considered principally as an indicator of the major interest in important areas—a vector toward significant desirable goals. The funds thus applied represent a firm indication of interest to universities, industry, and the national research complex as a whole. It is important, therefore, that these funds be applied wisely in the gross to assure the accuracy of the broad vector. By having a thorough knowledge of the overall national effort in the major technical topics, specific efforts can, however, be oriented to emphasize interest in specific areas of known void or areas of exceptional need.

Selectivity: The major problem confronting the R&D planner in this area is that of deciding which directions the R&D should progress, since one obviously cannot do research and development on everything. Selectivity is the key. This problem is very complex since research and exploratory development must be both responsive to specific needs and opportunistic with respect to the possibilities of new technology and science. The technical program must provide for the transition of new ideas from research into promising new or improved techniques, materials, and processes for future military applications. In addition, the total national effort must be considered in determining the course of the formal technical program.

On one hand, the technical program must generate the technology for the next generation of systems and subsystem components, and help to minimize the time between concept and operational capability. The major portion of the technological effort must, therefore, be oriented toward military problem areas to assure that efforts in the many independent areas of technology will

ultimately lend themselves to integration. The value of such effort depends largely on our ability to predict the capabilities desired in the future. For the near-term we can do this quite well; often the user is knocking at the door. For the long-term, unfortunately, our 20–20 vision fails a bit and only generalized concepts or broad mission area descriptions can be derived.

At the same time, another segment of the research and development effort covers exploration of the unpredictable, but intuitively promising effort that often leads to new techniques and occasionally "breakthroughs." This latter segment embraces a category of high risk—high gain effort which relies heavily on the technical competence and judgment of those managing the program. This latter category of effort is that which may generate the technological basis for the next family of desired operational capabilities.

In planning any technical program, management must decide upon the balance appropriate within research or development. The balance will vary from time to time, from one science or technical area to another, and will be influenced by the environment of the time. It is a function of corporate management to set the guidelines for establishing this balance, and in making sure the balance is, in fact, maintained.

In the selection of *opportunistic* types of effort, the man who knows best is the scientist or engineer who has day-to-day intimacy with science and technology. One relies heavily upon the judgment of the military engineer or scientist since: 1) he has a general understanding of problem areas facing the military, and 2) he is the most knowledgeable with respect to the scientific potential and technical risk.

In the selection of efforts to be *responsive* to operational needs or deficiencies, however, we move into an area that can be evaluated in a more quantitative manner. Here time-phasing becomes more important, technical risk takes on more meaning, especially with respect to the contribution expected in an operational sense, and costs for a unit of work usually are higher and may involve expensive facilities and large manpower resources. The major source of guidance used in determining areas for emphasis is the generalized statements of desired operational capability. These desired operational capabilities provide a planning framework for identifying the technology desired, the time-phasing required, and the relative importance of various needs in different areas of technology.

Before these objectives can be of direct use in management, they must be translated into supporting R&D programs that accurately reflect the appropriate research goals and directions. Thus, the desired capabilities provide the research and development manager something meaningful to consider in his judgement concerning the relative allocation of effort among the various candidate research and development programs. The essential ingredient here is that work is channelled toward creating something that will contribute to future operational capabilities.

Evaluation Procedure: The sections which follow describe an experimental evaluation procedure, QUEST, that is designed to provide "visibility" in the area of program distribution in the research and exploratory development categories. The procedure is primarily oriented to show the relevance and criticallity of an area of technology and the sciences that contribute to its military capabilities. The procedure is not absolute, nor optimal, and may not even be the decisive factor in planning and programming. It is, however, an extremely useful aid for the decision maker, regardless of whether he is in the laboratory or at higher echelons of management. It combines many subjective judgments into one overall picture—it remains a subjective approach. The procedure involves the assignment of quantitative values to judgments made by experienced people and brings together these judgments in an orderly, visible manner as an aid in making gross allocation decisions among technical programs in different areas of technology and among areas of science.

PURPOSE OF QUEST

The Need for a Rational Approach to Appraisal and Evaluation

A need exists for a logical means to allocate resource over the broad spectrum of research and development based on overall utility of each mission.

Congressional appropriation committees have requested quantitative justification from DOD as to the disposition of its resources system for dispensing DOD R&D funds.

The Present Method of Allocation of Resources is Based on Level Funding for Research or "Fire Drill" Funding for Exploratory Development and Leaves Much to be Desired.

I do not believe DOD has been appraising, evaluating, and allocating its research and development resources in the most objective manner. The traditional approach to this problem of resources allocation has been to give the researcher what he had last year, and the engineer fragmented funding on a "piecemeal justification" basis. The technological funding would be given to those areas whose champions could convince top management that their areas have greater requirements for resources than other areas. However, this approach has several serious deficiencies, the two most important of which are 1) its sensitivity to the salesmanship qualities of the lower management echelons and, 2) the tendency to base justifications on only one factor (like near-term military

utility). These funds should be allocated only after a complete evaluation of all three factors pertinent to project selection have been considered, which also include the probability of success and the costs involved, as well as military utility.

Most technical managers, both in and out of the Government, regard all research as "pure" and "valuable" for the future. "Frequently, such executives, counseled by the scientist themselves, refuse even to consider the problem logically for fear that interference from higher levels will damage their sacred cow."[12] Many times I have heard from research agencies or companies, "We fund the man not the work." This may be a good procedure for achieving results, but they may not bear any resemblance to the needs or goals of the Government or the company.

I firmly believe that research not only can, but should be planned.

I am of the opinion that research has a definite role in the Department of Defense, the great bulk of it must be guided along the lines of "relevancy to DOD missions," and yet not so constrained that it produced exclusively applied research.

A given percentage of the R&D budget, say 20 percent, should be unfettered for "knowledge for the sake of knowledge" in research and, for "technological opportunities" in the case of exploratory development, since relevance can be hidden deeply! Today's scientific curiosity may be tomorrow's military giant.

QUEST is designed to:

1) Define the purposes of the research and exploratory development programs and relate these to DOD missions or companies' goals or needs by

   a) providing a quantitative "relevance" number to each scientific discipline,

   b) providing a quantitative "contribution" number to each technological or functional area.

2) Develop a structure which will aid in the understanding of the relationships between the sciences, technologies, and the missions to which they contribute.

3) See that the scientific or technological areas are objectively evaluated to insure balanced support and continuity for long-term objectives.

4) Develop a mechanism to insure that *all* scientific and technological areas are considered so that no opportunities (voids) are overlooked.

5) To make available a logical technique which can be utilized in explaining to higher authority how, where, and why the resources were applied as they were.

---

[12] J. B. Quinn and R. M. Cavanaugh, "Fundamental research can be planned," *Harvard Business Review,* January–February 1954.

General Description of Methodology

Current research and exploratory programs are supported by DOD in order to have available the scientific and technological knowledge required to satisfy future needs of the military.

There is not any easy way to show adequacy as well as relevancy of science to missions or systems, without going through technology or functions, so that QUEST follows the rationale of using technology as the coupling between science and missions.

Prior to the allocation of funds, two pieces of information are required:

1) The potential *military value* of this technology or science, in the future, and

2) A technical *forecast* (including time and resources) of the *probability of achieving* (risk) technological objectives or useful scientific results.

Military Value or Relevance

One must first determine the future adequacy and relevant value of each technology to specific missions and then to each scientific discipline. Thus, military value is quantized for research and development in the macroview by two interdependent matrices:

Matrix 1. Value of Technology to Mission: The mission-oriented parameter of this matrix is the initial input and must be quantified by members of the military (CDC, CMC, CNO, SAC, and TAC, etc.[13]). These "figures of utility" assigned to each warfare category should be updated annually prior to budget time and must be based on a combination of the world situation, the most probable future scenarios, and the forecasted future environment. The number assigned to most important category should be 100; the rest should fall in appropriately. The "producer" commands of all three services (Army Materiel Command, Navy Material Command, Air Force Systems Command) should then assign relative contribution numbers of each technological area, from 0 to 10, to each mission. If the contribution number is multiplied by the figure of merit for each mission, the impact can be determined for each individual mission. When each individual mission is accumulated, the resultant summation determines the quantitative contribution of each technology to every mission.

Three "technology to mission charts" may well be required, one for now, one for five years from now, and one 10 years from now. This should aid in determining future adequacy. If a sensitivity investigation shows very little difference, this may be discontinued.

Matrix 2. Relevance of Science to Technology: The technology parameter should be filled in first using the

[13] Combat Development Command; Commandant, Marine Corps; Chief of Naval Operations; Strategic Air Command; Tactical Air Command.

contribution numbers evolved from Matrix 1. Then, the research branch of the services (Office of Naval Research, Army Research Office, Office of Aerospace Research) should determine the relevance (between 0 to 10) to each of the scientific disciples as it applies to each technological area. When the quantified technological area contribution is multiplied by the relevance number, the number generated will represent the significance of that scientific discipline to that particular technological area. The resultant summation of that discipline to all quantified technological areas would then represent the "mission relevance" number for each scientific discipline.

This procedure may also have to be repeated for three time frames (now, 5 years from now, and ten years from now), in order to permit long-term research a chance to show its impact on future systems.

Because this procedure includes technological transfer in the matrix, this criteria need not be broken out separately. Timeliness and responsiveness is also implicit in the "figures of utility" for each mission given by the operational inputs from each service.

Forecasts

In addition to military utility, it is incumbent on the programmer, before he allocates his funds to the scientist or engineer, to find out what the probability of success (risk) of the scientist achieving his goal(s) or objective(s) is. This can be done by requesting a technological forecast of a given area. A technological forecast may be defined as the prediction, with a given level of confidence, of the occurrence of a technical achievement within a given time with a specified amount of resources.

Scientific Forecast—Applied Research: A forecast in this area should consist of a background, present status, forecast, military implications, and references.

Technological Forecast—Exploratory Development: A forecast in this area should consist of a state-of-the art, status, forecast, operational significance, and references.

Detailed Description of QUEST

Let there be given a set of desired military capabilities or missions to be performed which satisfy the following assumptions:

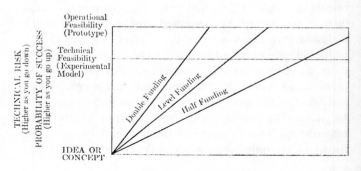

1) Each mission can be assigned a critical weight (W), based upon its *operational* importance.

2) The weights of the missions are additive (i.e., the importance of two missions, taken together, is the sum of their individual weights.) (See Attachment 5.)

Let there be given a set of technologies, defined such that the subtechnologies within each are relatively homogeneous. That is, they must be more like each other than they are like subtechnologies in other technologies. Further, each technology must be costed to arrive at the annual funding based preferably on a five-year projection. Lesser periods would apply to a technology area that is approaching termination prior to five years.

Then form a matrix as follows:

Technologies

		$T_{Ia(1)}$	$T_{Ia(2)}$	$T_{Ia(3)}$	$\cdots$	T_r
Military Capabilities (Missions)	m_1					
	m_2					
	m_3					
	.					
	.					
	.					C_{ij} / C^{*}_{ij}
	m_n					

At each intersection on the matrix between a technology (T_i) and a mission statement (m_i), the evaluation team considers the potential contribution of the technology to the mission. The contribution might, for example, be improvements in a system, subsystem, component, material, or a procedure needed to achieve the desired capability.

Then for each intersection the evaluation team must assign two separate quantitative judgments C_{ij} and C^{*}_{ij}. Attachment 3 provides numerical values to be used in expressing the criticality of the technology to the desired mission capabilities. The first judgment will be the criticality (C_{ij}) of the technology efforts progressing within the special Fiscal Years budget ceiling to the respective desired capability. Next, the team will estimate additional funding which could be used within current manpower ceilings and with existing facilities. The team will then judge the criticality C^{*}_{ij} of the technology that could be provided by the over-ceiling funding. The criticality value assigned to the over-ceiling effort should never exceed and rarely equal the criticality value assigned the in-ceiling effort.

Those items that receive a criticality value of 7 or 10 must be expressed as a brief verbal description on a separate backup for the matrix entry. (This should include, in the Navy for instance, the proposed goals for exploratory development that are being addressed.)

At the completion of this set, the matrix would look as follows:

W Mission Weighting		$T_{Ia(1)}$	$T_{Ia(2)}$	$T_{Ia(3)}$	$\cdots$	T_r
100	m_1	7 / 4	5 / 2	2 / 1		
20	m_2	10 / 1	2 / 0	0 / 0		
10	m_3	7 / 5	1 / 1	0 / 0		
70	m_4	0 / 0	10 / 4	10 / 0		
. . .						
2	m_n	0 / 0	0 / 0	4 / 4		
N_{Total}		970 / 470	1250 / 490	908 / 108		

For each intersection on the matrix the mission weighting (W_{m_i}) is multiplied by the criticality values C_{ij} and C^{*}_{ij}. The vertical column is then totaled to find N_{T_i} for each technology area specified at the top of the matrix for both in-ceiling and over-ceiling resource levels.

Each technology area is then ranked in decreasing order of N for the entire matrix. This ranking can be by in-ceiling only, over-ceiling only, or combinations of both. For purposes of explanation, consider the in-ceiling ordering only.

The specific Fiscal Years exploratory development funding corresponding to each technology area is provided for each entry as indicated in Table I. This resource entry includes both the contract and in-house support resources required for the effort.

TABLE I
IN-CEILING ORDERING OF TECHNOLOGY

	Decreasing N	Annual Rate Millions $
$T_{Ia(2)}$	1250	0.050
$T_{IIIe(4)}$	1100	0.100
$T_{Ia(1)}$	970	1.000
$T_{IVc(2)}$	900	0.500
$T_{Vb(3)}$	820	0.300
.	.	.
.	.	.
.	.	.
T_r	50	etc.

The next step requires the preparation of a visual display of the data arranged in Table I. First, the dollar column in Table I is added to some arbitrary accumulated total, for example, 50 million dollars. At this point, a graph is made of dollars versus technological area at the T_{Ia}, T_{Ib} level for this 50 million dollar increment. Next, the dollar column in Table I is added to the 100 million accumulative total and this increment is plotted on the same graph as the previous 50 million. This process is continued until the entire budget is included on the graph.

Obviously, the first 50 million increment shows the profile of those areas with highest direct relevance to the military problem areas used in the matrix. The last increment has the least *direct* relevance.

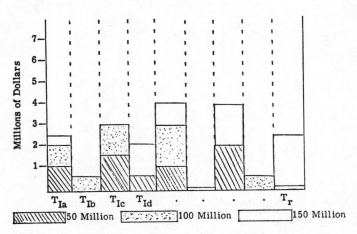

In similar manner the over-ceiling program can be displayed. Further, a combination in-ceiling and over-ceiling graphic presentation can be prepared from these same data.

If any proposed budget is applied as an overlay to the above series of profiles, one can observe either the similarity or dissimilarity of the funding proposed to the funding profile developed from the relevancy relationships. These dissimilarities, if they are found to exist, are areas that management should examine in greater depth and be able to explain.

Research

Using the set of technologies given previously, and a set of sciences, a technology-to-science matrix can be formed as shown here.

	S_1	S_2	$\cdots$	S_m
T_1				
T_2				
.			C_{ij} / C^*_{ij}	
.				
T_r				

At the intersection T_i and S_i, the evaluation team will consider the contribution of S_i to T_i. The team will then assign two quantitative judgments to these contributions. The numbers will be assigned according to the criteria in Attachment 4. The first judgment will be the criticality C_{ij} of the research efforts within the special Fiscal Year budget ceiling to the technology T_i. Next the team will estimate the additional resources which could be used within the current manpower ceilings and with existing facilities. The team will then judge the criticality C^*_{ij} of the research possible with the additional resources, using the criteria of Attachment 4. The criticality of the over-ceiling research resources should never exceed, and rarely equal, the criticality of within-ceiling research. For example, if the criticality of within-ceiling research is estimated to be 5, the criticallity of the over-ceiling research should not exceed 5 and usually will be less than 5.

If criticality of any research is judged to be 8 or greater, a supporting statement backing up this judgment will be prepared by the evaluation team.

Each technology will have received a score N_{Ti} during the evaluation of exploratory development. The products (N_{Ti}) (C_{ij}) are summed for S_j, giving a value V_j for each science. The sciences are ordered according to V_j, and science profiles prepared in the same manner as was explained above for exploratory development.

OMISSION AND WEAKNESS

1) This procedure does not consider changes in value per change in dollars. It is based upon the total value of a package per total dollar budget. Therefore, it does not develop an optimum balance in the program wherein each additional dollar expended produces the same improvement in value regardless of the discipline concerned.

2) The procedure does not consider technical transfer in a direct and visible manner. For example, having accomplished an event in materials may contribute to propulsion without receiving a direct value in the matrix.

3) The procedure does not provide for a special consideration of high potential "opportunistic" effort that does not lead itself, as yet, to mission-type objectives no matter how broad they may be. The feature can be added as a separate table.

4) The procedure does not show the amount of effort contributed from other agencies, but this factor is inherent in the cost estimating steps.

5) The procedure does not consider day-to-day management decisions concerning over-runs, impracticability of termination due to effort nearing completion, contract phasing, etc.

6) Corollary effort in another program area outside of research or exploratory development which may affect funding in research or exploratory development is not considered.

SUMMARY

Many procedures are being developed and used in and out of the Government and industry in allocating resources. Ultimately, the widespread installation of such procedures appears inevitable because of strong trends toward organizing and mechanizing information for long-range planning and because of the growing number of persons who are interested in these procedures.

It is obvious that efficient planning and programming of the overall research and development programs depend on the ability to handle large numbers of individual R&D projects in an efficient manner. Quantitative appraisal and selection techniques, such as this one, along with powerful computers now give the decision makers additional information on which to base their decisions.

ACKNOWLEDGMENT

The author is indebted to the other members of this interservice team for their valuable assistance in preparing this paper. In alphabetical order, they are:

Lt. Col. P. Caulfield, Research and Technological Division, Air Force Systems Command; H. Davidson, Army Research Office; Dr. H. Liebowitz, Office of Naval Research; Major J. Martino, Office of Aerospace Research; and L. Roepke, Headquarters Army Materiel Command.

ATTACHMENT 1

VALUE OF TECHNOLOGY TO MISSIONS

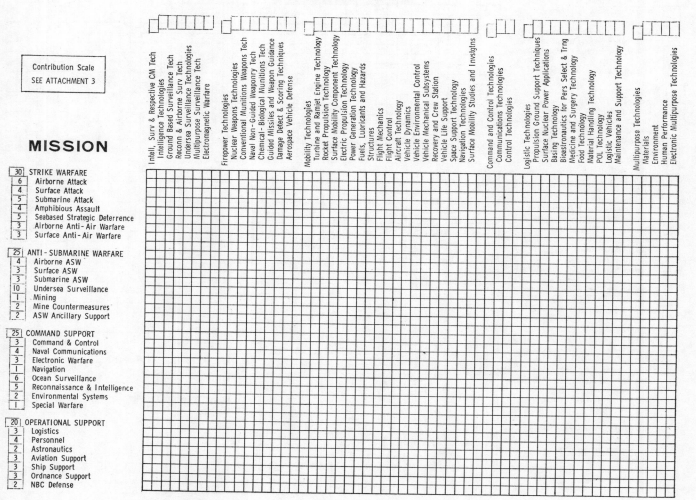

(The numbers assigned to each mission are dummy numbers for security reasons.)

ATTACHMENT 2

RELEVANCE OF SCIENCE TO TECHNOLOGY

SCIENCE

Relevance Scale
SEE ATTACHMENT 4

PHYSICAL SCIENCES
General Physics
Solid State Physics
Atomic & Molecular Physics
Quantum & Classical Wave Physics (new)
Acoustics
Plasma & Ionic Physics
Theoretical Physics
Relativity and Gravitational Physics
Quantum Fluid Physics
Instrumentation

Nuclear Physics
Cosmic Radiation
Elementary Particles
Nuclear Structures

Chemistry
Physical Chemistry
Organic Chemistry
Inorganic Chemistry
Analytical Chemistry
Solid State Chemistry
Biochemistry
Chemistry Techniques

Mathematical Sciences
Theoretical Mathematics
Applied Anal, Theoretical Mech & Math Phy
Biological Mathematics
Numerical Analyses
Math Statistics & Probability
Theories & Tech of Log Anal & Decis Making
Theories & Tech of Info Processing
Info Processing Systems & Devices
Meth Topics Relevant to Spec Mil Problems
Basic Methodology in Systems Research
Interdisciplinary Research
Communication & Control Systems

ENGINEERING SCIENCES
Electronics
Electromag Wave Propagation & Radiation
Electromagnetic Wave Detection
Phys Properties of Solids, Liquids & Gases
Electromag Materials & Components
Electronic Theory
Communications Theory

TECHNOLOGY

Intell, Surv & Respective CM Tech
Intelligence Technologies
Ground Based Surveillance Tech
Reconn & Airborne Surv Tech
Undersea Surveillance Technologies
Multipurpose Surveillance Technologies
Electromagnetic Warfare

Firepower Technologies
Nuclear Weapons Technologies
Conventional Munitions Weapons Tech
Naval Non-Guided Weaponry Tech
Chemical-Biological Munitions Tech
Guided Missiles and Weapon Guidance
Damage Detect & Scoring Techniques
Aerospace Vehicle Defense

Mobility Technologies
Turbine and Ramjet Engine Technology
Rocket Propulsion Technology
Surface Mobility Component Technology
Electric Propulsion Technology
Power Generation Technology
Fuels, Lubricants and Hazards
Structures
Flight Mechanics
Flight Control
Aircraft Technology
Vehicle Dynamics
Vehicle Environmental Control
Vehicle Mechanical Subsystems
Recovery and Crew Station
Vehicle Life Support
Space Support Technology
Navigation Technologies
Surface Mobility Studies and Invest

Command and Control Technologies
Communication Technologies
Control Technologies

Logistic Technologies
Propulsion Ground Support Techniques
Surface Nuclear Power Applications
Basing Technology
Bioastronautics for Pers Select & Trng
Medicine and Surgery Technology
Food Technology
Material Handling Technology
POL Technology
Logistic Vehicles
Maintenance and Support Technology

Multipurpose Technologies
Materials
Environment
Human Performance
Electronic Multipurpose Technologies

(Cont'd on next page)

RELEVANCE OF SCIENCE TO TECHNOLOGY

SCIENCE

Relevance Scale
SEE ATTACHMENT 4

TECHNOLOGY

Intell, Surv & Respective CM Tech
Intelligence Technologies
Ground Based Surveillance Tech
Reconn & Airborne Surv Tech
Undersea Surveillance Technologies
Multipurpose Surveillance Technologies
Electromagnetic Warfare

Firepower Technologies
Nuclear Weapons Technologies
Conventional Munitions Weapons Tech
Naval Non-Guided Weaponry Tech
Chemical-Biological Munitions Tech
Guided Missiles and Weapon Guidance
Damage Detect & Scoring Techniques
Aerospace Vehicle Defense

Mobility Technologies
Turbine and Ramjet Engine Technology
Rocket Propulsion Technology
Surface Mobility Component Technology
Electric Propulsion Technology
Power Generation Technology
Fuels, Lubricants and Hazards
Structures
Flight Mechanics
Flight Control
Aircraft Technology
Vehicle Dynamics
Vehicle Environmental Control
Vehicle Mechanical Subsystems
Recovery and Crew Station
Vehicle Life Support
Space Support Technology
Navigation Technologies
Surface Mobility Studies and Invest

Command and Control Technologies
Communication Technologies
Control Technologies

Logistic Technologies
Propulsion Ground Support Techniques
Surface Nuclear Power Applications
Basing Technology
Bioastronautics for Pers Select & Trng
Medicine and Surgery Technology
Food Technology
Material Handling Technology
POL Technology
Logistic Vehicles
Maintenance and Support Technology

Multipurpose Technologies
Materials
Environment
Human Performance
Electronic Multipurpose Technologies

Column headers (Science):

Info Processing
Electro-Acoustics
Plasma Electrodyn
Quantum Electronics

Materials
Organic Materials
Lubricants
Inorganic Materials
Metals & Alloys
Composite & Fibrous Materials
High Temperature & Specific Materials
Surface Phenomena, Corrosion & Prevent
Radiation Resistant Materials
Ceramics
Characterization
Macro Molecular Research

Mechanics
Flight Mechanics
Simulation Research
Hydroelasticity
Aeroelasticity
Biomechanics
Aeromechanics
Hydromechanics
Mechanics of Materials
Stress Analysis & Structural Stability
Continuum Mechanics

Energy Conversion
Fuels & Propellant
Single-Step Energy Transformation
Multi-Step Energy Transformation
Energy Utilization
Combustion Dynamics

ENVIRONMENTAL SCIENCES
Oceanography
Physical Oceanography
Chemical Oceanography
Marine Biology
Marine Geophysics & Chemistry

Terrestrial Sciences
Seismology
Geology

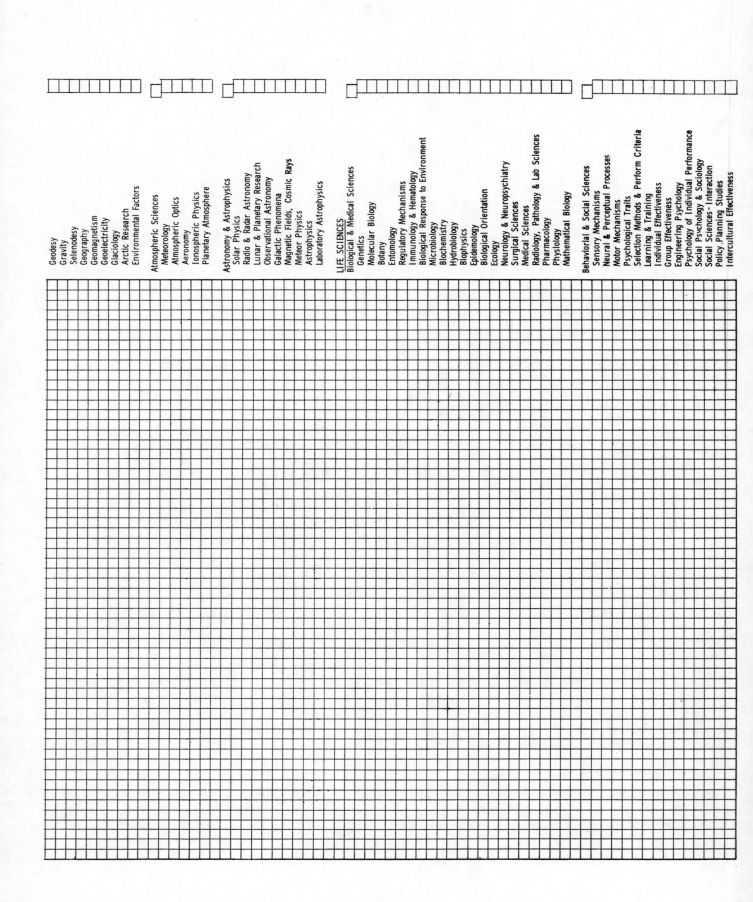

ATTACHMENT 3

CONTRIBUTION OF A TECHNICAL EFFORT TO A DESIRED OPERATIONAL CAPABILITY (MISSION)

(The assumption is that the objective of the technical effort will be accomplished.)

Absolutely Essential

Failure to have this technology will absolutely prevent the attainment of the capability desired...................... 10

Major Contribution

Failure to acquire this technology will result in a significant decrease in one or more of the major performance parameters needed to attain the capability desired. Such degradation *probably would prevent* receiving a favorable decision for development of equipment for the inventory................ 7

Cost Reduction

Success in achieving this technology will provide a major reduction in the cost of achieving the capability desired...... 5

Substantial Contribution

Failure to achieve this technology will result in the loss of a highly desirable but not essential capability. Such degradation, while important, probably would not prevent a favorable decision on the development of equipment for the inventory to attain the capability desired.......................... 4

Refinement of Capability

Achievement of this technology will result in some refinement of the present capability. The desired capability, however, could be achieved without this effort...................... 3

Indirect Contributions

Achievement of this technology will only be an indirect contribution to the capability desired......................... 2

Remote Association

This effort has only a remote association with the capability desired... 1

No Contribution... 0

ATTACHMENT 4

RESEARCH EVALUATION

No progress is possible in this technology without vigorously pursuing this science.................................... 10

Major improvements in this technology will require major advances in this science to achieve success................. 8

Current knowledge will permit only crude or cumbersome solutions to advanced technology requirements. New and significant knowledge is required to make satisfactory solutions possible... 5

Only minor and straightforward extension of existing knowledge is needed to permit this technology to meet advanced technology requirements................................. 3

Current knowledge in this science is adequate for advance of this technology.. 1

The technology does not draw on this science at all.......... 0

ATTACHMENT 5

WEIGHTING OF DESIRED OPERATIONAL CAPABILITIES (MISSIONS)

First, for each Service, a list of missions is generated. This list should cover the complete spectrum of wartime and peacetime missions of a particular Service. For each mission m_i, the Service staff will be asked to assign a relative weight W_i, according to the following procedure.

Given a list of missions, a committee of not over five persons will be asked to select the most important mission and assign it a weight of 100. They will next select the least important mission, and assign it a weight which indicates its importance relative to the most important mission (i.e., if it is half as important, it gets a weight of 50; if one-tenth as important, it gets a weight of 10). Next, each mission on the list is compared with the most important mission and assigned the appropriate weight, in the same manner as for the least important mission. When this process is completed, each mission is compared in turn with the least im-

portant mission, and the correctness of the previously-assigned weight checked. Adjustments may be made as necessary. If necessary, the process is repeated again with the most important mission. Eventually, the group will produce a set of weights for the missions. The set has two important properties. First, it is internally consistent, and second, the weights are additive. That is, the importance of two missions, taken together, is the sum of their separate weights. This feature will be used later in the methodology.

The weights will be given for a specified time frame, (e.g., 1971–76), but in actual fact will probably reflect current Service program emphases. The instructions to the group doing the weighting should specify that the weights are based on *operational* importance, should not reflect technological cost nor difficulty, and should be oriented to the specified time period rather than to the present.

A Classification System for Military Functions, Technologies, and Sciences

JOSEPH P. MARTINO, SENIOR MEMBER, IEEE

Abstract—Systems for classifying or categorizing areas of science and technology are required, not only for use in information retrieval operations, but also for methods used for R&D project selection and evaluation. This paper describes the background and development of one such system which was devised for information retrieval purposes. Either the system itself, or the methods by which it was devised, may be of use to others facing problems similar to those of the organization for which it was devised.

A METHOD FOR classifying scientific and technological activities into categories is required for purposes of information retrieval, for use in quantitative methods for evaluating the scientific and technological activities of R&D organizations, and for resource allocation or budget classification systems for R&D organizations. For purposes of information retrieval, it is necessary that a classification scheme cover the entire area of knowledge to be stored and retrieved, and that the classifications provided be unambiguous. That is, the categories should be exhaustive and mutually exclusive. Then a piece of information can be assigned to a category and retrieved at some later time without error or loss. Similarly, classification schemes for quantitative evaluation methods or for resource allocation or accounting procedures need the same characteristics of exhaustiveness and mutual exclusiveness. Only in this way can it be assured that all activities are included, that they are included once only, and that related activities are placed in the same classification category. Thus the classification scheme discussed below is pertinent to all three types of application.

This scheme was originally devised as part of an attempt to solve a recurring problem faced by many research organizations, including ours. We found that we frequently were asked to reply to questions of the type "What have you done lately for X?", where "X" is whatever problem currently of most concern to top management. The problem, of course, is one which was not anticipated by anyone, or it would not have precipitated a crisis. Furthermore, the question contains the implication that if the research organization has not done something lately for "X," then management will begin to have some doubts about the utility of the research organization. Fortunately, if the research organization has pursued a program of broad and fundamental research,

and if it has kept in mind the interests and peculiar needs of its parent organization, it is not too hard to compile a collection of examples of research results of relevance to "X," even when "X" was not anticipated. However, the effort of answering the question usually disrupts activity to a certain extent. It would be better to have some means of answering such questions, which did not involve obtaining information directly from the researchers, especially when the same information happens to be relevant to several questions.

As a normal practice, our organization prepares an annual summary of its research achievements. It was decided that the collection of these summaries would be the raw material out of which questions would be answered. The problem to be addressed then was one of devising a scheme for coding the achievements so that they could be retrieved to answer a well-defined question. That is, the achievements had to be classified in some fashion which would provide an almost automatic association with a properly-stated problem, instead of requiring some knowledgeable person to make a decision about each achievement relative to each question.

The first problem which had to be faced was the fact that knowledge itself, which is the major product of a research organization, does not solve problems or provide new capabilities. It is only the basis out of which new capabilities may be generated. Thus it was clear that there had to be some intermediate step between the scientific achievement itself, and the problem statement.

The ultimate result was a threefold distinction between functions to be performed, stated in a time-independent and technology-independent manner; technologies, i.e., tools, techniques, and procedures for performing functions; and science, i.e., knowledge about the universe which can be used to devise new tools, techniques, or procedures. The problem then became one of categorizing all the functions performed by the parent organization, in this case the Air Force; categorizing the technologies which have some application to carrying out those functions; categorizing the scientific research areas in which our organization worked; and defining the necessary connection between them.

This distinction among functions, technologies, and sciences appeared simple, but the appearance was deceptive. In looking at existing categorizations of functions, technologies, and sciences, we found many points where one was confused with another. For instance, reconnaissance is clearly a function to be performed. But among the technology organizations responsible for pro-

Manuscript received January 11, 1967. This paper was presented at the 18th Military Operations Research Symposium (MORS), Fort Bragg, N. C., October 1966.

The author is with AFOSR (SRGC), Office of Aerospace Research, Washington, D. C.

ducing equipment for use in that function, it was logical to categorize their effort as reconnaissance technology. But this alleged "technology" lumped together things like cameras and radar sets. A mapping radar, used for reconnaissance, and a fire control radar, used for air-to-air combat, are more like each other than either one is like a camera. As another example, we found considerable confusion between electronics research, which has to do with learning about the behavior of electrons, and electronics engineering, which consists of a set of tools and techniques, perhaps based on knowledge about behavior of electrons, for solving problems. In short, we found that in most existing categorizations, there was confusion, on the one hand, between the gathering of knowledge and the design of tools using that knowledge, and on the other hand, a function to be performed, and the collection of tools by which that function was currently being performed.

We concluded that it would be necessary to generate a new classification scheme for all three areas. Many of the existing categorizations would be useful as a starting point, but would have to be modified. It was necessary to produce list of functions, technologies, and sciences. These lists should be complete, in that nothing was left out; the fineness of the breakdown should be such that the number of items on each list was reasonable; and the categorization should be such that like things are lumped together, and each thing should appear in only one category.

We found that there was little difficulty in classifying the sciences, largely because the Department of Defense had already promulgated such a classification. It is shown in Table I, and is known as the defense research sciences. The breakdown we actually used was one step more detailed than the one shown in Table I, with several subcategories in each of the 14 DRS Subelements shown.

Similarly, for Air Force functions, we found that Air Force long-range planning documents were a fruitful source, as were manuals of doctrine. In these, the functions tended to be stated in a time-independent manner. The writers did a fairly good job of looking behind the technology which is currently used to perform the functions, and abstracting out the functions themselves. Table II lists the major categories into which we were able to divide all Air Force functions. Table III gives a finer breakdown of the tactical air warfare function.

The only area in which real problems were encountered was that of categorizing technologies. The existing lists, from which we started, tended to reflect the structure of technology-producing organizations. Furthermore, they tended to omit the "soft" technologies almost completely. They were directed almost exclusively to the hardware technologies. But since we did considerable research in life sciences and mathematical sciences, it was necessary to assure that the technologies drawing

support from these sciences appeared in the list. The final result was a set of major categories, shown in Table IV. Each of these is broken down further in Tables V through X.

The system described above has been implemented. Achievements are stored on edge-notched cards, coded by area of sciences, technology supported, and mission supported by the technology. The relations between sciences and technologies, and between technologies and missions, are developed on a pair of matrices which can be used easily in placing the coding notches on each card. In addition, special recurring requirements, such as an annual report for the UN Committee on Space Research (COSPAR), can be coded directly on the appropriate achievement cards. This system is still undergoing refinement, but it appears to be a satisfactory way of eliminating from our scientists the burden of supplying achievement information for both scheduled and unscheduled requests for information to be supplied to persons outside the research organization.

TABLE I

PHYSICAL SCIENCES
General Physics
Nuclear Physics
Chemistry
Mathematical Sciences

ENGINEERING SCIENCES
Electronics
Materials Research
Mechanics
Energy Conversion

ENVIRONMENTAL SCIENCES
Terrestrial Sciences
Atmospheric Sciences
Astronomy & Astrophysics
Oceanography

LIFE SCIENCES
Biological & Medical Sciences
Behavioral & Social Sciences

TABLE II

TACTICAL AIR WARFARE
STRATEGIC AIR WARFARE
AIR DEFENSE
PERSONNEL MANAGEMENT & TRAINING
RESEARCH, DEVELOPMENT, TEST, & EVALUATION
SEARCH, RESCUE, & RECOVERY
SPACE OPERATIONS
MILITARY ASSISTANCE
LOGISTICS

TABLE III

AIR-TO-GROUND OPERATIONS
Area Targets
Fixed Targets
Mobile Targets
Area Denial
Illumination

AIR-TO-AIR OPERATIONS

TACTICAL AIRLIFT

TACTICAL RECONNAISANCE
Target Acquisition & Marking
Damage Assessment
Intelligence Collection & Processing

ELECTRONIC COUNTER-MEASURES
Self-defense ECM
Offensive ECM
Supporting ECM

SPECIAL AIR WARFARE
Counterinsurgency
Psychological Warfare
Unconventional Warfare
Civic Action

COMMAND & CONTROL
Deployment Control
Battle Control
Communications Support
Command of Forward & Dispersed Units

BASE SECURITY
Intrusion Detection
Base Defense
Law Enforcement
CB Defense

AIRCRAFT MAINTENANCE

AIRFIELD CONSTRUCTION & REPAIR

TABLE IV

INTELLIGENCE, SURVEILLANCE, AND RESPECTIVE
COUNTERMEASURES TECHNOLOGIES

COMMAND AND CONTROL TECHNOLOGIES

MOBILITY TECHNOLOGIES

FIREPOWER TECHNOLOGIES

LOGISTICS TECHNOLOGIES

MULTIPURPOSE TECHNOLOGIES

TABLE V

Intell, Surv & Respective CM Tech
Intelligence Technologies
Ground Based Surveillance Tech
Reconn & Airborne Surv Tech
Undersea Surveillance Technologies
Multipurpose Surveillance Tech
Electromagnetic Warfare

TABLE VI

Command and Control Technologies
Communications Technologies
Control Technologies

TABLE VII

Mobility Technologies
Turbine and Ramjet Engine Technology
Rocket Propulsion Technology
Surface Mobility Component Technology
Electric Propulsion Technology
Power Generation Technology
Fuels, Lubricants and Hazards
Structures
Flight Mechanics
Flight Control
Aircraft Technology
Vehicle Dynamics
Vehicle Environmental Control
Vehicle Mechanical Subsystems
Recovery and Crew Station
Vehicle Life Support
Space Support Technology
Navigation Technologies
Surface Mobility Studies and Invstgtns

TABLE VIII

Firepower Technologies
Nuclear Weapons Technologies
Conventional Munitions Weapons Tech
Naval Non-Guided Weaponry Tech
Chemical-Biological Munitions Tech
Guided Missiles and Weapon Guidance
Damage Detect & Scoring Techniques
Aerospace Vehicle Defense

TABLE IX

Logistic Technologies
Propulsion Ground Support Techniques
Surface Nuclear Power Applications
Basing Technology
Bioastronautics for Pers Select & Trng
Medicine and Surgery Technology
Food Technology
Material Handling Technology
POL Technology
Logistic Vehicles
Maintenance and Support Technology

TABLE X

Multipurpose Technologies
Materials
Environment
Human Performance
Electronic Multipurpose Technologies

On Relating Research Problems to Mission Requirements

RODERICK W. CLARKE

Abstract—A concept for relating research programs sponsored by the military services to future military mission requirements is described. Developed by the Office of Research Analysis, this concept is currently being used to assist its parent command, The Office of Aerospace Research, in insuring that the Air Force's basic research program is relevant to future aerospace missions and that the Air Force systems planning agencies are aware of the operational implications of basic research results.

ORA's approach involves the use of operations research techniques to perform mission, systems, and research analyses which would ideally result in the definition of future international environment, system cost effectiveness, research and exploratory development opportunities, and system implications from research results. However, several factors currently block full realization of this goal even though significant results have been achieved.

OVER THE PAST few years pressures from a number of sources have caused research scientists and program managers in the Department of Defense to pay a great deal more attention to the relations of their activities to military weapon system needs than they had typically done before. Known as "coupling" or "relevance" activities, they explicitly recognize the fact that research for its own sake has no place in programs sponsored by the military departments. This is not to say that irrelevant research programs were commonplace in the past. Such was not the case. However, sometimes the appearance of this was evident and as such cast doubt on the need for the military sponsorship. Deliberate action was required to remove all doubt as to the value of basic research for a strong national defense posture.

The purpose of this paper is to acquaint individuals interested in the improvement of research and development management with a concept of relating research problems to operational mission requirements. This concept has evolved at the Office of Research Analyses (ORA) over the past few years. ORA is one of the five principal research laboratories of the Office of Aerospace Research (OAR), the Air Force's prime agency for the conduct and sponsorship of basic research. In the subsequent discussion, ORA and its problems are used as a model for illustrative purposes. Although much work needs to be done on this approach to the problem before it is perfected, it is believed that it has much wider appli-

cation than is presently being realized. It is hoped that the following presentation will stimulate others to suggest and implement improvements.

TERMS OF REFERENCE

The environment for the wider application of ORA's concept is centered around a military research agency. It can either be at command level, such as Hq OAR, or at laboratory level. The one constraint is that the research program have a disciplinary rather than mission orientation. The agency is faced with the external requirement that its research programs be relevant to the accomplishment of military missions in a demonstrable way. Further, the agency typically enjoys decentralized, nondirective management.

The nature of basic research is taken to be a process oriented toward the discovery of new knowledge. Two principal types of activity are seen—pioneering and supporting research. Pioneering research is concerned with opening up new fields of science. Its nature and application are unknown, or more likely, unknowable a priori. Supporting research is concerned with providing new knowledge for which a need has been identified. For the former, the lead time or interval between research program inception and weapon system application of the results accruing from the program is 10 to 20 or more years; for the latter it is more on the order of 3 to 5 or more years.

Still another attribute of research is that there is no direct path for applying its results. Figure 1 is an extension of Shapero's model in which the results of research flow into a pool of knowledge from which subsequent R&D activities draw relevant items as needed.[1] Here later R&D activities follow a similar practice, both drawing on and contributing to the pool of knowledge. The size of the arrows is intended to suggest the degree to which this is true. The dashed arrows further suggest that there is probably some direct transfer between activities. Could it be that we are really concerned with increasing the flow via this route?

Manuscript received January 11, 1967. This paper was presented at the 18th Military Operations Research Symposium (MORS), Fort Bragg, N. C., October 1966.

The author is with the USAF Office of Research Analyses, Office of Aerospace Research, Holloman AFB, N. Mex.

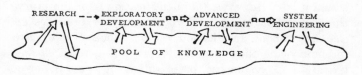

Fig. 1. A model of the R&D process (after Shapero).

ORA and Its Mission

To provide perspective for the concept being presented, an overview of ORA would seem appropriate. ORA is an in-house operations research group numbering about 45 people. Of these, 30 are civilian and military scientists representing a wide range of disciplines and experience. The present organization has evolved from a series of prior groups largely concerned with providing precise, independent evaluations of military weapon systems.

As a result of the insistence of the Congress that the military services demonstrate the relevance of their research programs to future mission accomplishment, ORA was requested to investigate and propose a way in which it could contribute to the realization of that objective. From this investigation a concept emerged based on two objectives: 1) to provide decision information to the Commander, OAR to assist in insuring that the Air Force basic research program is relevant to future aerospace missions and that Air Force systems planning agencies are aware of the operational implications of basic research results, and 2) to develop methods for the identification of mission-relevant research opportunities and for the timely application of research results to aerospace weapon systems.

To fulfill these objectives ORA performs work in three principal areas. It conducts *system analyses* to determine the technical validity, operational feasibility, and cost effectiveness of proposed future aerospace weapon system concepts. It performs *research analyses* to identify promising opportunities for relevant research programs and to determine cost effective applications for accomplished or on-going research. Finally, under the title of *mission identification,* studies are made to identify future aerospace mission and system concepts which are responsive to the needs generated by the interaction of national objectives and the projected economic, political, and sociological environment.

Relationships Between ORA Functional Activities and End-Products

Figure 2 shows the relationships between the ORA functional activities and the end-products they seek. From mission identification, insight is gained for 1) future international political, social, and economic environments; 2) predictions of U. S. goals, policy, and doctrine; 3) the various types of threats—military and nonmilitary—to these; and 4) the concepts for mission systems to counteract the foreseen threats. Most of these are inputs needed for placing subsequent analysis on a logical basis and to minimize the number of unfounded assumptions. However, the identification of nonmilitary threats is thought to have value for other branches of the Government. In addition, the only method now seen for influencing the initiation of pioneering research activities is a systematic presentation of the predicted

future international environment to scientific research workers and planners. In this way we would seek to be catalytic agents that stimulate the thought processes of creative people and provide them with a basis for specifying relevance.

From system analysis we obtain cost effectiveness evaluations of specific systems by exploiting the relevant technology and economic data bases. In addition, the implications of their operational procedures and doctrine and the technological barriers to their timely acquisition and increased cost effectiveness are identified. The relationship between system and research analysis pivots on this latter item. Here the concept is that through research analysis, technological barriers can be translated into opportunities for research and exploratory development programs. It is in this way that we seek to influence the "supporting" research activities.

Another aspect of research analysis is determining specific applications for accomplished research results and the operational implications of these. Here we are seeking to influence both the system and research planner by identifying potentially attractive system capabilities which could be available if the necessary investment in advanced development were made. Both the technological barrier and research applications aspects of research analysis are discussed in more detail below.

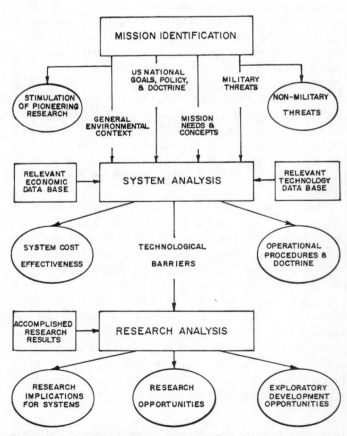

Fig. 2. Relationships between ORA functional activities and end-products.

MISSION IDENTIFICATION

Mission identification is the newest element of the ORA program. It has been undertaken because of the insistance by the Congress and DOD that basic research programs be relevant to Air Force missions and the 10 to 20 or more year lead time associated with basic research.

World conditions are becoming increasingly complex. More than ever before, it is now necessary to consider the context of the future world environment when studying weapon systems in depth. All future weapon systems will have to operate in a world significantly affected by policies and conditions which could be vastly different than the world we know today. Among the conditions most likely to change are the extent of nuclear proliferation and arms control agreements, the increasing disparity between the rich and the poor nations, and the rising expectations of all mankind. These conditions and policies place constraints and limitations on the characteristics and effectiveness of weapon systems. If the common features of the possible future worlds can be forecast with some accuracy, systems analyses relating to future weapon systems become more realistic and credible.

The approach being employed in mission identification is shown in Fig. 3. It consists of three sequentially

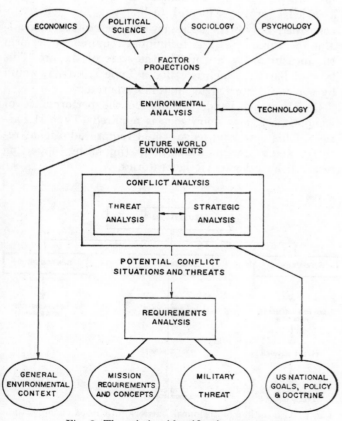

Fig. 3. The mission identification process.

accomplished elements: environmental, conflict, and requirements analysis.

By projecting the various factors of the international environment such as economics, political, and other behavioral sciences, together with advancing technology, one can derive alternative models of the future world. Stated another way, one can determine a wide range of possible future world environments that could be realized. We call this type of study, environmental analysis. It should be recognized that we are not saying that the future world will be like any of these models; only that it could be. We are looking for areas of commonality that will make our subsequent analysis relatively insensitive to what the future holds. But we are also interested in the limiting cases or extremes.

After the future world environments are defined, the task becomes a problem of identifying areas of potential conflict. Conflict analysis involves a comparison of U. S. goals, policies, and objectives with the divergent goals *and* means of other nations. The possible resulting conflict might range from low-intensity diplomatic sanctions to full-scale wars.

Conflict analysis logically leads to the requirements for future military missions and systems. In considering the latter, one is beginning to enter the domain of systems analysis. It is important to understand that there is no clear-cut line of demarcation between those functional activities, and that overlap and interchange between them is both unavoidable and desirable.

The current status of progress for mission identification at ORA is best described as in the methodology development stage. The mission identification process is clearly one that is never ending because of the dynamic nature of our world. However, we expect to have completed one whole iteration by November, 1968, with a statement of the World of 1985 available in November, 1967.

RESEARCH ANALYSIS

The next major area of discussion is research analysis which is defined as the identification of promising opportunities for mission relevant research and the determination of cost effective applications for accomplished or on-going research. As its definition suggests, research analysis consists of two parts: 1) technological barrier studies which evolve from the analysis of a major weapon system, and 2) research application studies which deal with the application of basic research results to USAF system requirements.

Technological barriers and research applications are closely related. Figure 4 shows the origin and terminus of both types of studies. Technological barriers originate from the sensitivity analysis of the factors influencing the performance and cost of a major system. Technological barriers indicate what research must be accomplished in order to expedite the development of a system or to make a system more effective for a given budget level.

Research applications studies have their origin with an advance in a particular scientific area. The method used in a research application study is to devise a conceptual system based on the scientific advance and to compare this conceptual system with alternative methods of accomplishing the same task.

The types of systems ORA typically deals with are too complex to study by considering all aspects in great detail simultaneously. Therefore, they are considered first at the subsystem level. The individual subsystems are optimized considering relevant parameters and then are combined to determine the overall system characteristics and performance. One of many outputs of a systems analysis might be the graph as shown on the lower part of Fig. 5.

Technological barrier studies normally start with a sensitivity analysis of the effects of varying subsystem characteristics on the overall system performance. An elementary hypothetical example is shown. To perform sensitivity analysis, reasonable increases in performance are postulated for the various subsystems. If the total system performance demonstrates a relatively large change with a change in a particular subsystem performance, a possible technological barrier is indicated. The hypothetical example on the bottom of the illustration shows the effect of a subsystem performance gain of twenty percent on that of the total system. The total payoff is more responsive to the improvement of subsystem 2. Therefore, if the technology used to construct subsystem 2 can be improved, the total system becomes more attractive.

Translation of Technological Barriers into Research Opportunities

The translation of technological barriers into research opportunities follows no set patterns. One approach is to break the subsystem down into components. Through coordination with the Air Force Systems Command's Research and Technology Division (RTD) and OAR laboratory personnel, attempts are made to determine the "weak" subsystem components. Research necessary to improve the component's performance or to develop new, superior components is then taken to be the key to improved capability.

Technological barriers may be of two basic types as shown in Fig. 6. For example, the type of barrier limiting the performance of component 1 requires no new knowledge or experimental techniques. The barrier is concerned only with necessary but heretofore unavailable measurements. The techniques required to perform the measurements are within the state of the art. This type of barrier, which is called a Type I barrier, would by typically referred to an RTD laboratory.

On the other hand, to improve the performance of component 2, new knowledge is required (Type II barrier). This new knowledge would require additional research and represents a means of stimulating supporting research by other OAR laboratories.

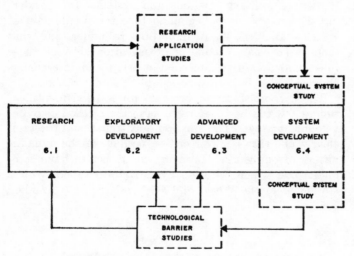

Fig. 4. Flow diagram for research analysis.

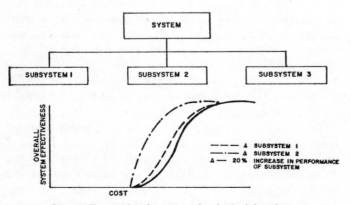

Fig. 5. Determination of technological barriers.

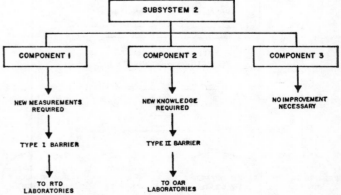

Fig. 6. Translation of technical barriers into research opportunities.

Utility of Technological Barrier Studies

The question may still remain, "What is the utility of a technological barrier?" In answering this question, it is meaningful to demonstrate utility in relation to hardware systems development. System development personnel are well acquainted with PDPs (Program Definition Phase) and development cycles. However, even before entering the PDP phase, a proposed project must satisfy certain long-range criteria such as 1) outstanding problems must be of an engineering rather than experimental nature, 2) the technology for assembling the system building blocks must be in hand, 3) mission and performance envelopes must be defined and optimized, and 4) the best technical approach must be selected. These criteria must be considered years before PDP approval can be anticipated. For example, experimental problems usually require 3 to 7 years before satisfactory solutions can be gained; therefore, experimental problems must be addressed at least that far ahead before PDP approval can be assured. Solution of problems such as the development of building block components and technology and other criteria listed also require long lead times.

ORA analyses deal with systems that are some 3 to 10 years away from the PDP point. By outlining the technological barriers, it is felt that this Office can assist OAR and RTD in rapidly and efficiently moving toward the point of PDP approval and help to insure that the development of necessary AF systems are accomplished in a routine fashion rather than on a less efficient crash basis.

Research Application Studies

Research application studies are typically performed upon the request of the OAR Scientific Laboratories which includes the AF Office of Scientific Research. Studies are also suggested by some of the ORA investigators as a result of insight gained through their system analysis studies. Headquarters OAR has not yet suggested any studies; however, it is believed that this would be a fruitful source because of its overall monitoring of the research program and its frequent and close contacts with Hq USAF and DDR&E.

Initial contact with the OAR laboratories is usually made with a Laboratory Chief or the Plans and Programs Office. Since there are a large number of possible research applications studies, ORA relies upon the Laboratory Chiefs or the Program Managers to accomplish the preliminary screening of study candidates.

After a research application study is initiated, the ORA analysts attempt to work closely with the individual scientists concerned. We feel that the research scientists can make excellent inputs and suggest valuable modifications to the application study. In addition, the close working relationship between the systems analyst and the research scientist brings more realism and credibility to the analysis as well as broadening the understanding and outlook of the affected individuals.

The methodology used for the research application study is shown in Fig. 7. The first step is to employ the specific results of an OAR research program in a conceptual system designed to perform a specific Air Force mission requirement. The conceptual system is then compared with alternative (existing or proposed) ways that have or could perform the same function. Specific mission profiles are proposed and the several systems are analyzed in terms of their effectiveness. Finally, the systems are priced and compared with the previous results to determine their cost effectiveness.

Groups performing research application studies must be continually aware of current on-going research, the state of technology, cost trends, and future Air Force requirements. ORA feels that previous and current analysis work with future weapon systems has placed it in an excellent position to conduct such studies. Considering the broad scope of the total OAR research program, the number of research application studies that could be performed greatly exceeds ORA's capacity. ORA intends to continue to perform carefully selected application studies, to more fully develop and refine the methodology and to disseminate the results of the studies. It is anticipated that OAR laboratory program offices will themselves perform application studies in the future with the assistance and guidance of ORA as required and thus significantly increase the output and benefits of this type of analysis.

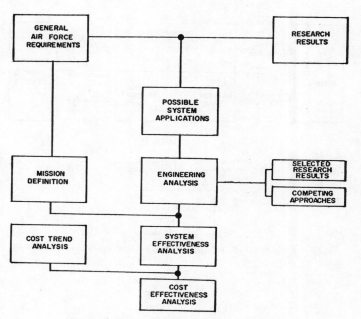

Fig. 7. Research applications methodology.

SUMMARY

Now that the elements of the overall concept have been described, the interrelationships between the elements will be summarized. In addition, the outstanding problem areas that impede the fully effective implementation of the concept are presented to conclude the present discussion. However, it is hoped that these remarks will, in fact, open the discussion of such topics as to the wider application of ORA's concept of operation and ways that we of the IEEE and MORS R&D Management Working Groups might mitigate or overcome some of the outstanding problems.

ORA Concept of Operation

The three ORA mission elements are seen to be mutually supporting and interact under *ideal* circumstances to serve a number of clients with widely differing objectives and requirements. Emphasis is placed on the word ideal because ORA is small in relation to the size of the problem we are dealing with. However, we believe we have made an auspicious start which should point the way for other groups that could do similar things.

As shown in Fig. 8, ORA considers three types of starting inputs: potential research applications from research agencies; system objectives and requirements from system planning agencies; and technological alternatives from technology agencies. In turn, ORA provides these organizations with several types of output.

For the research and technology agencies, opportunities for mission-relevant research are identified. Also provided is future environmental context derived from mission analysis. This also provides an input to system analysis in the form of requirements for future systems.

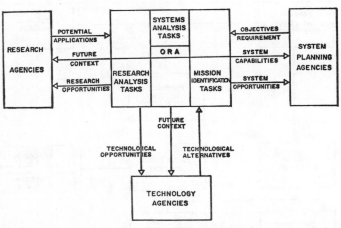

Fig. 8. ORA concept for relating research problems to mission requirements.

For system planning agencies, system analysis provides decision information relative to cost effective weapon system alternatives to perform specific future missions. It also identifies technological barriers which are translated into the research opportunities, and the means by which the operational implications of research results are assessed.

It is important to understand that these outputs have both direct and indirect applications. By direct application, we mean that it serves a client's immediate needs. By indirect application we mean that it has a residual value as a data base for future studies, to advance the operations research methodology and as an input to subsequent analysis.

Problem Areas: Opportunities for Management Science

Without question, the most difficult problem facing ORA is how to obtain coverage of the whole science–military mission spectrum with its limited resources and without sacrificing quality. Our experience suggests that quality requires analysis in depth and this is mutually exclusive from breadth given fixed resources.

In the area of mission identification, the principal difficulties involve reasonably tractable methods for projecting environmental factors into the future and identifying mission requirements based on conflict situations which develop as a consequence of these projections. The triservice meeting on long-range forecasting held at the AF Academy in August, 1966, was a start but much more needs to be done.

In the area of research analysis, identification of pioneering research applications is a complete blank. Only the possible catalytic action of environmental context briefings has been identified and its value is not demonstrable. The translation of technological barriers into supporting research opportunities is another area where a gap between theory and practice exists. The so-called "confrontation" method proposed by Hq OAR[2] holds promise but it has yet to be tested. Still another area of difficulty is the identification of *nonobvious* applications for research results. In some cases the reaction to the research applications considered by ORA has been "what else is new?". The solution to this problem most likely lies with closer liaison between the scientist and the analyst but the exact mechanism remains to be discovered.

REFERENCES

[1] A. Shapero, "Diffusion of innovations resulting from research," Stanford Research Institute, Stanford, Calif., July 1965.
[2] Unsigned, "Coupling by confrontation," Hq OAR Staff Paper, April 1965.

A Program of Research on Coupling Relations in Research and Development

ALBERT H. RUBENSTEIN, SENIOR MEMBER, IEEE AND CHARLES F. DOUDS, SENIOR MEMBER, IEEE

Abstract—As part of a continuing program of studies of R&D, one area for field research has been identified that is concerned with coupling the flow of ideas about new materials, products, and processes from the laboratory through the steps to utilization. The various complex communication phenomena involved—liaison, interface, coupling, technology transfer (LINCOTT)—are treated in a series of eleven studies. Each has a unique focus and set of variables. They cover a variety of environments—commerical and military laboratories, U. S. firms overseas, and R&D in developing countries. But all the studies share the common goal of increasing understanding of communication and information exchange between functionally related science, engineering, production, and management groups, with the eventual goal of providing tested propositions for improved organizational design.

INTRODUCTION

IN THE PAST few years, members of the Program of Research on the Management of Research and Development at Northwestern University have been studying, from a number of viewpoints, the general problem of information transfer and coordination among the various phases of the R&D process including application of the results of research. The set of problems that this work covers is known by various names, including "coupling," "interface," "liaison," "diffusion," "transition," "technology transfer." We use the acronym LINCOTT to describe our interest in this field.

By nature, the research and development process is a series of linked functions, as indicated in Fig. 1, with a roughly sequential flow of work—e.g., research, development, design, engineering, tooling, production, marketing, and use. Within each function there are people with their own specialties, values, objectives, styles of operation, loyalties, interests, and capabilities. The linkage between these functions depends to a large extent upon accommodation between the individuals in the separate functions, especially those that are adjacent in the flow of work—e.g., the researchers, the developers, and the designers—and also those who may not be directly adjacent—e.g., the researchers and marketers. *Communi-*

Manuscript received July 1969; revised August 1969. Part of this paper was presented to the Working Group on Research and Development Planning, 22nd Military Operations Research Symposium (MORS), December 1968. The latter part of the paper draws extensively on "Coupling relations in research and development: Second technical report" for the Army Research Office, May 1969. This work was supported by the Army Research Office, the National Aeronautics and Space Administration, and the National Science Foundation.

The authors are with the Department of Industrial Engineering and Management Sciences, Northwestern University, Evanston, Ill.

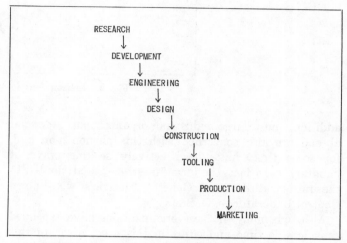

Fig. 1. The research-to-marketing linkage of R&D.

cation and *decision making* are principal activities that occur across the linkages. Prompt, accurate, relevant information is required to flow across these interfaces. Clear, organizationally beneficial, timely decisions are required to achieve effective "liaison," "interface," "coupling," or "technology transfer" (LINCOTT) relations.

In all of our studies of the research and development process over the past 18 years, problems in this area have been recognized. In our 10–12 current projects or subprograms we encounter various aspects of this phenomenon. In some cases, they are critical; in others, merely constraining parameters on the subphase of the process we are studying—e.g., information-searching behavior of researchers, project selection, idea flow, effects of environmental factors on research and development groups, the organization of research and development in newly developing countries, etc.

Parallel to our *research* concern with this general phenomenon of diffusion, interface, or liaison, there has been increasing attention among mission-oriented R&D-supporting and R&D-performing organizations to specific *practical* aspects. These efforts are also manifested under various titles such as Technology Utilization, Coupling, and Spin Off. Chief among the large federal research and development supporters who have been concerned with these phenomena have been NASA, DOD, NIH, AEC, the British DSIR, and other foreign equivalents, and the various branches of the Department of Commerce that support and/or perform R&D. The British and Dutch efforts go back 25–30 years. In

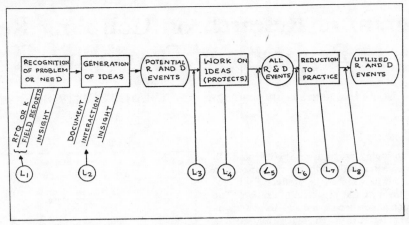

Fig. 2. Liaison function entry points, *K*-contract.

addition, most large industrial organizations here and abroad are also concerned with this phenomenon and, for some time, have been actively seeking ways of handling it. In fact, the term "interface" is attributed to the former director of General Electric's well-known Central Laboratories, G. Suits.

Although many of these organizations have expended considerable time and effort in this area, much of this effort has been *solution* oriented, rather than problem or *research* oriented. That is, much effort has been expended in trying to find massive quick answers to this set of inadequately defined and understood problems.

We have been active in research related to this subject for some time, and have recently begun to accelerate and broaden our efforts on this critical problem area in R&D management. One aspect of the subject—liaison relations—was considered early in our work [14]. A model from a more recent paper is illustrated in Fig. 2 [7].

The more than 30 members of the Program of Research on the Management of Research and Development are all either teachers or graduate students. Our research is integrated into our academic programs—theses, dissertations, and faculty research. It is all basic research, oriented toward increasing understanding of the nature of the research and development process and related phenomena.

Although the Program has been structured around a dozen major programmatic subproblems of the research and development process, the ultimate choice of an individual research topic is that of the investigator (the thesis student or faculty member). Recently, a number of graduate students and several staff members have become very interested in this general area, and there are indications that this interest will continue and grow.

Previous Program Work in the LINCOTT Area

Over the past few years on a modest scale, the principal investigator and his associates have been attempting to formulate this set of problems in more rigorous

terms, establish testable propositions about the processes involved, and make a beginning on a sound set of theories about the subject. Our approach has been 1) to draw on the best available knowledge of the subject from the fields of the practitioners and the work of organization and system theorists, 2) to construct propositions that are both plausible in view of the available evidence, and significant in terms of the value of the potential solutions, and 3) to test these propositions in rigorously designed field studies in operating R&D organizations of industry and government.

Four studies, two from other areas of our program, completed during the last four years, relate closely to the LINCOTT area and have provided useful inputs in content and methodology to our current studies. The first of these (below) is a study by D. Kegan involving the effect of information-seeking behavior of scientists on technology transfer from outside organizations to their own. Subsequently, the other three are very briefly described.

Kegan studied how a group of radiochemists and related specialists in the life sciences get and *use* technical information from the literature [9]. It started as an "inside-out" study, in which we were attempting to trace the path of information generated by Argonne National Laboratory into the laboratories of potential users. It soon became evident that such tracing was not feasible within our resources, and the study evolved into an examination of the sources of information and the decisions to *use* information by a group of people who were one set of potential users of Argonne's output.

For one month, ten researchers in an industrial research and development laboratory recorded a sample of the written technical information items that they received. Four months later they were interviewed to see which of these items had proved useful, and in what ways.

The data showed that a researcher will call an item "useful" even if he does not cite the item, report information from the item, or take some other action based on the information in the item. He will call the item useful when it has had some effect on him or significance for him. Thus, studies that restrict their measures of information usefulness to externally observable behavior may not be validly representing usefulness to the researcher.

Retrospective studies have often had trouble in tracing the sources of ideas or the end use of particular research work. The data of this study indicate that an item may prove useful, not because of the information objectively contained in that item, but because the item causes a cognitive restructuring of the researcher's mind, or a "free association." The item may "release" an idea in the researcher, although another reader without the same stored information or ability may not have the new idea by reading the same item.

In a related study, arrived at from quite a different set of interests, R. Martin did a dissertation related to the sources of ideas for changes in production processes or products [10]. His sample comprised about two dozen technically based manufacturing companies in the Chicago area—electronics, electromechanical, and mechanical.

His respondents were chief executives, chief engineers, or other executives who are responsible for such changes. He succeeded in getting some coefficients for a model that contains a number of factors which the literature and previous studies indicate have some effect on the decision to accept and use such ideas.

R. C. Mills completed an analysis of data that we collected by remote field studies in connection with Phase II of Project Hindsight [11]. He examined questionnaire, interview, and document data relating to the liaison, interface, or coupling relations of a sample of the R&D Event Groups in several large government laboratories (Army, Navy, and Air Force). In addition, he reformulated some earlier models we had constructed, and generated new propositions for test from the results of his study.

In a staff study, R. Lewis and the authors, in cooperation with the RAND Corporation, focused on a very specific interface, the one occurring between systems designers and research and development people—that is, the people in the actual laboratories [19]. Here we were concerned with a number of aspects of the flow of design specifications and requirements, and the return flow of state-of-the-art information between the various groups involved in the planning process as in Fig. 3.

Research Questions

Some of the research questions pursued by members of the group are listed below. Each of the larger research questions has a number of corollary subquestions and related research propositions for test in rigorously designed field studies.

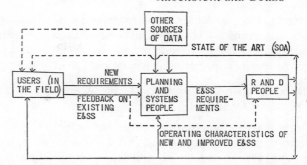

Fig. 3. An abbreviated schematic of some information flows in the complex "systems" R&D process, emphasizing communication links between users, planning and systems people, and R&D. (E&SS = Equipment and Subsystems.)

Need for Formal or Systematically Organized Coupling Between Functional Areas and Organizations

How can communication or coordination gaps be recognized? Is there a threshold of difficulty or conflict above which a formal coupling arrangement is needed? Are communication problems symptomatic of coupling gaps? How does phase of a project affect the need for formal coupling? How much of a gap is tolerable before attempts are required to bridge it formally? Under what circumstances are informal coupling arrangements preferable?

Nature and Organization of the Coupling Function

Where should such an activity be located? How should skill composition of the activity (group) relate to the nature of the projects and/or groups being coupled? Are different organizational arrangements needed for fire fighting versus longer range coupling? How innovative and how aggressive should the coupling group be in its activities? How "visible" should the coupler be? How large should the group be (from one to many people)? What are the effects of multiple (possibly redundant) coupling channels?

Measuring the Effectiveness of the Coupling Group or Activity

What criteria can be used? Do formal couplers aid or impede communication? What are the desirable and undesirable side effects of coupling arrangements? How can we identify successful coupling activities and associate organizational design factors with their success? Who should perform the evaluation? How does effectiveness of coupling relate to overall organizational effectiveness?

Kind of People Needed in Coupling Roles

To what extent do and should managers act as coupling agents? Should couplers be from the groups that are to be coordinated or from other groups—i.e., what are the effects of group loyalties? What kinds of unique training and personality characteristics are needed? How important is the organizational status of coupling agents? Do some individuals have a natural "propensity" for performing coupling activities?

Effects on the Coupling Activity of Differences in Environmental Conditions

How do coupling requirements and effectiveness relate to organizational and cultural differences—e.g., government versus industrial and U. S. versus international? What environmental factors tend to interfere with coupling—e.g., special languages and styles of operation? How does the nature of the organizational environment affect coupling? How does the emergence of informal couplers depend on the environment? How do coupling problems vary between disciplines and different technological specialties?

Possibilities of Simulating the Coupling Process

Is it feasible to develop a dynamic simulation of the coupling or technology-transfer process? Would such a simulation (or set of simulations) help in increasing understanding of the process, training people for it, or solving specific coupling problems? Can the dynamics of the process, related to project or program phase, be adequately simulated?

Some of these questions have already been designed into thesis or staff studies. They are described in the following sections.

CURRENT STATUS OF STUDIES

The overall purpose of our studies of LINCOTT phenomena is to increase understanding and to provide improved bases for organizational design in this complex area of the R&D process. Other aspects of the R&D process are important to its success—e.g., funding methods, individual creativity and productivity, internal organization—but the transfer of information between the various elements in the process is critical.

The studies described here focus on a wide range of aspects of the coupling process, including the need for coupling, the nature of the coupling process, the kind of people involved, and the effects of the environment. We hope that all of them will eventually contribute to an improved basis for designing and managing coupling processes in R&D.

The studies are viewed as a group by the researchers involved for several reasons. In broad terms they are all concerned with the same phenomena even though the substantive focus of particular studies is quite different. Eventually the underlying theories and findings should complement and supplement each other, though the specific propositions may be quite different. Another important reason for viewing the studies as a group is that the methodologies and field-research techniques developed are especially relevant to each other. The problem of "instrumentation" in behavioral studies is diffi-

cult. With a focus on the same phenomena, even though in widely different settings, the instrumentation and methodology developed in each of these studies is of particular value in contributions to the problem of developing valid and believable conclusions in these and future studies of liaison and coupling processes in government laboratories, industrial companies, and elsewhere.

The eleven current LINCOTT studies, focusing on a variety of situations, are grouped here into four areas: studies of government laboratories; studies of U. S. industrial operations; studies of U. S. industry involved in intercultural coupling; and studies of foreign technology transfer.

All of the following studies are currently underway or being developed. As yet, there are no definite findings or tests of propositions to report. In a few cases, there has been sufficient preliminary field work to allow tentative findings to be presented.[1]

Studies of Government Laboratories

The following two research studies are directly concerned with LINCOTT phenomena, primarily in government laboratories. A limited amount of data are also being collected in commercial R&D operations. These two studies are designed so that they form a single coordinated research project. Data are being collected from the same sites and the same respondents. They both focus on the same *dependent* variable—"effectiveness" of work-related communication—sharing data on this variable and certain other parametric data. Upon completion of the individual studies, the data on the independent variables will be pooled in a staff study extension of the project.

1) R. T. Barth, "The effects of differences in intergroup relationships on communications, coupling, and technology transfer activities between RDT&E groups."
2) C. F. Douds, "The effects of work-related values on communications between RDT&E groups."
3) Staff project, "Study of the information transfer process in RDT&E organizations."

Studies of United States Industrial Operations

The three current studies in this area are centrally concerned with LINCOTT phenomena and are directly relevant to problems faced by administrators in R&D operations, both in their own laboratories and in conjunction with contractors. The first study reported below is of particular interest as it deals with the introduction of "high" technology into the managerial decision-making process (i.e., operations research) and the role of the operations research manager, as well as others, in the

---

[1] Short descriptions of the individual studies are contained in our working paper 69/34. Copies may be obtained from A. H. Rubenstein.

process of gaining acceptance and implementation of these techniques in the organization. The second study deals with "high" hardware technology—the numerically controlled machine tool—in production operations. The third study deals with the relations of engineering and scientific organizational functions to a nonengineering and nonscientifically trained function; specifically, the marketing function in the commercial firm and its relations with R&D.

1) A. S. Bean, "Liaison relations between industrial operations research (OR/MS) groups and their clients: A study of the relationship between liaison design and organizational development."
2) J. Ettlie, "Technology transfer in the machine tool industry: The implementation of new numerically controlled machine tools."
3) H. C. Young, "The effect of improper information transmission and reception on the relations between research and marketing departments."

Studies of United States Industry Involved in Intercultural Coupling

The studies in this group substantively deal with liaison, coupling, and technology-transfer problems existing between the headquarters of U. S. firms and their foreign affiliates. In these circumstances, significant cultural differences may exist, along with a variety of other factors such as differences in patent and legal systems. These studies offer the opportunity to significantly broaden the scope of our understanding of LINCOTT phenomena. Some of the specific propositions are likely to be directly transferable and testable within the context of research operations in the United States. To the extent that other propositions represent "extreme" cases for situations in the United States (we have subcultures in organizations and in various geographic regions) they will contribute to the underlying theory. Also, of particular interest is the development of specific methodologies and data-elucidation techniques that are likely to become necessary under these somewhat more difficult field conditions.

1) W. A. Davig, "Transfer of technology to U. S. company affiliates in Mexico."
2) R. P. Forster, "Factors influencing the composition of the R&D portfolios of American R&D laboratories in Europe."
3) E. C. Young, "An analysis of factors influencing the decision to adopt new production technology in selected chemical firms in Mexico and Colombia."

Studies of Foreign Technology Transfer

This pair of studies is concerned with factors affecting the technology-transfer process within the foreign country, not necessarily involving the movement of technology out of any one particular country to the focal country. In broad terms, the basis for the theoretical structure is similar to other LINCOTT studies—the establishment of information networks among people, similarities and changes in orientation, and decisions regarding problem recognition, search, change, adaptation, implementation, and acceptance.

1) A. K. Chakrabarti, "Analysis of socio-economic factors influencing implementation of research results in selected Indian industries."
2) A. D. Jedlicka, "Technology transfer at the level of the community in developing countries."

OTHER PROGRAM ACTIVITIES

In addition to the specific research projects, a variety of other activities support the work in the LINCOTT area. Seminars, sessions with visitors, internal research sessions, special projects, trips, etc. constitute part of our own liaison, coupling, and technology-transfer activities.

Seminars, Research Sessions, and Visitors

Various types of group sessions are conducted for the benefit of members of the Program of Research on the Management of Research and Development. These sessions range from informal discussions with 3–5 participants to formal lectures for audiences of 20–30 or so conducted for a variety of purposes—informal exchange of ideas, more formal critiques of proposals, providing assistance, in organizational design, etc.

Program Research Designs

Many of the questions in the LINCOTT area involve the communication of new information and new ideas within the organization. Another important set of questions is concerned with the transfer of "worked-out" ideas from one organization to another—the problem area of technology transfer. A research design of this process for a real-time study extending over several years was developed this year [17].

Much of the existing literature on the technology-transfer process takes a broad overview of the process or depends upon the survey approach. This has provided an understanding of some of the problems involved, but more from an academic standpoint than from a practitioner's standpoint. Two recurrent and key aspects of vital importance to managers in the military and in industry for many types of technology transfer are the *time lags* from the introduction (or development) of the new process to its on-stream effective utilization and the *costs* involved. The key problem, of course, is to shorten the time lags within acceptable costs.

The proposed design is for a series of real-time field studies of the technology-transfer process in the aerospace-electronics, military production, or commercial industries. The main focus of the study will be on the behavioral dynamics of the transfer process in the receiving organizations. Specific "pieces" of technology —e.g., clearly identifiable materials, machines, production methods, instrumentation, etc.—that are new to the receiving organization will serve as the unit of focus. The unique characteristics of the study are 1) the real-time feature, 2) the focus on time lags, 3) the focus on specific pieces of technology, and 4) concern wtih behavior.

Studies of Organization Design Methodology

In addition to research activities aimed at developing a fundamental understanding of the R&D process, work for the past two years has also been proceeding in our program on the development of methodologies for organizational design. A series of "experiments" has been conducted in the development and application of a somewhat formal methodology for solving problems in organizational design. These trials have been carried out in a sequence of courses in which small groups of students deal with actual field problems of local organizations or, in one class, simulated problems typical of actual experience. The methodology involves developing a set of criteria derived from objectives of the organizational function in question, a set of design features based on manipulable aspects of the given situation, and a set of design parameters based on relevant but nonmanipulable characteristics of the situation. The design features and parameters are linked to the criteria by design propositions. Insofar as possible, these propositions are derived from organization theory and management of R&D literature. The various experiences of several groups in the first year of this activity are described [6].

In the 1968–1969 academic year, five students participated in a two-quarter sequence in which they dealt with actual field problems in two different corporations. Both of the field problems, which were established by the "clients," involved transfer of technology and communications between corporate and divisional R&D. In one case, the problem was communication within the laboratory of about 300 personnel and the enhanced selection of projects to better satisfy the needs of commercial divisions. In the other case, the problem involved communication between the central laboratories of this world-wide organization and its divisional laboratories. A potentially significant indicator of the nature of the problem in one organization was noted when the students were denied access to the divisional laboratories to collect data for the study.

Specific recommendations were developed from the criteria derived from the managers' stated objectives, and data bearing on these criteria obtained through interviews and questionnaires from a number of the people in the laboratories. These recommendations were presented formally to the managers involved. They both reported that they considered the exercise worthwhile.

Proposition and Instrument Inventories

Two additional activities supporting the LINCOTT activities, as well as the research program as a whole, are the development of inventories of propositions and instruments. The nature of the "science" involved in behavioral studies is such that there are many approaches possible to any particular topic, resulting in a wealth of potentially valid and useful propositions. A file of such propositions relevant to the LINCOTT area has been established, drawing upon a variety of sources. It includes tested propositions from the behavioral science literature, propositional statements extracted from the writings and comments of operating managers, scientists, and engineers and potentially testable propositions developed in the course of programmatic work.

Another problem area in the conduct of organizational research is the development of reliable valid instruments. It is characteristic of much of the work in this field for each investigator to generate his own instruments. This arises for a number of reasons. As one step towards improving this situation within our own program, a central depository of research instruments was established. These instruments (questionnaires, rating scales, structured interview schedules, unobtrusive measures, etc.) were collected from a search of research journals, books, our own research projects, personal contacts, and other sources. Whenever possible, data on the reliability, validity, and other uses of the instrument were included. This depository now has over 200 items. Additional items are added as they are encountered.

A computer-aided information-retrieval and indexing system is being adapted for use with the research instruments. The indexing will involve search dimensions such as author, title, variables measured, and type of instrument.

Summary

Liaison, coupling, organizational interfaces, and technology transfer, the various LINCOTT phenomena, are all aspects of a related set of complex phenomena having to do with information exchange and communication in the research-to-production process. Of course, these phenomena are not limited to R&D; they are prevalent in various forms in all types of organizations. The phenomena involved are of great interest to organization theorists because of the central importance of communication within and between organizations in understanding organizational behavior. They are of great interest to many practicing managers who recognize that many of their problems lie in this area.

R&D provides a particularly promising area in which the organizational LINCOTT process can be studied. R&D is a dynamic process, chartered to create new ideas for materials, products, and processes. It is committed to inducing change in the organization and in the social system. Particularly in developing military systems, but also in many commercial systems, its products are highly complex, produced on tight time schedules and with constrained budgets. In such circumstances, it is very important that technology be transferred from one organization to another, or from one part of an organization to another, through effective coupling processes. Yet, in such an environment, the opportunities for ineffective communication are great. It is remarkable that the process works as well as it does.

In our Program of Research on the Management of Research and Development, we have initiated a number of studies in this area. Our prior research in a number of other areas of R&D has repeatedly uncovered problems in this area and provided useful preliminary insights. Eleven currently active studies concerned with various aspects of the LINCOTT phenomena in a variety of environments have been described. Individually, they constitute basic research into the phenomena involved. Collectively as these and future field studies and field experiments mature, information for application in organizational design will become available to the practitioners of R&D. Of course, there will then remain the problem of technology transfer from the academic community to the field.

Some Program Papers on Lincott

[1] R. T. Barth, "Design of a study to investigate the role of the coupling (liaison) agent in military and aerospace R&D," paper 69/22. Dept. of Ind. Engrg. and Management Sci., Northwestern University, Evanston, Ill., May 1969.

[2] A. S. Bean, "Some considerations on the management of management science groups," notes on a presentation to the 16th Internatl. Meeting of the Inst. of Management Sci. (New York, March 1969), Dept. of Ind. Engrg. and Management Sci., Northwestern University, Evanston, Ill., 1969.

[3] A. Chakrabarti, "Proposal for collaboration between Northwestern University and National Chemical Laboratory, Poona, in a study of the socio-economic factors influencing utilization of research results in Indian chemical industry," paper 69/2, Dept. of Ind. Engrg. and Management Sci., Northwestern University, Evanston, Ill., 1969.

[4] ——, "Report on the exploratory field study on the study of socio-economic factors influencing the diffusion of technological innovations in Indian industry," paper 68/47, Dept. of Ind. Engrg. and Management Sci., Northwestern University, Evanston, Ill., 1968.

[5] C. F. Douds, "An approach to a theory of organizational interfaces," paper 67/32, Dept. of Ind. Engrg. and Management Sci., Northwestern University, Evanston, Ill., March 1967.

[6] ——, "Structure and process in organizational design: Observations on some trials," paper 68/3, Dept. of Ind. Engrg. and Management Sci., Northwestern University, Evanston, Ill., March 1968.

[7] C. F. Douds and A. H. Rubenstein, "Some models of organizational interfaces in the R&D process," paper 66/6, Dept. of Ind. Engrg. and Management Sci., Northwestern University, Evanston, Ill., March 1966.

[8] D. Hardin, R. C. Mills, and H. C. Young, "A pilot study of relations between marketing departments and research departments in business organizations," paper 67/63, Dept of Ind. Engrg. and Management Sci., Northwestern University, Evanston, Ill., May 1967.

[9] D. L. Kegan, "The usefulness of written technical information to two groups of chemical researchers," M.S. thesis, Dept. of Ind. Engrg. and Management Sci., Northwestern University, Evanston, Ill., 1969.

[10] R. B. Martin, "Some factors associated with the evaluation of ideas for production changes in small companies," Ph.D. dissertation, Dept. of Ind. Engrg. and Management Sci., Northwestern University, Evanston, Ill., 1967.

[11] R. C. Mills, "Liaison activities at research and development interfaces: A model, some empirical results, and design considerations for further study," M.S. thesis, Dept. of Ind. Engrg. and Management Sci., Northwestern University, Evanston, Ill., 1967.

[12] M. Radnor, "The control of R&D by top managers of large decentralized companies," Ph.D. dissertation, Northwestern Tech. Inst., Northwestern University, Evanston, Ill., August 1964.

[13] M. Radnor, A. H. Rubenstein, and A. S. Bean, "Integration and utilization of management science activities in organizations," *Operational Res. Quart.*, vol. 19, June 1968.

[14] A. H. Rubenstein, "Liaison relations in research and development," *IRE Trans. Engineering Management,* vol. EM-5, pp. 72–78, June 1957.

[15] ——, "Integration of operations research in the firm," *J. Ind. Engrg.*, vol. 11, September–October 1960.

[16] ——, "Organizational factors affecting research and development decision-making in large decentralized companies," *Management Sci.*, vol. 10, pp. 618–633, July 1964.

[17] ——, "A real-time study of technology transfer in industry," paper 69/5, Dept. of Ind. Engrg. and Management Sci., Northwestern University, Evanston, Ill., March 1969.

[18] A. H. Rubenstein and C. F. Douds, "A bibliography on interface, liaison, and technology transfer," paper 68/28, Dept. of Ind. Engrg. and Management Sci., Northwestern University, Evanston, Ill., November 1968.

[19] A. H. Rubenstein, C. F. Douds, and R. Lewis, "A preliminary field investigation of some models of organizational interfaces in the R&D process," paper 67/17, Dept. of Ind. Engrg. and Management Sci., Northwestern University, Evanston, Ill., 1967.

[20] A. H. Rubenstein, S. D. Hill, A. Chakrabarti, W. Davig, W. Hetzner, T. Schlie, and E. C. Young, "Some data on applied research institutes in developing countries," (for presentation at the meeting of ORSA), paper 69/18, Dept. of Ind. Engrg. and Management Sci., Northwestern University, Evanston, Ill., November 1969.

[21] A. H. Rubenstein, M. Radnor, N. R. Baker, D. R. Heiman, and J. B. McColly, "Some organizational factors related to the effectiveness of management science groups in industry," *Management Sci.*, vol. 13, April 1967.

[22] E. C. Young, "Progress report on LINCOTT research project," Northwestern University, Evanston, Ill., February 1969.

Technology Transfer in Practice

HERMAN BIEBER

Abstract—Many government and industry leaders now feel that poor transition of technical data and know-how from fundamental and exploratory R&D into commerical utilization is a prime cause of poor research effectiveness. Particularly in the large corporate or Federal laboratory, good research is often "wasted" because no innovation results. Given the current research cost spiral, society can ill afford under-utilized research; in fact, multiple applications on R&D should be the goal.

The prime thrust of this paper is that technology is primarily transferred by *people*, not via organization charts or formal reports.

IT is fashionable today to undertake theoretical studies of technology transfer. Much of this work is in universities and, for practical reasons, is heavily oriented toward technology transfer within large Government agencies or from these agencies to the civilian sector. This paper will adhere to the industrial viewpoint and cover

1) the need for technology transfer (or "coupling," as it is sometimes called),

2) how corporations perceive and respond to this need,

3) the activities and special problems of the coupling agent, and

4) his training and career outlook.

The practices and problems described in this paper are a composite of large company behavior and do not necessarily reflect the practices or policies of Esso Research.

Even though much of the literature on coupling has emanated from Federal laboratories, or has been sponsored by Federal agencies, industry is equally concerned[1] with this vital part of the innovation process. Given today's research cost spiral, the large corporation can ill afford under-utilized research. Yet much good research is still "wasted" because no innovation[2] results. The coupler or technology-transfer agent can play a critical role in securing wider commercial applications of new technology.

It is legitimate to inquire why a large corporation would need to worry about coupling as a specific function. One can argue that the competent research manager would intuitively create any necessary linkages between new technology and market needs as part of his job. This was true at one time, and still is, in many small companies. However, as the corporation grows, it is more and more difficult for the research manager, or vice-president for research to perform the necessary technology-transfer duties.[3]

The need for a separate coupling function stems from both external environmental factors and internal problems with corporate giantism. The external problems include the following.

a) *Mushrooming Technical Literature*—The exponential growth of technical material makes it impossible for anyone to be current in other than a very narrow specialized area. But the research manager must be able to separate the wheat from the chaff. He must pinpoint those technical events that are truly timely and significant (e.g., relevant) to his corporation. The further and further subdivision of the traditional technical fields of mathematics, chemistry, physics, and biology accentuates the problem. Each subfield develops its own journals, and its own specialized technical jargon. This compounds the problems of the generalist manager who is trying to fathom business relationships between two apparently dissimilar fields. The acquisition, handling, storage, and retrieval of technical information is in itself a specialty, which the average research manager is ill-equipped to handle directly.

b) *Time Compression of Technological Advance*—The gap between innovation and invention is shrinking so that it is no longer possible to rely on universities to codify new technical knowledge for transmittal to the next generation of students. Real-time information systems are needed.

c) *Technical Obsolescence*—As a corollary of the preceding, it is more and more difficult for the graduate engineer or scientist to remain technically alert and up to date. More technical people are becoming obsolete sooner, particularly outside of their immediate work responsibilities. Technical education must be a life-long process, but how is one to choose from the varied menu of subject matter available?

Many of the same factors operate internally but on a smaller scale. As corporations grow, communication lines become strained and lines of authority and responsibility fuzzy. Geographical spread accentuates the problems of internal corporate communication. Although it is understood by many that technology is transferred primarily by people, there is more and more reliance on organizational charts and formal report systems. The multiplicity of internal reports re-

Manuscript received July 1969; revised August 1969.

The author is with the Department of Corporate/Government Research, Esso Research and Engineering Company, Linden, N. J.

[1] *Forbes Magazine,* November 15, 1968.

[2] In this paper *innovation* refers to the commercial introduction of a new process, product, or service, in contrast to the *invention* of a novel concept. Invention is only one step in the innovation process.

[3] D. L. Schon, *Technology and Change,* contains a lucid development of this thesis.

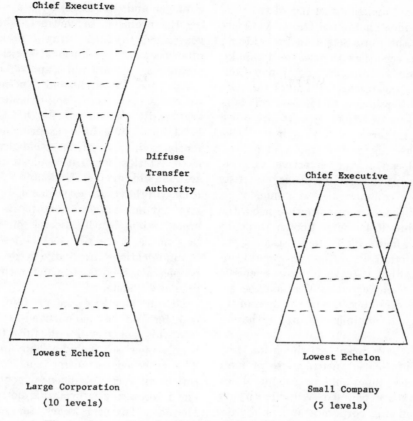

Fig. 1. Attenuation of communication—small or large company.

sults in filtering systems, which, in themselves, introduce impedance and noise into the communication system. This situation has been described as shown in Fig. 1. In the small company there is at least *some* communication and direct influence between the Board of Directors and the bench scientists and engineers. But the large corporation interposes many levels. Middle management becomes a gate valve for information, each layer adding its impedances and extraneous noise. Everything is designed to promote corporate stability and resist change. Successful innovation in such a situation is often predicated on changing the system (as in the "free-form" corporate structure typified by Litton Industries) or in devising informal ways to end run the barriers. The maverick inventors, the "change-makers," the coupling agents will do this, often at considerable peril to their career.

From an examination of the literature of R&D transfer, as well as from many personal field contacts, I would classify corporations in three groupings.

a) *Happily Ignorant*—These companies have not worked on the problem. They may not even be aware that there is a problem. Often such companies are in an intermediate growth phase where things have not quite yet got out of hand, or else they are run by the original owner–entrepreneur who is still able to handle the innovative function personally.

b) *Concerned*—Some companies are beginning to be aware that their performance is less than optimal, and that communications between research, manufacturing, and marketing need "improvement." However the situation is still perceived as a problem that management can exclusively handle within the context of existing organizational frameworks.

c) *Have Reacted to Improve Transfer*—A few companies have recognized the coupling problem in the context of the overall innovation process, have researched the problem in light of their specific organizational structure, and have made appropriate management and/or staff changes to promote technology transfer.

Four basic techniques (or combinations of these) seem to have evolved:

1) As typified by Bell Telephone Laboratories,[4] careful control of spatial/organizational bonds and barriers can pay rich dividends. Interaction between development and manufacturing groups can be enhanced by deliberately locating them in the same building. However, because of their distinctly differing roles and time frames, these groups should report to separate managements. Where geographic separation is unavoidable, communication may be fostered by having two groups report to the same management.

[4] J. A. Morton, *A Model of the Innovative Process.* NSF Publ. 67-5.

2) Rotation of personnel makes direct use of the personal enthusiasm of the idea champion. Dr. J. A. Goldman, former director of the Ford Scientific Laboratory, favors getting the basic scientists themselves to make the appropriate technology transfer and innovation. This can only happen if the researcher knows the corporate problems and goals relevant to his work. This is fostered by encouragement of attendance at corporate business meetings and deliberate short- to immediate-term rotations in engineering and manufacturing departments. This method can be very effective, but unfortunately there are many productive basic scientists with little inclination for commercial development.

In addition to becoming aware of corporate need, the "rotational" scientist himself becomes known throughout the company, and is more likely to be used in the future as a valuable internal consulting resource. Conversely, some companies that kept their basic scientists in an ivory tower have been forced to abandon the activity after a number of years because of the lack of innovative "fallout," i.e., a tangible return on the research investment.

3) Several companies have been experimenting with the use of semiformal information networks to promote technology transfer across functional or product lines. Information researchers[5] are charged with identifying, interpreting, and transmitting corporate and public domain technical information. They are more than technical librarians answering reference calls. They actually take the initiative in passing out information and suggesting fruitful areas for corporate research. Often they can present the research manager with relevant facts that he did not anticipate or answer important questions that he could not verbalize. At 3M, divisional information scientists meet regularly for informal meetings to discuss patent problems and research breakthroughs and bottlenecks. This has frequently resulted in invention and innovation via multiple use of technology, quite independent of the formal company communication channel.[6]

4) Finally, specific technology transfer activities can be organized as staff functions. General Electric,[7] for example, has specialized staff groups to enable the corporate vice-president to "hot-house" new innovations until they become obviously attractive to an established product line, or become the basis for a new product line. Such staff functions may include liaison groups charged with promoting interdivisional information transfer, technical feasibility and market development groups, and new business development organizations that can actually initiate new ventures. The point here is that all these functions report to the same manager and, therefore, have a vested interest in solving the problem. In contrast, when innovation is subcontracted to an existing functional group, the task often becomes an additional workload outside of the corporate main stream and is apt to receive short shrift.

At Esso Research and Engineering Company, research is organized along product lines, but it is geographically centralized in the Linden–Florham Park, N. J., area. We have experimented with, or are currently trying, all of the technology-transfer techniques cited. At this point, it would appear that some hybrid system will evolve. Undoubtedly, each large corporation will have to experiment to develop the specific strategy most appropriate to its needs and particular organization. Much research on innovation remains to be done, and creative techniques to supplement formal communications are badly needed. But the truism that people, not reports, transfer technology must predominate any system.

Having identified the need for organized technology transfer and having outlined some evolving methodology, this paper will now turn to the function of the coupler per se, including his personal characteristics. The technology-transfer agent is often described as sort of an overt intelligence agent collecting, evaluating, and interpreting information both internal and external. He has a natural knack for separating the relevant from the extraneous and for synthesizing trends and action recommendations from bits of discrete data. To do this, he must first adapt, translate, and package the information before it can be effectively transmitted across an organizational interface. He matches technology with need.

Often successful technology transfer or coupling requires an "invention by analogy" before the utility of the information becomes apparent. For example, one large corporation solved a costly problem in fabricating transformer laminations by observing operations in a plywood manufacturing plant. The information scientist, therefore, bridges the gap between the general and specific. He walks the narrow line between the generalist and the specialist.

What kind of a person is this? What are the elements of a job description for technology transfer?

First, the individual selected must be technically competent and objective, but he also needs a good knowledge of business. He should be broadly aware of company programs and personalities. In short, he must possess very wide interests and a lively curiosity.

He is a self starter, able to define problem needs, and to develop answers before he is asked. Because he operates across company lines, he must be politically astute in order to promote his goals effectively. Technology transfer is thus a demanding assignment, and requires a seasoned company engineer–scientist who is obviously also well qualified for other important com-

[5] G. H. Cloud and W. T. Knox, *"Information Research— A New Tool,"* Fifth World Petroleum Congress, paper 15, ch. 9.
[6] Personal communication.
[7] A. M. Bueche, *Natl. Conf. on Industrial Research* (Chicago, Ill.), 1968.

pany staff or managerial jobs. For this reason, coupling is usually not a career assignment, but rather a rotational position.

There is also some evidence that the effectiveness of a full-time coupler tops out after a few years. Perhaps rejuvenation is possible via a return to the bench or some other line of staff work. Generalizations are hazardous here, but a company would probably be wise to arrange for a continual introduction of new blood and new ideas into the liaison/technology-transfer function.

The author feels that many elements of technology transfer could be successfully taught. Perhaps some day an enterprising university will offer a technology-transfer minor as an MBA option. But as there is currently no college course dealing with technology transfer or coupling per se, most "practitioners" are home grown and evolve into the position. Undoubtedly, as the technology-transfer operation becomes more sophisticated, it will become more important for colleges and universities to pay some attention to this function in their curricular development.

No discussion of coupling is complete without considering some of the frustrations and satisfactions involved in the job. Promoting technology transfer truly entails many frustrations. One is always battling the NIH (not invented here) factor. Further, the coupler's impact on the corporation may be quite diffuse in contrast to the scientist making a well-characterized breakthrough in the laboratory. For this reason, it may be difficult to obtain management recognition.

The coupler may also lack peer approval, since the nature of the job is not widely understood. It is often perceived as a high-level clerical or librarian job. Sometimes, one must plant a seed of an idea somewhere else to get anything accomplished. When it matures and results in an action program, it may be difficult to share in the credit.

It is often difficult to measure job effectiveness. Some information can be measured directly in dollars, for example, the acquisition of a license or know-how permitting termination or curtailment of a redundant laboratory program. But what is the "value" of supplying top management with information that may only improve their judgment and general business knowledge in a vague way? At Esso Research, considering *only* those aspects of information research that can be quantified, returns on "investment" were commensurate with scientists and engineers doing lab/pilot plant R&D.

For all of the foregoing reasons it is difficult to attract competent people into the job. Sometimes one can find a diamond-in-the-rough, a latent coupler who underachieves in a narrowly specialized assignment. But the "good man" is likely to view the job as not being challenging or in the corporate main stream. This is another reason why the rotational assignment is often the only way to entice a high-rated employee to consider such a staff function. It goes without saying that the use of the technology-transfer staff as a "shelf" for managers who did not cut the mustard is deadly. Such men are hardly likely to assume the risks inherent in effective coupling.

Yet, in spite of all of these problems, the technology-transfer activity offers much personal satisfaction for the competent gregarious multifaceted individual.

Relating Organization Goals and Technological Forecasting for Research and Development Resource Allocation

C. M. SCHOMAN, JR., D. N. DICK, MEMBER, IEEE, AND T. R. McKNIGHT

Abstract—This paper discusses a simple and logical method for using Navy Exploratory Development Goals (EDG) and the Navy Technological Forecast (NTF) for the allocation of resources to technology to meet future requirements. First, the military worth of the various EDG in meeting Navy objectives is determined. Second, the utility of the various technologies to the EDG is determined by systems design and scientific/engineering offices. The military worth and technology utilization values are then combined into an Index of Worth value indicating the worth of the various technologies in meeting Navy objectives. A mathematical model is suggested as a future refinement.

INTRODUCTION

RECENTLY many new factors have entered into the defense research and development resource allocation problem. Funds are needed for social programs, air pollution, water pollution, highways, airway safety, transportation, and a host of other nondefense programs. Suddenly resources are limited. There is just not enough money to support everything. Since it is difficult to relate the early phases of research and development (Exploratory Development) to end use—to make its value visible to all management levels—it becomes a prime candidate for budget cuts.

Mr. McNamara, then Secretary of Defense, in testifying to Congress concerning Exploratory Development stated [1] that the management problems involved are complex and that he has "never been fully convinced that we are getting full value from this 1-billion-a-year effort." He stated that although he recognized that exploratory development had contributed significantly to our military strength, the effort was so diverse, large, and decentralized (more than 12 000 active tasks at the present time) it was difficult to evaluate all of the results in relation to the costs.

Sen. Gordon Allott (R–Colo.) stated that: "Congress and the taxpayer have a right to expect that their research program has some strong overall direction and control." He warned: "Unless the taxpayer and their elected representatives know what they are buying, a reaction will cause a severe cutback in funds." He also

Manuscript received July 1969; revised August 1969. This paper was presented at the 22nd Meeting, Military Operations Research Society, Navy Postgraduate School, Monterey, Calif.

The authors are with the Advanced Planning and Analysis Staff, Naval Ordnance Laboratory, Silver Spring, Md.

indicated: "There are not sufficient dollars to fund every research program regardless of merit or priority."

These are only a few of many statements that could be listed saying the same thing: "Resources are limited; priorities must be established; the reasons for these priorities clearly understood by all; and what we will get for our money made visible."

Resource allocation is a prime management responsibility. It is basically a problem of establishing priorities and communication at various organizational levels. The allocation of resources to the early phases of research and development is particularly complex because of the communication problem among managers and scientists/engineers. To make the situation more complex and urgent there is

1) the rapid advance of technology,
2) the shortening of time between technological discovery and application,
3) the socio-technological interface, and
4) the limitation of resources.

All of these strongly indicated that past methods of resource allocation by intuition, consensus, tradition, personality, prejudice, and other factors generally described as "political" may not be satisfactory in the future.

SYSTEM ACQUISITION

In the allocation of resources to research and development the Research, Development, Test, and Evaluation (RDT&E) System Acquisition Spectrum must be understood. In this spectrum the closer you are to research, the more difficult it is to make resource allocation decisions, based on specific end uses or requirements, and the greater the communication problem between the manager/decision maker and the scientist/engineer. The following are the Navy definitions [2] for the early phases of research and development.

1) Research—includes all effort directed toward increased knowledge of natural phenomena and environment and efforts directed toward the *solution of problems in the physical, behavioral, and social sciences.*

2) Exploratory Development—includes all effort directed toward the *solution of specific military problems,* short of major development projects. This type of effort may vary from fairly fundamental applied research to quite sophisticated bread-board hardware, study, programming, and planning efforts.

EXPLORATORY DEVELOPMENT RESOURCE ALLOCATION

This paper is primarily concerned with the allocation of resources to the exploratory development phase of the system acquisition process. Exploratory Development is the phase between research and advanced development that provides the technological building blocks with which improved and/or new systems are built. It serves as the all important bridge between wide-ranging research areas and the advanced development of specific systems.

There are general considerations concerning any resource allocation method for research and development. The underlying thoughts incorporated into this method are as follows.

1) Any resource allocation method must be simple, logical, understandable, and usable in the present organization.

2) Any resource allocation system *must provide* for a) supporting known technologies to meet anticipated future needs, and b) exploiting new technologies as they become available.

3) What is in the future is largely a matter of opinion and judgment. Numerical values may be assigned to opinion and judgment, but this does not make them any more accurate.

4) Resource allocation models should be in keeping with the accuracy of the input data. No degree of mathematical complexity will make the data more valid.

5) The end result of any resource allocation method is the establishment of priorities at various management levels. No amount of semantic or numerical manipulation can avoid the necessity to establish a ranked relationship between resources and requirements.

6) The resource allocation model must provide required guidance and information to all levels of management for decision making.

There are two basic roads to the future. One is by recognizing requirements and supporting science and engineering in a manner that has the maximum probability of meeting these requirements; and the other by exploiting scientific and engineering advances to create new items and systems, new requirements, and a new future.

The Navy is taking both roads. In the publication of Navy Exploratory Development Goals [3], the requirements are stated; in the publication of the Navy Technological Forecast [4], the advances that might be obtained in various areas of technology are stated. This paper indicates how these two efforts can be related to provide a system for allocating resources. The general procedure will be as follows.

1) Determine relevant technologies.
2) Determine the worth of the technology to future requirements; that is,
  a) what requirements are supported?
  b) how important are these requirements?
  c) how well does the technology support the requirements?
3) Determine advance possible in the technology; that is
  a) what advances can be made, when, and with what funding?
  b) how can the technology be exploited?
4) Determine how worth and advance of technology can be related in a systematic manner for resource allocation. *Specifically the system to be described will indicate how the Exploratory Development Goals and the Navy Technological Forecast can be used for allocating resources today to meet future requirements.*

EXPLORATORY DEVELOPMENT GOALS (EDG)

The basic purpose of the EDG is to translate the broad and intentionally general statements given in a number of Navy planning documents into specific quantitative terms that are useful in planning an exploratory development program that is responsive to Navy requirements. The goals can be looked at as a transformer that translates general requirements into specific objectives such as range, launch depth, damage criteria, etc. These are the system operational parameters the Navy desires to obtain to carry out its missions. The goals have been divided into the following five basic divisions, called functions

  a) target data collection,
  b) command and control,
  c) counteraction,
  d) mobility, and
  e) support.

Each goal provides information on

  a) operational mission supported,
  b) technical capability,
  c) environment,
  d) relationship to other goals, and
  e) a brief of rationale.

The goals are *need* oriented, and it is not implied that *all* Exploratory Development should be devoted to satisfying these goals. This indicates that the Navy recognizes that technology may be exploited to create new needs. The percentage of Exploratory Development resources that should be need oriented or based on the EDG is a management decision. It depends to a large extent upon the confidence management has in the completeness of the EDG.

Navy Technological Forecast (NTF)

The Navy Technological Forecast predicts, within a stated level of confidence, the anticipated occurrence of a technological achievement, within a given time frame, and with a specified level of support.

The first NTF was prepared by the Navy technical community in 1968 [5]. The Navy Technological Forecast consists of two approaches: 1) the Basic Forecast and 2) Technological Needs Identification Studies. The Basic Forecast is divided into three parts:

Part I—Scientific Opportunities;
Part II—Technological Capabilities;
Part III—Probable Systems Options.

Part II is primarily concerned with exploratory development and is organized into the following sections.

a) Background—introduction to the field.
b) Present Status—state of the art—where are we now?
c) Forecast—projection of technology—where can we go?
d) Operational Implications—what does it mean?
e) Associated Activities—where are the capabilities?
f) Reference—where did information come from?

Resource Allocation System

In the Navy EDG, goals based on needs are stated; and in the NTF the technological possibilities are indicated. It remains for us to describe a system that will join these two together to determine how resources should be allocated. Since any resource allocation system is actually the establishment of priorities at various management levels, the following questions immediately arise.

1) How important are the goals to objectives?

2) How important are the various technologies to the goals?

3) What advances can be made in the various technologies, how important are they, are how much will they cost?

These questions can be answered by conducting 1) An Index of Worth forecast, and 2) An Index of Advance forecast. The central thought of the allocation method is a dual view of technology from both military utilization and the possible technological advance. The Index of Worth Forecast indicates the military utility of the technology area. The Index of Advance forecast indicates the possible control of technological advance by resource allocation. The two indices are coupled into a decision model to assist in determining resource allocation alternatives.

Index of Worth Forecast

The Index of Worth forecast determines the quantitative worth of technologies in supporting stated Navy objectives. The Index of Worth I_{W_i} for the various

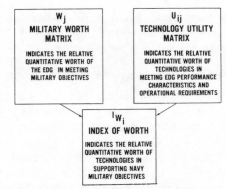

Fig. 1.   General method for determining the Index of Worth I_{W_i}.

technologies is determined by developing both a Military Worth Matrix and a Technology Utility Matrix (Fig. 1).

The Military Worth W_i indicates the relative quantitative worth of the EDG to stated military objectives. The Technology Utility Matrix U_{ij} indicates the relative quantitative worth, based upon key technological parameters of the various technologies in meeting the EDG performance characteristics and operational parameter requirements.

The Military Worth Matrix and the Technology Utility Matrix are combined mathematically to obtain an Index of Worth Matrix I_{W_i}. This matrix contains Index of Worth values for the various technologies that indicate their quantitative worth in supporting stated Navy objectives.

Military Worth Matrix

The Military Worth portion of the Index of Worth Forecast will now be described. The Military Worth Matrix is a column matrix containing the quantitative worth values of each of the 137 EDG. These values provide the relative importance of each EDG (compared to the other 136) and therefore represent a ranking and weighting of the EDG. The development of the Military Worth Matrix involves obtaining weight values for each EDG.

One question is who should determine the value of these weights? The Navy organization most qualified to make judgments concerning both the worth of military missions and the worth of Exploratory Development Goals to military objectives is the Chief of Naval Operations (CNO). As stated in the Navy's RDT&E Management Guide [2], CNO's mission includes "the determination of the military requirements of and priorities of things to be procured" by the Navy. They are most familiar with the Navy doctrines concerning operational activities and overall military objectives (Fig. 2).

How would CNO go about evaluating the relative military worth of 137 Exploratory Development Goals? The solution to this problem lies in subdividing the EDG into smaller groups that are more suitable to the value judgments that must be made in the weighting process.

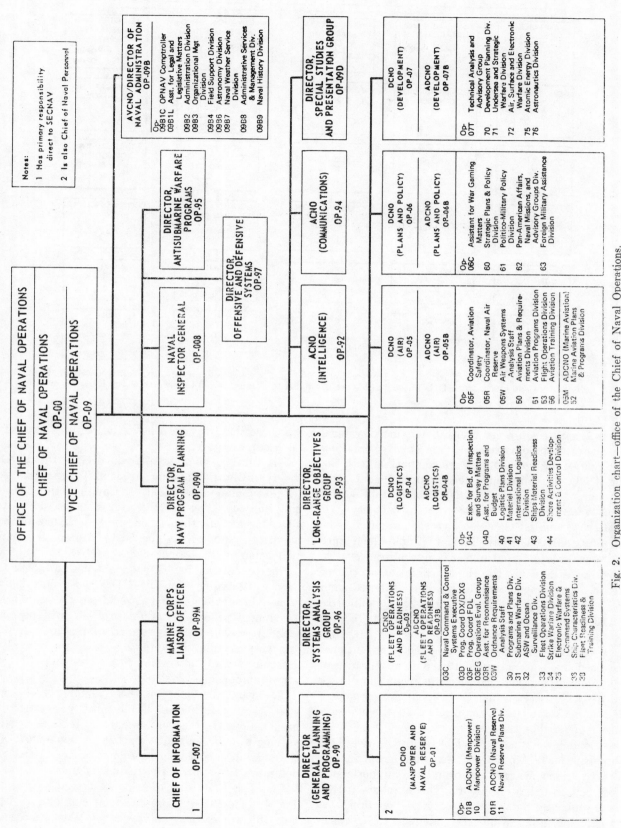

Fig. 2. Organization chart—office of the Chief of Naval Operations.

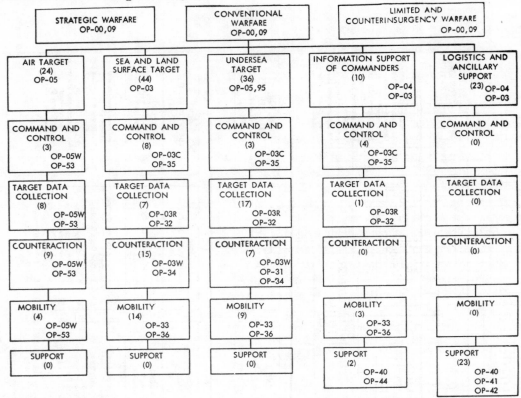

Fig. 3. The military worth W_i is obtained by various CNO offices weighting warfare areas, target/support areas, military function areas, and EDG. These weights are combined to obtain the military worth of the EDG for meeting Navy objectives.

CNO is organized in a structure that is more systems related than technology related (Fig.2). By breaking the EDG down into groups that are compatible with the existing CNO organization, each group of goals will "find a home" somewhere in CNO where suitable expertise is available to evaluate the grouping category.

Fig. 3 shows one EDG breakdown that might be employed. Since CNO is more likely to think along lines of the importance of types of warfare, the first level in the breakdown is to list the three general categories of warfare: Conventional, Strategic, and Limited and Counterinsurgency. Strategic Warfare is here defined as a major no-holds-barred conflict between the United States and another major power (or powers) in which strategic nuclear weapons are employed. Conventional warfare is defined as major conflict without the use of *strategic* nuclear weapons. However, it includes military action in which *tactical* nuclear weapons are employed. Limited and Counterinsurgency refers to the military actions not covered by the first two categories.

The second level breaks the EDG into the five Target/Support areas: Air Target, Sea and Land Surface Target, Undersea Target, Information Support, and Logistics and Ancillary Support. The numbers in parentheses indicate the number of EDG contained in each particular group while the indicated CNO offices are those that appear to have the required expertise for the group category.

The third level of breakdown divides the EDG into the five Military Function Areas of Target Data Collection, Command and Control, Counteraction, Mobility, and Support. The fourth level of breakdown is the EDG level. This, then, is one scheme that could be employed for subdividing the EDG into small groups for evaluation by the various offices of CNO.

The procedure that CNO might use to develop military worth values for the EDG must now be determined. It should be emphasized from the start that the assignment of weight values to EDG will be no easy task. Assessing the importance of mission capabilities is a very complex undertaking—one that depends on a great number of factors having a significant effect on the overall importance level.

To ensure that most of these factors will be considered, the weighting of EDG must be systematically broken down into several separate steps, each step involving a value judgment at that particular level. Then, the overall weight value assigned to each EDG will be determined by considering value judgments made at all levels. The EDG breakdown just described is shown in Fig. 4. This structure is somewhat similar to a decision tree [9], where the four levels are Warfare Area, Tar-

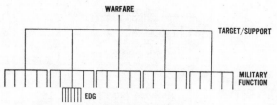

Fig. 4.　Weighting can be viewed as a tree-like structure starting with warfare areas and branching to the EDG.

get/Support Area, Military Function Area, and the EDG level. The evaluation method employed will involve making a value decision at each level. The final EDG military worth value will then be determined by a mathematical analysis of the value judgments made at all four levels.

One question that arises is: "How does a group of CNO experts come up with weight numbers such as these that are representative of the consensus of their opinions?" There are a number of ways this could be accomplished. A procedure similar to the so-called Delphi technique [7] might be employed. A complete description of an application of this technique to the problem at hand has been included in the report titled "Planning an Exploratory Development Program (Resource Allocation)" [8]. This technique utilizes certain aspects of the Delphi technique and also employs the Churchman–Ackoff [9] method to ensure consistency of evaluation.

The Delphi method employs the systematic repeated polling of the intuitive judgment of a group of well-informed experts. Briefly, it begins by providing each member of the group with a questionnaire to be filled out in secret. The experts respond to a number of questions using their own intuitive judgment on each subject. There is no discussion among the experts. The results of this poll are then tabulated and averaged. Each member of the group is then presented with the same questionnaire, only this time the results of the first polling are included so that each expert can see how his first response compared with the averaged response of the group. The experts then respond to the same questions a second time. This time their answers may be changed to reflect any change of thinking that has resulted from knowledge of the average group response. In this same manner, a number of iterations of this procedure are performed until a general convergence of opinions is obtained, and final results are averaged and recorded as typifying the group judgment.

Technology Utility Matrix

The discussion of the Military Worth Matrix reviewed the EDG from an operational point of view. To derive the second factor of the Index of Worth, the Technological Utility Matrix, the entire task from the technology aspect will be reviewed.

The primary consideration is the determination of

technology areas. In an exploratory development program, what are the specific areas to be supported? This question is of critical importance if the Navy laboratories are to have competence in technologies that will support future systems not yet defined.

Technology is relative to one's needs. The technology necessary to support one type of product will necessarily differ from the technology supporting another. For our discussion, the important features of the problem are the end product and the nature of exploratory development. The primary end product of the Naval Ordnance Laboratory (NOL), which is the author's area of concern, is Navy weapon systems.

The purpose of the exploratory development phase of the system-acquisition process is to provide the basic building blocks for future systems. To satisfy such a broad base, two types of technologies must be defined.

a) Product technologies—The technologies that serve as the integral functional parts of systems; for example, fuzing, propulsion, etc.

b) Multipurpose technologies—The technologies that serve several system functions and the processes necessary to produce systems; for example, organic materials, fabrication techniques, etc.

There are approaches to the overall problem that can simplify the definition of technological areas. One approach is to take an EDG (or a small group of EDG) and propose specific systems to meet the goal(s). Based upon the systems proposed, identify the technologies required and specify these technologies as the exploratory development technological areas. This is certainly a valid approach, and there is no doubt that the systems so produced would meet the goals. After all, this is the way military systems are normally defined for advanced development. However, this method of defining technologies for exploratory development is based upon specific systems. It is dependent upon specific interpretation of the goals and, hence, today's interpretation of needs. It does not necessarily allow any approach to meeting the goal or the changing of goals. An exploratory development program should be responsive to changing needs and changing technologies. The Navy exploratory development areas are the Navy's technological base from which many alternative technological approaches can grow to meet changing military needs.

A method recognizing that systems are the natural bridge between technology and the EDG, without the restrictions of specific systems, is the *functional analysis approach*. The method requires the identification and definition of the system functions necessary to satisfy the goals. The functional analysis approach is based upon the premise that hardware configurations can and do change, but basic functions remain and always need to be satisfied. By identifying the system functions, the basic technological needs supporting the function can be defined and supporting technological areas can be determined.

The functional approach requires, by design, very broad considerations. To place constraints on the problem and to ensure a method compatible with the real world, several restrictions were adopted. First, to the extent possible, any method developed would be based upon, and be compatible with, present documents and procedures of the Navy Exploratory Development Program. A method whereby a major new data-collection effort would be required was not desired. Next, the area of primary interest to the Navy Ordnance Laboratory (NOL) is weaponry. It is assumed that the Counteraction function is satisfied by the successful deployment of a weapon system; the weapon system here meaning the weapon suit, not the platform.

The general considerations necessary to define a weapon system for the Counteraction EDG are indicated in Fig. 5(a). The terminology is broad enough to include all types of weapons. Also shown is a translation of the considerations into a conventional vocabulary [Fig. 5(b)] that can be used to describe weapons existing today. The terminology used is similar to the subareas of the Exploratory Development Planning Structure (EDPS) for weaponry [10].

Using the system functional analysis approach, a portion of the EDG was analyzed. The EDG area selected for analysis was the Counteraction function. Present and proposed systems in the Undersea, Surface-to-Air, and Strategic areas were analyzed to determine their system functions and whether the functions could be described using the major subareas of the EDPS. The analysis indicated the three types of systems can be described by the same function, and functions can be the subareas of the EDPS. Also, the EDPS subareas are similar to the Broad Area Categories of the Navy Technological Forecast (NTF), part II [11]. The definition of the system functions in terms of the NTF breakdown permits the NTF to be interpreted as forecasts of system functions.

The technologies necessary to support the system functions of the three types of systems were derived. Fig. 6 illustrates EDPS subareas, typical supporting system functions, specific system types, functions support areas, and base technologies.

The levels of the weapon systems breakdown are the rudiments of an overall structure, which, of course, is not complete to view a laboratory's technology base. The structure is *not* an exploratory development program. It *does* allow the categorization of normal laboratory efforts to determine exploratory development areas. It *does* provide for an overall view of contiguous effort that relate applied research through exploratory development areas to Naval weapon systems.

The overall exercise of taking specific weapon areas and determining generic functions common to all weapon areas indicated the basic functions can be inter-

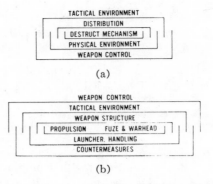

Fig. 5.   Weapons systems can be described by system functions, thus eliminating the necessity of relating technology to specific weapons systems. (a) General weapons considerations. (b) Conventional weapon relationships.

preted within the vocabulary of the EDPS. The process is one of reorienting definitions or comfortable phrases for the various areas necessary to support Navy systems. The merging of the EDPS/NTF and weapon system functions into a common reference area suggests the following.

1) The EDPS subareas/NTF broad areas can be used to describe gross system functions of weapon systems.

2) At least one NTF is available for each system function giving the transfer of scientific technologies to system functions.

3) The EDPS is the focal point between operational systems and Navy technology and as such must be sensitive to the natural evolution of systems and the technologies that support them.

These three significant conclusions indicate the thread of logic that *can* be used to indicate the role of each area of technology in meeting Navy needs. The utilization of the EDPS and NTF breakdown to relate scientific approaches to system functions permits the first step in relating the utility of technology to meet the EDG. This step is the transfer of various scientific and engineering technologies to system functions. Relating system functions to the EDG would complete the desired conversion of technology to EDG.

There is theoretically an infinite number of ways (specific systems) available to relate system functions to EDG. For this reason a "method" of conversion is really an "approach" that should 1) establish (or provide a basis for) the basic relationship between system functions and EDG, and 2) not constrain any technological approach to satisfy the EDG (by relating technologies to specific systems).

The consideration of the approaches to the technology/EDG conversion reveals there is a spectrum of possibilities available. At one end of the spectrum, one could use a suitable genius. Assuming one is intelligent enough, he can relate each field of technology to each EDG and thereby establish the desired relationship. Unfortunately, this type of people rarely exists. At the other end of the spectrum one could take each area of

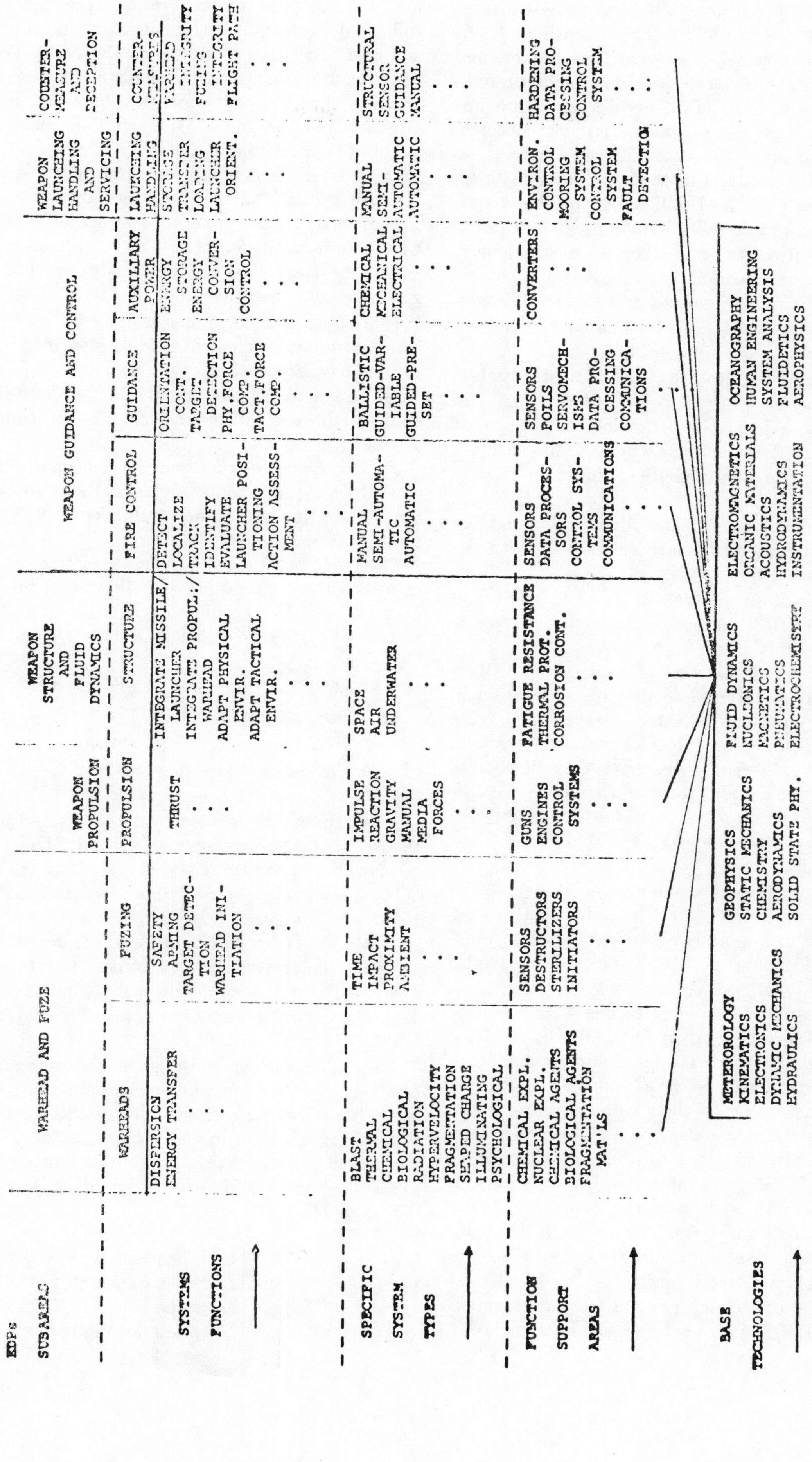

EDPs:

SUBAREAS

	WARHEAD AND FUZE		WEAPON PROPULSION	WEAPON STRUCTURE AND FLUID DYNAMICS	WEAPON GUIDANCE AND CONTROL			WEAPON LAUNCHING HANDLING AND SERVICING	COUNTERMEASURE AND DECEPTION
	WARHEADS	FUZING	PROPULSION	STRUCTURE	FIRE CONTROL	GUIDANCE	AUXILIARY POWER	LAUNCHING HANDLING	COUNTERMEASURES

SYSTEMS FUNCTIONS →

- WARHEADS: DISPERSION, ENERGY TRANSFER ...
- FUZING: SAFETY, ARMING, TARGET DETECTION, WARHEAD INITIATION ...
- PROPULSION: THRUST ...
- STRUCTURE: INTEGRATE MISSILE/LAUNCHER, INTEGRATE PROPUL./WARHEAD, ADAPT PHYSICAL ENVIR., ADAPT TACTICAL ENVIR. ...
- FIRE CONTROL: DETECT/LOCALIZE, TRACK IDENTIFY, EVALUATE, LAUNCHER POSITIONING, ACTION ASSESSMENT ...
- GUIDANCE: ORIENTATION CONT., TARGET DETECTION, PHY.FORCE COMP., TACT.FORCE COMP. ...
- AUXILIARY POWER: ENERGY STORAGE, ENERGY CONVERSION CONTROL ...
- WEAPON LAUNCHING: STORAGE TRANSFER, LOADING, LAUNCHER ORIENT. ...
- COUNTERMEASURE: VARIED, FUZING INTEGRITY, FUZING INTEGRITY, FLIGHT PATH ...

SPECIFIC SYSTEM TYPES →

- WARHEADS: BLAST, THERMAL, CHEMICAL, BIOLOGICAL, RADIATION, HYPERVELOCITY, FRAGMENTATION, SHAPED CHARGE, ILLUMINATING, PSYCHOLOGICAL ...
- FUZING: TIME, IMPACT, PROXIMITY, AMBIENT ...
- PROPULSION: IMPULSE, REACTION, GRAVITY, MANUAL, MEDIA FORCES ...
- STRUCTURE: SPACE, AIR, UNDERWATER ...
- FIRE CONTROL: MANUAL, SEMI-AUTOMATIC, AUTOMATIC
- GUIDANCE: BALLISTIC, GUIDED-VARIABLE, GUIDED-PRESET ...
- AUXILIARY POWER: CHEMICAL, MECHANICAL, ELECTRICAL ...
- WEAPON LAUNCHING: MANUAL, SEMI-AUTOMATIC, AUTOMATIC
- COUNTERMEASURE: STRUCTURAL, SENSOR, GUIDANCE, MANUAL ...

FUNCTION SUPPORT AREAS →

- WARHEADS: CHEMICAL EXPL., NUCLEAR EXPL., CHEMICAL AGENTS, BIOLOGICAL AGENTS, FRAGMENTATION MAT'LS ...
- FUZING: SENSORS, DESTRUCTORS, STERILIZERS, INITIATORS ...
- PROPULSION: GUNS, ENGINES, CONTROL SYSTEMS ...
- STRUCTURE: FATIGUE RESISTANCE, THERMAL PROT., CORROSION CONT. ...
- FIRE CONTROL: SENSORS, DATA PROCESSORS, CONTROL SYSTEMS, COMMUNICATIONS ...
- GUIDANCE: SENSORS, FOILS, SERVOMECHANISES, DATA PROCESSING, COMMUNICATIONS ...
- AUXILIARY POWER: CONVERTERS ...
- WEAPON LAUNCHING: ENVIRON. CONTROL, MOORING SYSTEM, CONTROL SYSTEM, FAULT DETECTION ...
- COUNTERMEASURE: HARDENING, DATA PROCESSING, CONTROL SYSTEM ...

BASE TECHNOLOGIES →

METEOROLOGY	GEOPHYSICS	FLUID DYNAMICS	ELECTROMAGNETICS	OCEANOGRAPHY
KINEMATICS	STATIC MECHANICS	NUCLEONICS	ORGANIC MATERIALS	HUMAN ENGINEERING
ELECTRONICS	CHEMISTRY	MAGNETICS	ACOUSTICS	SYSTEM ANALYSIS
DYNAMIC MECHANICS	AERODYNAMICS	PNEUMATICS	HYDRODYNAMICS	FLUIDETICS
HYDRAULICS	SOLID STATE PHY.	ELECTROCHEMISTRY	INSTRUMENTATION	AEROPHYSICS

Fig. 6. The exploratory development planning structure (EDPS) provides the basis for relating technology to system functions.

technology and prepare a normative technological forecast [12] for each specific EDG. This is entirely feasible, but would be extremely costly in time, talent, and funds. In reviewing the more probable techniques to relate technologies to the EDG, certain facts are apparent. First, analysis using quantitative methods can at best be only an approximation. Second, there is no specific quantitative analysis method that applies to all cases. Any method developed will be essentially a procedural framework for exercising human judgments.

Any approach used to gain the desired judgment must recognize the real world. It should reflect a natural process to the individuals involved and not require consideration outside their areas of experience. One approach is as follows.

1) Classify the EDG into areas that lend themselves to analysis by experts.

2) Determine the levels of technological areas that coincide with the application areas where experts exist.

3) Identify experts (or activities) for each EDG/technology area.

4) Provide information for and direct the judgment of experts, so that the results are compatible with desired resource allocation methods.

5) Establish results in a format easily digestible into the resource allocation method and for broad assessments of validity.

The portion of the EDG of major concern to NOL is the Counteraction function. The previous discussion of technology determination indicated that, in satisfying the Counteraction function, the NTF weapon technologies can be used to describe the basic functions of a weapon system. To apply these technologies to the EDG, there are several ways in which the counteraction functions can be divided for analysis by the technological experts.

To identify and confine areas for judgment, the EDG are divided into platform/target duels for analysis by experts. This relationship allows the Counteraction function to be divided into a 3-by-3 array of platform versus target. The matrix gives nine selected categories. Each box in the matrix is identified as Undersea-to-Undersea, Air-to-Surface, and so forth. For each of the nine matrix categories there are parameters common to the EDG. By arranging the EDG of each platform/target category according to their common parameters, the relative effect of the variation of each parameter can be compared to present state of the art of systems. Categorization of Navy weapons applications in this manner is compatible with present laboratory tasks. Personnel are available who are familiar with the problems associated with the applications area.

Using the Platform/Target matrix as the EDG classification, the level of technology used to relate technology to EDG is the Broad Area Forecasts of the NTF

[4]. The selection of these areas recognizes the availability of experts plus the concentration and organization of information available in the NTF. For the specific resource allocation methods used here, the NTF provides the necessary interlock between the Index of Advance and the Index of Worth—the pacing parameter(s) of the technology areas.

Experts on technology (or groups of experts) with experience in the platform-target category are selected. The experts are required to associate the effect of the EDG requirements on their fields of technology.

The evaluation is to be conducted under certain guidance constraints.

1) Judgment is to be based upon the pacing parameter(s) of the technological field as identified in the Navy Technology Forecast.

2) The area of the projection of the technological state of the art to be considered is the time frame of the EDG.

3) The judgment of a specific field of technology relative to other necessary technologies is to be made on the assumption that other technologies will not exceed their projected state of the art.

4) Under the preceding three constraints, the expert expresses the required state of the art of his technology area for each EDG as being in one of the following four states: [*Note:* State of Art (SOA)]

a) SOA Required > SOA Predicted

b) SOA Required $\cong$ SOA Predicted

c) SOA Required < SOA Predicted

d) Technology Area does not apply.

A matrix can be formed by the expressed judgment of the expert's relating technologies and EDG. The matrix relationship is the relevance of the effort required in the field of technology to meet the EDG. It is defined as the Relevance Matrix R. In order to integrate this information into the Index of Worth (and therefore the allocation method) the matrix must be converted into a numerical array, with the array standardized to unity for each EDG. The standardized numerical array is the Technology Utility Matrix U.

To convert the expert judgment to a numerical matrix, any set of SOA-to-number equivalents can be used, or the experts can express their judgment numerically as a probability of being in the various states. For example, let each element of R, r_{ij}, have the following relationship [*Note:* State of Art Required (SOAR), State of Art Predicted (SOAP)]

$$r_{ij} = \begin{cases} 4, & \text{when SOAR} > \text{SOAP} \\ 2, & \text{when SOAR} \cong \text{SOAP} \\ 1, & \text{when SOAR} < \text{SOAP} \\ 0, & \text{when not related.} \end{cases}$$

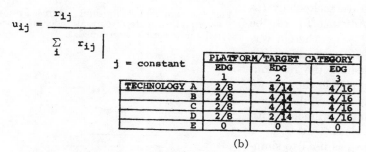

	PLATFORM/TARGET CATEGORY		
	EDG 1	EDG 2	EDG 3
TECHNOLOGY A	2	4	4
B	2	4	4
C	2	4	4
D	2	2	4
E	0	0	0

4, SOAR > SOAP
2, SOAR ≈ SOAP
1, SOAR < SOAP
0, NOT RELATED

(a)

$$u_{ij} = \frac{r_{ij}}{\sum\limits_{i} r_{ij}\Big|}$$

j = constant

	PLATFORM/TARGET CATEGORY		
	EDG 1	EDG 2	EDG 3
TECHNOLOGY A	2/8	4/14	4/16
B	2/8	4/14	4/16
C	2/8	4/14	4/16
D	2/8	2/14	4/16
E	0	0	0

(b)

Fig. 7. Technologies can be related to EDG by technical personnel developing a relevance matrix. The relevance matrix (a) is normalized (standardized) to obtain the technology utility matrix (b).

Utilization of these numerical values in defining R gives the Relevance Matrix shown in Fig. 7(a). The conversion of this matrix into the Utility Matrix requires that the array be standarized for *each* EDG. The EDG standardization is necessary because of the manner in which the Index of Worth is defined in the resource allocation method. The reduction of R to obtain U is gained by deriving each element of U_{ij}, by

$$U_{ij} = \frac{r_{ij}}{\sum\limits_{i} r_{ij}\,|\,j} = \text{constant.}$$

The Utility Matrix obtained by this conversion is shown in Fig. 7(b).

There is a variation available in determining the Utility and Relevance Matrices. It is conceivable that experts may have trouble associating technological areas with sets of EDG. If this is the case, the information can be presented in a more detailed form, perhaps one that is technically easier to relate.

For each of the nine matrix categories there are operational parameters common to the EDG. By arranging the EDG of each platform/target category according to their common operational parameters, the range of the variation of each EDG operational parameter can be compared to the technology state-of-the-art pacing parameters. This allows a parameter relative assessment of the demands of each EDG. A matrix can then be derived between the technological areas and operational parameters. This approach will allow technical experts to visualize different EDG in an orientation that may be more comfortable in expressing judgments.

The Index of Worth should describe the operational importance of accelerating the rate at which a technology is advancing. The relevance numbers that have been defined provide just this kind of information. A low weight is given to technologies that are expected to be more advanced than necessary if current efforts continue throughout the time period. Similarly, a high weight is given to those technologies that will have to be advanced at a faster rate if they are to meet needs.

The relevance numbers relate operational parameters to technologies. There are at least three ways of combining these numbers to relate technologies to EDG.

1) Identify the parameter that is most deficient and use its relevance. This has been called the "worst-case" approach.

2) Average the parameter relevances.

3) Rank the operational parameters according to their military importance and then take a weighted average of the parameter relevances.

The first approach is aggressive. It will give a higher probability of solving the major problems than the second approach; but if the predictions are overly optimistic, some technologies that contribute to many aspects of system performance may not receive enough effort. On the other hand, the second approach makes sure that those areas that apply to many different aspects of the systems receive high weights. The drawback of this method is the possibility that a few deficiencies that seriously affect specific aspects of system performance may remain at the end of the time period.

To get a measure of the utility of a technology to the Navy's total mission, the technological utility to each EDG is weighted by the relative military worth of that EDG. Cross support is considered by summing these individual utilities. These sums are called the Index of Worth of the technology.

The Index of Worth tells whether the current effort in the technology will give a reasonable probability of meeting the needs that the technology has to fulfill.

Index of Advance Forecast

The Index of Advance for the ith technology is determined from the Navy Technological Forecast. Using the pacing technological parameter of the ith technology (as indicated in the NTF), an Index of Advance I_{A_i} can be defined. The particular definition of I_{A_i} used herein was selected to be compatible with the resource allocation method. I_{A_i} is determined by establishing the relationship between the advance that can be made in the technological parameter at a given funding level and the advance that could be made in the same parameter with unlimited funding in the same time period.

An exponential function decaying to 1 is used to simulate the variation of I_{A_i} with funding. It is likely that the additional returns derived from putting more and more money into research in a particular area during a fixed time period will decrease (Fig. 8). An exponential function shows diminishing returns, is mathematically convenient, and can be determined by a single point. An estimate of the fraction of the maximum attainable advance that can be achieved with current funding would normally be used for this reference point. The equation used to describe the diminishing returns is as follows:

$$I_{A_i}(X_i) = (1 - e^{-X_i/D_i}).$$

where X_i is the funding level and the parameter D_i is the funding that achieves 63 percent of the advance in the technology. Without going into the algebra, it should be apparent that an estimate of the Index of Advance at any funding level will determine the constant D_i. Substituting values for $I_{A_i}^0$ and X_i^0 leaves D_i the only variable in the equation. In some cases, current funding will be used for this purpose.

Some possible variations on the simple model and ways of handling them are presented on Fig. 9. In the first case, there is a cost associated with establishing a program in this area. Curve 1 shows the kind of returns that might result. Curve 2 is the kind of exponential that can model the situation.

In the second case, it is necessary to provide some minimum support to research in the area. For certain reasons, it is not feasible to do work in the area unless at least this much money is provided. A simple constraint $X_i > X_i'$ is sufficient to make the solution possible.

Resource Allocation Model

The Index of Advance expresses quantitatively the prediction of the fraction of possible advance that can be obtained at various budget levels. It relates rate of advance to funding. Therefore, weighting the Indexes of Advance by the Indexes of Worth, and summing creates a meaningful measure of total value.

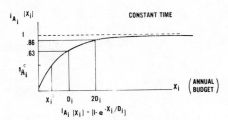

Fig. 8. Simulated diminishing returns. From the current funding level and estimate of current Index of Advance I_A the exponential curve can be determined.

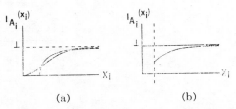

Fig. 9. Two special cases of the Index of Advance curve are (a) curve 1, requiring a price of admission, and (b) curve 2 where a minimum support level is determined for each technology. Both cases are considered in the model.

The allocation model weights Index of Advance curves for each technology with the relative worth of that technology I_{W_i}. Inasmuch as both I_{A_i} and I_{W_i} are standardized to the range between 0 and 1, the results for the various technologies are numerically comparable. A payoff function is defined as the sum of these terms:

$$P = \sum I_{W_i}(1 - e^{-X_i/D_i}) \quad \text{or} \quad P = \sum (I_{W_i})(I_{A_i}).$$

This payoff is maximized, subject to a budget constraint $\sum X_i = C$. This constraint simply indicates that total funds available are fixed.

Congress allocates money on an annual basis. Therefore, the funding levels X_i referred to are annual budgets. The maximization of the payoff function P gives an indication of the best way to allocate funds next year to meet the long-range requirements expressed in the EDG. These considerations suggest that funding decisions consider the military and technical judgments within the context of an idealized model. In practice, there is considerable cost involved in varying funding widely from one year to the next. Therefore, changes should be made in the direction suggested but probably not to the extent suggested by the model. When following budgets are being developed, results can be assessed and further changes made based on the additional information that has been gained in the previous year.

The variables are the annual budgets to the *technologies*. One might ask why annual budgets enter a calculation that has seemingly been based on the total time period between the present, and the time the EDG refer to. The point is that budgets are reviewed annually. A goal twenty years in the future is reached by twenty sequential appropriations. Each budget must be developed

TECHNOLOGIES \ EDG WEIGHTINGS	1/2	3/8	1/8
Weapons Structures and Fluid Dynamics	2,2,0,2,0	4,2,0,1,0	1,4,0,4,0
Propulsion	2,2,0,2,0	4,2,0,2,0	1,4,0,4,0
Guidance and Control	2,2,2,2,2	4,2,4,2,2	1,4,4,2,4
Warhead and Fuze	2,2,4,0,0	2,1,1,0,0	1,4,0,0,0
Launching, Servicing, and Handling	0,0,0,0,1	0,0,0,0,2	0,0,0,0,1

Fig. 10. Relevance of technologies to EDG. Relevance numbers: 0—the technology is not related to the parameter; 1—the forecast predicts the parameter should easily be surpassed; 2—the forecast provides that the parameter could just be met with the current effort; 4—the forecast predicts the parameter can not be met with current efforts.

so that as much progress as possible, within resource limitations, is made during that year. It is recognized that relevance numbers will change due to the annual allocation of resources. This will be taken into consideration in exercising the model for the next annual allocation.

The mathematical problem of the model has been solved using the method of Lagrange multipliers. The solution is programmed in FORTRAN for a time-shared computer system, so that different parameters can be tried and real-time solutions attained.

Fig. 10 shows relevance numbers[1] of five technologies for which technology Index of Advance curves were derived for a group of EDG. The values of W_j describing the relative rankings of the EDG, are presented at the top of the columns.

Allocations are obtained by substituting these value judgments and the Index of Advance curves that were derived from the computer model. Fig. 11 shows the fractions of budgets ranging between 30 percent and 200 percent of the current budget, which are distributed to each of the five technologies. The averaged parameter relevances are used. Minimum funding levels were set to 0 so that a true variation could be obtained.

This resource allocation model is capable of relating the technologies defined by the "Broad-Area" section of the NTF to the Navy missions defined quantitatively in the EDG. Budgets to the functional technologies are determined through an evaluation of military needs. The key translation is the specification of system functions

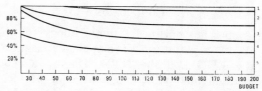

Fig. 11. Allocations of resources to Navy technologies as a function of budget level are obtained from model. This is only a guide to suggest direction of change. One must remember that both the Index of Worth and the Index of Advance are based on human judgment. "Computer magic" does not change this fact. 1—launching, servicing, and handling; 2—weapons structure and fluid dynamics; 3—warhead and fuze; 4—propulsion; 5—guidance and control. The percentages represent a fraction of budget optimally allocated to indicated technology.

that are sufficient to meet the operation requirements. Given such a translation, the functional parameters in the NTF can be compared to the operational parameters and the necessary judgments obtained. Below this level, the model presented is not directly applicable. The basic structure necessary for intelligent planning has, however, been laid.

A technical manager given a block of funds to study a technology area, such as fuzing for example, can find out which EDG require advances in his system function. He will therefore be able to tell whether the problem is primarily one of size, of detection range, of depth, of sensitivity to countermeasures, or whatever it may be. This knowledge can direct his work. He can also look at the system analysts' opinions about the range of parameter values that must be obtained. This knowledge will tell him whether evolutionary development of the current state of the art or major innovation is necessary. For example, if the necessary advances are within the predicted state of the art, then he should probably

[1] Both the relevance numbers and the Index of Advance curves are hypothetical. Numbers were selected for use as examples that seem reasonable, but have no basis in fact.

spend most of his budget ensuring that those advances are obtained and a smaller fraction developing new concepts. On the other hand, if evolutionary development would not be sufficient, then a larger part of his staff should be developing new approaches and testing them out. The point is that it should be up to the technical expert to determine what constitutes a feasible attack on the stated objectives in the budget he has been given.

One must always keep in mind that Exploratory Development is a probabilistic process. As programs develop, additional information will be learned that may make the results drastically different from the predictions. Therefore, budgets probably should not vary as much from year to year as the model output may suggest. With budgets being allocated yearly, the objective should be to make adjustments in the direction suggested by the model without creating large, wasteful fluctuations. The decision maker must optimize the expected value of the work to be done in the year, considering military priorities, the technical situation, and the costs involved in diverting effort from one program to another.

Conclusions

This paper has outlined a methodology for the planning of an exploratory development program based upon the EDG and the NTF. The main thought of the allocation method is the dual view of technology, from both military utilization and possible technological advance. An Index of Worth was described that indicates the military utility of the technology area. An Index of Advance was defined that indicates the possible control of technological advance by resource allocation. The two indices were coupled into a decision model to assist in determining resource allocation alternatives. Fundamental to the entire method is the information content and format of the EDG and the Broad Area forecasts of the NTF. The relationship between the EDG and NTF is based upon certain major necessary characteristics of these documents.

The Exploratory Development Goals are as follows.

1) The goals are not oriented toward a specific system or type of system.

2) The operational parameters of each EDG specify completely all critical operational parameters necessary to meet the goal.

3) The values of the operational parameters represent those values beyond which an operational deficiency will exist.

The Navy Technological Forecast utilization was based upon the following features of the NTF.

1) The broad-area forecasts are defined so that the technology areas can be interpreted as system functions.

2) Pacing technology parameters are identified that serve to bridge between scientific discipline parameters and operational parameters.

3) The pacing parameter(s) is projected in time as a function of funding levels.

4) The growth saturation asymptote of the pacing parameter is identified. Any utilization of the resource allocation method described in this discussion must keep these features of the EDG and NTF in mind.

The purpose of this study was to determine the utility of the EDG and the NTF for resource allocation. A method has been outlined to use the EDG in conjunction with the NTF to plan an exploratory development program. The method described in this paper has the following features.

1) EDG critical to military objectives are identified.

2) Technologies critical to meeting the EDG are identified.

3) EDG for which current forecasts cannot be met within a specific time period are identified.

4) The EDG/Technology relationship is independent of specific system designs or types of systems.

5) Each technological area's worth is related both to its utility in meeting a goal and the importance of that goal.

6) The capacity of each technology area to support many EDG has been determined.

7) The allocation model suggests funding levels based upon advancing the most important technologies at a faster rate than other technologies.

8) The allocation model discriminates against technologies that have reached diminishing returns.

The resource allocation method presented is, by design, useful at the macroscopic and microscopic levels. With a slight reorientation of thinking about the Worth and Advance considerations coupled into the allocation model, the method is applicable at the Department, CNM, System Command, and laboratory levels. A significant factor concerning this approach is that each organizational level can apply the method independently of the others.

The resource allocation system presented conserves and strengthens the spirit of exploratory development—to provide the building blocks for improved and new systems without limiting technological approaches and tying technology to preconceived systems. Exploratory Development, and its planning, is the backbone of the Navy in-house technical capability. Without this technical capability, new systems could either fail or look like old systems. Tying requirements and technology together in a strong in-house exploratory development program provides the Navy with the capabilities and responsiveness necessary to meet its future destiny.

Acknowledgment

The authors wish to acknowledge the contributions of Dr. T. E. Phipps and W. C. Carlson to the resource allocation model and for their general critique of the method.

References

[1] Secretary of Defense, Hon. R. S. McNamara, Testimony to Congress, FY 1969 Budget.
[2] Department of the Navy, RDT&E Management Guide NAVSO P-2457 (Rev 7-67).
[3] CND letter MAT:031:RJM Ser. 002967, November 3, 1967 w/e NOFORN Publ. "Exploratory development goals."
[4] NAVMAT letter 031C:MJC, "Navy technological forecast," October 1, 1968 promulgation.
[5] NAVMAT instr. 3910.10, "Implementation procedures for the Navy technological forecast program," August 29, 1967.
[6] PATTERN: "Long range corporate planning," AM 97, Department of Military and Space Sciences, Honeywell, Inc., September 1967.
[7] N. Dalkey and O. Helmer, "An experimental application of the Delphi method to the use of experts," *Management Sci.*, September 1963.
[8] NOLTR 68-164, "Planning an exploratory development program," (Resource Allocation), U. S. Naval Ordnance Laboratory, November 1, 1968 .
[9] C. W. Churchman and R. L. Ackoff, "An approximate measure of value," *J. Opt. Res. Soc. Am.*, vol. 2, pp. 172–187, 1953.
[10] NAVMAT instr. 3910.12, "Exploratory development program planning structure," January 5, 1968.
[11] NOLTR 67-166, "An organization and method of accomplishing advanced planning," U. S. Naval Ordnance Laboratory, November 1, 1967.
[12] M. J. Cetron and T. I. Monahan, "An evaluation and appraisal of various approaches to technological forecast," in *Technological Forecasting for Industry and Government*. Englewood Cliffs, N. J.: Prentice-Hall, 1968.

Technological Forecasting—Practical Problems and Pitfalls

MARVIN J. CETRON AND DONALD N. DICK, MEMBER, IEEE

Abstract—Technological forecasting is becoming a widespread activity in business and the military. The actual accomplishment of the forecasting task is increasing in methodological sophistication. This article presents many practical problems and pitfalls encountered in planning and preparing technological forecasts. The authors examine the factors to be considered in the initial stages of implementing forecasts, the validity of previous forecasts, summarize recent advances, point out new hazards, evaluate the forecasting technique, and include some realistic suggestions for improved technological forecasts.

WHEN a corporation decides to utilize a technological forecast as an input to planning decisions, the administrators are faced with some very fundamental questions. What do we ask for? How is it accomplished? Who should be assigned to the task? How can we ensure a useful product? Or as one questioning manager put it, "How much time will it take from productive work?"

A primary consideration that affects all of these questions is the forecast content. The prescription for the contents can determine its overall utility. During 1968 the U.S. Navy prepared and published its first technological forecast. Other military services and several corporations had prepared forecasts prior to this and the Navy had profited from these efforts. The Navy's product covered three different types of forecasts, comprising over six hundred individual forecasts prepared by twenty-three separate R&D activities. The format used by the Navy required a complete assessment of each field of technology as well as a forecast of the state of the art. In retrospect, this work did present some experiences that can contribute to the learning process of management and the technical communities, and it can be used as a vehicle for discussion of the practical problems and pitfalls that can develop in the preparation of technological forecasts.

I. The Forecast—Something for Everyone?

To ensure that a technology forecast is useful to technical, operational, and management personnel, the Navy required that each forecast be . . . *"the prediction, with a stated level of confidence, of the anticipated occurrence of a technological achievement, within a given time frame with a specified level of support"*[1], . . . Supporting information was required for all forecasts. Each forecast comprised five categories. The categories included all aspects of the technology under examination from the history of its application to the implications of the forecast to the areas of application. The following paragraphs discuss the five major categories and their desired contents from corporate and military viewpoints.

Manuscript received July 1969; revised August 1969. This paper was published originally in *European Business*, Paris, France, April 1969

M. J. Cetron is with the Headquarters Naval Material Command, Exploratory Development Division, Washington, D. C.

D. N. Dick is with the Advanced Planning and Analysis Staff, U. S. Naval Ordnance Laboratory, White Oak, Silver Spring, Md.

[1] See References section.

A. Background

This section should identify the organizational goals and other objectives to which the fields of technology being forecast can contribute. It should discuss the present fields of application of the technology in areas of interest to the organization. A description of the significant factors influencing past developments, and those factors which would tend to emphasize or deemphasize further developments should be included.

For the Navy forecast, the fields of technology were related to military operational objectives. This work was assisted by the existence of Navy quantitative development goals and consisted of identifying each technological area forecast with one or more of the goals.

B. Present Status

Here, the field of technology's current state of the art should be quantitatively described. The inherent advantages or disadvantages (safety, stability, etc.) must be listed, and a description of existing or potentially troublesome technological barriers or gaps should be included. Also, this section should describe the efforts made by competitors to utilize the technology and how these efforts have affected their share of the market. One example of technology utilization with a marketable difference is the variety of approaches to the construction of television sets. The hand-wired and printed-circuit technologies are each advertised as having greater advantages than the other.

The military planner must consider the technological advantages, disadvantages, and susceptibility to counter actions by potential aggressors. This involves quantitative statements of current status of a nation compared with its potential adversaries, and identification of gaps where technological advances over present barriers would present clear advantages.

C. Forecasts

The forecast consists of a projection of the state of the art as a function of time and cost with an indicated level of confidence. Only relevant and accurately identified pacing technological parameters should be projected. These parameters could be strength, weight, specific impulse, shaft horsepower per unit volume, or any other parameter that typifies the advance of the technology areas. The discussion of the pacing parameter should be quantitative and directed to the effects of changes in complexity, cost, performance, and any other factors that may alleviate or cause limitations. Charts and graphs should be used to clarify projections and enhance communication. Adequate supporting data are an essential requirement for preparation of a valid forecast.

An example of a technological pacing parameter is illustrated in Fig. 1. The actual and anticipated gains in certain characteristics of air-cushion vehicles are shown. Air-cushion-vehicle (ACV) performance, in terms of a factor of merit, is projected for a vehicle with a bare bottom and with a skirt and trunk system. Significant improvements in ACV performance have resulted from the development of skirts and flexible jet extensions. Aerodynamic problems associated with these developments have been largely resolved, but finding suitable materials for the air-cushion devices is a continuing problem.

D. Product Implications

This section should describe the effect on the corporation of the technological advances projected in the forecast. The corporate or product goals discussed in the Section I-A should be quantitatively related to the forecast. Factors affecting manpower requirements, training, effectiveness, or operating efficiency should be described. Graphic techniques should be used where applicable. The implications of new products, market share, profits, and economics of scale should be discussed quantitatively.

In military forecasts, this section would discuss the implications to operating forces. The operating environment would be discussed in terms of threat-accommodation parameters such as target range, target accuracy, operating speed, and operating depth. For instance, if Fig. 1 (a projection of the technology of air-cushion vehicles) was expressed in operational terms, the illustration could represent captured air-bubble aircraft carriers with an operational parameter of speed indicated in knots. Of course, this is a purely hypothetical example selected to show how a technology could be exploited and defined in terms that are meaningful to the user—in this case, the Navy.

E. References and Associated Activities

The publications from which authoritative direction has been elicited should be cited. List the technical documents in the field that add credibility (hence utility) to the forecast. The corporate divisions and competitors who have contributed or have interest in this technological area are to be included. Also, government activities, universities, consultants, and their point of contact should be listed. The Navy forecast requires its contributors to identify all laboratory reports. The references also include other applicable references with the names of the contributory activities.

The factual content of the forecasts is quite extensive. For each technological field, a history of its application, projections of the state of the art, relative corporate goals, marketing information, possible new applications, and present shortcomings are essential parts of the package. It is this breadth of the technological assessment that allows the forecast to be beneficial to a

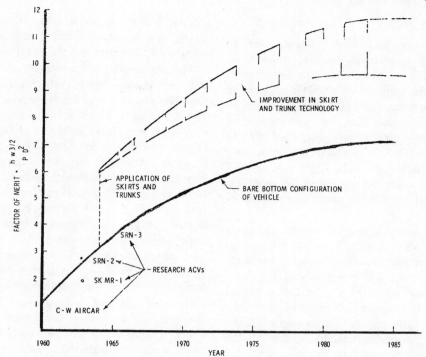

Fig. 1. Air-cushion vehicle performance. Typical trend correlation/extrapolation forecast curve: h = mean height above surface (feet); w = gross vehicle weight (pounds); P = total installed horsepower; D = effective diameter (feet) at skirt or bottom surface of vehicle [5].

diverse audience. The manager, technical expert, systems analyst, and marketing expert can each use the forecast as an aid in planning. In contrast, if the content of the forecast was just a state-of-the-art projection of a technological area without background, present status, and operational implications, its usefulness would probably be limited to the technical community.

In recognizing a technological forecast designed for wide utilization that will require the variety of information indicated in the five categories, we gain an appreciation of the nature and extent of the effort involved. The actual mechanics of conducting such a task must be directed by the talents and training of the specific individuals involved. No attempt to prescribe an all-encompassing step-by-step procedure to avoid pitfalls will (or can) be made, but a discussion of what appears to be the inherent problems of such an undertaking, and an indication of some solutions that were found to be applicable in preparing the Navy forecast are presented here.

The broad-area-forecast concepts of "something for everyone" may best be summarized by an analogy as illustrated in Fig. 2. One input results in two distinct outputs, whose applications are vastly different. The first, dairy products, could be considered as the primary output. The second, fertilizer, is a by-product of the operation. The end item paying for the input is the dairy products industry; however, the fertilizer applica-

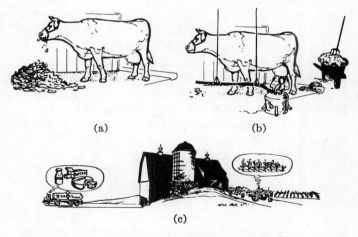

Fig. 2. (a) Input. (b) Output. (c) Application.

tion will assist in growing more crops, which in turn serves to increase the input. For military purposes, the primary reason to pursue technology is to provide weapons systems for national defense. The secondary output is an increased bank of technological knowledge aiding in further systems development. The cycle may be perceived from vastly different viewpoints, indicating the necessity for any forecasting effort to have a communications common denominator. The establishment of such a reference plane is accomplished through the art of structuring.

II. STRUCTURING—THE KEY TO UNDERSTANDING

Perhaps the most important factor to consider in directing or preparing a forecast is the problem of structuring. In technological forecasting, the aspects of structuring permeate all levels of effort. It begins when management states the areas in which forecasts are to be prepared. (Here we assume that the implementation of a technological forecasting program would attempt to assess a broad corporate technological base.) The manner in which the various fields of technology are defined will affect the type of forecasts prepared, its content, and the overall effect of policy and goals of the corporation.

Structuring, as used here, is the art of putting one's mind and communications in order. It is the attempt to describe the mutually exclusive and collectively exhaustive sets that define the breadth and depth of the forecasting effort. Stated another way, a good technological forecast structure will be a good definition of the technological areas to be forecast. As an example of the nature of structuring, consider the hierarchy of the various factors that can be used to describe food for human consumption. A conventional arrangement may begin with the categories of fruit, vegetable, meat, etc. These major categories are then broken into their parts, and these parts are further broken into their parts. Fruit could be divided into apples, oranges, bananas, etc. Apples, in turn can be structured into Red Delicious, Winesap, Jonathan, etc. The structure, to have high utility, must be as complete as possible. In general, the first few items fall into place quite easily, then as completeness is approached the task is much more demanding as the inevitable rearrangements occur and the search for all-encompassing terminology is conducted.

When attempting to define a structure to accommodate an area to be forecast, it is convenient to view the corporate product (or groups of products) as a system or systems. This system view simply means the product is viewed as being composed of separable items that are fully integrated in their contribution to the product. The task is to take each product, separate it (mentally of course) into its components, look for commonality across product components, and request a forecast for each component. As an example, an automobile can be viewed as being composed of a transmission, engine, body, etc. Any structuring problem in the example appears to be one of fineness of division, which might be considered trivial in such a well-defined product. This would be true if the problem in hand was so well constrained.

Here, the main object is to prepare a forecast. This implies that concern is directed toward the future. The dependence upon present-day configurations of products becomes uncertain, and complexity is added to the forecasting task as we move our forecasting further into the future.

The Navy forecast covered operating capabilities twenty years ahead. During such a lengthy period supporting technologies can change drastically.

The problem of future uncertainty is not insurmountable but it does complicate forecasting. It will require that the corporate product be viewed as a system in a broader sense than just its physical components. It should be visualized in terms of the functions necessary to accomplish the product objectives while the product is in operation in its environment. The fundamental premise of the functional approach is: "components may come and go, but basic functions remain and need to be satisfied." This look at system functions in an operational environment is sometimes referred to as the systems approach. In prior times it was probably regarded as part of competence. As an example of the difference between the views one can take, let us return to the automobile. The individual who views the auto as an integration of components such as the engine, steering, brakes, etc. is indeed thinking "systems." There are many variations available within this framework to accomplish the desired product performance. However, the individual who views the auto as one part of a transportation system, composed of propulsion, guidance, and control, etc. is thinking functionally. Long-range forecasting requires functional thinking.

The distinction between components and functions is a relative matter. Words such as function, component, and system are multilevel. One man's system is another man's subsystem or one man's function is another's system. Functions, as used here for technological forecasting, are the product requirements independent of technological approach. (For example, a function could be defined as a market share increase and attainment need not be tied to any particular product or products. As a military illustration one could define a neutralization function to be achieved without specifying the particular weapons required.) Thinking functionally for the structuring of the major portion of the forecast areas will not solve all problems. It will help avoid many dead ends and much wheel spinning by taking that first big step.

One should be aware of some side effects of this process. Structuring of the type discussed here can set the framework for creative contributions to end products. It will not guarantee creativity; however, it will provide a field for its development. A good functional structure will point out gaps or holes and will tend to ensure completeness of product coverage. Further, everyone will be looking at the corporate product from a common but individually different view. This in itself may be worth the forecasting effort. Another effect will be a definite need to state explicitly and quantitatively the corporate operational objectives. A valid structure cannot be obtained without a clear understanding of the objectives. Product functional structuring may also force consideration of the company's future direction. As an example, if a group is required to think functionally about house refrigerators and house air-conditioners, it will not be too long until the consideration of house refrigeration as a corporate product could arise. It is not a small effort to determine whether the company should be going in this direction in the future. Creativity and explicit product (or corporate) goals seem to be the type of activity that any corporation would encourage. The fact is, many establishments do not have a formalized procedure to handle such demands. The result can be overall frustration for both the manager and the technical innovators.

III. A Rose by Any Other Name...

A fairly logical argument can be made for structuring a product as if it consisted of a series of functions operating as a total system within a described environment. The extension of this concept to the actual forecast may not be as straightforward. As a matter of fact, strict adherence to a set of functions may artificially constrain the broad view inherent in a forecast. In general, much of this concern can be alleviated when one attempts to define "what is technology?"

A general consensus of the scientific, technical, and management communities will agree that solid-state electronics, lasers, and hydrodynamics are fields of technology. Also, communications, automatic data processing, and ship-hull design are regarded as fields of technology. We are faced with the chicken/egg problem when considering that solid-state electronics can contribute to automatic data processing, but there is no functional relationship—just one of several techniques. This suggests the functional area forecasts should be complemented with other forecasts. These are forecasts of technologies that in one way or another contribute across several functions. They are multipurpose technologies and can be described as support technologies. As an example, an automobile functional forecast would be complemented by forecasts in areas such as organic materials and materials fabrication. The support technologies should, as a minimum, cover 1) areas that can constitute the physical end product, 2) the activities necessary to produce the product, and 3) the *total* environment in which the product operates (human, natural, competitive, etc.).

To summarize the thoughts on the identification and definition of technological areas to be forecast, there are two complementary approaches. One is the functional structure based upon the corporate product(s). These are forecasts of scientific applications to specific corporate problem areas. The other approach is the preparation of forecasts in technology areas that support product development and use. These tend to be forecasts of scientific/engineering areas such as materials, hydrodynamics, acoustics, etc. For a complete assessment of technology impact upon the corporation, both are required. When defining the technology areas of interest to a corporation, it is important to consider the ramifications of the various ways it can be done. Two illustrations of structuring are shown in Fig. 3. Note that one major category is concerned with support for product engineering. This is composed of the multipurpose technologies that support products developed under either structure. Note also the structures in the illustrations are the type that might be developed by a production-oriented manager. A research engineer would probably view the corporation as being in the energy-conversion business and proceed from there. Both views are necessary to develop a common structure. For conflicting views, as in this example, corporate goals would be the modifier between the views.

With an understanding of what areas are to be forecast, the question of the type of forecast can be addressed. The depth of penetration into each technological area will be variable. Also, no one person or group of people has or should have a peer's license in identifying technology areas of interest to the corporation. These considerations can be accommodated by allowing different types of forecasts to be prepared.

The corporate goals indicate a certain area for operations, and a forecast should be prepared for each functional area identified by the structuring of the product. This ensures that the corporate strategy (as it is visualized at present) is covered. The functional area forecasts will tend to be normative (need-oriented) forecasts. They should provide a reasonable indication of the corporate technological capabilities in the product field. Further, to ensure completeness and because functional forecasts are product oriented, additional forecasts should be solicited for technological areas that could support several functions or that could have an effect on the overall corporate operations. These forecasts would tend to be exploratory in nature.

Both the functional area and support forecasts should be at a broad level. For simplicity, this type of forecast can be identified as a *Broad-Area Forecast*. The definition of the areas to be forecast should be a joint effort between management and technical departments. Any one breakout will not satisfy everyone, but each should be able to interpret the final framework in terms of their area of responsibility.

A second type of forecast should be included to allow excursions in depth into each functional or support area as need dictates, and also as a forum to express new product ideas. These *In-Depth Forecasts* can be considered as avenues for spontaneous efforts of technological opportunities, as well as part of any overall program of forecasting.

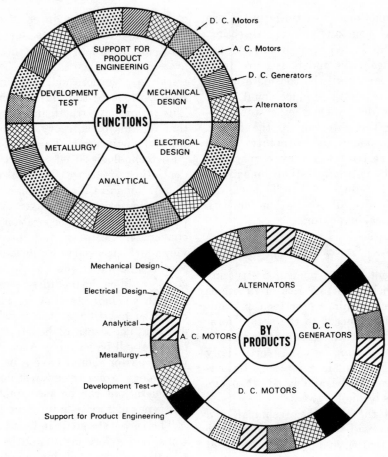

Fig. 3. Two different R&D structures.

IV. SELL SCIENCE!

The forecast presentation will, to a large extent, be governed by the methodology used to project the field of technology. The methods used to forecast the future state of the art are generally categorized as intuitive, growth analogy, trend extrapolation, and trend correlation. Within each of these categories there are several techniques [2].

A. Intuitive Forecasting

This method projects the state of the art by expert advice using one or a group of individuals who are experts in a technology area. Fig. 4 represents the time projection of ship shaft horsepower per unit weight. The curve is based upon a consensus of technical experts in the ship propulsion area. The curve also indicates the step-wise nature of some technological innovation developments.

B. Growth Analogies

This technique represents forecasts where the projection is based upon the familiar s-shaped saturation curve. Fig. 5 indicates a projection of fuel-cell power plants that follow this type trend. Generally, the saturation level is a theoretical or practical limit, which the

curve approaches asymptotically. A great number of developments can be represented in this way.

C. Trend Correlation

The comparison between two or more trends to confirm one or determine a third is used here. Fig. 6 is an example of trend correlation where it is assumed that marine technology for gas turbines in the future will follow the known development of aircraft gas turbines. Trend correlation has the advantage that the extent of correlation between trends can be established statistically.

D. Trend Extrapolation

Forecasts in this method are projections using curve-fitting techniques or simply extensions of present trends. Fig. 1 is an example of both trend correlation and trend extrapolation. Trend extrapolation assumes present and past data define the future.

The saying "a picture is worth a thousand words" is especially valid in presenting a technology forecast. By intent, the forecast will be reviewed (and interpreted) by people with diverse needs and backgrounds. The forecaster should present the projection of the state of the art and product implications in a graphic display if at

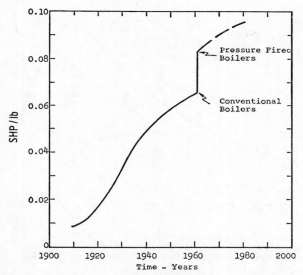

Fig. 4. Marine steam-propulsion systems. Typical intuitive forecast curve [7].

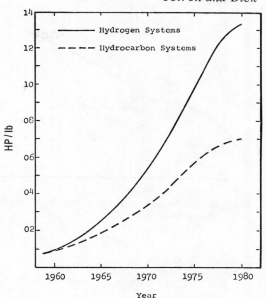

Fig. 5. Fuel-cell power plants. Typical growth analogy forecast curve [7].

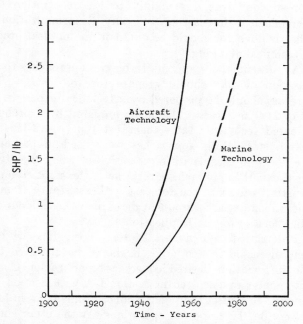

Fig. 6. Simple cycle gas turbine. Typical trend correlation curve [6].

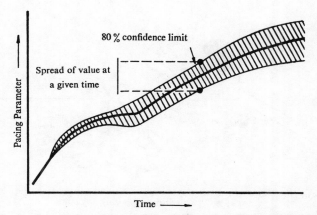

Fig. 7. Level of confidence shown where time is the critical parameter.

all possible. Further, the forecaster should use the display to convey as much qualification as is deemed necessary and to bring attention to significant points. For example, consider the Navy forecast requirement to express the forecast as a level of confidence. The requirement can be used by a forecaster to ensure his forecast is interpreted as a projection to an area—not a point. Fig. 7 indicates how confidence limits about a "best estimate" (spread of value at a given time) can be displayed to portray the approximate nature of the projection where time is critical. Fig. 8 is a way to indicate confidence of time (spread of time for a given value) where the value is critical. Display techniques can be used to guard against misinterpretation or to

crystallize concepts. For instance, a planner wants to know how fast a train could travel in the year 1975. The forecaster would present the projection as shown in Fig. 7 with the pacing parameter and operating speed, given as a spread (say 175 to 200 mi/h). If on the other hand, the planner wanted to know when he could operate at 200 mi/h, the forecast would be given as a spread of time (say 1974–1976) for the operating speed as shown in Fig. 8.

At some point in time the top management of a corporation will want to review the technological forecast. It would be a waste of time to submit all sections of all forecasts. It would be wiser to present to top management the portion of the forecast that will be useful in making decisions at the corporate level. For this, a separate summary should be prepared. The summary should cover new ideas and an assessment of what corporate goals can be met. This is a different view than

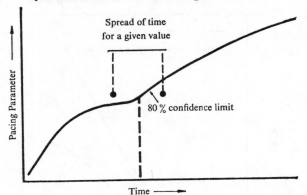

Fig. 8. Level of confidence shown where the value of the pacing parameter is the critical factor.

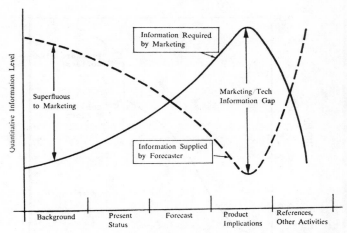

Fig. 9. Forecast sections comparing outputs and inputs. (This comparison shows one user's needs—Marketing Department; other users, such as systems analysts, would not indicate the same gaps.)

Fig. 10. Two children playing in the same room with the same toys; not two children playing together.

the technical community would desire. However, the needs of top management are reasonably covered in the *Product Implications* section of the forecast. If the section is prepared with the top management review in mind, the executive summary can be composed entirely of the *Product Implications* section.

V. Who, Me?

Having covered what a forecast should contain, the areas to be forecast, and the various types of forecasts available to serve the corporate needs, our attention can turn to who should do it. It is doubtful that a general request will generate a stampede of volunteers. The reaction of the technical community is likely to be unenthusiastic. The initial response of many technical people in laboratories to a request for technological forecasts could be described as . . . pessimism [3]. However, after preparing the forecasts, many found it to be a useful ex-

perience. It appears that a considerable portion of the "conversion" was due mainly to the recognition that technological forecasting is really a formalization of what is done (or should be done) in the natural process of technical planning.

At present, there appears to be two approaches to the question of *who* should prepare the forecast. 1) The forecast should be prepared by a technical expert in the field. 2) The forecast should be prepared by a product-oriented technical staff (generalists) or operations research staff. Both approaches were used in preparing the Navy forecast, with most activities using the "technical expert" approach. Several activities used technical experts to prepare the forecast with assistance from an operations research group to determine Operational Implications (Product Implications).

Referring to the five categories of the forecast content discussed in Section I, it should be observed that the information desired covers a broad range. Corporate goals are discussed in Section I-A with Section I-D devoted to a discussion of the effect of advances in technology on the corporate operations. At the other end of the spectrum, Sections I-B and I-C require rather detailed discussions of the technology area. If any one type of person prepares the forecast it is likely to make severe demands on his depth and breadth of knowledge.

This demand was reflected in the results of the Navy's forecast. Fig. 9 shows the relationship between the five sections of the forecast and desired quality. Quality was measured as actual content versus requested content. As indicated in the figure, the relative quantitative quality of Section I-A, I-B, and References was more than adequate. The forecast discussed in Section I-C drops off from the desired quantitative (not quality) level of the specific user with the product implications in Section I-D low enough to require additional effort beyond the first submission of most forecasts. It is appar-

Fig. 11. Two men talking to themselves; not to each other.

ent the individual technical experts encounter difficulty in translating their technical expertise into product implications terms.

On the basis of the Navy experience and consideration of the extent of information required to prepare a technology assessment type of forecast, it appears, the preparation may require the joint effort of two distinct types of people. 1) A technological area expert to be primarily concerned with Sections I-B and I-C. 2) A system analyst (Operations Researcher, Generalist, etc.) to assist in the *Background* and *Product Implications* sections. A joint effort of the two can have some beneficial side effects. A communication problem always seems to exist between people in general, as shown in Fig. 10, or managers and the technical community, as illustrated in Fig. 11. The joint effort can help open a dialogue between the two groups. It is not coincidental that the forecasting format is in itself a forcing function between the two groups to help ensure overall utility.

The task of anyone preparing a forecast can be lightened by a good clear statement of specific and quantitative corporate or product goals. The Navy's recently published "Exploratory Development Goals" provided the product goals for the Navy Technological Forecast. The goals allow the forecast to be related directly to the needs, resulting in a normative forecast. Although a normative forecast has many advantages, it does have one distinct disadvantage. If the goals change (or are misstated, or misinterpreted), the forecast may have minimal utility or be entirely misleading. A reasonable compromise is to have the actual forecast of the state of the art (Section I-C) exploratory to the greatest extent possible. All specific quantitative goal orientation should be placed in Section I-D.

Just as the goals can influence the forecast, so can the forecaster [4]. There should be an effort on the part of the forecaster to be as objective as possible. "Axe grinding" either by commission or omission should be avoided. The forecast should predict what is probable and possible, not what one wants or does not want. This concern is exemplified in the scientist's responsibility to society in the area of weaponry. From a management view, the scientist should "be on tap—not on top" in policy decisions. When preparing a forecast, the forecaster should consider what is feasible, not the social implications. However, once the forecast is objectively prepared, avenues should be open for the scientist to express his social views.

VI. Quantification—The Key to Utility

Sections I-C and I-D are the heart of the technology assessment type of technological forecast. The first indicates, within the stated probability limits, the growth of the technology. The latter is a projection of the effect of this growth on the corporation. It should not take a great deal of persuasion to convince most people that a forecast increases in utility according to the degree with which it is quantified. A statement such as . . . "commercial aircraft will fly higher, faster, and carry more passengers than at present . . ." does not contain information of great value. Whereas the statement "commercial aircraft will be capable of speeds of Mach 3 at altitudes of 70 000 feet while carrying up to 400 passengers . . ." contains information that can be used by a diverse audience.

It may appear simple and straightforward to state the need for, and obtain, quantification of forecasts. Experience has indicated otherwise. One reason quantification of the forecast is difficult is because the pacing parameter(s) to quantify is usually not apparent. The forecaster should spend a considerable portion of the time allowed for the task identifying the pacing (key) parameters of the technology. Pacing parameter identification may require a tradeoff study between all major technology parameters. In general, it is not a simple task. When the pacing parameters are not identified, a technique used by some forecasters is to project many parameters. Going the extreme in this direction and

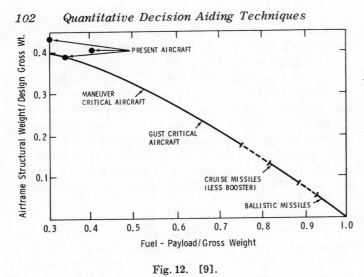

Fig. 12. [9].

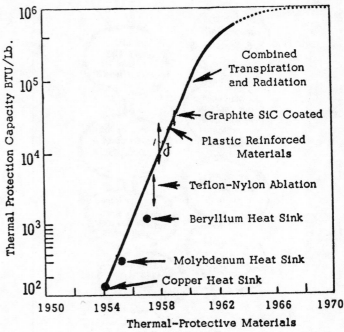

Fig. 13. Requirements changed and thermal protection became a less controlling factor [8].

overpowering the reader with data will severely limit the forecast's usefulness. Another factor influencing quantitative discussions is the natural reluctance of the technical community to state a precise number in a forecast when there is doubt about overall accuracy of the projection. Any quantitative discussion, or any forecast, is expressed as a prediction with a *level of confidence*. This qualification must be kept in mind by both the user and the forecaster.

VII. Hindsight Into Foresight

Many technological forecasts have been prepared by government and industry. An area of concern is their utilization. One issue is whether the preparation of the forecast will be self-fulfilling. Will the forecast, consciously or unconsciously, be used to guide development? We do not know of any correlation studies that indicate whether they are or not. Certainly there have been forecasts stating certain things could not be done that did not stop others from doing them. This can be seen from von Karman's committee on gas turbines (see Appendix I). On the other hand, Fig. 12 is a representation of weight trends of certain types of air vehicles that was prepared in 1945. A technical reviewer in 1967 indicated the curve is still valid for present fighter aircraft. The curve was contained in the von Karman Army study conducted by an august group of scientists (see Appendix II) to indicate new developments in the future. Because of the high stature of the group who prepared the report, it may have been self-fulfilling. The general feeling toward self-fulfillment of technological forecasts: if the forecast was prepared by a laureate in the field, the chances for self-fulfillment increase; if the forecast is prepared by an individual who has equal competence but little recognition in the technology area, the chances decrease.

Another issue is the development of forecasting methodology to ensure a reasonable degree of credi-

bility. There have been some forecasts that were completely out of phase with actual developments. We can assume forecasts of this type will continue. However, if the forecasting is approached in an objective scientific manner, one can place a reasonable degree of confidence in the forecast. Figs. 13–16 are curves taken from forecasts prepared eight years ago. With each curve is the comment of a technical reviewer's 1968 hindsight. The figures indicate a cross-section of forecast usefulness. They represent projections of what was feasible in 1961. Note that feasibility does not mean advancement will happen. A need must be present to ensure development.

The preparation of a technological forecast is not a single-shot affair. It should be considered a continuing effort. Each forecast should be reviewed periodically and updated as required. A specific time period cannot be stated for all forecasts. It will depend upon the dynamic nature of the area. Any updating procedure should include a reassessment of the areas to be forecast to ensure compatibility with current needs.

Finally, there seems to be an issue over whether one should attempt to forecast technology at all. It is a relatively new field where military and industry have expanded in a hasty and haphazard fashion. Consequently, technological forecasting bears close scrutiny if for no other reason than it may not warrant the load on the time of the people required to prepare them. Critical to the entire issue is the need and utility of forecasting. As to the need, decisions are made that require an assessment of technology whether a forecast exists or not. As

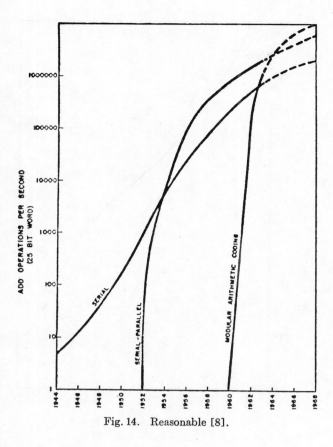

Fig. 14. Reasonable [8].

agement. An objective technological forecast can provide a valuable input to the future direction of the corporation—an area of vital importance to all management levels of the corporation.

APPENDIX I

"In its present state and even considering the improvements possible when adopting the higher temperatures proposed for the immediate future, the gas turbine could hardly be considered a feasible application to airplanes mainly because of the difficulty in complying with the stringent weight requirements imposed by aeronautics.

"The present internal-combustion-engine equipment used in airplanes weighs 1.1 lb/hp, and to approach such a figure with a gas turbine seems beyond the realm of possibility with existing materials. The minimum weight for gas turbines even when taking advantage of higher temperatures appears to be approximately 13–15 lb/hp." *The Committee on Gas Turbines, Appointed by the National Academy of Sciences, June 10, 1940.*

was indicated previously, a forecast is nothing more than a formalized scientific procedure of activities that are normally utilized either in a fragmented manner or informally in making decisions concerning the future state of the art of technology. As to the utility, this is a function of the overall effort. If a valid objective quantitative forecast is available it will be used. Quantification and objectivity can be attempted. Validity cannot be guaranteed, but face validity can be approached by iterative updating. Actual validity can never be proven because of self-fulfillment. Technological forecasting is not a panacea, but neither is it useless. It is, like other systematic analyses, an attempt to quantify to the extent possible the state of technology. As such, it can aid in decisions that might not be made as well if the forecast did not exist.

The various types of problems discussed here should crystallize several important points about technological forecasting. First, there is no cheap and quick way of producing a technological forecast. There are many factors to consider. The forecast effort should be planned and conducted with entire corporate operations in mind. Second, a technological forecast should serve a wide audience. It is not worth the investment if it cannot be or is not used. The forecast content should be as broad an assessment of technology as is practicable within corporate goals. Finally, a comprehensive forecasting effort is not possible without the backing of *all* levels of man-

APPENDIX II

AAF SCIENTIFIC ADVISORY GROUP

Dr. Th. von Karman
Director

| Colonel F. E. Glantzberg | Dr. H. L. Dryden |
| Deputy Director, Military | Deputy Director, Scientific |

Lt. Col. G. T. McHugh, Executive
Capt. C. H. Jackson, Jr., Secretary

Consultants

Dr. C. W. Bray	Dr. A. J. Stosick
Dr. L. A. DuBridge	Dr. W. J. Sweeney
Dr. Pol Duwez	Dr. H. S. Tsien
Dr. G. Gamow	Dr. G. E. Valley
Dr. I. A. Getting	Dr. F. L. Wattendorf
Dr. L. P. Hammett	Dr. F. Zwicky
Dr. W. S. Hunter	Dr. V. K. Zworykin
Dr. I. P. Krick	Col. D. N. Yates
Dr. D. P. MacDougall	Col. W. R. Lovelace II
Dr. G. A. Morton	Lt. Col. A. P. Gagge
Dr. N. M. Newmark	Lt. Col. F. W. Williams
Dr. W. H. Pickering	Major T. F. Walkowicz
Dr. E. M. Purcell	Capt. C. N. Hasert
Dr. G. B. Schubauer	M. Alperin
Dr. W. R. Sears	I. L. Ashkenas
	G. S. Schairer

Layout and Illustration

Capt. M. Miller
Capt. T. E. Daley

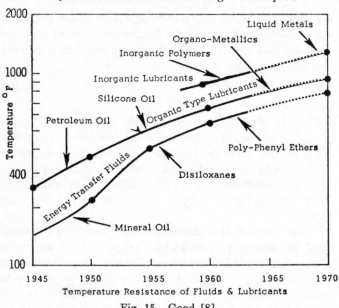

Fig. 15.   Good [8].

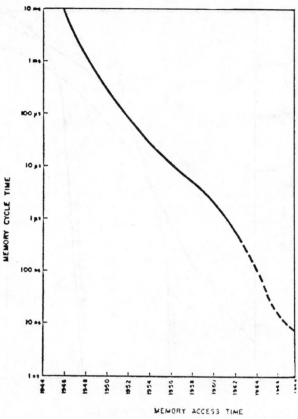

Fig. 16.   Too optimistic [8].

References

[1] M. J. Cetron *et al.,* "A proposal for a navy technological forecast," pt. I, Summary Rept., Naval Materiel Command, Headquarters, Washington, D. C., May 1966.

[2] M. J. Cetron and A. L. Weiser, "Technological change, technological forecasting and planning R&D—A view from the R&D manager's desk," *The George Washington Law Rev.—Technol. Assessment and the Law,* vol. 36, no. 5, p. 1091.

[3] M. J. Cetron and T. I. Monahan, "An evaluation and appraisal of various approaches to technological forecasting," in *Technological Forecasting for Industry and Government,* J. F. Bright, Ed. Englewood Cliffs, N. J.: Prentice-Hall.

[4] M. J. Cetron and E. B. Mahinske, "The value of technological forecasting for the research and development manager," *Futures,* vol. 1, September 1968.

[5] M. J. Cetron *et al.,* "A proposal for a navy technological forecast," pt. II, Backup Rept.; Naval Materiel Command Headquarters, Washington, D. C., May 1966.

[6] M. J. Cetron, "Using technical forecasts," *Sci. and Technol.,* p. 60, July 1968.

[7] F. A. Hansen and D. Smith, "Long range research and development planning," Naval Ship Research and Development Center, Annapolis, Md., 1966.

[8] R. Lenz, Jr., "Technology for tomorrow," Air Force Systems Command, USAF, Wright-Patterson AFB, Dayton, Ohio, 1961.

[9] Th. Von Karman, "Towards new horizons," Army Air Corps, Washington, D. C., 1945.

The Need for Allocating Resources to "Combat-Effectiveness Measurements" from Initial R&D to Obsolescence

NORMAN K. WALKER AND CHARLES R. PHILLIPS

Abstract—Operations analysts and weapons designers all agree on the extreme difficulty of collecting "hard" data on the performance of weapons systems. This paper presents case studies from World War II through Southeast Asia, which illustrate the prevalence of the problem and also show how, for the lack of quite minor detailed information, incorrect conclusions have been reached in operations analysis reports, leading to unnecessarily costly operations.

I. INTRODUCTION

IN EXPLORING the subject of this paper in more detail, the title and emphasis have changed several times. This is not surprising. There is general dissatisfaction with the feedback of Weapons Systems Effectiveness information from the field and even more dissatisfaction with the results when they are received, and yet it is not clear what is wrong.

All the services insist that a new system fulfills the design and performance requirements specified in the contract, and require an acceptance test by service personnel in addition to a demonstration test by the contractor.

Furthermore, all the services recognize that there is an additional requirement for testing the system in an environment as like combat as possible, and under a variety of simulated combat conditions. Such tests are required to demonstrate system vulnerability, survivability, and effectiveness, and the results are of value to the operating organizations to establish tactics and techniques, to logistics to establish logistical and maintenance R&D, to system developers to prepare improved design parameters for new systems, and on to the planners for war planning factors and force requirements.

Certainly the problem is not necessarily lack of funds. Dr. Foster, in testimony before Congress estimated that $500 000 000 would be spent in FY 1969 on user tests and on the retrieval of combat data, and this is not a negligible proportion of a $700 000 000 Research, Development, Test and Evaluation budget.

The authors believe that the problem is one of the direction of effort and the organization of effort. The right kinds of data—the critical requirements—have never been properly identified and fed into the Test and Evaluation (T&E) system, and the best form of instrumentation has not been provided.

It is important to remember always that the final output of a weapons system is combat effectiveness, and this combat effectiveness must be achieved by means acceptable to the purchaser and user.

II. CASE HISTORIES

The authors have personally located and investigated five cases from World War II, Korea, and Vietnam where, because of the lack of quite minor information, incorrect conclusions on operational effectiveness were reached leading to dubious tactical conclusions.

To avoid invidious present-day illustrations, which may be embarrassing, the authors propose to discuss in detail only one system, the employment of heavy guided bombs in World War II and Korea, but remind the reader again that data are generally available on present-day systems where similar costly mistakes have been made.

A. AZON Bomb in World War II (1944–1945)

The AZON bomb was first introduced into World War II in Northern Italy when an attempt was made to cut the Brenner Pass railroad by destroying the viaduct at AVISIO—a particularly heavily defended target.

A 35-mm film of the bomb runs, plus impact data and personal contacts 15 years later showed that operational instructions to fly straight and level while lining up the bomb sight and while controlling the bomb to impact were unofficially disregarded, and control abandoned after 5 seconds giving very poor results—though better than unguided bombing.

A simple device monitoring the system operation[1] would have disclosed the early abandonment of control, and a simple reconsideration of the system would have shown that provided course changes were small, large variations in aircraft speed and altitude after dropping the bomb were permissible.

Such revised instructions could have encouraged the crews to control all the way to the target, and could have led to a reduction in Probable Deflection Error (DEP) from 605 to 100 feet. This would have justified

---

Manuscript received July; 1969, revised August, 1969.
The authors are with the Applied Systems Corporation, Rockville, Md.

[1] This was in fact used during the contractor trials at various proving grounds.

the substitution of AZON for all normal bombs in this mission.

B. *RAZON Bomb in Korea (1950–1952)*

The RAZON guided bomb was developed in 1944–1945 and was mothballed. It was introduced in Korea in 1950 to attack bridges and power stations. The RAZON featured direct control laterally and a pseudo-control system in pitch that did eliminate some range errors.

The Far Eastern Air Force had excellent strike coverage, and excellent Operations Analysts although no Missile Systems Engineer was available with a good knowledge of the design principles of RAZON. The results showed a DEP of 5 mils and a Probable Range Error (REP) of 18 mils, and FEAF Operations Analysts concluded that the number of bridges destroyed could be increased somewhat by using low-level bombers with conventional bombs; to which the enemy responded very easily with strong light anti-aircraft gun defenses causing many losses.

Had it been realized that the RAZON system was predicated on the use of the Douglas DB-18, an aircraft which was obsolete in 1942, the REP could have been cut to 5 mils by using a simple maneuver that was well within the compass of the B-29 aircraft, and that had already been used in the successful German F-X 1400 bomb project of 1944. In this case, the recommendation could not have been in favor of low-altitude level bombing, the enemy counter would have been more difficult, and U. S. losses could have been greatly reduced.

III. Current Examples of Good Practice

With the current considerable expenditure on Operational Test and Evaluation it would be surprising if some of these types of problems were not under attack.

A. *UK-BULLPUP*

The United Kingdom is very conscious of the need to economize in missiles and in training procedures. As a result only picked men fire BULLPUP in the Royal Navy, and each flight is recorded by a special cine camera mounted in the nose of the firing aircraft.

All data on all practice firings are sent to the Royal Naval Air Station at Lossiemouth, and every firing is analyzed.

Since through this process only effective operators are retained on BULLPUP, funds permit frequent practice firings and a high level of efficiency is maintained.

B. *UK-SEACAT*

The SEACAT is a human-operator-cum-autopilot controlled guided missile for the close defense of ships against aircraft. Results of acceptance trials were good but have been greatly surpassed by actual service firing trials.

The standard SEACAT installation includes not only a simulator for frequent practice on board, but a cine camera mounted coaxially with the acquisition radar, and a recorder to monitor the actual signals transmitted to the missile in flight, which are also played through the simulator to give lateral and vertical errors during the trajectory.

This system evidently includes the main features necessary for good OT&E, including combat data.

C. *CARDS*

The USAF is currently instrumenting certain aircraft with CARDS, the 100-channel Combat Aircraft Recording Data System. For aircraft fitted with an inertial navigation system, CARDS will provide almost all the information needed to evaluate weapon performance—such as before, during, and after strike photographic coverage, functions of firing gear and sight, and position attitude and velocities in space axes.

Channels are also available for physiological monitoring.

An elementary system with eight channels has been used by the British Navy for some years on the Buccaneer aircraft.

D. *FULLCAP–CARDS*

The special pod known as FULLCAP was designed to supplement CARDS with a completely independent Inertia Navigation System plus LORAN (Radio Long-Range Navigation) update for aircraft without this facility. Some units have been built, but development is now held up. It is possible that a more desirable solution is to ensure that all Service aircraft carry a lightweight inertial navigation system.

An improved system developed by Ling-Temco-Vought called TERCOM is also available.

IV. Information Needs

It is clear that the type of information needed is generally provided as a matter of course to the developer in his tests.

Let us consider the five major test conditions as recognized by the U. S. Army.

1) Engineer Tests/Service Tests (ET/ST)—Army Material Command: Tests conducted by Army Material Command to verify that the contractor has met the specifications for a new system. Full data are obtained from special instrumentation as required to define the performance of the system and the operator. The environment is normally benign, but a few tests will be made under specified extreme conditions.

2) Confirmatory Tests (CONARC): These are rather small-scale tests to confirm that the specified objectives attained under ET/ST conditions are also met with appropriately trained Service personnel in a typical operational environment. The tests usually provide information on training and maintenance requirements on overall effectiveness and on limiting weather conditions.

3) Troop Tests (CONARC): These are Minimal Instrumentation Major Field Exercises with normal Service personnel under realistic conditions (accuracy and reliability data only, with minimal instrumentation).

4) Field Experiments or OT&E (Combat Developments Command and CDCEC): Special field experiments conducted by CDC Experimentation Command to determine whether the tactical doctrine and objectives originally envisaged for the weapon system are sound in an environment as close to combat conditions as can be arranged. Very elaborate range instrumentation is often used, but missile information is often marginal and mainly confined to accuracy and reliability.

5) Combat: The true test of a system is its effectiveness under combat conditions. Unfortunately at the present time we normally recover less than 1 percent of the potential information on accuracy and much less on effectiveness. Instrumentation is almost confined to gun cameras (now few) strike photos and Bomb Damage Assessment from post-strike reconnaissance photographs.

The other Services have similar comprehensive test programs up to the Troop Tests and Confirmatory Tests and the interest of the developing agency is usually far more obvious in the other user trials in the case of the Army. However, the Navy and the Air Force tests do not include the elaborate field exercises staged by CDCEC simulating combat conditions. Navy and Air Force testing capabilities have been limited primarily to questions of lethality of weapons systems under ideal conditions for the attacker, using Service personnel. Emphasis has not been placed on the vulnerability or the survivability of the attacking system, and the USN and USAF targets do not have means of then simulating return fire. (However, the USAF at Eglin AFB is developing a specially instrumented range for Air Force Weapons Effectiveness Testing (AFWET), which will ultimately permit fairly realistic two-sided tests with multiple engagements.)

Each of the first four types of tests listed is designed to serve the needs of one user, and of that user only. In fact, one could say that each derives only from the one above, and recently—in the name of avoiding bias—there has been a strong tendency deliberately to avoid any "contamination" from preceding tests.

Unfortunately, as has been seen from the case history cited, this leads to a complete lack of communication between the user and the designer of the system, which currently is only being overcome by special efforts on a crash basis, once the sheer accumulation of poor data has shown a solution must be found.

The real difficulty seems to be that two major systems are in conflict. The weapons designer would like combat data, but finds his attempts to get information from which better systems can be designed frustrated by the user, who wants to fight the war *now*, and does not want to take time off for pie-in-the-sky projects.

The user would like better effectiveness data so that his current mix of weapons can be used more efficiently.

These are not incompatible, but the current OT&E tests plus crash programs will not do the job.

V. SUGGESTED SOLUTION

Firstly, one must plan, from the start, to obtain the necessary data. The techniques required are much the same as those needed in the early R&D stages of a project, but the equipment and trained personnel must be carried on as an essential component through Service Test, Troop Tests, OT&E, and on into combat. It is of considerable operational importance to decide whether each system should carry its own test equipment or whether some universal system, such as CARDS, should be used.

The choice is a "user" choice, but the Weapons Designer must know of this choice and arrange for the necessary inputs to the CARDS system, if adopted.

All data need not be evaluated, but all must be available. However, if the "Instrumented Missile" approach is used, it would be good enough to instrument 10 percent of production since at present impact data for less than 1 percent of missiles fired are recovered.

Secondly, suitable changes must be made in Personnel structure to ensure that when the data are available, the correct decisions are made. The detailed advice of a Missile Systems Engineer familiar with the particular system under consideration must therefore be available. This is most easily made available by continuing contact through the original developers.

Thirdly, we must realize the OT&E on a fully instrumented range is not a direct step on the way to combat data, but an important vantage point from which a survey of probable combat results can be made, with conditions under our control.

Full use must be made of the system instrumentation provided to confirm that this will give good results in combat by comparison with the instrumented range data. However, once the instrumentation is checked, the burden of data reduction on the range will be greatly reduced.

Fourthly, to implement these changes, continuing support must be given to "Combat Effectiveness Measurements" from the earliest R&D phase through into obsolescence for every system.

Since this will imply a very full degree of acceptance across the board, it seems likely that the planning of OT&E tests and the collection and evaluation of combat data will tend to be one of the most concentrated areas of activity within the Department of Defense.

Research Project Cost Distributions and Budget Forecasting

BURTON V. DEAN, SAMUEL J. MANTEL, JR., AND LEWIS A. ROEPCKE

Abstract—The purpose of this paper is to determine the nature of actual research project costs, their probability distributions, and corresponding parameter values so that long-range budget forecasts and variances can be provided. The distribution and parameters of the research project costs for 1963 through 1967 have been developed and are discussed.

A description of the present Army budgeting system is presented. The budget forecasting problem is defined and a mathematical model is presented.[1] The essential elements of the model are described in terms of parameters and coefficients, which are obtained from the 1963 through 1967 budget data. Four variations of the basic model are developed and compared.

This paper contains a list of computer program statements specifically designed 1) to derive the necessary parameters from historical data, and 2) to forecast these parameters for each of five years into the future. The program, its operation, and features are discussed with sample outputs provided for illustration purposes.

I. Introduction

AN EXTENSIVE mythology has long surrounded the subject of research. Among other elements of this mythology is the notion that the results of research activities and the costs associated with these results are highly unpredictable. In the face of this assumed unpredictability, and perhaps because of it, institutions conducting and financing large scale research activities have been under pressure to introduce planning techniques and methods, which will allow funding agencies some measure of control in their budgeting process.

The mythology further insists that the more basic the research, the less predictable will be the output and the associated costs. Research conducted in some sciences is considered to be more or less predictable than research in others.

This paper is concerned with the nature of research costs, their probability distributions, and corresponding parameter values, with an aim to developing methods of long-range research budget forecasting models.[2]

Research can be categorized in many ways. The degree of orientation toward "the increase of knowledge in science" as opposed to "the application of knowledge . . . directed toward a solution to an existent or anticipated" problem determines whether the research is classed as "basic" or "applied."[3] It can be classified by the area of science central to the research project. It can be categorized by the programmatic area to which it may contribute. The source of monetary support, government or private, may be used to classify research efforts. There are, of course, many other dimensions through which research can be considered. The paper will view research cost distributions across several dimensions and show that *the same general form of distribution describes research costs independently of the dimension used.*

The Army research budget is successively divided to form five distinct levels of classification. From the highest (most aggregative) to the lowest (least aggregative) these levels of classification are called

1) categories,
2) program elements, occasionally broken down into subelements,
3) projects,
4) task areas, or tasks,
5) work units.

The term "category" generally differentiates research activities between basic and different levels of application. The "6.1" category would identify a research activity as "basic research, while the "6.2" category would identify it as "exploratory development" work.

Program elements refer to the general mission orientation of the research. For example, either basic or applied research may be carried out under a program element devoted to underwater weapon mobility. Under such a program element might come many "projects," each concerned with the ultimate development of a different general method of achieving the program element.

Manuscript received July 1969; revised August 1969. This report was prepared as part of the research activities of the Department of Operations Research, Case–Western Reserve University under Contracts 542-2518 with the Army Materiel Command, 542-2104 with Project Themis, and 542-2510, Department of Defense, Washington, D. C. with the Office of Naval Research.

B. V. Dean is with the Operations Research Department, Case–Western University, Cleveland, Ohio.

S. J. Mantel, Jr., was with the Economics-In-Action Program, Case–Western Reserve University, Cleveland, Ohio. He is now with the Department of Management and Quantitative Analysis, College of Business Administration, University of Cincinnati, Cincinnati, Ohio.

L. A. Roepcke is with the Technical Planning Branch, U. S. Army Materiel Command, Washington, D. C.

[1] The mathematical model employed here was originally developed by B. V. Dean, H. Mann, and B. D. Corwin, "*A management control system for estimating research and development manpower requirements,*" for Babcock and Wilcox Company, Department of Operations Research, Case–Western Reserve University, Cleveland, Ohio, Tech. Memo. 85, May 1967.

[2] The nature of the output of research activities is considered in two papers: B. V. Dean and L. Hauser, Tech. Memo. 65 and B. V. Dean, Tech. Memo. 70, Department of Operations Research, Case–Western Reserve University, Cleveland, Ohio.

[3] Army Regulation 70-9, *Research and Technology Resume-Work Unit Level,* Department of the Army, May 1966, p. 10.

Within each project, there are a number of more specific "tasks" that must be accomplished. These might include guidance systems, launch systems for missiles, and communication devices. And, finally, to achieve any given task, it may be necessary to undertake a number of different "work units" of research in military, industrial, or academic research laboratories, They are the work units that are identified as "basic," "applied," etc.

Note these two general comments about the classification scheme. First, any individual work unit may be the only research done to solve a given problem, or it may be one of several work units conducted in parallel and all oriented toward answering the same general question. Second, the distinction between "basic" and "applied" research tends to become less clear when speaking of specific work units.

The researcher may be motivated in his efforts by his desire to understand a phenomenon, while the funding agency may wish to solve a fairly well-defined problem. To the researcher, the work would be "basic," while the agency might define it as "applied." Throughout this paper, the authors have used the categorization adopted by the funding agency.

II. WORK-UNIT COST DISTRIBUTION— ARMY RESEARCH OFFICE DATA

The objective of this section is to determine the probability density function of the cost of research work units. Given the random variable x, where x is the cost of a work unit, the probability density function $f(x)$ for work-unit costs will be determined. It will be shown that the *log-normal distribution* gives an excellent fit to the observed values of $f(x)$.

Army research work unit-cost data were analyzed for the 1964, 1965, 1966, and 1967 fiscal years. For each year, two research categories (1 and 2, corresponding to "basic" and "exploratory development") were considered separately and together. The data were grouped into classes by size of funding level, and frequency distributions were fitted to the observed frequencies. Class intervals of $100 000, $200 000, and $300 000 were used. For example, the observed frequency in class 1 using an interval of $100 000 is the number of work units whose cost is less than $100 000; the observed frequency in class 2 is the number of projects whose cost is between $100 000 and $200 000, etc.

The data were fitted to two frequency distributions, log normal and gamma. The log-normal curve was significantly better than the gamma curve in all cases, although the gamma curve was fairly good. The data fit the log-normal distribution within a 1 percent significance level.

The log-normal distribution considers the cost of a research work unit x to be a random variable. The log-normal probability density function is

$$f(x) = \frac{1}{\sigma \sqrt{2\Pi}} \exp\left(-\frac{1}{2\sigma^2}(\log x - \mu)^2\right) \qquad 0 < x < \infty.$$

The two functional parameters are μ and σ^2. It is called a log-normal distribution because the logarithm of the variable x has a normal distribution with mean μ and variance σ^2. The mean of the x variable is given by $\exp\left(\mu + \frac{1}{2}\sigma^2\right)$ and the corresponding variance is $\exp\left(2\mu + 2\sigma^2\right) - \exp\left(2\mu + \sigma^2\right)$.

Maximum likelihood estimators were used to estimate μ and σ^2. The estimate of μ is

$$\frac{\sum_i \log(x_i)}{N},$$

where x_i is the cost of work units and N is the total number of work units. The estimate of σ^2 is

$$\frac{\sum_i (\log(x_i) - \mu)^2}{N - 1}.$$

The range of μ is from 6.34–6.92 and of σ^2 from 1.27–1.95.

Using the estimated values of μ and σ^2, the expected frequency in each interval is calculated so that it may be compared to the observed frequency. Since $f(x)$ is a probability density function,

$$\int_0^\infty f(x)\,dx = 1.$$

The integral of the area under the density function over a specified interval is the probability that the variable will fall in that interval. Thus, the expected frequency in an interval is

$$N \int_a^b f(x)\,dx,$$

where a and b are the end points of the interval.

The expected frequency can be shown as a line fitted to the observed data and the goodness of this fit can be measured. The Kolmogorov–Smirnov goodness of fit test was used here. In this test a statistic D is defined, where

$$D = \max |F_N(x) - F(x)|,$$

and $F_N(x)$ is the observed cumulative distribution function. $F_N(x)$ is equal to the number of data points with value less than or equal to x, divided by the total number of points. $F(x)$ is the cumulative distribution function of the log-normal curve with μ, σ^2 as parameters, where

$$F(x) = \int_0^x f(y)\,dy.$$

The smaller the value of D the better the observed data fit the log-normal curve. For this particular application D ranges from 0.029 to 0.075, which is within the 1 percent significance level for all the distributions.

Sensitivity of the Interval

The Kolmogorov–Smirnov D statistic varies with the class interval used. The authors consider the "best" interval to be that which yields the smallest D statistic. In seven out of twelve cases the best interval was 200 ($200 000). Even where the "best" interval was 100 or 300 the D statistic for the 200 cases was at the 1 percent

TABLE I
LOG-NORMAL FUNCTION

Year	Category	Sample Mean for x_i	Sample Variance for x_i	$\hat{\mu}$	$\hat{\sigma}^2$	D	Interval*
64	1	1616	3 481 016	6.6691	1.9542	0.062	300
65	1	1766	3 355 173	6.9245	1.4657	0.075	200
66	1	1689	3 020 208	6.9095	1.2748	0.074	100
67	1	1716	3 297 852	6.8952	1.3841	0.058	200
64	2	1434	2 727 947	6.6524	1.5076	0.033	200
65	2	1322	2 082 145	6.6006	1.4480	0.038	300
66	2	1236	2 413 019	6.4915	1.5650	0.033	200
67	2	1029	1 037 615	6.3372	1.7365	0.064	200
64	1 and 2	1471	2 869 667	6.6558	1.5892	0.034	100
65	1 and 2	1410	2 350 928	6.6646	1.4618	0.039	300
66	1 and 2	1319	2 543 503	6.5681	1.5328	0.029	200
67	1 and 2	1156	1 516 113	6.4406	1.7131	0.055	200

* Thousands of dollars.

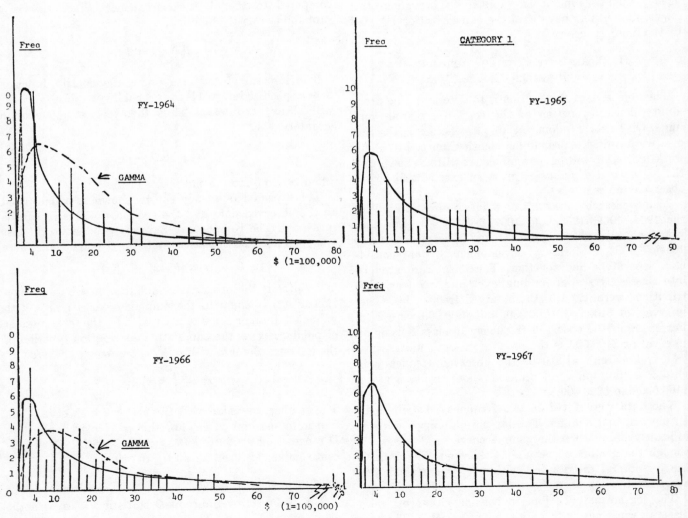

Fig. 1.

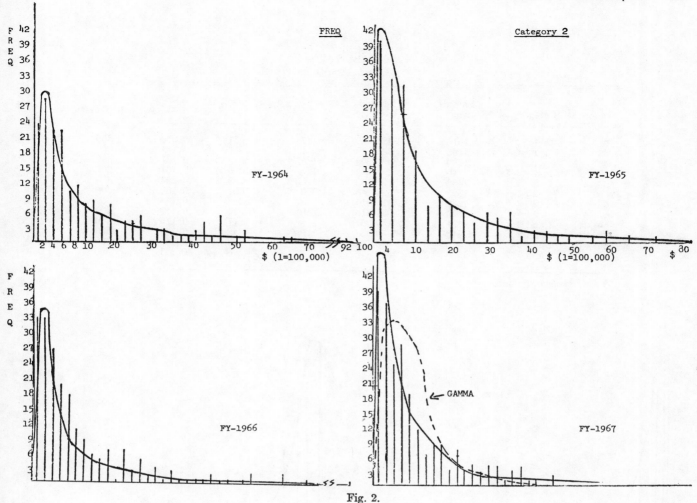

Fig. 2.

level. Consequently, the 200 value is considered the best interval for overall cost fitting purposes.

Table I shows the statistical results for applying the log-normal density function. Figs. 1, 2, and 3 show the observed frequencies and the fitted expected frequencies for each of the four years for category 1 (basic research), category 2 (exploratory development research), and categories 1 and 2 combined.

Gamma Distribution

The gamma probability density function is

$$f(x) = \frac{1 x^{\alpha-1} e^{-x/\beta}}{\Gamma(\alpha)\beta^{\alpha}}.$$

The parameters of the density function are α and β. The mean is $\alpha\beta$ and the variance is $\alpha\beta^2$. After the value of α is estimated by a recursive technique, β is estimated using a maximum likelihood relationship, where the estimate of β is

$$\frac{\sum_i x_i}{N}.$$

A grid with intervals of 0.1 was used to estimate α. A finer grid with intervals of 0.02 was tried for some cases. The finer grid gave a better fit with a smaller D statis-

tic but the improvement was minor and did not approach the goodness of fit of the log-normal distribution.

The expected frequencies and the D statistic are computed for the gamma distribution the same way as for the log-normal distribution. Some of the graphs have the corresponding gamma curve drawn in for purposes of comparison. In general, the gamma curve peaks later and lower than the log-normal curve. In the gamma curve there is a higher concentration of mass at the mode.

The value of α ranges from 1.7 to 2.1. The β value depends on the sample mean and ranges from 500 to 1000. The D statistic had values between 0.13 and 0.2. In general, the gamma curve improves as the size of the intervals increases. Ten of the "best" intervals were 300, the other two were 200. The gamma distribution might be even better with larger intervals, but information is lost if the data are aggregated too much. Table II shows the results of the gamma density function.

Trend Analysis

Drawing conclusions about trends over time on the basis of only four years is rather difficult. The statistics of projects in category 1 act differently than those in category 2, as may be seen from the tables. The mean is

TABLE II
GAMMA FUNCTION

Year	Category	Sample Mean	Sample Variance	α	β	D	Interval*
64	1	1616	3 481 016	1.7	951	0.200	300
65	1	1765	3 355 173	2.1	841	0.138	300
66	1	1689	3 020 208	1.85	913	0.137	300
67	1	1716	3 297 852	1.7	1010	0.161	200
64	2	1434	2 727 592	1.89	759	0.164	300
65	2	1323	2 082 145	2.0	661	0.150	300
66	2	1236	2 413 019	1.8	686	0.144	300
67	2	1029	1 037 616	2.0	514	0.147	200
64	1 and 2	1471	2 869 667	1.8	817	0.175	300
65	1 and 2	1410	2 350 928	1.9	742	0.144	300
66	1 and 2	1319	2 543 503	1.8	733	0.146	300
67	1 and 2	1156	1 516 113	2.0	578	0.141	300

* Thousands of dollars.

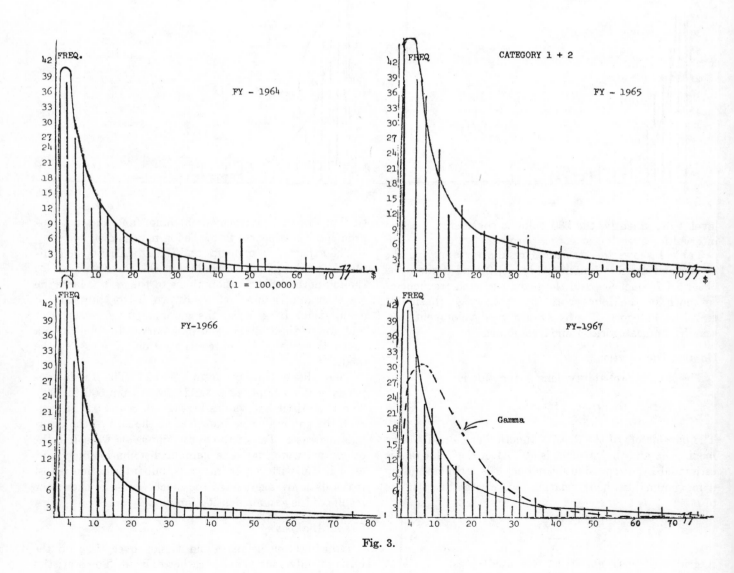

Fig. 3.

decreasing for category 2 and increasing for category 1. During this period, the sample variance is decreasing overall.

III. RESEARCH WORK-UNIT COST DISTRIBUTION—OFFICE OF NAVAL RESEARCH

The Office of Naval Research (ONR) distributes its research funds to eight science divisions within the organization, thence to programs within each of the divisions, and finally to research work units. The data appearing in Figs 4 and 5 were taken from the Ocean Science and Technology Division, and in Figs. 6 and 7 from the Physical Oceanography Program within that division. (The suggestion to use data from this division and program came from the ONR and was motivated largely by considerations of the ease of data collection and processing.)

Cost information for 178 work units funded through the Ocean Science and Technology Division for fiscal year 1967 were examined. A class size of $10 000 was used for work-unit costs. The cost distributions were then plotted on probability paper and appear to be log normal.

Since the ratio of total research costs to the number of professional man years involved in the project is often used as an index for research costs, the distribution of cost-per-professional man year for the Ocean Science Division and for the Physical Oceanography Program appear to be log normal.

ONR expends research funds through 33 "codes," which are subscience areas within the eight science divisions. A study of ONR research activity contained data on the total and average amount spent for research work units under each of the 28 codes that existed in FY 64.[2] The distribution of the average expenditure under these also appears to be log normal (Fig. 8).

IV. RESEARCH EXPENDITURES AND THE LOG-NORMAL DISTRIBUTION—A BEHAVIORAL COMMENT

It is interesting to consider the question of why the log-normal distribution should occur with such regularity as a feature of research cost analysis. There is, of course, a mechanistically obvious reason why these distributions should uniformly exhibit a positive skew. Costs are constrained to be greater than zero and less than some number that is quite large when compared to the average amount spent on any one work unit. But this mechanistic explanation of the positive skew is not particularly satisfying.

A number of interviews conducted with program and project directors who have the immediate responsibility of working with research performers revealed several behavioral phenomena, which are more or less obvious when taken separately, but which lead to the unobvious log-normal cost distributions when taken together.

1) An agency's research budget is apportioned on a more or less a priori basis, between the several major programs or basic science areas which are of interest to the agency. These funds are further allocated to projects or subsciences. This gives each of the project or subscience managers a pool of funds which he can then assign (or recommend for assignment) to specific research work units falling within his area of interest and competence.

2) Each of the research managers has a reasonably specific notion of what is an appropriate size of work unit in the areas he manages. While this notion does not impose a severe constraint on his funding behavior, it does provide him with a mental benchmark from which he deviates only for cause.

3) These benchmarks are usually known to scientists proposing to do research in the various programmatic and subscience areas. If they are not known in advance of submitting a proposal, conversation or correspondence with the project managers communicates them rather quickly.

4) The cost benchmarks differ markedly and characteristically for programmatic or scientific areas. While manpower costs are quite similar across fields, the costs of equipment typically associated with research in different scientific areas vary widely.

5) Program managers tend to adopt a philosophy that leads them to spread the risks—rather than to put "all their eggs in one basket." They have a strong preference in favor of funding several medium size or small projects rather than one or two large ones. If the project manager's cost benchmark is, for example, approximately $30 000, two $30 000 work units are considered preferable to one $60 000 work unit. Three $30 000 work units are strongly preferred to one $90 000 etc., unless there is an overriding reason to the contrary.

Clearly, the attitudes noted above will tend to produce cost distributions which exhibit positive skew when costs are collected within a scientific area, for a given programmatic area, or when the costs are categorized as basic or applied. The program manager's attitudes are reinforced by the behavior of scientists who "learn" rather quickly the cost benchmark characteristics of different funding agencies, scientific fields, and program managers.

While attitudes 1)–4) explain why the cost distribution is positively askewed, they do not explain why it fits a log-normal form so well. To explain the log-normal form, the authors suggest tentatively that the desire of program managers to spread their risks would tend to produce a log-normal distribution if the proper assumption about the relative undesirability of larger and larger research project costs is made.

Conclusions

From the materials presented above, it appears that the distribution of the costs of research projects tends to be log normal. Such a distribution is consistent with the observed behavior of those who fund research projects. In all cases considered, the data fit the log-normal distribution with a type-I risk of less than 1 percent.

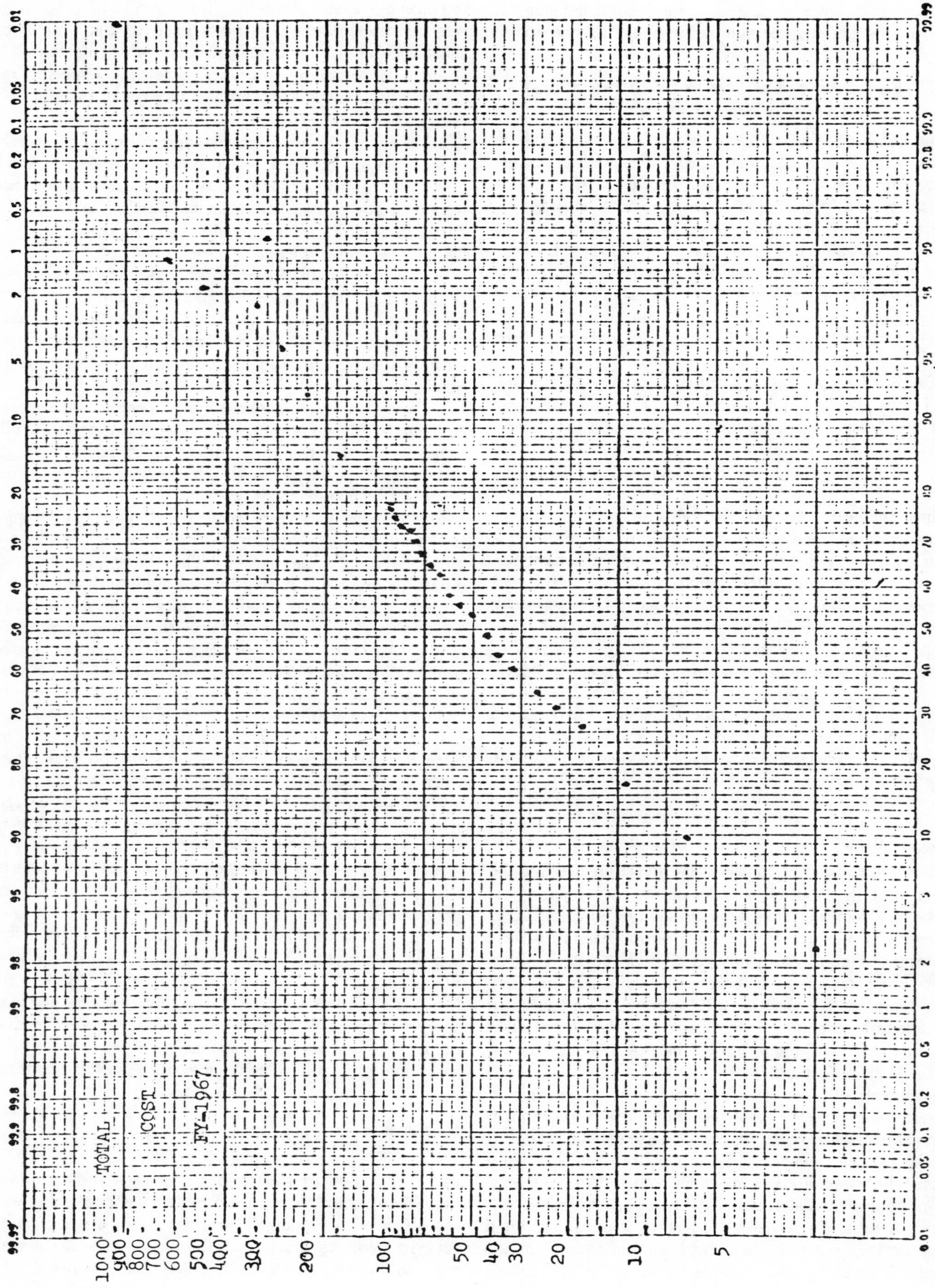

Fig. 4. Ocean science and technology division—cumulative probability.

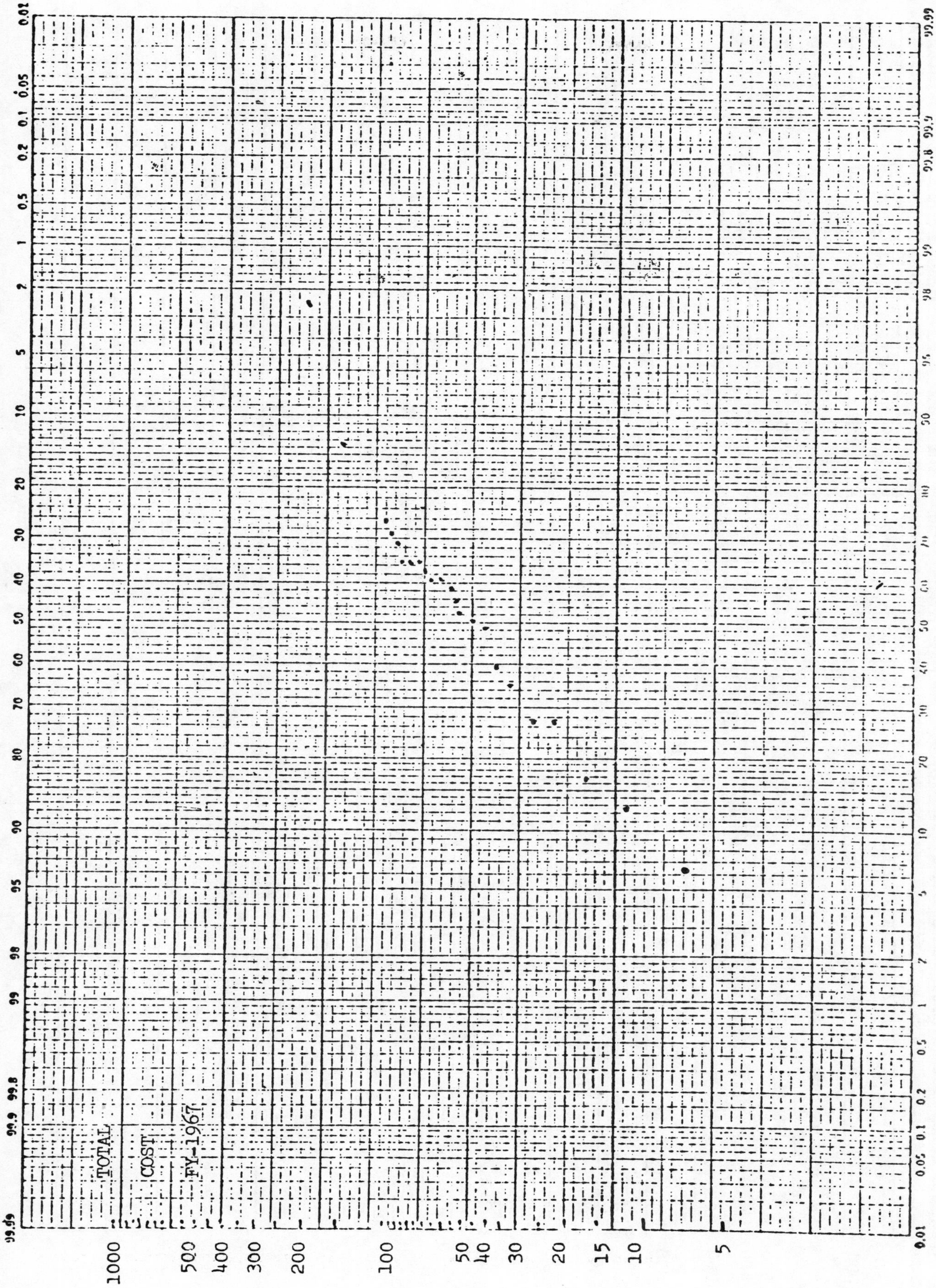

Fig. 5. Ocean science and technology division—cumulative probability.

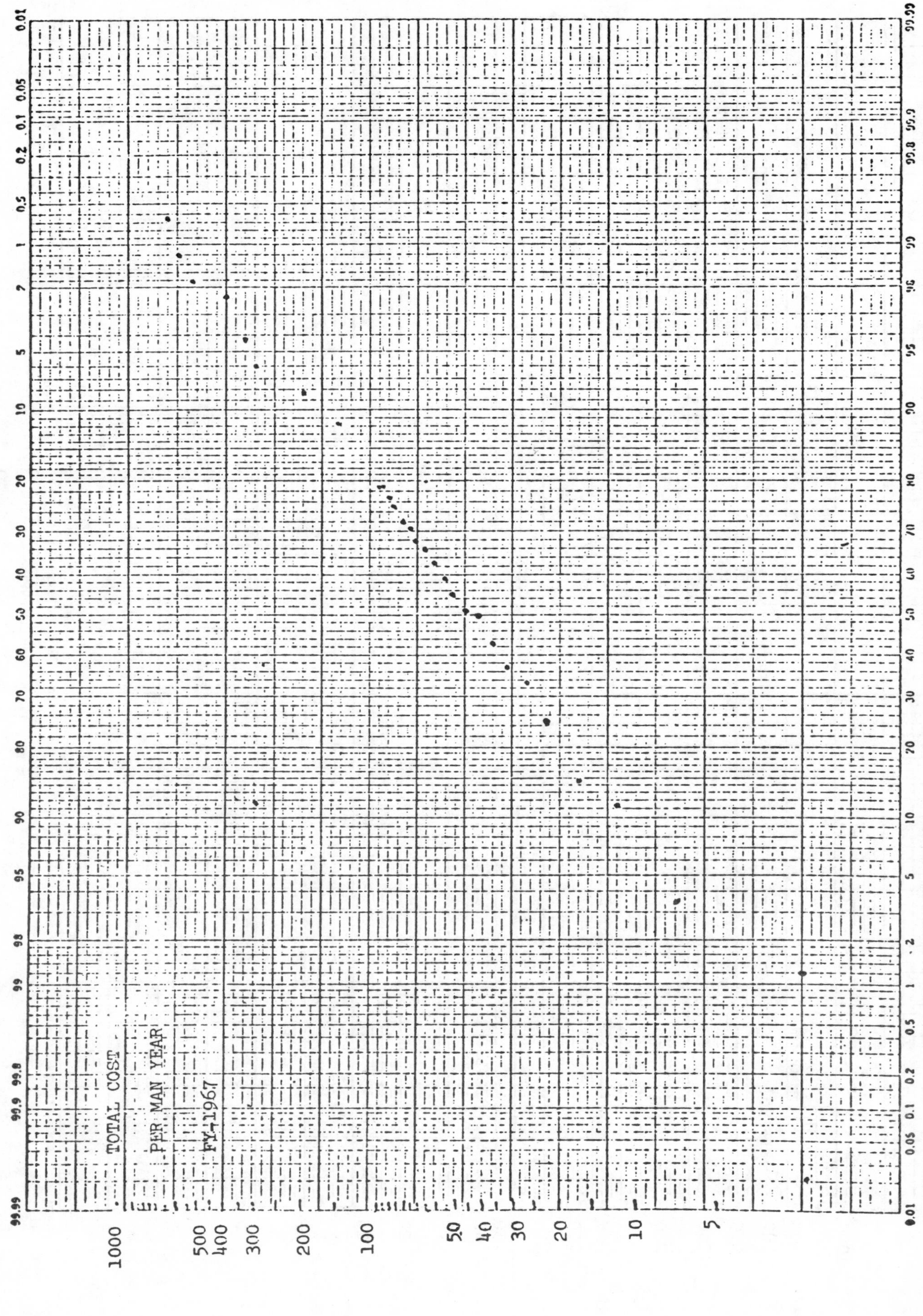

Fig. 6.   Physical oceanography subscience—cumulative probability.

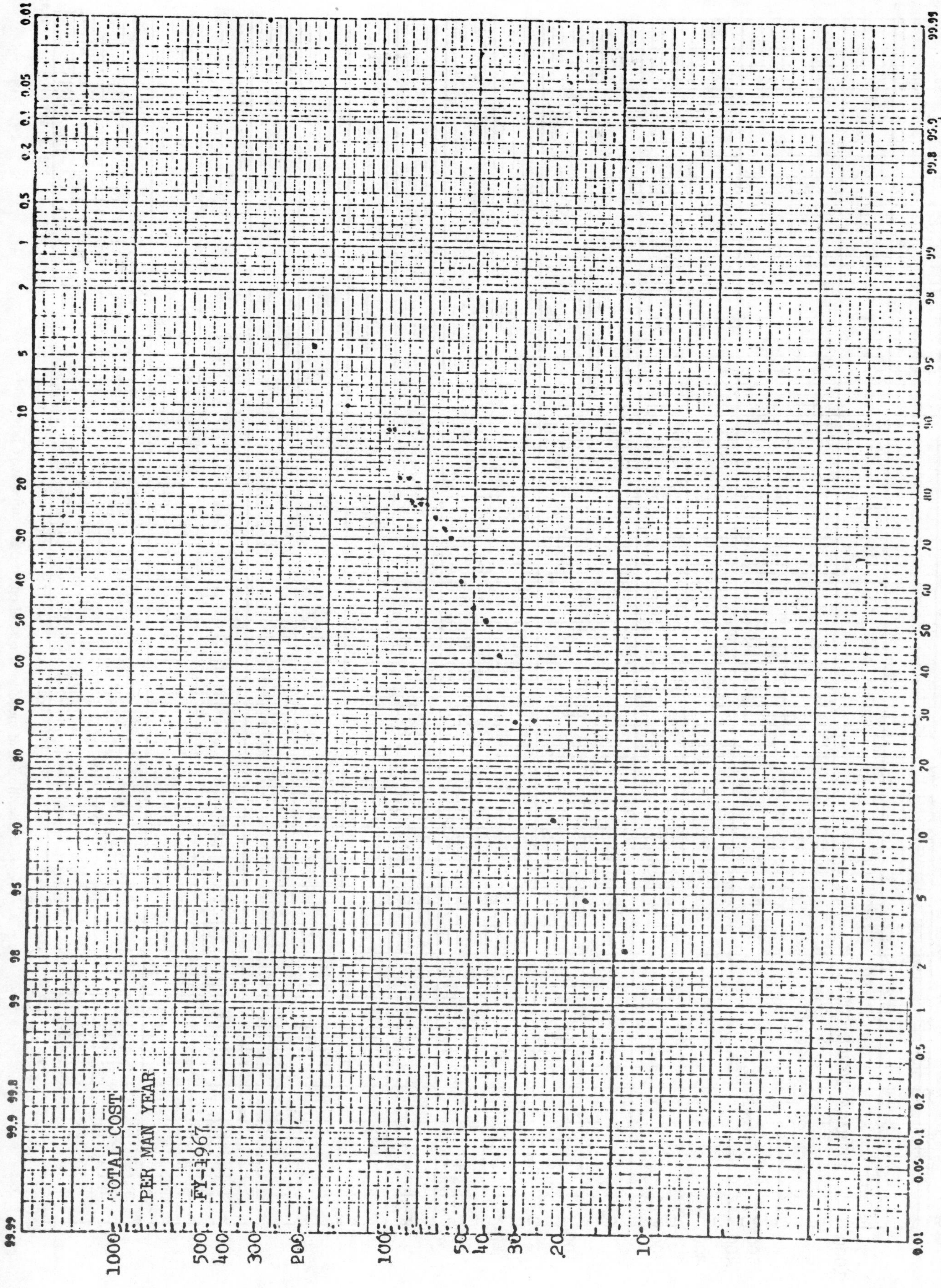

FIG. 7.   Physical oceanography subscience—cumulative probability.

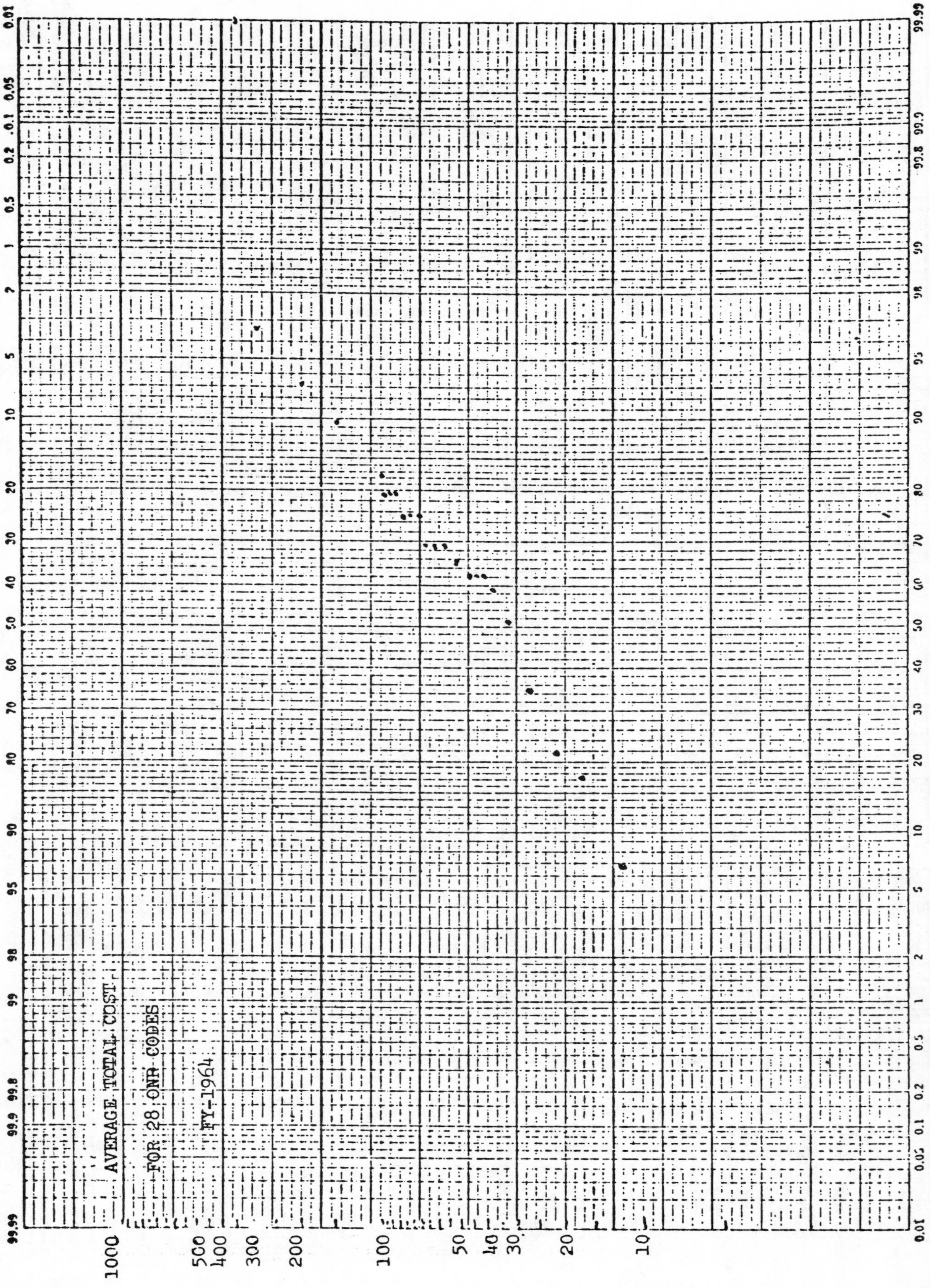

AVERAGE TOTAL COST

FOR 28 ONR CODES

FY-1964

Fig. 8.   Distribution of mean total cost of our codes—cumulative probability.

TABLE III
TRANSFER COEFFICIENTS FOR CATEGORY 1, ELEMENT 1

From	To Element 1 Task 1	Element 1 Task 2	Element 1 Task 3	Element 1 Task 4	Year	Definition
Element 1	8695 0.8678 0.8678	100 0.01 0.01	1170 0.1168 0.1168	55 0.0055 0.0055	1963	(1) (2) (3)
Element 1	8453 0.8453 0.8565	100 0.01 0.01	1392 0.1392 0.1280	55 0.0055 0.0055	1964	(1) (2) (3)
Element 1	9145 0.8239 0.8449	25 0.0023 0.0072	1780 0.1604 0.1395	150 0.0135 0.0084	1965	(1) (2) (3)
Element 1	8335 0.8172 0.8380	100 0.0098 0.0079	1695 0.1662 0.1461	70 0.0069 0.0080	1966	(1) (2) (3)
Element 1	8300 0.8137 0.8332	95 0.0093 0.0082	1560 0.1529 0.1475	245 0.0240 0.0112	1967	(1) (2) (3)
	0.7927 (0.0908)* 0.8218 (0.0582)	0.0078 (0.0042) 0.0069 (0.0040)	0.1769 (0.0675) 0.1594 (0.0529)	0.0226 (0.0262) 0.0118 (0.0092)	1968 Estimate	(2) * (3) *
	0.7791 (0.1161) 0.8131 (0.0744)	0.0077 (0.0054) 0.0063 (0.0051)	0.1868 (0.0863) 0.1674 (0.0677)	0.0264 (0.0336) 0.0132 (0.0118)	1969 Estimate	(2) * (3) *

* Figures in parentheses are standard deviations: (1) dollar value, (2) yearly transfer coefficient, (3) cumulative transfer coefficient. Totals may not add to 1 because of round-off error.

V. RESEARCH BUDGET FORECASTING

Budget Forecasting Model

The Army research budget supports numerous research programs and projects which may require funding over a period of years. It would be helpful to develop a method of forecasting the required funds for future programs and projects in a given time frame. The method employed here involves estimates of the transfer coefficients, where a transfer coefficient is the fraction of a total budget allocated to a particular line item.[1] Before defining the transfer coefficients and their estimation, we reiterate the Army budget classification.

The Army research budget is successively divided to form five distinct levels of classification. The levels of classification, from highest to lowest are called 1) categories; 2) program elements; 3) projects; 4) tasks; and 5) work units. The interrelation of these classifications for a given set of research programs may be conveniently represented in a diagram as a tree, spreading from left to right. The highest level, or left-most node of the tree, represents the total, and the right-most branch ends represent the lowest classification or level, i.e., work units. Assume that each work unit has been allocated some fixed amount of funds. Then moving down the tree (moving to the left) to the task nodes, one can determine the amount of funds allocated to the tasks. The task allocations are the sum of the alloca-tions to the work units which can be researched from the particular task node. Similarly, the allocation to a project is determined by summing the funds allocated to tasks whose nodes can be reached from the project node, and so on down the tree.

Transfer Coefficients

A transfer coefficient is a fraction assigned to a work unit, task, project, or program element such that when multiplied by the budget of the next higher level item, the resulting product is the budget for the respective work unit, task, project, or program element. In this model, categories are considered separately and transfer coefficients are defined only for levels 2)–5). Further, transfer coefficients are defined only for adjacent levels. For example, the coefficient relating say work unit m to program element k is not explicitly defined. The above coefficients are called "yearly transfer coefficients" in this report.

Another coefficient called "cumulative transfer coefficients" is used, where the cumulative transfer coefficient is the fraction of the accumulated expenditures over more than one year.

Prediction

Under the Department of Defense Program Budgeting System, the Army is required to forecast detailed

TABLE IV

TRANSFER COEFFICIENTS FOR CATEGORY 1, ELEMENT 2 TO 14 PROJECTS

From		1	2	3	4	5	6	7	8	9	10	11	12	13	14	Year	Definition
		0.3069	0	0	0.0568	0.0847	0.0325	0.0900	0	0.0232	0.0688	0	0.3180	0.0191	0	1963	(2)*
		18578	0	0	3437	5127	1469	5448		1405	4163		19254	1158			(1)
		0.0888	0.0015	0.0614	0.0664	0.1296	0.0736	0.1183	0.0206	0.0242	0.0775	0.0003	0.3190	0.0184	0	1964	(2)
		5713	96	3948	4273	8340	4733	7612	1324	1559	4985	20	20529	1215			(1)
		0.0881	0.0042	0.0699	0.0661	0.1292	0.0871	0.1220	0.0205	0.0264	0.0736	0	0.2897	0.0232	0	1965	(2)
		6018	285	4775	4518	8827	5951	8340	1404	1802	5032		19801	1587			(1)
		0.0920	0	0.0658	0.0698	0.1343	0.0907	0.1228	0.0178	0.0264	0.0738	0	0.2905	0.0161	0	1966	(2)
		6207	0	4441	4712	9063	6120	8288	1200	1782	4977		14598	1085			(1)
		0.0830	0	0.0573	0.0626	0.1238	0.0787	0.1180	0.0198	0.0221	0.0640	0.0003	0.2742	0.0218	0.0744	1967	(2)
		6132	0	4236	4624	9148	5817	8720	1461	1633	4727	21	20263	1611	5500		(1)
Element 2		0.0016	0.0001	0.0596	0.0689	0.1452	0.1054	0.1324	0.0184	0.0245	0.0675	0.0001	0.2634	0.0206	NA	1968 (3)	linear
		0.0058	0.0067	0.0670	0.0763	0.1526	0.1128	0.1398	0.0258	0.0319	0.0750	0.0076	0.2709	0.0280	NA	1968 (3)	linear adjusted
		0.2098	0.0041	0.0383	0.0540	0.0926	0.0414	0.0978	0.0209	0.0181	0.0510	0.0009	0.2612	0.0208	NA	1968 (3)	quadratic
		0.2168	0.0029	0.0453	0.0610	0.0996	0.0544	0.1048	0.0279	0.0251	0.0580	0.0079	0.2682	0.0278	NA	1968 (3)	quadratic adjusted

Column group heading: **To** (columns 1–14).

* Figures in parentheses are standard deviations: (1) dollar value, (2) yearly transfer coefficient, (3) estimate.

TABLE V
SAMPLE TABLE OF COEFFICIENTS OF CATEGORY 2—1967 UNADJUSTED LINEAR YEARLY TRANSFER COEFFICIENTS

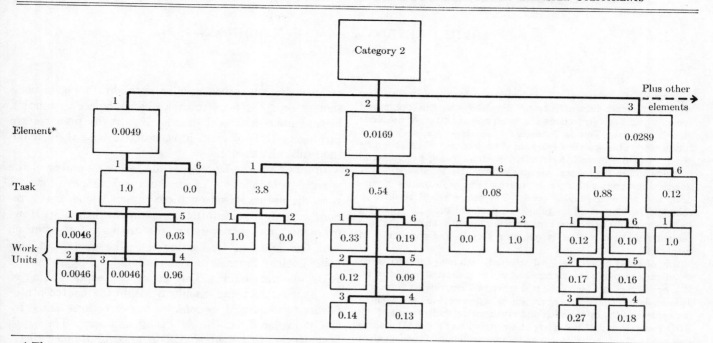

* There are no "projects" in this set of elements. Coefficients may not sum to 1 because of round-off error.

research budgets down to and including the work unit level for five years in advance. It has been shown that the detailed budget for year t can be forecast, provided that we have a set of estimated transfer coefficients. The method employed in this paper to estimate the transfer cofficients is the method of least square curve fitting.

Budget data for expenditures have been collected for the five fiscal years 1963–1967 and least square curves have been derived. The data indicate that the transfer coefficients, both yearly and cumulative, tend to be quite stable over time.

In Tables III–V transfer coefficients are shown for category 1, element 1 by both yearly and cumulative coefficients base on linear fits. In addition, coefficients are shown for category 1, element 2 fund transfers to 14 projects. Finally, a chart is drawn of unadjusted linear element transfer coefficients for category 2. This chart shows the "funding tree" from work units to tasks to elements to categories. (Only 3 of 29 elements have been shown in order to conserve space).

VI. AREAS FOR ADDITIONAL RESEARCH IN BUDGET FORECASTING

At the present time the confidence limits for the transfer coefficient curves are not determined in either the linear-adjusted or quadratic-adjusted cases. Though the confidence limits for least square curves have been derived, the necessary curve adjustments made to meet the constraints introduces an additional error term in the estimate of the curve variance. Therefore, the usual confidence limit equations do not hold in this case.

Further, the additional error term is certainly a function of the method of adjustment and it may be true that some other method of adjustment is more appropriate. The program does not presently force the curves through the points 0 and 1, through which points they should pass in theory. (This latter restriction should cause no trouble in this particular application.)

An alternate approach to the adjustment problem is to formulate the transfer coefficient as a constrained optimization problem to be solved using quadratic programming. Even here, however, the problem of confidence limits remains. It appears that the most appropriate method is to derive the confidence limit equations for the various adjustment methods and employ that adjustment method that yields the narrowest limits.

The program as written could be reduced quite significantly once a particular model was selected. At the present the program generates four models, two models using the yearly transfer coefficients (one linear and one quadratic), and two models using the cumulative transfer coefficients (one linear and one quadratic). Beside the reduction of the present program, additional features may be incorporated. Two such features that appear most appropriate are a routine to generate actual budget forecasts, given a total budget for year t, and a routine to order unsorted input data.

ACKNOWLEDGMENT

The authors wish to acknowledge the contributions of Mary Green and J. Svestka to this paper and thank them for their general critique of the method.

Technological Forecasting in a Dynamic Environment

MARVIN J. CETRON AND JACOB N. JOHNSON

Abstract—Government and industry are developing many new ways to forecast future technical developments, but the payoff comes when these projections are incorporated as part of the R&D planning process. This is done on two levels—when deciding on future work in a specific development project and when assigning priorities to the overall R&D effort. Systems being developed in industry and in the federal government are able to integrate technological forecasts with data on future needs, probabilities of success, and potential funding levels. The computerized result is a complete ranking of all on-going and potential projects according to their overall worth. But care must be taken to ensure that the computer printout retains its role as a servant and not a ruler of managers.

One of many normative (goal-oriented) technological forecasting techniques currently being examined will be discussed in this paper. It is hoped that this technique will serve two interrelated purposes: 1) to explore the structure of project-selection decision problems in the context of the information and organization environment of the R&D manager and 2) to explore characteristics of the R&D process that are relevant to the design and implementation of management system for planning and controlling resource allocation among various R&D projects.

Background

OVER the past five years, both government and industry have become fascinated with the potential of technological forecasting as an aid in planning R&D budgets [3], [6], [11]. As laboratories expanded and budgets grew, managers found that many of the traditional ways of allocating their resources of men and money seemed inadequate. But most attempts to build better allocation systems foundered on the following two basic questions. Which research areas are most likely to be the source of significant technical breakthroughs? Which breakthroughs are most likely to bring an important new development?

The realization that technological forecasting methods could help answer these questions was catching hold slowly when many R&D planners were rudely shaken by a new reality—a leveling off or even a cutback in most government-sponsored research efforts. With the NASA post-Apollo projects whittled back, the United States Department of Defense (DOD) research budgets cut

Manuscript received July 1969; revised August 1969. This paper was prepared originally for presentation to the International Conference of the Institute of Management Science (TIMS) and appeared in *Technological Forecasting: A Practical Approach*, M. J. Cetron. New York: Gordon and Breach, 1969, ch. VIII.

M. J. Cetron is with the Headquarters Naval Materiel Command, Exploratory Development Division, Washington, D. C.

J. N. Johnson is with the Synergistic Cybernetics Inc., Alexandria, Va.

extensively, and other usually expanding budgets on a shorter rein, the need to make hard choices in funding became more critical than ever. Now many planners are turning to technological forecasting to help them make their difficult selections.

In many previous presentations, a large number of the specific techniques used to make a technological forecast were discussed. Based on these presentations, many requests for further information were forthcoming. However, most requests were not for further information on how technological forecasting could be made, but how technological forecasts once made could be integrated into R&D planning efforts. This paper will explain some of the approaches being examined within the United States government as well as some of the directions being actively explored in United States industry. The truth is, however, this field is still in an evolutionary phase and most work now being done in one organization cannot be modified enough for adoption in others. At best, what is being done can provide many helpful hints for planners grappling with their own problem of using technological forecasts in allocation problems [4], [5].

It is vital to remember that a technological forecast is not a picture of what the future will bring. Instead, it is a prediction with a level of confidence in a given time frame of a technical achievement that could be expected for a given level of budgetary and manpower support.

The tenet underlying technological forecasting is that individual R&D events are susceptible to influence. The times at which they occur, if they can occur at all, can be modulated significantly by regulating the resources allocated to them. Another basic tenet of technological forecasting is that many futures are possible and that the paths toward these futures can be *mapped* [7].

In use, a technological forecast can be looked at from two vantage points. One, in the present, gives the forecast user a view that shows the path that technological progress will probably take if it is not consciously influenced. In addition, the user will see critical branch points in the road—the situation where alternative futures are possible. He will also gain a greater understanding of the price of admission to those branching paths.

The second vantage point is in the future. The user selects or postulates a technical situation he desires. Looking backward from the point, he can then discern the obstacles that must be overcome to achieve the result he wants. Once again, he is brought up against the hard realities of what he must do to achieve a desired result. As one user has said, "The process substitutes forecasting for forecrastination."

MAKING BASIC FORECASTS

At this point, it is worth reviewing some of the basics of making technological forecasts. This idea is not new. Leonardo da Vinci is probably the prime example of the scientific and technical forecaster whose knowledge and imagaination enabled him to foresee many developments far in the future. Science fiction writers from Jules Verne to Arthur Clarke have also peered into the future, often with great success [7]. As long as one remains within the general bounds of knowing natural laws, he is safe in forecasting almost any technical achievement and enjoying some success. But a highly developed imagination offers little help for the technological planner—the odds are not good enough.

To reduce the odds, most technological forecasts today fall into four categories: intuitive, trend extrapolating, trend correlating, and growth analogy [11].

In intuitive forecasting, an individual may make an educated guess, or he may call on polls or panels of experts for advice. A technique that promises to produce more objective intuitive forecasts is the *Delphi* method, developed by Helmer of the RAND Corporation. In one version, a group of experts in a chosen field might be asked to name technical breakthroughs or inventions urgently needed and realizable within the next 50 years. The experts are polled by written questionnaires, eliminating the open debate generally found in panel decision making. As a result, the influence of certain psychological factors is reduced—a persuasive speaker, unwillingness to abandon publicly expressed opinions, or the bandwagon effect of majority opinion. In a second round of questionnaires, participants are asked to give a time scale for achieving each of the items selected. They are also asked the reasons for their earlier opinions. These data are correlated and fed back to each with a request that he reconsider his earlier beliefs and submit new estimates. The result is usually some sort of a consensus [12].

The strength or weakness of Delphi or other polling systems rests upon the knowledge or intuition of selected experts. It assumes that the consensus estimate is generally correct without an examination of basic data. Most other forecasting methods are tied directly to basic technical data. The *trend-extrapolation technique,* for example, is based on two fundamental assumptions: 1) the forces that created the prior pattern of progress are more likely to continue than to change; 2) the combined effect of these forces is more likely to extend the previous pattern of progress than it is to produce a different pattern.

One difficulty in using this technique, however, is that the longer the period of the forecast, the greater the probability that one or more of the assumptions made will become invalid. The yield strength of a material, for example, will go up as its density is increased, but there is a theoretical limit.

The *trend-correlation method,* on the other hand, uses two or more identifiable trends in a technical field and tries to determine the probable relationship of one to the other. Plotting the speeds of military and transport aircraft indicates that the transports lag by a predictable amount. Therefore, looking at current or future military aircraft gives a good insight into the future of airliners.

Finally, forecasting by *growth analogies* recognizes that progress in a specific technical development has an exponential characteristic initially, then changes its slope and tapers off toward a horizontal asymptote. This approach, however, is good only for a short term—ten years at the most. In many cases, a new development will take over the improvement rate as the old one is running out of steam. Mercury vapor lamps, for example, started improving dramatically just as incandescent lighting had reached its limit.

The four techniques discussed have one common aspect. They all depend on historical data and projection. There is no provision in them for the systematic introduction of management plans and actions. To take these into account, the forecaster must still rely on intuitive judgment. Newer and more sophisticated attempts at forecasting, however, include a systems analysis and a mathematical-modeling approach. Basic to these methods is the interaction of human awareness of economic, social, and geopolitical needs with the technical state of the art. The technical inputs are formulated by methods like those mentioned above, but they are then examined for nontechnical feasibility.

PUTTING FORECASTS TO WORK

In most cases, a manager does not have a total system with which to work. Instead, he has the results of trend extrapolations or other regular technological forecasting projections. How does he use these data? While there are many approaches, the following is one which the Navy Department is examining to determine which techniques can best help decide which R&D projects to fund.

We begin with a technical planning flow chart (Fig. 1) that shows the "shredding out" of some of the bits and pieces that comprise the construction of a sea floor site. Assume that we have a technological forecast for each and every parameter of the shred out. The forecasts, at each level of the breakdown, are the probable paths that various technologies will take. Armed with this type data, a meaningful discourse can ensue between the user and producer. For a given set of operational requirements and performance characteristics called for by the user, the technical planners can respond with data that tell the user by what alternative means his needs can be satisfied, and when he can expect these to be accomp-

CONSTRUCTIONAL OBJECTIVE

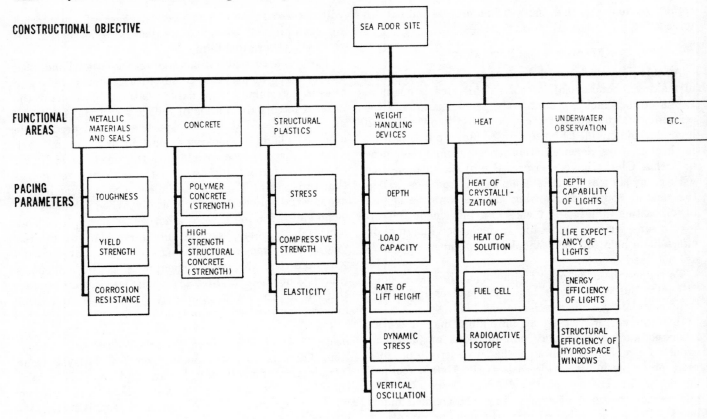

Fig. 1.   Technical planning flow chart.

lished. Many of the trade offs—between metals, plastics, and glass, for example—become clear.

Construction officers, however, are not usually quite so acquiescent in accepting what a planner sees ahead. When faced with a military threat, or an anticipated threat, they want an effective answer to that threat by a specified date. The same holds true if they wish to create a new force of their own. In these situations, planners are taking a vantage point at some time in the future and are trying to discover if they will have the technology they need by that time. Quite likely, an examination of the technological forecasts to that point in time will reveal that the users are not likely to get what they want. Now, this is useful information in itself, and represents an approach that is not yet widely used in industry.

However, this view of the technological forecasting task is not the only one. There is the question of which path we should take to achieve a desired result. By deciding on our needs in the future and looking at the forecasts, we can spot the principal obstacles standing in our way, and the magnitude of those obstacles. The inference is clear; if the given goal is to be achieved in a given time the efforts must be applied in the areas containing the major obstacles. Or, we can settle for something less with clear knowledge of what that something less will be. Often, this analysis will show that two or more paths may be taken to achieve the needed or acceptable capabilities. The point here is that an environment of flexible choice is engendered—choices of which

the user was not previously aware. A truly comprehensive technological forecast is backed up not only by material and data that were used in generating the specific forecasts, but also by supplementary analysis of various subfactors that could influence each technological forecast. Forecasts like these help indicate the future posture of an enemy or competitor. While you do not know what he *will* do, you at least have a better idea of what he *could* or *could not* do.

MECHANICS OF DECISION MAKING

Now let us turn to an example and see how a specific decision can be analyzed, based on some technological forecasts generated by the Naval Civil Engineering Laboratory [15]. Forecasts for metallic materials and seals are given in terms of toughness, yield strength, and corrosion resistance. The next consideration might take us into the area of concrete and ultimate concrete strengths for, say, structural concrete versus polymer concrete, or possibly plastic composites. We also might want to consider forecasts of weight-handling devices, heating for sea floor sites, and underwater observations. Each of these functional considerations key into the total sea floor site construction problem, in the same manner that each of the pacing parameters key into each functional area. In this fashion we can work our way through the chart (Fig. 1), eventually going into any degree of detail or considering as many functional areas as we wish.

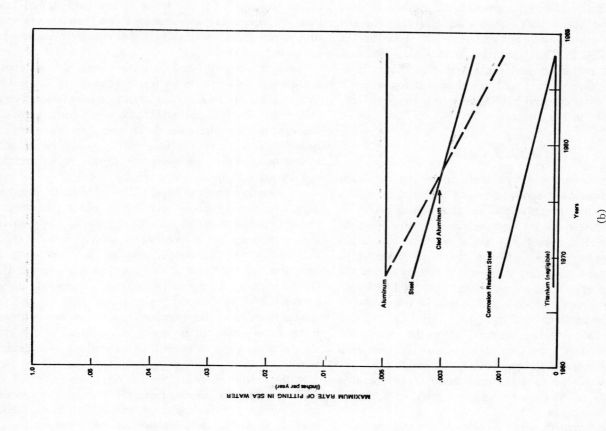

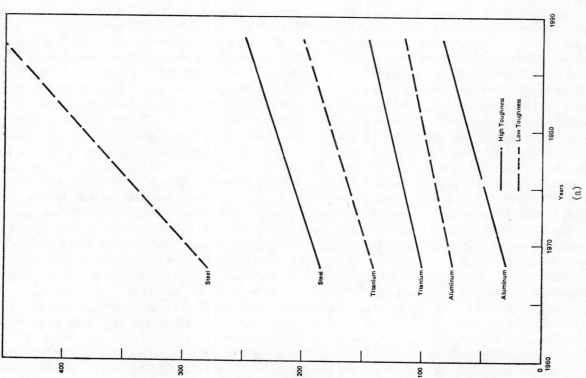

Fig. 2.   Parametric forecasts of metallic materials. (a) NASL forecast of strength of ship structural materials. (b) NASL forecast of corrosion resistance of ship structural materials.

This information is used for very practical decisions. For instance the pacing parameters of toughness, yield strength, and corrosion resistance are forecast for the functional metallic materials and seals are shown in the graphs of Fig. 2. The complete technological forecast on metallic materials and seals and five other functional areas covered in Fig. 1 are shown in Appendix I. All the materials covered in the Navy technological forecast are shown in Fig. 16.

THE OVERALL PICTURE

Up to this point we have been discussing the technological forecasting needed for one problem in a laboratory. But any organization has many such problems [13]. Here the question becomes one of allocation of resources of men, money, and materials. The evaluation scene, therefore, shifts from the technical specialist to the department manager, the head of research, and the overall planners. The forecast data must be fitted into their overall planning approach if it is to be really useful.

When management problems are simple, a decision maker can examine the various factors he must consider with relative ease. One man, such as the hermit in a cave, the individual homeowner, the small businessman, or the teacher in a one-room school, may be able to interrelate all of the necessary information and succeed in his endeavors.

As the management scope becomes larger and the complexity of problems increases, more and different factors must be considered to reach a decision. Soon, staff and management procedures are needed to assist in all phases of management. Eventually, the point is reached where any one decision affects many facets of the operation; all efforts become interrelated to an alarming degree.

Increasing complexities are particularly true with programs or projects that must operate under a fixed government or corporation resource ceiling. Choices must be made on alternative approaches, specifically, which efforts should proceed and which should be dropped or delayed. Since numerous efforts are interrelated in time, resources required, purpose and possible technical transfer one to another, choices must be made with consideration of the total effect. Whether he be a manufacturer, a service industry director, government administrator, or university professor, every manager seeks the greatest payoff for resource investments.

What alternatives does a manager have for developing resource-allocation approaches? The resource-allocation problem is usually too big to keep in one man's head and often inputs come from levels completely outside of his control. Hundreds of inputs can be involved when the alternatives are examined in depth.

A familiar resource-allocation approach is termed the *squeaking-wheel* process. One can cut resources from every area (one can be sophisticated and cut some areas more than others) then wait and see which area complains the most. On the basis of the loudest and most insistent squeaking, the manager can then restore some of the resources previously withdrawn until he reaches his ceiling budget.

Another common approach develops the minimum noise level and results in fewer squeaks by allocating this year's resources in just about the same manner as last year. The budget perturbations are minimized and the status quo maintained. If this *level-funding* approach is continued very long within a rapidly changing technological field, the company, group, or government agency will end up in serious trouble.

An effortless version of the preservation of management security approach to resource allocation seeks to perpetuate the *glorious past*. Last year, or the year before, or perhaps several years ago, a division or organization had a very successful project, therefore why not fund the unit for the next five years on any projects that they advocate? The premise is "once successful, always successful." This method really means that no analysis should be made of the proposed project or its usefulness; instead, projects will be assigned resources solely upon the basis of past record of an individual or organization.

Still another way to allocate resources is called the *white charger* technique. Here the various departments come dashing into top management with multicolor graphs, handouts, and well-rehearsed presentations. If they impress the decision maker, they are rewarded with increased resources. Often the best speaker or the last man to brief the boss wins the treasure [2].

Finally, consider the *committee approach,* which frees the manager from resource-allocation decisions. The committees tell the manager to increase, decrease, or leave all allocations as they are. A common danger is that the committee may not have enough actual experience in the organization or sufficient information upon which to base its recommendations. If the committee is ad hoc or from outside the organization, the members can also avoid responsibility in not having to live through the risky process of implementing their recommendations.

Obviously, the described allocation methods are neither scientific nor objective, though they are utilized quite extensively. These naive approaches point up the need of the manager and his staff for an aid to bring information into a form upon which judgment may be applied. It is a common experience for an organization to have numerous reports on specific technical subjects that recommend increased resources for the particular area. But the direct use of this data only compounds the manager's problem when he tries to allocate resources among the many technical areas. If he is operating under a fixed budget ceiling, to increase funding for one technical area requires that either one or more technical areas must be correspondingly decreased.

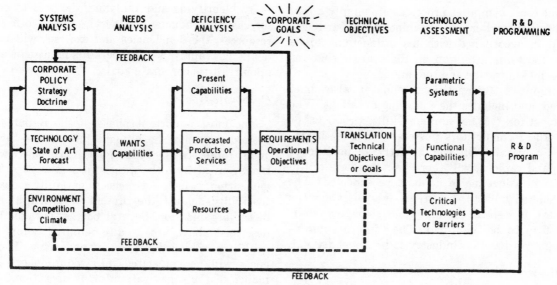

Fig. 3.   Long-range R&D planning.

TECHNOLOGICAL RESOURCE-ALLOCATION SYSTEM

A more sophisticated alternative approach involves the use of staff or specialists in operations research. Information they assemble can be used to significantly assist managerial judgment. This is the point where quantitative evaluation techniques enter the picture. Each major aspect of a program can be examined, first separately and then as it is interrelated to competing factors. Items such as timeliness, cost utility or payoff, confidence level or risk, personnel, facilities, etc., can be evaluated by specialists in each field and the total picture made available as a basis for decision. Greater payoff areas can be identified and problems can be highlighted. Inputs can be accurately recorded, made clearly visible and analyzed for assisting the final decision.

The use of quantitative techniques permits input factors and possible outcome to be reexamined readily and different managerial emphasis applied. The manager can still hedge his "allocation selections" by allocating resources through such criteria as increased resources to previously successful groups, backing a high-risk effort, i.e., a high-cost project with slim chances of success that might yield gigantic results. The decision maker can incorporate any desired additional criteria, such as the politics of selection, competitive factors, or technological barriers.

The question now becomes one of allocation of the resources of men, money, and materials. Fig. 3, the long-range planning diagram, which is really a broad allocation diagram, shows the interactions of numerous managers from the technical specialist to the department manager, the head of research, and the corporate planners. The data must be fitted into an overall planning approach if it is to be really useful. Corporate goals are the main topic and occupy the central position in the chart. In order to establish corporate goals, the preliminary steps of systems analysis, needs analysis, and deficiency analysis must be accomplished. After the goals and technical objectives are established, technology assessment and R&D programming take place to complete the R&D resource-allocation process. Each of these steps will be explained in greater depth.

Systems Analysis

Corporate policy must be considered. It involves philosophic and strategy questions, including the following. Shall I be the industry leader? Shall I keep abreast of the industry technically and see if a major market develops? In the overall environment competitors' actions must be followed closely, but there are other factors such as interest rates, business expectation, economic forecasts, etc. to be identified [1]. Fig. 3, viewed as the corporate planning chart, shows a recommended organization of considerations.

The technology forecasting element acts as a catalyst in setting and implementing overall corporate goals. At present, only a handful of the largest corporations are really utilizing their full corporate technical potential. The next question is: How to relate the technological forecasts with appraisal in this total picture? A discussion of the numerous appraisal methods would be a long story in itself. For example, all systems employed by the Department of Defense utilize three major factors in the appraisal or normative forecasting process—military utility, technical feasibility, financial acceptability. Each of these factors is amenable to quantification, and can be fitted into a model that compares the value of each component, project, or system. Due to the complexity of the analysis, it is necessary to program the job on a computer to get usable information quickly. It must be remembered, however, that these computer processes are simply a tool to aid the decision maker; the machine merely arranges the material in accordance with his instructions so he can quickly focus his attention on those areas that require his special knowledge and judgment.

The environment (competition, climate) also must be considered, and includes the following questions. Who are the competitors? What unique skills, products, or finances do these competitors possess? What is the industry-wide climate? Will the industry demand continue to expand rapidly, will there be a sudden drop in demand, or will a leveling of demand be expected? The factors considered under the systems analysis allow the needs (wants) as well as the unique or strong capabilities of the firm to be identified. The "future environment" for the construction industry is in Appendix VII.

Needs Analysis

Analysis of the wants or desirable areas of growth for the firm is equally as important as defining the areas where no growth or decline is expected. The national or international economy provides the broadest scope for analysis of the needs for the firm's products or services. The stage of development in the country, the requirements from related industries, the availability and cost of capital and governmental controls may all require attention for the process of determining what the firm "wants" to do.

The industry share of the market for the firm relates directly to its volume. That is, in an industry of rapid growth the individual firm may grow while remaining constant relative to its competitors. Conversely, the share of the market may need to be greatly increased to remain at a level stage in a declining industry.

Finally, the desire of the firm and of the individual groups within the firm can be assessed. However, these desires may not be attainable within the capability of the firm. Thus, the wants need to be balanced against the capabilities.

Deficiency Analysis

After the wants of the organization have been established, the capabilities available must be delineated in order that areas of deficiency can be identified. Ordinarily, the present capabilities of an organization will be known, but often effort is required by management to obtain a comprehensive statement of its technological capabilities in terms of men, money, and machines. Because we are dealing with futures, the products and services such as new manufacturing methods, new materials, and advanced skills that are forecasted to be available must also be carefully identified. Other resources available to the organization will also be important information. Skills or manufacturing processes or equipment, etc. may exist that could be available from outside the organization when and if required.

By identifying and analyzing the present capabilities, forecasted products and services, and other available resources, the deficiencies and excesses will become evident. The analysis now permits management to focus upon realistic corporate goals.

Corporate Goals

The most important phase of the resource-allocation system may now be brought into focus—the corporate goals (objectives). These goals may be viewed by top management from the wants (desires or needs) of the organization, which have been carefully considered for feasibility against the present or potential capabilities of the organization. Several passes through the analysis described above are usually required before acceptable goals are achieved by top management. The corporate goals will be translated into requirements for performance of the organization, or as operational objectives.

Technical Objectives

The idea of applying quantitative approaches to resource allocation has too long been suspect by management. Currently, both industry and government are seeking tangible improvements in the results from use of available resources. Economy drives and/or cost/benefit analyses have resulted in pared budgets with the need more critical than ever to make hard choices among alternative programs. The application of objective measurements to resource assignments has too long been classified as visionary and impractical. For example, how does a corporation decide whether its allocation this year for research and technology is adequate? How does it decide the right balance between the research and development or manufacturing projects?

A prime example of lack of quantitative data exists in the area of assessing technological effort. Querying the scientist or engineer and requesting a justification of his selection of a program or a task (including projected benefits to a mission or product-oriented organization) has often been construed as an assault against the scientific professionals' prestige and prerogatives. Today, scientists and engineers are beginning to realize that they are accepted at the highest organization levels and that one of the signs of this ascendancy is their high visibility and responsibility to the interrogation of criteria and rational judgments. The technical managers' intuition can no longer be accepted as infallible and beyond managerial review [2].

Several project-evaluation and selection techniques have as their basis a belief in the efficacy and acceptance of Bayesian statistics and theories of probability [4], [5], [13]. Bayesians believe that it is correct to quantify feelings about uncertainty in terms of subjectively assessed numerical probabilities. Thus, assessments are made of probabilities for events that determine the profitability or utility of alternative actions open to the decision maker.

For example, there is a necessity to assess the criterion of whether a piece of research is technically feasible (technological forecasts) or what the probability is that it will be successfully accomplished (level-of-confidence criterion). Bayesian theory believes that it is possible for an "expert" in the field being assessed to assign a figure of merit or "subjective" probability number that the event will actually occur. This theory states that on this very subject matter an expert can assign a "subjective" probability number from a scale, for example, between 0 and 10. Men of considerable experience in a field usually have no difficulty in utilizing a Bayesian probability scale. In a like manner, other criteria, such as the utility of the research to the objectives of the organization, or relevance to desired priority systems or corporation products, are assessed (criterion of utility).

The use of Bayesian subjective probabilities makes feasible the incorporation into the decision process, in a formal and visible way, many of the subjective and objective criteria and variables previously taken into account by the decision maker informally and without visibility.

The probability assignment, a number between 0 and 10 to each facet, factor, criterion, or parameter inherent to a rational decision, reflects the degree of belief held by the individual expert(s) that the above objective will be met.

Thus, the experience, knowledge of the subject, and judgment of the various experts are summarized by the subjective probabilities that they assign against the respective criteria. The final or top decision maker then has a clear view of the alternatives and can use the results of the probability assignments of the different experts. A computer can be used to summarize the choices or probabilities of the experts. The computer can also be used to determine "consequences" if the probability assignments are changed, or if the final decision maker adds new information or weighting factors, etc.

Advocates of allocation and selection procedures are accused of assuming that the myriad of quantitative estimates of scientific relevance, importance, feasibility, etc. can be collected and manipulated [14]. Apparently the academic community also believes in the above assumption. For example, in the field of education, the university admission policy is based on a "myriad of quantitative estimates."

R. Freshman, one of the U. S. Air Force Laboratory planners who was previously a professional educator, relates the following example [2]. High school students are admitted to universities based on the quantitative judgments of teacher grades as the key criterion. These teachers grade about 5 subjects a year, for 4 years of high school—thus, 20 teacher judgments. Different teachers, different subjects, different tests, different subject matter taken in high schools throughout the nation, are fused into one. Teacher opinions on how to grade, biases and prejudgments, oral recitations, grades on nonstandardized unstructured subject matter, and tests are all injected into the above conglomeration to form the individual teacher's final grade in one subject. High school grades for the four years are averaged to come up with one number—the high school average—the *magic number,* which has great influence in college admission. More miraculous is that there is a good positive correlation between this magic number and success in college. It is recognized that this "quantitative estimate" of many judgments is the best single criterion or indicator of success in *college;* but again, it is just an aid to the decision maker. The personal interview, college boards, or extra curricular activities also affect his judgment prior to making a final decision.

Opinions and judgments can be and should be weighed by every decision maker in his final decision. Several quantitative techniques gather and summarize the opinions and judgments to enable the final decision maker (like the university dean of admissions utilizing teacher judgments) to visualize and weigh, as one input to his decision, the judgments of numerous people on diverse factors.

Two main points on quantitative decision making should be emphasized.

1) The quantitative management techniques discussed *do not make decisions,* but provide a basis of information upon which decisions can be made.
2) A validity check cannot be made since once the resources are allocated, the plan becomes self-fulfilling.

Technology Assessment or Subsystem Analysis

Assessment of technology or subsystem analysis is employed to answer the question: Which, when, and how many resources should be allocated among the alternative projects? Since the topic is multifaceted, it is necessary to draw information from a variety of sources including operations research, project-selection techniques, and technological forecasting.

Technology assessment is not official jargon. The expression "assessment of technology" is not found listed in the tables of contents or indexes of texts on management. Nor is it identified and found in the general literature of management or in official planning, programming, and policy documents of the government agencies.

Assessment is commonly considered to mean "setting a value to." Assessment of technology, then, means setting a value to technology. Technologies include areas of special knowledge such as gas turbines, diesels, thermionics, thermoelectrics, fuel cells, and energy conversion, as opposed to the areas of science that include

TABLE I

Basket 1	Fruit Cost (cents/unit)	Basket 2
5 apples	10	10 apples
8 oranges	20	2 oranges
6 bananas	30	9 bananas

TABLE II

Boat 1	Boat 2
25 knots	20 knots
80 decibels	50 decibels

items such as alloy theory, surface physics, cryogenics, and magnetism. The kinds or measures of value attributed to technologies will be discussed later. Also, it can be demonstrated that the nature of the assessment of technology depends on who assesses, why the assessment is performed, and the nature of the technology itself.

How is Technology Assessed?

One simple technique of assessing technology uses an analogy and a rather trivial example. To assess the value of two baskets of fruit with contents as listed in Table I, first assess or determine the value of the baskets in one of many respects such as weight (a critical criteria for submarines), volume (a critical criteria for space craft), calories (a critical criteria for weight-watchers), and cost (a critical criteria for budgeteers). For this example, assessment can be readily done in terms of financial cost with monetary cost values assigned to the individual items as follows:

$$\text{value (1)} = (5 \times 10) + (8 \times 20) + (6 \times 30)$$
$$= 50 + 160 + 180$$
$$= \$3.90$$
$$\text{value (2)} = (10 \times 10) + (2 \times 20) + (9 \times 30)$$
$$= 100 + 40 + 270$$
$$= \$4.10.$$

The analogy is made by having the baskets of fruit represent technologies; the fruits represent characteristics or parameters of the technologies; and the cost values of the fruit represent their "relative importance factors." The value for each basket can be represented by the formula:

value = sum of [(relative importance factor)

$\times$ (criteria or parameter)].

This illustration introduces the terms "importance factors" and "parameters" and demonstrates (assuming the analogy is valid) that the parameters, while different from each other, provide measures of technology that can be taken collectively to determine a single numerical value that can be compared to a similarly derived value of another technology. Note again that the assessment could have been made for the purpose of comparing other importance factors—values of weight, volume,

calories, etc. It is easy to see that the selection of the relative importance factors is dependent upon the parameters (kinds of fruit, in the example), and upon the purpose of the assessment. This latter dependency will be discussed further in addressing the question: Why (or for what purpose) assess technology? Please note that the above example does not add together apples and oranges, rather importance factors have been constructed to cancel the different units of fruit in the multiplications, and does add like units of cost associated with each different fruit.

Another *hypothetical* example of technological assessment is provided by K. Ellingsworth of the Annapolis Division of the Naval Ship Research and Development Center, Division Planning Office [8]. This one is not in the form of an analogy, nor is it trivial. It concerns the design of a boat for river warfare use in Vietnam. The design has proceeded to the point where a choice must be made between two parameters of two boats, as illustrated in Table II.

The two boats have speeds and noise levels of 25 knots, 80 dB and 20 knots, 50 dB, respectively. Here it appears difficult to assign relative importance factors, but there are methods that can be used. In this case, a mission analysis can allow us to determine the relative importance factors. Imagine the boat patrolling a river "looking" up and down the river with its radar. Its mission is to prevent enemy junks from crossing the river. The more noise the boat makes, the farther up the river the enemy can hear the boat. The farther away the boat can be heard, the more time the enemy has to escape by crossing the river or by ducking back into a shallow creek where our boat cannot go, and the faster our boat must be to catch the enemy. It is simply a matter of physics and geometry to determine, say, for a given boat noise, the speed required to achieve a stated level of mission effectiveness. The results of a mission analysis might be stated as for every 16 dB of noise, 4 knots of speed are required in order to be able to intercept those junks up to a mile away and in the middle two-thirds (width) of the river. In other words, 4 dB of noise are equivalent to 1 knot of speed, and these are the relative importance factors needed. The boat is then selected, as illustrated in Table III. Calculations of value from data follow.

$$V(1) = (25 \times 4) - (80 \times 1) = 20$$

$$V(2) = (20 \times 4) - (50 \times 1) = 30.$$

TABLE III		
Boat 1	Importance Factors (decibels/knots)	Boat 2
25 knots	4	20 knots
80 decibels	1	50 decibels

TABLE IV
TECHNOLOGY—BATTERIES

Parameter	User	Manager	Designer	Engineer
Volume	3	2	10	8
Cost	0	10	2	2
Time between recharging	10	2	4	1

Note that speed adds to the boat's value, noise subtracts. The above assessment indicates the choice of Boat 2. It is a slower boat, but its reduced noise makes it more effective by the criteria established. This sort of assessment might be done to determine operational capabilities, to determine design criteria, or, in resource allocation, to determine the appropriate levels of effort in the two technological areas of boat power and noise reduction.

Who Assesses Technology? Why? For What Purpose?

Intuitively, nearly everyone assesses technology at some time, for some purpose, and to some degree of sophistication. The "man on the street" for example may essentially assess the aggregates of the technologies of color versus black and white television. He may consider the collective value of parameters such as cost, picture quality, repair frequency, and pressure from his wife in order to choose which, if either, to buy. That nearly everyone has different values was pointed out by Guth and Tagiuri [9].

1) The personal values that businessmen and others have can be usefully classified as theoretical, economic, aesthetic, social, political, and religious.
2) The values that are most important to an executive have profound influence on his strategic decisions.
3) Managers and employees often are unaware of the values they possess and also tend to misjudge the values of others.
4) The executive who will take steps to better understand his own values and other men's values can gain an important advantage in developing workable and well-supported policies.

Earlier it was stated that the assessment of technology depends on who assesses, why the assessment is undertaken, and on the nature of the technology itself. A hypothetical situation that provides some illustration of the range of assessors, and how assessment might vary over this range is provided in the following example. This example also illustrates one of the difficulties in assessing technology that results from variations of people and purposes involved.

Consider the technology of batteries and three of its parameters—volume, cost, and time between recharging. A broad range of assessors might be the following in the situations described.

Technology Involvement	Situation
User	Lieutenant USN—Commanding Officer of a boat that contains batteries; drifting on a Vietnamese river on night patrol;
R&D manager	Chief of Naval Development—responsible for Navy's total Exploratory Development Program (Applied Research) considering each year's fiscal budget;
Boat designer	Naval Architect—Naval Ship Systems Command, designing a boat for use in Vietnam;
R&D engineer	Project engineer—working in a Navy R&D laboratory to improve the general performance of batteries.

These four people might assess battery technology using the same quantitative techniques, where 10 is the highest value that may be assigned and 0 the lowest (Table IV).

Table IV shows the relative importance factors that the four persons might assign to the parameters based on intuition. The differences shown by the variations of relative importance are possibly true, while perhaps exaggerated. The importance factors were chosen considering the following rationalizations.

The boat operator's life depends to a large extent on his boat. He is probably very concerned when, in the situation described, he must start up his *loud* engines to charge the batteries. He therefore considers the necessity and the time between recharging very important. He is probably not too concerned with the volume of the batteries as long as they do not infringe significantly on ammo storage space. He probably does not care what the batteries cost, much less the cost of the battery R&D effort.

The R&D manager is likely to place more importance on cost and less importance on individual performance characteristics. This is probably due to his responsibility for a large number of R&D programs and proposed programs involving many different parameters of many different technologies and the common element among these is cost.

The boat designer is concerned with the overall performance of the boat. He must be assured that all components required fit onto the boat, and he, therefore, considers volume relatively more important than cost or time between recharging.

Column 1 - Categories General Operational Requirements (GORs)	Column 2 Impact of Task Contributions										Column 3 Value to Individual Category
	1.0	.9	.8	.7	.6	.5	.4	.3	.2	.1	
31 - STRIKE WARFARE											
6 - Airborne Attack											
3 - Surface Attack											
5 - Submarine Attack											
4 - Amphibious Assault											
7 - Sea Based Strategic Deterrence											
3 - Airborne Anti-Air Warfare											
3 - Surface Anti-Air Warfare											
31 - ANTISUBMARINE WARFARE											
5 - Airborne ASW				✓							3.5
4 - Surface ASW						✓					2.0
5 - Submarine ASW						✓					2.5
10 - Undersea Surveillance								✓			3.0
2 - Mining											
3 - Mine Countermeasures											
2 - ASW Ancillary Support									✓		0.4
23 - COMMAND SUPPORT											
3 - Command and Control											
4 - Naval Communications											
4 - Electronic Warfare											
1 - Navigation											
4 - Ocean Surveillance											
5 - Reconnaissance & Intelligence											
1 - Environmental Systems											
1 - Special Warfare											
15 - OPERATIONAL SUPPORT											
2 - Logistics											
4 - Personnel											
2 - Astronautics											
2 - Aviation Support											
2 - Ship Support											
2 - Ordnance Support											
1 - NBC Defense											

4. TOTAL VALUE TO NAVAL WARFARE = 11.4

Scale of Definitions for "Impact of Task Contribution" (Column 2):

Points - Descriptors

1.0   Creation of radically new mission concepts (meets overriding critical need)
.7   Revolutionary extension of capabilities
.4   Incremental or marginal improvement of capabilities
.2   Increase in economy

Fig. 4.   Appraisal Sheet 1—value to naval warfare.

The project engineer is concerned with many characteristics of batteries; he is concerned with the improvement of batteries in general. It is not particularly required of him that he produce a profit. Therefore, he may not be particularly cost conscious. It is not required of him, perhaps, that he produce the smallest possible boat battery, and, therefore, he places less importance on volume than does the boat designer.

The above considerations suggest that the selection by a person of relative importance factors for parameters describing a technology is highly influenced by the environment in which the person is involved. Key expressions taken from the above for the persons described are

user	life, Vietnamese river (warfare),
manager	total R&D program, command,
designer	performance of boat (system made up of many technologies), engineering center,
R&D	many characteristics of one technology, laboratory.

A difficulty in assessing technology, illustrated above, is the problem of obtaining and maintaining an alignment of relative importance factors between the users of technologies and those responsible for improving the capabilities of technologies.

In the *hypothetical* example, the R&D engineer may not have been aware of the degree of importance of a particular parameter to a particular user. In other words, an R&D engineer may not recognize the need for a particular technological improvement. The importance of such need recognition as it contributes to the successful development of weapon systems is well illustrated by the comprehensive technology-source study Project Hindsight conducted by Isenson and Sherwin of the Department of Defense [10].

R&D Programming

To reiterate, three factors used by the Department of Defense to evaluate systems programs are military utility, technical feasibility, and financial acceptability. These factors are also important when planners evaluate research and development. However, it is necessary to quantize these factors so that they may be compared for different research and development programs.

Probability of Success

☐ 80 - 100% Chance of Meeting TAO.

☑ 30 - 80% Chance of Meeting TAO.

☐ 0 - 30% Chance of Meeting TAO.

Number of Different Concurrent Approaches

☐ 1   ☐ 3   ☐ 5   ☐ 7   ☐ 9

☐ 2   ☑ 4   ☐ 6   ☐ 8   ☐ 10 or more

Sacred Cow?   Who Says?

S-1 ☐ President   S-4 ☐ ASN (R&D)(Asst Secretary   S-7 ☐ CND (Chief of
                                      of Navy for Research   Naval
S-2 ☐ Congress   and Development)   Development)

S-3 ☐ DOD (Department of S-5 ☐ JCS (Joint Chiefs   S-8 ☐ Other _____
           Defense)   of Staff)

                          S-6 ☐ CNO (Chief of Naval
                                      Operations)

Appraisal Summary

No. of GORs ___5___

Value (V) ___11.4___

Probability of Success (Ps) ___0.9375___

Expected Value (EV) ___11.4 x 0.9375 = 10.7___

Optimum Funding ___2 Million___

Desirability Index (D) ___5.35___

Fig. 5.   Appraisal Sheet 2.

One of the simpler techniques being investigated by the Navy utilizes Appraisal Sheet 1 (Fig. 4), which addresses the problems of military utility. Military utility with respect to development atmosphere is a measure of R&D work in terms of its usefulness in meeting U. S. Navy general operational requirements (GOR). To be useful, hardware or information must provide a new or improved capability in the shortest possible time after its need is recognized. Thus, military utility is made up of three interdependent criteria—value to naval warfare, responsiveness, and timeliness. In this condensed version, we will consider value to naval warfare.

This criterion considers the extent of the contribution of a task area objective (TAO), a unit of work, in terms of its inherent value as well as its military operational value. The importance of a task is measured by its relative impact on any individual naval warfare category as well as the number of categories receiving a contribution from the task objective. This is done by multiplying the assigned value of the warfare category by the impact value of the contribution to arrive at a value for each individual category. The sum of these values will determine the value of the task area objective. (The figures of merit, or point values assigned to each naval warfare category (Column 1) are dummy figures; they were assigned for this example only. The actual total number of points assigned these 29 naval

categories are equal to 100, and they are assigned for test purposes on the basis of the importance of each of these categories in the 1975 and 1980 time frames since this is when most of our current exploratory development work will find its way into the fleet. The operational users provided the test figures based on the present world situation and their estimates of the most probable future situations.)

When the warfare area specialist filled in Column 2, the impact of the task area objective contributions, he considered the descriptors under the Scale of Definitions. In some cases the 4 descriptors do not adequately describe the contribution; in those cases he interpolates between these numbers.

The credibility of the ratings of technical feasibility and the probability of success increase if they are rated by personnel who have the necessary technical expertise and competence, as they can best judge these factors on the basis of the ability and experience of the individuals and/or organizations carrying on the development efforts under consideration.

The top half of Appraisal Sheet 2 (Fig. 5) solicits the opinion of the technical specialist regarding the probability of achieving the total task area objective that is being undertaken. It considers whether the task could be successfully accomplished from a scientific and technical feasibility point of view. Technical risk also takes into consideration the degree of confidence or prediction that the remaining portion of the total objective can be attained. The degree of confidence or prediction that the remaining portion of the total task objective can be attained usually assesses the factors of the present state of the art, either implicit or explicit. This technical appraisal is naturally based on technical forecasts and includes time factors and resource levels, as well as the competence of the investigating team.

Therefore, the technical specialist checks the box that best describes his opinion regarding the task area objective being evaluated, as well as the number of different concurrent approaches being taken, which are also a measure of probability of success.

The areas called "sacred cow?" and "who says?" were also considered in what we call the "management environment." This section solicits opinions on the acceptability of the effort in the management structure. Here, the evaluator is asked to give what he believes to be "the Washington environment" considerations concerning this effort, and he checks the applicable box.

The Appraisal Summary of Fig. 5 is then analyzed. The total program is calculated by value, expected value, and desirability index for three funding levels, by the computer. The inputs for military utility come from Fig. 4.

For example, suppose the proposed task area objective (TAO), or R&D effort, is to devise a system able to detect submerged submarines a given distance away from a sensor, say 20 miles. We shall consider the criterion "value to naval warfare." Of the 29 naval general operational requirements shown in Column 1 of Fig. 4, the TAO would be of value and contribute only to five GOR —airborne ASW, surface ASW, submarine ASW, undersea ASW, and ASW ancillary support.

With respect to airborne ASW, the success of the R&D venture in this hypothetical example is considered a revolutionary extension of capabilities, and is accorded 0.7 point. At the same time, airborne ASW is said to contribute 5 out of the 100 units assigned to all the GOR. Thus, the value of the TAO to naval warfare with respect to airborne ASW is $0.7 \times 5 = 3.5$. The outer categories can be similarly evaluated for their contributions, and the total value of this TAO to naval warfare is summed at 11.4, as shown in Fig. 5.

For our calculation of the probability of success (P_s) in meeting the TAO, we use the probability chart shown on Table V. In this chart, n is the number of concurrent approaches used to accomplish the TAO, and C is a number arbitrarily assigned to the chances of succeeding in a given approach. We use

80–100 percent chance of success	$C = 0.8$
30–80 percent chance of success	$C = 0.5$
0–30 percent chance of success	$C = 0.2$.

We assume that all approaches n have the same chance

TABLE V
TABULATION OF P_s

n	C 0.8	0.5	0.2
1	0.80000	0.50000	0.20000
2	0.96000	0.75000	0.36000
3	0.99200	0.87500	0.48800
4	0.99840	0.93750	0.59040
5	0.99968	0.96875	0.67230
6	0.99993	0.98438	0.73786
7	0.99997	0.99219	0.79029
8	0.99999	0.99609	0.83223
9	0.99999	0.99805	0.86578
10	0.99999	0.99902	0.89263

of success, and therefore, the same value of C. If each n were to have a different C, a more involved calculation would have been necessary. The number assigned to the probability of one approach failing is then $(1 - C)$. The number assigned to the probability of n approaches failing is $(1 - C)^n$. Further, if we assume that at least one of the approaches taken will succeed, then the number assigned to the probability of success P_s is $1 - (1 - C^n)$. This figure for P_s is filled in under the Probability of Success column in Fig. 5.

Example: On Appraisal Sheet 2, we might have had 4 approaches $(n - 4)$ with a 30–80 percent chance of meeting TAO $(C - 0.5)$. Then the number corresponding to the probability of success is 0.93750 or 93.75 percent. From our previous example, we calculated the total value of a given TAO to be 11.4. Therefore, the expected value is $11.4 \times 0.9375 = 10.7$.

The preceding has been a discussion of concurrent approaches. If the task area were made up of phased or sequential operations, these probabilities would be handled in a different manner.

Three funding levels are utilized in the concurrent approach—actual/optimum, maximum, and minimum.

The actual/optimum consists of the latest approved fiscal data. For each subsequent year, funds are entered based on what is estimated as necessary to achieve the completion date if the task area is supported at an optimum rate. An optimum rate is one which permits aggressive prosecution using orderly developmental procedures, not a crash program.

The maximum consists of what could effectively be expended in advancing task area completion date. Maximum funding is the upper limit in which unlimited resources are assigned in order to accelerate the accomplishment of a task area.

The minimum consists of what could be effectively utilized to maintain continuity of effort and some progress toward fulfilling the task area objective. Minimum funding is the threshhold limit below which it would not be feasible to continue further efforts in the task area. The simplified formula is

N A V M A T   P R O G R A M   E V A L U A T I O N   R E P O R T
(RANKING OF 6524PU12 BY TOTAL WARFARE VALUE MR. CETRON 6TYPE)

TASK AREA NUMBER	TITLE	SC	EXP. VALUE	FUNDING						RANKING#
				MAX	CUM	OPT	CUM	MIN	CUM	
WF1151175l (U)SPACE SYSTEMS ENGINEERING WF0190101			26.446875	300	300	300	300	300	300	27.3
XF0322200l (U)COMMUNICATIONS SATELLITE SUPPORT XF019090R			22.050000	2000	2300	1375	1675	1000	1300	25.2
WF032227sl (U)SATELLITE COMMUNICATIONS WF0190101			10.350000	350	2650	350	2025	0	1300	21.8
WF125527sl (U)SATELLITE OCEANOGRAPHIC DATA COLLECTION WF0190202			9.375000	900	3550	700	2725	150	1450	12.5
WF125517s2 (U)SOLAR RADIATION MONITORING SATELLITE WF0190202			8.000370	3000	6550	2800	5525	1200	2650	11.9
WF0323275l (U)SATELLITE NAVIGATION WF0190101				2250	8800	2250	7775	0	2650	10.2
WF125517sl (U)METEOROLOGICAL SATELLITE DATA READOUT WF0190202			8.750000	600	9400	200	7975	150	2800	10.0
WF021127sl (U)ADVANCED TECHNIQUES FOR SPACE OBJECT DETECTION AND IDENTIFICATION WF0190102			2.800000	850	10250	850	8825	0	2800	5.6
WF021117s2 (U)OCEAN SURVEILLANCE SYSTEMS ANALYSIS WF0190202				5500	15750	5000	13825	4000	6800	4.8
WF0531175l (U)SATELLITE INTERCEPTER SYSTEMS ANALYSIS WF0190102				500	16250	500	14325	200	7000	1.0
WF0537275l (U)ASTRO-DEFENSE THREAT STUDIES WF0190102				300	16550	200	14525	100	7100	1.0

Fig. 6.   Example—Computer printout ranked by value and expected value.

86080126000 1
C

N A V M A T   P R O G R A M   E V A L U A T I O N   R E P O R T
(RANKING BY OPT DESIRABILITY)

TASK AREA NUMBER	TITLE	SC	F U N D I N G						RANKING*
			MAX	CUM	OPT	CUM	MIN	CUM	
SF08452002	(U)ACOUSTICAL SILENCING (INTERNAL SHIPS SYSTEMS).	S6	320	320	220	220	185	185	.266477
SF08452004	(U)ACOUSTICAL SILENCING, SHIP ISOLATION DEVICES	S6	535	855	435	655	333	518	.181034
XF10532001	(U)TEST EQUIPMENT	S3	2400	3255	1300	1955	770	1288	.124614
SF08452005	(U)ACOUSTICAL SILENCING, HULL VIBRATION AND RADIATION	S6	955	4210	680	2635	610	1898	.093750
SF02132001	(U)DIRECT VIEW IMAGE INTENSIFIER TECHNIQUES	S4	400	4610	300	2935	65	1963	.080000
SF08452001	(U)SHIP SILENCING MEASUREMENTS, ANALYSIS AND PROBLEM DEFINITION	S6	1360	5970	1095	4030	860	2823	.072602
WF02132601	(U)IMAGING RECONNAISSANCE SENSOR DEVELOPMENT	S3	1000	6970	750	4780	200	3023	.056666
RF08412002	(U)DEEP RESEARCH VEHICLE PROGRAM	S6	1700	8670	1510	6290	1180	4203	.048344
SF01121003	(U)DOMES AND SELF NOISE	S6	600	9270	550	6840	540	4743	.041236
XF10545001	(U)ADVANCED ACTIVE DEVICES AND TECHNIQUES	S3	4000	13270	2600	9440	2000	6743	.039711
PF11521004	(U)IMPROVED NAVY STAFFING CRITERIA	S6	500	13770	500	9940	253	6996	.038400
SF01121007	(U)SYSTEM ANALYSIS AND ENGINEERING	S6	1000	14770	850	10790	500	7496	.037058
SF08452003	(U)ACOUSTICAL SILENCING, EXTERNAL SHIP SYSTEM	S6	1920	16690	1735	12525	1412	8908	.033789
TF10531001	(U)CARGO MOVEMENT AND DISTRIBUTION	S6	700	17390	550	13075	300	9208	.018039
SF01121004	(U)TRANSDUCERS AND ACOUSTIC POWER GENERATORS	S6	4500	21890	4009	17084	2700	11908	.011785
SF01121002	(U)SONAR SIGNAL PROCESSING AND CLASSIFICATION	S6	7000	28890	6520	23604	5800	17708	.007246
SF01121001	(U)UNDERWATER SOUND PROPAGATION	S6	6400	35290	6000	29604	4800	22508	.005250
SF09443004	(U)NUCLEAR PROPULSION PLANT MATERIALS DEVELOPMENT	S4	1100	36390	1100	30704	0	22508	
SF09443001	(U)NUCLEAR PROPULSION PLANT TECHNOLOGY	S4	1000	37390	1000	31704	0	22508	
SF09442003	(U)SURFACE SHIP REFUELING EQUIPMENT AND PROCEDURES DEVELOPMENT	S4	2200	39590	2200	33904	0	22508	

Fig. 7. Example—Computer printout ranked by desirability.

value $(V) \times$ probability of success (P_s)

$$= \text{expected value } (EV)$$

$$\frac{\text{expected value } (EV)}{\text{funding level } (C)} = \text{desirability index } (D).$$

Completing the analysis of the rating sheet, GOR represents the number of general operational requirements affected by the project; P_s, as previously stated, is read off a probability chart; and the optimum funding level is determined according to the resources needed to complete the project in the time span of the study. The final desirability index numbers now provide a way to compare a great multitude of current and proposed R&D projects. By carrying out similar evaluations on the basis of responsiveness to expected needs, the timeliness of the projects, and other criteria, it is possible to combine all the information about the project and come up with its "total warfare value."

The end results of a research and development planning effort like this are computer printouts (Figs. 6 and 7), which rank every project according to its value in the overall program. In the Navy, this comes to over 700 separate R&D projects. It would be a mistake, however, to think that the impressive-looking computer printouts are taking over the final decision-making job. *Most of those who design and work with information systems like the one described, fully realize that technological forecasts and quantitative estimates of project value are no more or less than a planning tool, and only one of many that a manager must use in making final decisions.*

Conclusions

We are well aware of many of the omissions and weaknesses of these quantitative-selection or resource-allocation techniques. It should be stressed again that they were not intended to yield decision, but rather information that would facilitate decision. Indeed, these techniques are merely thinking structures to force methodical meticulous consideration of all factors involved in resource allocation. *Data* plus *analysis* yield *information*. *Information* plus *judgment* yield *decisions*.

We are firmly convinced that if we had to choose between any machine and the human brain, we would select the brain. The brain has a marvelous system that learns from experience and an uncanny way of pulling out the salient factors or rejecting useless information. It is wrong to say that one must select intuitive experience over analysis or minds over machines; really they are *not* alternatives, they complement each other. Used together, they yield results far better than if used individually.

A close look at a few "facts" concerning the quantitative resource-allocation methods shows these approaches to be merely experimental management techniques. The fact that a computer or an adding machine may be used to facilitate data handling should in no way distract from the basic fact that human subjective inputs are the foundation of these systems. Accurate human calculation, as opposed to use of a computer for the calculations of all the interrelationships considered, would not alter the basic principles of these management tools in any respect. Yet, I often hear the reactionary complaint that quantitative measurements cannot be applied to management processes because human judgment cannot be forsaken and machines cannot replace the seasoned experience expertise of the manager [14].

The real concern should be directed toward using the collective judgment of technical staffs (technological forecasts) and decision makers in such a manner that logically sound decisions are made, greater payoff is achieved for the resources committed, and that less, not more, valuable scientific and engineering time expended. To make an incorrect decision is understandable, but to make a decision and not really know the basis for the judgment is unforgivable. The area of good resource allocation certainly must have advanced beyond this point; otherwise, a pair of dice could replace the decision maker.

Most of the managers who design and work with information systems fully realize that technological forecasts, quantitative estimates of project value, and other aids to resource allocation are merely a planning tool, and only one of a brand new kit of advance decision-making devices.

Even this caveat, however, does not defuse critics of the whole idea—and there are some very vocal ones around in government and business. Some of the criticism is in reaction to the fear of "mechanization" of a task felt to be rightfully in the province of human evaluation. Other critics claim that building up a logical system, computerizing the output, and quantifying what are essentially intuitive and judgment decisions may insulate some managers with a false sense of security. The validation of the process will not be continued and management responsibility will be abandoned. Another criticism stems from the use of estimates as basic figures in the analysis. This kind of objection can also be applied to a decision based on "experience" and made without a quantitative approach.

Technological forecasting and systematic analysis tend to force managers to consider their resource-allocation tasks more comprehensively and highlight problem areas that might easily be overlooked by more traditional approaches. However, regardless of the high degree of sophistication that is being attributed to these planning devices, managers should use the devices with caution.

Appendix I[1]

Metallic Materials and Seals

Background

In order to successfully construct and maintain structures on the ocean bottom at great depths for extended periods of time, behavior at depth of materials of construction and the limitations of construction designs and methods must be well defined.

Many of the parameters affecting the corrosion of metallic materials such as O_2 concentration, pH, pressure, salinity, temperature, etc., were found to vary extensively in the deep ocean. These parameters change with location, depth, and season. In order to better define the behavior of construction materials in the deep ocean, test exposures of 10 995 specimens of 500 materials have been made at 2500 and 6000 feet in the Pacific Ocean off the coast of southern California for varying periods of time up to 1064 days. Evaluation of these specimens has shown that the corrosion behavior of materials at these two depths is different in both degree and nature, and is different from their behavior in sea water at the surface.

One particular area of inadequate information pertinent to the installation and maintenance of structures in the deep ocean is that of the behavior of seals and gaskets during long-term loading while exposed to sea water.

Investigation of the long-term seal loading and deterioration effects in the deep ocean is underway at NCEL. In July, 1968, 40 specimens of 15 static seal configurations constructed from five flange materials will be exposed to the deep ocean at a depth of 6000 feet. This initial exposure is scheduled to be six months in length.

Metal components of sea floor structures and equipment will be subjected to very severe environmental and service conditions, and are likely to be covered with plastic or paint coatings, where practical, to protect them from corrosion. Such coverings will be subject to abrasion, and impact damage and the bare metal thus exposed will be subject to rapid corrosion unless protected by some system such as cathodic protection.

Present Status

Materials: Of the 500 materials exposed to date in the deep ocean test program, many have shown promise for application in the deep ocean. However, as in all applications of materials in a corrosive environment, a material selection must be made by evaluation of pertinent performance data, material requirements, and actual exposure conditions (environment, stress, crevices, and galvanic corrosion possibilities).

Corrosion data from the six deep ocean exposure tests has added significantly to the body of corrosion knowledge used in material selection for deep ocean

[1] The illustrations in all appendixes are unclassified material.

TABLE VI

Material	Density (no./in4)	Strength (psi) Available now	Strength (psi) Available 1970–1980
Steel	0.283	130 000–180 000	300 000
Titanium	0.160	110 000	160 000
Aluminum	0.100	70 000	90 000
Fiber reinforced plastic (FRP)	0.080	100 000	150 000
Glass	0.090	100 000	250 000

This table and associated projections are extracted from the Technical Development Plan (46-36X), Deep Ocean Technology Project, May 1968.

structures. Note the available strengths of steel, titanium, and aluminum in Table VI.

Seals: Evaluation of the present seal technology has revealed a dearth of published information about the use of seals for external pressure applications and for long-term loading and deterioration effects in sea water. A compilation of the limited available service data for seals in the deep ocean, taken primarily from deep submersible vessel applications, indicates the major difficulty in the design of a seal that will be effective without maintenance for long periods is the corrosion of the flange faces and not the deterioration of the actual sea material. Seals of the O-ring type are considered to be of primary importance for deep ocean applications. The deep ocean performance of this type of static seal in various configurations is presently being investigated by this laboratory. Preliminary tests have confirmed the usefulness of static O-ring seals for deep ocean use, as there were no seal failures in the laboratory short-term hydrostatic loading tests simulating depths up to 10 000 feet.

Cathodic protection has been quite an effective method of corrosion control for steel ships, piling, buoys, etc., in shallow sea water applications, but in deep ocean exposures only small test specimens have been cathodically protected to date, and relatively little is known about cathodic protection in such environments.

Forecast

Materials: The deep ocean corrosion data obtained in the previous exposure tests has made it possible to predict long-term behavior in the deep ocean for many materials in environments similar to those in which the corrosion tests were made. However, many materials were found to corrode in such a way that long-term generalized predictions of corrosion are impossible, e.g., increasing pitting rate or increasing corrosion rate. Also, due to the wide variation of corrosion-related parameters, long-term, and in many cases short-term corrosion behavior can only at best be approximated from present corrosion data and theory. Corrosion exposures for extended periods and in numerous locations will better define the corrosion behavior of metallic materials throughout the deep ocean. Laboratory tests that to date have been stifled by inability to maintain corrosion-related parameters at desired values may prove to be of great future value in this definition of corrosion behavior if proper testing equipment can be designed.

One particular aspect of the corrosion behavior of materials in the deep ocean and indeed in any marine environment, which will require future investigation in order to clearly define actual corrosion behavior, is that of galvanic or metal-couple corrosion. Since nearly any structure of apparatus must be constructed of more than one material, the possibility of accelerated corrosion of one or more of the materials exposed to the sea water must be considered in any realistic materials selection. The dearth of present information on this subject may in the future be studied in two ways; either actual metal combinations must be exposed to the environment or the electrochemical behavior of each of the metals to be investigated must be determined by measurements taken on the metals at intervals during their exposure.

The development of new alloys, which by virtue of their high strength, low density, or supposed corrosion resistance, will require testing by either deep ocean exposure or by exposure in a well-regulated simulation facility in a laboratory, if the latter proves to be a reliable means of predicting corrosion behavior in the deep ocean.

Seals: The development of a static seal system that is reliable from a deterioration standpoint over extended periods in the deep ocean should be the result of the present investigation at NCEL. Seal flanges constructed of corrosion-resistant materials and compatible with most proposed construction materials are now being tested and are hoped to prove successful. Other proposed methods of improving flange life are cathodic protection, painting, and development of a seal system that eliminates corrosion-accelerating crevices. Development of a dynamic shaft-type seal that is reliable for long periods in the deep ocean should be undertaken in the near future. The main problem envisioned in this development is that of an elastomeric material to affect the seal. Problems of flange corrosion should be well delineated by a test on static seal systems.

In general, the values in Table VI are based on forecasts from the sea-bed study. For present state-of-the-art materials, particularly glass, strengths less than accepted laboratory values are indicated. In the case of glass, the scatter of data is so great (i.e., 60 000–350 000 psi for simple compression joint tests of chemically strengthened glass) that a nominal fracture stress of 100 000 psi was used.

Analyses of known materials and configurations of pressure-resistant structures, coupled with predicted R&D support for their use in operational vehicles, indicate the following projected capabilities.

1) In the present time frame, fiber-reinforced plastic and massive glass are the best candidate materials for 20 000-foot operations.

2) Development of high-yield-strength aluminum (150 000 psi) will permit its use for cylindrical hulls with W/D = 0.5 to operating depths of 20 000 feet.

3) The development of a higher strength titanium will permit its use of cylindrical hulls with W/D = 0.4 to operating depths of 20 000 feet.

4) A metallic or FRP cylindrical or spherical hull capable of 10 000-foot submergence can be envisioned within 5 years.

5) A metallic of FRP cylindrical or spherical hull with 15 000-foot depth capability can be available within 10 years.

6) A 20 000-foot depth capability, with various hull configurations and material options is possible within 15 years.

7) The development paths which can minimize the time/depth demonstration sequence are 6000 feet, 4 years, steel cylinder or sphere; 10 000 feet, 5 years, steel cylinder or sphere; 15 000 feet, 5 years, FRP cylinder; 20 000 feet, 8 years, FRP or glass sphere.

The Naval Applied Science Laboratory (NASL) has submitted Fig. 2 (a) and (b) to show yield-strength and corrosion-resistance predictions for structural aluminum, steel, and titanium alloys. The difference between the high- and low-toughness materials referred to in the yield-strength curve is that the former are estimated to be capable of sustaining a minimum of approximately 7-percent plastic deformation before fracture. For later refinement of data, see the NASL technological forecast on materials.

Cathodic protection systems will be used in conjunction with other corrosion-control measures (coating, sheaths, inhibitors, etc.), to reduce costs and obtain the most dependable level of protection.

Operational Implications

The definition of the corrosion behavior of metallic materials in many deep ocean environments will enable the construction of a deep ocean structure with a long projected life span.

The definition of the behavior of many seal systems in many deep ocean environments will provide seal and flange materials for construction of a deep ocean structure with a long projected life span.

References

"Deep ocean civil engineering," NCEL Tech. Rept. 345, Back-up Rept., Undersea Technology Panel, Project Sea-bed, September 1964.

"Properties of materials in the deep ocean environment, a progress report," NCEL Tech. Note N-380, March 1960.

"Properties of materials in the deep ocean environment, a progress report," NCEL Tech. Note, July 1962.

"Preliminary examination of materials exposed on STU I-3 in the deep ocean (5640 feet of depth for 123 days)," NCEL Tech. Note N-605.

"Effect of the deep ocean on the corrosion of selected alloys," NCEL Tech. Note N-781, October 1965.

"Visual observations of corrosion of materials on STU I-1 after 1064 days of exposure at a depth of 5300 feet in the Pacific ocean," NCEL Tech. Note 793.

"Corrosion of materials in hydrospace—I, Irons, steels, cast irons and steel products," NCEL Tech. Note N-900, July 1967.

"Corrosion of materials in hydrospace—II, Nickel and alloys," NCEL Tech. Note N-915, August 1967.

"Corrosion of materials in hydrospace—III, Titanium and titanium alloys," NCEL Tech. Note N-921, September 1967.

Associated R&D Organizations

NASL, Brooklyn, N. Y.
NRL, Washington, D. C.
NSRDC, Washington, D. C.
NAMC, Pensacola, Fla.
NAEC, Philadelphia, Pa.
Lockheed Aerospace and Missiles Co., Sunnyvale, Calif.

Appendix II

Concrete

Background

For the past 40 years concrete has been used as an ocean construction material for coastal and harbor installations. The performance of underwater foundations, piers, and piles, which were poured in place at depths to 200 feet using the methods of tremie, bucketing, and pumping, have shown good structural integrity except for a number of incidents where concrete members exhibited major deterioration. In all these cases the cause for deterioration could be directed to low-quality concrete. High-quality concrete (high cement factor, low water–cement ratio, high density, etc.) not only resisted deterioration but also attack by marine organisms.

Experience has also been gained using concrete as a pressure hull material for subaqueous transportation tunnels. Tunnels have been constructed from large precast sections at depths to 120 feet, although high factors of safety were always present with static working stresses below 500 psi.

Present Status

The feasibility of deep ocean concrete installations was shown in research studies on model spherical hulls subjected to hydrostatic loadings. Concrete hulls developed stresses on the order of 14 000 psi, while the strength of the concrete from uniaxial cylinder tests was only 10 000 psi. Present developments in concrete technology, such as polymer concrete or plastic impregnation of concrete, may eliminate the problem of sea water premeating through the material, and also increase the ultimate strength of the material to 24 000 psi. Further developments in fiber-reinforcement techniques and sandwich-construction methods offer the potential capability of concrete installations to undergo dynamic and cyclic loading conditions.

Forecast

Within 20 years, technological advances for concrete will allow working stresses on the order of 12 000 psi and will eliminate the problem of concrete premeability to sea water. Major developments in construction techniques, such as assembling concrete pressure hulls from prefabricated elements or mixing and pouring concrete on site using sea floor aggregate and sea water as materials, will have significant impetus in broadening the applications for concrete as a construction material in the oceans. Underwater semipermanent and permanent installations will range in size from small instrumentation capsules to large "gymnasium-size" manned habitats. Very large pressure hulls are feasible insofar as the wall of a concrete hull can be constructed to any thickness. It is foreseen that concrete structures will be employed to maximum operational depths of 3000 feet, even though the material is capable of withstanding hydrostatic pressures at operational depths of 10 000 feet and greater.

Design data obtained from extensive research on the physical properties and structural behavior of concrete under hydrostatic loading will be available for predicting the behavior of any concrete structure in the ocean. Future trends in development work on polymer concrete, glass fiber-reinforced concrete, and other unknown methods will not only continue to increase the strength of the material (Fig. 8,) but also the economic advantages and the reliability of the material for sea floor installations.

Operational Implications

Permanent installations on the ocean floor are technically feasible if constructed from high-quality concrete. Advantages of fixed ocean floor habitats are that personnel can be transferred to and from the surface easier than an entire habitat can be transported, the structure does not have to undergo cyclic loading, and certain structures such as nuclear-reactor containment vessels will be negatively buoyant, and therefore designed on the criterion of a permanent underwater pressure hull.

Very large underwater concrete structures can be fabricated by cast in-place techniques or precast methods of assembling sections *in situ*. Large hulls constructed from other materials have maximum size limitations because of a lack of welding technology for thick walls or elastic instability problems that require many hull stiffeners. The need for tall wide installations could be for oil-drilling operations, which house man and equipment.

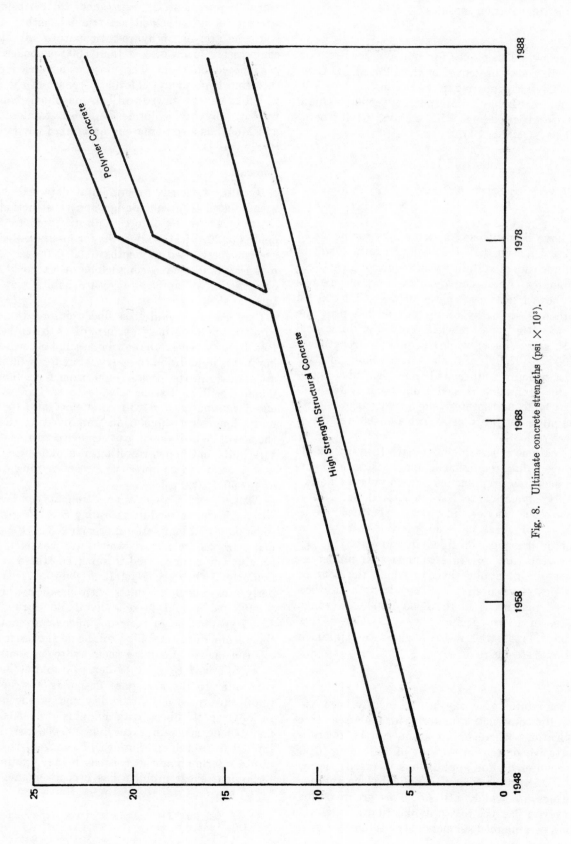

Fig. 8. Ultimate concrete strengths (psi $\times 10^3$).

Buoyant concrete pressure hulls can have application within continental shelf regions as long-term subsurface buoys and instrumentation capsules.

References

B. C. Gerwick, "Techniques for concrete construction on the ocean floor," presented at the 1967 ASCE Conference on Civil Engineering in the Oceans.

J. D. Stachiw, "Behavior of spherical concrete hulls under hydrostatic loadings," U. S. Naval Civil Engrg. Lab., TR-547, October 1967.

APPENDIX III

STRUCTURAL PLASTICS

Background

Plastics have been utilized in structures for undersea use for several decades. Where high strength-to-weight ratio and dimensional stability was required, glass fiber epoxy laminates were employed whose mechanical properties showed tensile strengths of up to 150 000 psi and compressive strengths of up to 100 000 psi. The premium strengths were reached only by directional windings of glass fibers, while for lower strengths of 20 000–40 000 psi hand-laid glass cloth and matting sufficed. The structures fabricated from glass fiber epoxy and polyester laminates ranged from fairings for submersibles to large underwater buoys and capsules with depth capabilities of up to 5000 feet and 0.3 weight-to-displacement ratio.

For applications where high strength-to-weight ratio is not the overriding requirement, but resistance to corrosion and economy are, plastics like polyvinyl chloride, acrylic, and polycarbonate have displaced, in a large measure, the much heavier and expensive corrosion-resistant metals. Polyvinyl chloride plastic battery containers, motor housings, oil-filled instrumentation capsules, cable reels, and pressure-compensated piping are typical examples of applications to which the nonreinforced plastics have been put. The strength of these nonreinforced plastics is in the 3000–15 000 psi range; but, because of their specific gravity (which is just slightly above 1) a strength-to-weight ratio approaching that of mild steel is realized.

Present Status

Glass fiber reinforced epoxy has frequently been used for nonmetallic construction material for undersea structural applications where no corrosion can be tolerated and compressive or tensile stresses of less than 40 000 psi are encountered. For applications where no permeability by water can be tolerated, polyethylene and neoprene coatings are widely utilized. This group of materials, however, has yet to see application as the main pressure hull of a manned submersible or habitat.

Nonreinforced plastic materials are usually considered for undersea structural applications where the primary requirement is resistance to corrosion, while stresses to be withstood are triaxial—either of hydrostatic nature, or of hydrostatic nature with tensile or compressive loads of less than 5000-psi magnitude superimposed on them. The most widely used plastic of this kind is polyvinyl chloride. Because of the ease with which it can be sawed, drilled, machined, bonded, and welded, polyvinyl chloride displaced stainless steel 316 and Monel as a construction material of low-stress structural members.

Forecast

By 1978 sufficient experimental data will have been accumulated to permit design and construction of man-rated glass fiber reinforced plastic pressure hulls for depths to 2000 feet, while hulls for instrumented capsules are routinely used to depths of 20 000 feet. The same material would have completely displaced steel in the construction of ambient pressure habitats on the continental shelf.

By 1988 man-rated glass fiber reinforced plastic pressure hulls will routinely perform dives to depths of 10 000 feet. New currently unknown glass and other fiber plastic laminates in addition to epoxy laminates will make their appearance in the ocean engineering field. The new laminates will be less permeable to sea water than the epoxy laminates, and will be subject also to less creep under long-term submersion. Improved fabrication methods will make it possible to achieve construction of pressure hulls and buoys resulting in a monolithic structure with tensile and compressive stress carrying capabilities of 40 000–50 000 psi.

Tensile and Compressive Strengths and Modulus:[2] Although elastic moduli exceeding 5×10^5 psi are rare, some polyimid laminates approach $2–3 \times 10^6$ psi. Modified carbons, many of which are considered organic copolymers, are expected to supersede these values, particularly if they are crystalline (whiskerized) and properly crosslinked. Products with elastic moduli of $5–10 \times 10^6$ psi should become available during the next 10–20 years. Due to their polynuclear aromatic nature, their temperature stability will be on the order of 1000°C or even higher, providing their hydrogen content is low.

Whiskerized Graphite Fiber: Graphite fiber composites offer to the aerospace designers a structural material unsurpassed in modulus and strength-to-weight ratio. Graphite fibers, with modulus of 50–50 000 000 psi and tensile strength exceeding 300 000 psi, have been limited to usefulness, however, because of the low-composite interlaminar shear strength they exhibit. The interlaminar shear problem has been overcome through a

---

[2] Extracted for "Technological forecast on organic materials," NSRDC, Annapolis, Md.

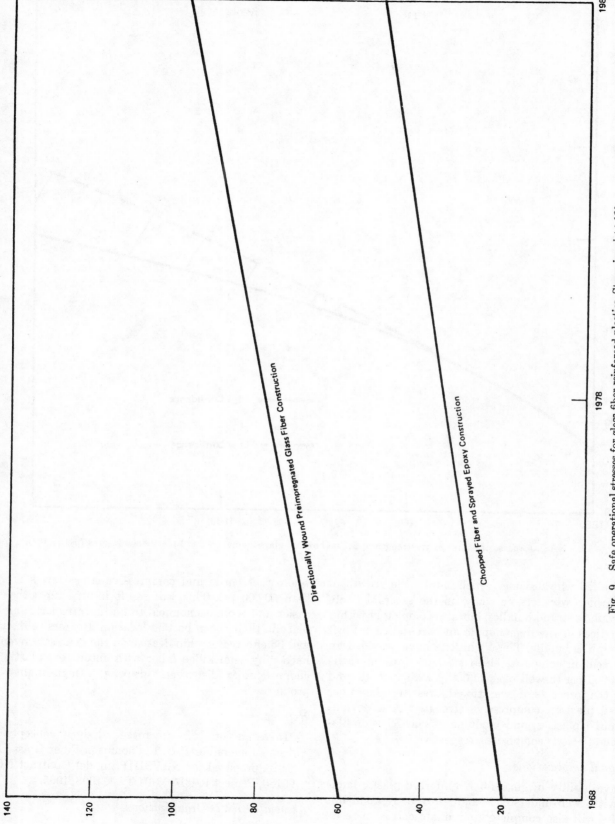

Fig. 9. Safe operational stresses for glass fiber reinforced plastics. Stress is psi $\times 10^3$.

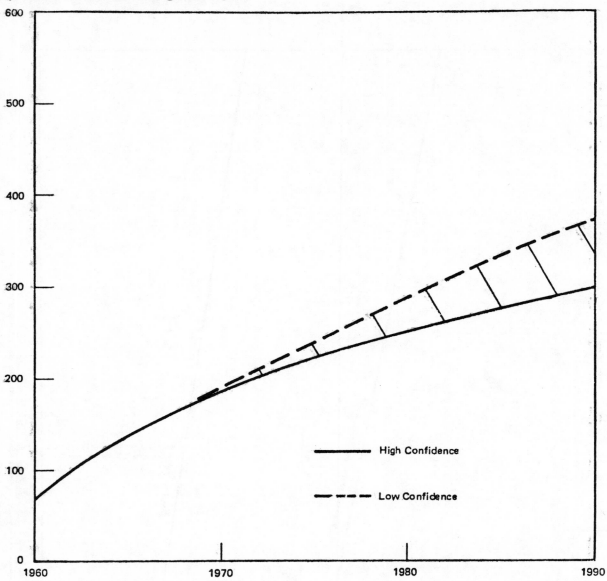

Fig. 10.   NASL forecast of compressive strength of 2:1 orthogonal glass filament wound plastic composites (psi × 10³).

process called whiskerizing, which entails the growth of silicon-carbide whiskers not only on the external fibers of the graphite strand bundles, but also completely within the interstices of the fiber bundle and around each fibril in the graphite bundle. These whiskers have provided an improvement in composite shear strength from approximately 3000 psi to well over 11 000 psi. Figs. 9, 10, and 11 show the forecasts of operational stress for glass fiber reinforced plastics, compressive strengths of glass filament wound plastics, and modulus of elasticity of filament wound plastic composites, respectively.

Operational Implications

The availability of glass fiber reinforced plastic laminates with well-understood and proven reproducible properties will also completely eliminate corrosion-resistant metals from underwater habitats and vehicles where the tensile and compressive-stress levels are less than 50 000 psi. This will result in structures that are easier and more economical to build, transport, and emplace in their ocean bottom location. Repairs to damages will be effected on ship deck or in the nearest convenient harbor by semiskilled labor with automated plastic and chopped fiber dispensers insuring a high-quality end product.

References

"Investigation of advanced design concepts for deep submersibles," H. I. Thompson Fiber Glass Company, prepared for NAVSHIPS under Contract NObs-90180, Project R-007-03-04 Task 1008, 1965.

Associated R&D Organizations

NSRDC, Carderock and Annapolis, Md.

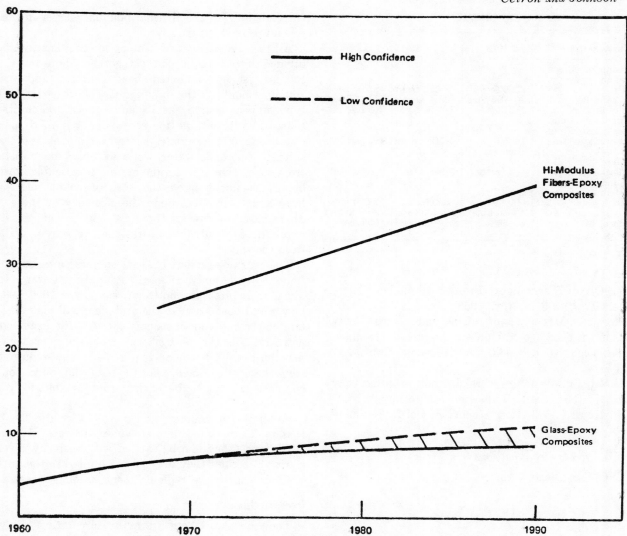

Fig. 11. NASL forecast of modulus of elasticity in compression of 2:1 orthogonal filament wound plastic composites (psi $\times$ 10⁶).

Appendix IV
Weight-Handling Devices

Background

The conventional way to place and remove objects of all kinds into and out of the ocean is from ships. As these objects have become heavier, however, and the desired depths greater, there has developed a need for considerably improved handling devices and techniques. Existing devices do not have sufficient capacity, and ship motions introduce dynamic stresses in the cables and undesirable motions in the object being handled. Also, as construction operations are performed within the ocean, rather than from the surface, there will be a need for new weight-handling devices that operate in the hydrospace without any support from the surface.

Present Status

The present state of the art concerned with weight-handling devices may be evaluated in terms of three potential realms of operation: the ocean surface; the ocean bottom; and the water column from surface to bottom.

Surface-supported suspension systems utilize long lines (cables, etc.) to transmit the lifting force to the bottom. Theoretical prediction of the stresses in these lines has been formulated, but testing and evaluation have been carried out only to the 1200-foot depth. Techniques for manufacturing, spooling, and storing high-capacity (large-diameter) long-length cables are inadequately developed.

Forecast

See Table VII for the predicted data.

Operational Implications

Increased weight-handling capacity and control will allow the Navy to place in the ocean larger and more sophisticated equipment and facilities with greater capability. It will also allow the Navy to recover heavier objects from greater depths.

TABLE VII

Characteristics	1973	1978	1988
Surface-supported subsystem			
Depth	6000 feet	12 000 feet	18 000 feet
Load capacity	20–100 tons	400–600 tons	600–900 tons
Rate of lifting	1–3 ft/s	2–4 ft/s	3–5 ft/s
Maximum dynamic stress in cable (percent of static stress)	10–50 percent	5–10 percent	4–6 percent
Maximum vertical oscillation of object	1–2 feet	0.1–1.0 feet	0.1–0.5 feet
Surface-independent subsystem			
Depth	600 feet	6000 feet	12 000 feet
Load capacity	10–30 tons	50–100 tons	200–400 tons
Height of lift	30–50 feet	50–100 feet	1000 feet

References

Deep Ocean Technology Project, Technical Development Plan 46-36X, April 1968.

P. Holmes, "Mechanics of raising and lowering heavy loads in the deep ocean: Cable and payload dynamics," NCEL Tech. Rept. R-433, Port Hueneme, Calif., April 1966.

B. J. Muga, "Mechanics of raising and lowering heavy loads in the ocean: Experimental results," NCEL Tech. Rept. R-543, Port Hueneme, Calif., September 1967.

Associated R&D Organizations

NUWC, San Diego, Calif.

APPENDIX V

HEAT

Background

The heat-supply system is one of the most important requirements of sea floor engineering. Heat is required for underwater operations in a variety of ways; e.g., to provide a warm comfortable environment in the cold hostile surroundings, and hot water for various uses of the personnel living and working at the ocean depths. In other instances, efficient means of heat rejection are needed for equipments that generate heat during their operation. All types of rotating machines fall in this category. In yet other instances, efficient means of heat transfer are required in power generating equipments that use fluids to convert the heat obtained from burning various fuels into electric power. With the exception of batteries and fuel cells, the memory of all power sources depends largely upon the efficiency of the predominant mode of heat transfer in the equipment. Often the heat-transfer rates are limited by either the critical heat flux or the mechanism of condensation in heat-transfer phenomenon involving phase changes, and by the resistance of the thermal boundary layer in the case of convective heat transfer.

All possible sources of heat or thermal energy may be divided into three broad categories: shore-based heat sources; surface-tendered heat sources; and *in situ* (emplacement of the ocean floor) heat sources. Each type of heat source has its advantages and limitations that make it suitable for use under a limited range of conditions. For example, shore-based heat sources are suitable for underwater work at only short distances from the shore, the maximum practicable distance being dependent upon the cost of connecting supply lines and their effect upon the efficiency of the system. Shore-based sources, therefore, lack the flexibility required for salvage operations at large distances from the shore.

The surface-tendered heat sources are useful for limited depths only. If used to supply hot water to the diver or habitat at depths of, say, over 1000 feet, the power and heat losses in the umbilical will make the system inefficient and uneconomical. *In situ* heat sources, however, offer the most efficient means of generating and distributing heat where required. If the requirements from the heat source are not too high, the source could be compact enough to be easily transportable to various locations.

Small power sources, in general, offer the flexibility that make them useful even under the most demanding conditions. They can be carried with them by divers on short notice, but they are usually limited to the duration of their use before replenishment becomes necessary.

Present Status

The divers are kept warm by circulating hot water through their suits. The hot water for this purpose is produced on board a barge or ship and sent to the diver through a rubber umbilical. The technology is not advanced enough to produce efficient, compact, and reliable heat sources that could be placed at the ocean depths near the habitat or the diver's working area. Similarly, because of the absence of dependable underwater heat sources, the habitat heating requirements are met by electrical heaters powered from surface-located energy sources.

Forecast

Heat sources based upon the heat of crystallization or heat of solution may become a practical reality in the next 10 years for application where small amounts of heat are required over relatively short periods of time. For example, a diver's suit may be made by sandwiching lithium nitrate between two sheets of flexible insulating materials and then using the heat of crystallization to keep the divers warm for 2 hours. Heating systems using heat of solution may also be developed for keeping divers warm using a closed cycle loop. These

TABLE VIII

| Power Source | Forecast | |
	1978	1988
Heat of crystallization	May keep divers warm for 2–3 hours	May be successfully used for 4–5 hours
Heat of solution	May keep a diver warm for 3 hours	May be successfully used for 4–5 hours
Radioactive isotope	Too expensive to be of practical value	Too expensive to be of practical value
Fuel cell	20 percent improvement in specific weight and volume	50 percent improvement in specific weight and volume

TABLE IX
Cost of Nuclear Power Plant
(Millions)

Power (kilowatt)	Operation of Depth (feet)	Present [1]	1978 (projected)	1988 (projected)
30	2000	5.8	5.2	4.6
30	20 000	8.1	7.3	6.5
100	2000	6.2	5.6	5.0
100	20 000	10.1	9.1	8.1
300	2000	6.6	6.0	4.9
300	20 000	15.8	14.2	12.6

systems, however, are required to be regenerated after a few hours of use making their uninterrupted long-term use difficult.

Radioactive isotopic heating is at the demonstration stage at this moment and may become feasible during the next 10 years. However, the cost of radioisotopes will forbid the applications of this system of heating for undersea operations since other less expensive methods are available. The use of radioactive isotopic heating, therefore, cannot be foreseen during the next 20 years.

The fuel cell principle may also be used to generate heat for undersea work. At the 30-kW power level, an estimated specific weight of 55 lb/kW will be required. This figure does not include the weights associated with the fuel storage and waste products. For the larger energy requirements, these will constitute a major portion of the equipment weights and volumes. During the next 10 and 20 years, however, extensive development work may increase the efficiency of the system sufficiently to reduce the system weight and volume requirements by 20 and 50 percent, respectively. The improvements in various sources for small power requirements during the next 10 and 20 years are compared in Table VIII.

The nuclear-reactor plant has been proved to be a very important and successful source of heat and power for undersea applications. Energy storage with the nuclear reactor requires very small weight and volume. It is the only practical self-contained power source for power and energy levels required at ocean depths. It is almost certain that nuclear energy will be the most widely used, and the least expensive, source of electrical power in the next decade or so. With wide use of nuclear energy, and the accompanying development work in better heat-transfer surfaces, the cost of producing heat may be reduced significantly during the next 20 years.

The actual cost of power per kilowatt from a nuclear reactor will depend largely upon the type and size of the reactor and the conditions under which it will be used. It is estimated that cost improvements of 10 and 20 percent may be safely expected during the next 10 and 20 years, respectively. These improvements are significant in view of the fact that dramatic developments

are not expected in the foreseeable future. These improvements in cost, weight, and volume are expected to be caused by a series of small developments in the fairly advanced art of reactor heat transfer. These improvements are shown along with the present costs in Table IX.

Operational Implications

Dives of up to 600 feet were achieved during 1968. Developments during the next 10 and 20 years may make it possible to operate at depths to 5000 and 20 000 feet, respectively, using mechanical equipments. These developments will have to come in areas other than heat transfer since the heat-generating equipment is not the restricting criterion.

The present-day pressurized-type water reactors could be reduced in weight and volume by an improved understanding of the boiling mechanism and its dependence upon the boundary-layer behavior. Similarly, advances in the art of achieving drop-wise condensation for indefinite periods will reduce the condenser sizes by a factor of 2–10, depending upon the level of research efforts and the application of the equipment. These are the high payoff areas where adequate financial support may lead to greater potential gain and an earlier improved operational capability.

In summary the maximum payoff will result from improved reactor design through steady advances in heat-transfer technology.

References

"Conceptual study of electrical power transmission systems to deep ocean installations (U)," General Dynamics Corporation, Electric Boat Div., Rept. CR 68.004, Contract N62399-67-C-0015, August 1967.

Appendix VI

Underwater Observation

Background

Operations in the sea can be observed directly by men looking through viewports at scenes illuminated by lamps; or indirectly, with television (assisted by buoys, acoustic sensors, and photography). In some instances the equipment is exposed to ambient, in others it must be protected from pressure or fouling. Such equipment has evolved from other industrial uses, e.g., television systems, or from military surveillance systems, (high resolution sonar). Remote systems require hard wire telemetry links between the coast site and the viewer (observer).

Present Status

Today's lamps are common tungsten filament incandescent lights, mercury vapor, quartz iodine, tungsten halogen, and thallium iodide. The efficiency of these illumination sources varies from 10 lumens per watt for the incandescent to 80 lumens per watt for the thallium iodide. The length of useful life of these illumination sources varies greatly from 10 hours for arc lights to 1000 or more hours for the incandescent lights.

Viewing distances of 10–20 feet are considered normal for the unaided eye while distances of 25 and 35 feet are approximate distances, respectively, for the vidicon and image orthicon.

The underwater viewing (visual display) capability of sonar devices has not been applied to ocean floor engineering. An ultrasonic telemetry system has recently been developed and is in prototype stage for use in depths greater than 6000 feet. The system has 3 channels and provides 10 percent of full-scale accuracy. Ultrasonic holography is in the R&D stage.

Acrylic windows of conical frustum shape seating in steel flanges with conical cavities are considered standard for submersibles. Design factors in the range of 8–18, based on short-term implosion pressure at room temperature are considered to be acceptable design criteria for such windows. Although a factor of 12 is looked upon as standard, it is known to be overconservative.

Other acrylic window shapes, like flat-disc and spherical-shell sectors have been investigated under short-term loading. As a result, flat-disc acrylic windows are also being utilized in a few shallow-depth submersibles, diving bells, and hyperbaric chambers. The spherical-shell sector acrylic windows have found no application yet in operational systems, although they are being considered for some.

Glass windows find only very limited application. Their use is limited almost exclusively to diving bells and hyperbaric chambers of less than 1000-psi pressure capability. But even there they are being displaced by acrylic material whose behavior under the combination of stresses found in a hydrospace window is more repeatable than that of currently available glass.

Fouling of the window's surface exposed to sea water limits the optical usefulness of windows to about 24 hours. A recently introduced tributyl tin oxide transparent coating extends the optical usefulness of windows to somewhat in excess of 100 hours. No difference in resistance to fouling has been found between glass, acrylic, or polycarbonate materials.

Forecast

By 1978 the light source will increase 50 percent in efficiency and 100 percent in length of life. The main area of improvement will be to match the wavelength of the generated light with the band in which the receiving sensor has its greatest efficiency. (See Figs. 12 and 13.)

The pressure case will become 20 percent lighter. The electrical connection will become 95 percent reliable. (See Fig. 14.)

Acrylic windows, regardless of their shape, will be completely understood and detailed design standards and specifications will be available for their design and fabrication. Factors of safety of 6–8 (compared with present design factor of 12) will encourage the incorporation of larger windows in submersibles. (See Fig. 15.)

Spherical-shell sector shape acrylic windows will further increase in size permitting the occupants of submersibles to have a panoramic view of hydrospace. Window diameters of up to 8 feet for continental shelf depths, and 1 foot for abyssal depths will become state of the art of acrylic windows. Very little improvement in acrylic windows beyond the state-of-the-art forecast for 1968 will be feasible unless the limitation imposed by the mechanical properties of the currently available acrylic are lifted.

Research conducted on the basic mechanical properties of glass, and the effect of triaxial stress fields with local stress concentrations on its failure will result in flat disc glass windows of 4–8 inches diameter and up to 5000-feet depth capability. Nevertheless, for the same diameter and thickness the acrylic windows will still be capable of withstanding greater depths than glass windows.

Other transparent plastic materials will produce several promising candidates with 20–50 percent higher mechanical strength properties of 20–50 percent less time-dependent strain than currently available acrylics.

Fouling of windows will be eliminated for periods of at least 1000 hours by the development of slow leaching transparent overlays applied to the high-pressure face of the windows.

By 1988 nuclear and gas power sources will become standard equipment. The length of life will be expanded from weeks to years for small energy supplies. The light-source efficiency will be increased to 250 lumens per watt. The length of useful life will be expanded five fold by introduction of better cooling methods, cold light sources, and better materials.

For underwater television cameras techniques such as time and range rating, to eliminate some "close" back scattering, may improve range to a limited degree.

For underwater ultrasonic telemetry, 1.0 percent of full scale accuracy appears entirely feasible. Many channels of information will be multiplexed on one ultrasonic carrier using FM-FM techniques. Since most phenomena being monitored are dynamically slow, time sharing will be utilized to increase the amount of information.

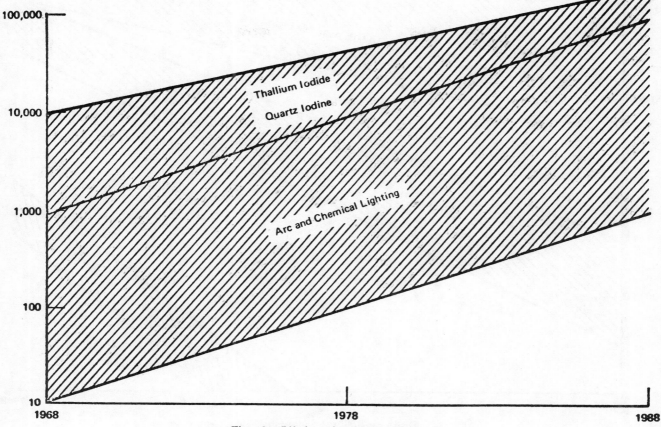

Fig. 12.   Lifetime of underwater lights.

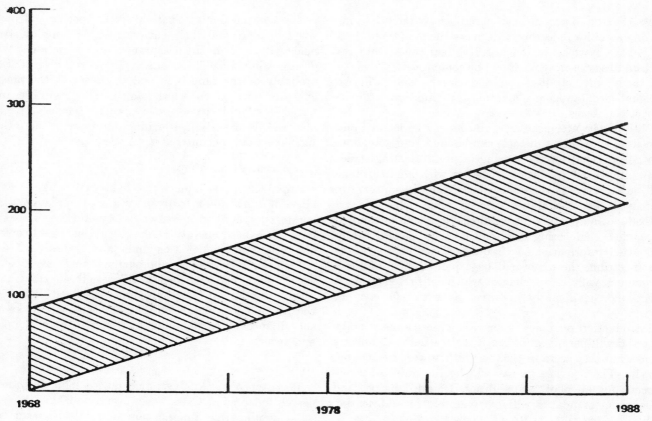

Fig. 13.   Energy efficiency of underwater lights (lumens/watt).

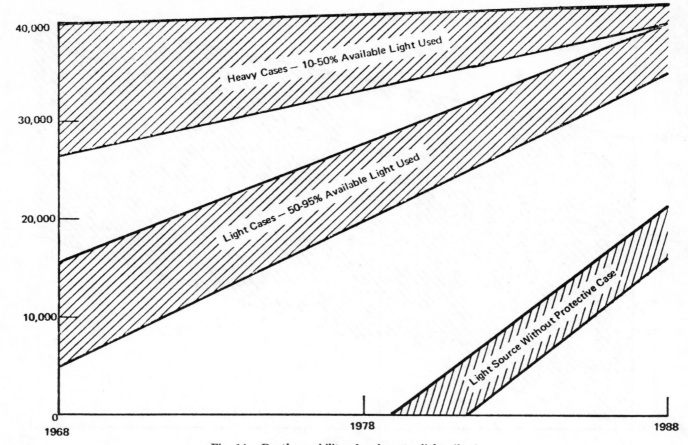

Fig. 14.   Depth capability of underwater lights (feet).

Surface radio buoys or other radio-link facilities, including satellite repeaters, will make the monitored data available anywhere in the world in real time. Data reduction to engineering units will be computerized.

Control of activities on the ocean floor will be accomplished by using ultrasonic techniques on a "two-way street" basis.

With underwater acoustics, objects can be located and dimensioned, readout of tools can be used, and guidelines can be provided for the mating of prefabricating structures. Improved resolution, together with greater range will be achieved as the dimension of the transducers are increased. The techniques used in mine detection and antisubmarine warfare ultrasonic devices will be adapted to sea floor engineering requirements. The use of digitally formatted information, at frequencies within the heaving spectrum, the diver will be exploited. Use of these techniques will free packages, which he presently must carry and significantly improve the work efficiency of divers.

Introduction of a new transparent plastic as window material will permit an increase in the window diameters from what they were in 1968 when they were made from acrylic. The increase in size will be the order of 20–50 percent for all depth capabilities. Detailed design and fabrication standards will be available for fabrication of hydrospace windows from the new materials.

The continued investigation of the mechanical properties of glass and their behavior under complex stress fields will result in the acceptance of glass on a par with plastic windows. The available glass windows will be probably of the same size and thickness as the plastic ones for any given depth range. They will be preferred for applications where water temperatures go above 75°F or sustained loading durations or more than 1000 hours are encountered in service.

Operational Implications

Improvement of underwater lights will make surveillance of surrounding hydrospace more complete and accurate and result in increased safety and ease of operations. Enhanced operating areas would be vessel control, data acquisition, navigation, and search and salvage.

Panoramic visibility approaching that of airplane cockpits and car windshields will permit safer operation of submersibles in close proximity to fixed objects on the ocean floor. Ocean bottom habitats will make the surveillance of surrounding hydrospace more complete and accurate.

References

R. Hitchcock, "Analysis of a pulsed light deep ocean search system," NCEL Tech. Rept. R-209.

——, "Submarine illumination and television in har-

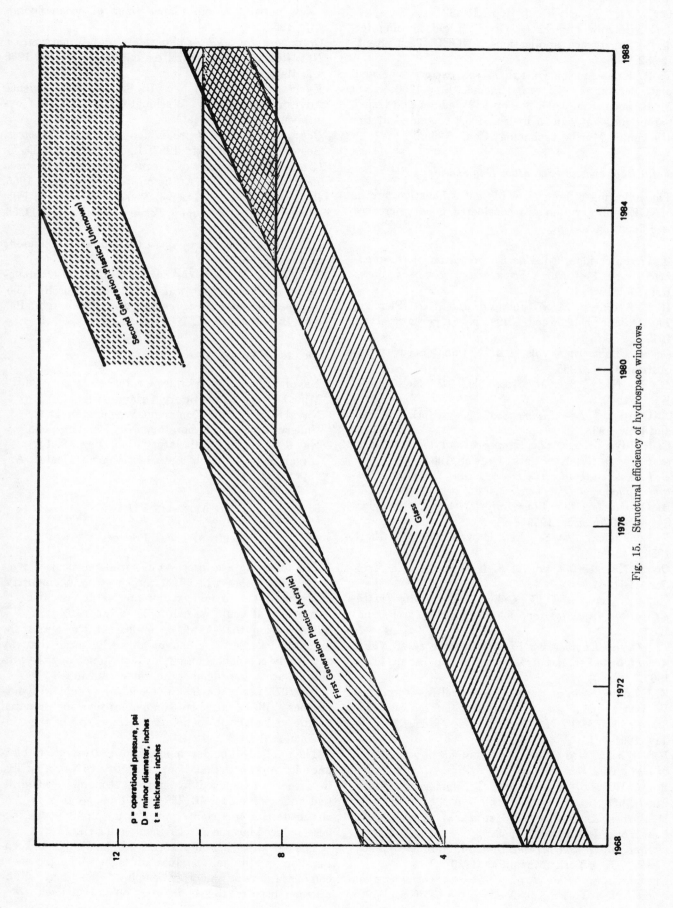

Fig. 15. Structural efficiency of hydrospace windows.

bor water," NCEL Tech. Rept. R-432.

J. D. Stachiw and K. O. Gray, "Light housing for deep-submergence applications," NCEL Tech. Rept. R-532.

T. R. Kretschmer, "DOTIPOS sea performance and plate bearing test," internal memo., June 1960.

M. R. Snoey and J. D. Stachiw, "Windows and transparent hull for man in hydrospace," presented at the 4th Annual Marine Technology Conf., 1968.

General References on Sea Floor Engineering

The following references, while not exhaustive, are in the NCEL library and are considered good references on sea floor engineering.

R. W. Fairbridge, Ed. *The Encyclopedia of Oceanography*, vol. 1 of *Earth Sciences Series*. New York: Reinhold, 1966.

H. V. Sverdrup, M. W. Johnson, and R. H. Fleming, *The Oceans*. Englewood Cliffs, N. J.: Prentice-Hall, 1942.

Ocean Engineering, vols. 1–4. National Security Industrial Assoc. 1965.

M. N. Hill, Ed. *The Sea*, vols. 1–3. New York: Wiley, 1962.

J. Cousteau, *The Living Sea*. New York: Harper and Row, 1963.

C. P. Idyll, *Abyss, The Deep Sea and The Creatures that Live In It*. New York: Crowell, 1964.

T. F. Gaskell, *Under the Deep Ocean; Twentieth Century Voyages of Discovery*. New York: Norton, 1960.

B. C. Heezen, *The Floors of the Ocean*. Geological Society of America, 1959.

V. Zenkovick, *The Sea Bed*. Lawrence and Wishart, 1959.

Ocean Engineering, vols. 1–8. North American Aviation, 1964.

C. L. Hayen and C. L. Cohen, *Sea Bottom Instrumentation Investigation*. Challenger Research, Inc., 1967.

The Ocean Engineering Program of the U. S. Navy; Accomplishment and Prospects. Oceanographic Office, 1967.

E. J. Long, *Ocean Sciences*. U. S. Naval Institute, 1964.

W. Bascom, *A Hole In the Bottom of the Sea: The Story of the MOHOLE Project*. New York: Doubleday, 1961.

IGY World Data Center A: Oceanography Catalogue of Data, vols. 1–5, 1967.

R. L. Wiegel, *Oceanographical Engineering*. Englewood Cliffs, N. J.: Prentice-Hall, 1964.

H. Barnes, *Apparatus and Methods of Oceanography*. New York: Interscience, 1959.

Oceanography and Marine Biology; A Book of Techniques. New York: Macmillan, 1959.

Oceanography, 1959 Proc. Internatl. Oceanographic Cong. New York: Am. Assoc. Advan. of Sci., 1961.

"New portrait of our planet (map of ocean floors), *Life*, 1960.

Oceanography, and Achievements and Opportunities. Nat. Res. Council, Committee on Oceanography, 1966 and 1967.

Effective Use of the Sea, U. S. Presidents Science Advisory Committee. Washington, D. C.: U. S. Government Printing Office, 1966.

Oceanography: An Introduction of Marine Sciences. Boston: Little, Brown, 1962. L. M. Hurs and D. G. Groves, Eds. *Glossary of Ocean Sciences and Undersea Technology Terms*. Arlington, Va.: Compass, 1965.

B. B. Baker, W. R. Deebel, E. D. Geisenderfer, Eds. *Glossary of Oceanographic Terms*. Washington, D. C., 1966.

C. A. King, *Oceanography to Geographers*. London: E. Arnold, 1962.

J. R. Dean, *Down to the Sea; A Century of Oceanography*. Glasgow: Grown, Son and Ferguson, 1966. *Marine Sciences Instrumentation*. Pittsburgh, Pa.. Am. Instrument Soc., 1962–1965.

Associated R&D Organizations

Naval Underwater Warfare Center, Pasadena, Calif.
Mine Detection Laboratory, Orlando, Fla.
Naval Ship Systems Command, Washington, D. C.
Underwater Sound Laboratory, New London, Conn.
Naval Electronics Laboratory, San Diego, Calif.
Naval Ship Research and Development Center, Annapolis, Md.

Appendix VII

Environmental Forecasts

The following are forecasts of social–political changes in the 1970's that will affect the construction industry. (See Fig. 16 for a matrix of material discussed in the forecasts that could be available in the 1970's.)

The notion that hard or unpleasant work must be tolerated because it is unavoidable will be on the way out. Many companies may find they cannot pay the premium that workers demand for unpleasant jobs.

By 1975 professional and technical people will outnumber skilled craftsmen. Companies must be prepared to hire and train personnel at the lower end of the educational scale.

The public will be developing a lower frustration tolerance for anything that impairs ability to work, to live in decency, as judged by current economic standards, and to express oneself. There will be no tolerance of circumstances created by poverty, unemployment, sickness, reduced income at retirement, and strikes.

The cost of laying off a worker will be as high as keeping him on the job because of higher unemployment compensation and the other benefits; hence, there will be a strong incentive to keep industry on an even keel.

FUNCTIONS / APPLICATIONS

MATERIAL	Homogeneous	Composite	Armor	Propulsion & Power	Piping & Auxiliary	Corrosive Service	Low Temp. Service	High Temp. Service	Protection	Wire Rope, Wire, Etc.	Electrical	Unique Properties	Camouflage & Identification	Energy Absorption & Insulation
	Structural			*Machinery*		*Environmental*				*Miscellaneous*				
ALUMINUM	X	X		X	X	X	X			X	X			
ANTIMONY												X		
BERYLLIUM	X	X		X	X	X	X	X		X		X		
BISMUTH												X		
CADMIUM						X					X	X		
CESIUM												X		
CHROMIUM		X		X	X			X						
COBALT		X		X	X	X		X		X		X		
COLUMBIUM		X			X			X				X		
COPPER		X		X	X	X	X			X				
GALLIUM											X	X		
GERMANIUM												X		
GOLD		X				X						X		
HAFNIUM								X			X	X		
INDIUM											X	X		
IRIDIUM											X	X		
IRON	X	X		X	X	X	X	X		X				
LANTHANUM											X			
LEAD						X					X			
LITHIUM												X		
MAGNESIUM	X	X		X	X	X		X				X		
MERCURY											X	X		
MOLYBDENUM	X			X	X			X			X			
NICKEL	X	X		X	X	X	X	X		X				
NIOBIUM											X			
OSMIUM											X	X		
PALLADIUM		X			X	X		X				X		
PLATINUM		X			X	X		X				X		
POTASSIUM												X		
RHENIUM						X					X	X		
RHODIUM												X		
RUTHENIUM											X	X		
SELENIUM												X		
SILICON											X			
SILVER		X				X					X	X		
SODIUM												X		
STEEL — SEE IRON														
TANTALUM				X	X	X	X				X	X		
TECHNETIUM											X			
TELLURIUM												X		
THALLIUM											X	X		
TIN						X					X	X		
TITANIUM	X	X		X	X	X	X	X		X		X		
TUNGSTEN				X	X			X			X	X		
URANIUM											X	X		
VANADIUM				X				X			X	X		
ZINC						X					X			
ZIRCONIUM											X	X		
ADHESIVES		X							X		X			
COATINGS									X					
COMPOSITES		X	X	X					X			X	X	
FIBERS & TEXTILES									X					
HYDRAULIC FLUIDS				X					X					
LUBRICANTS				X					X					
PLASTICS	X	X	X	X					X			X	X	X
WOOD	X	X												

Fig. 16. Materials technology matrix identifying functions/applications for materials discussed in the 540 series of forecasts. The X indicates material function covered.

The public will expect more attention be paid to safety in design. Industry will be expected to pay more of the social costs of problems it helped create, such as air pollution, water pollution, and traffic congestion.

The government will have an increasing say in where new plants are to be located. They will compel location in rural development areas, will control land usage and pollution, and will have much more influence on building codes.

There will be farming in the oceans.

There will be mining on the moon.

There will be less leadership from business and more from government, research centers, and universities.

We will near the end of democratic government as people lose interest and leave decisions to an intellectual technological elite.

There will be an emergence of new more dangerous weapons, permitting even poor countries to destroy any other country.

References

[1] H. I. Ansoff and J. M. Stewart, "Strategies for a technology-based business," *Harvard Business Rev.*, pp. 71–83, November–December 1967.
[2] M. P. Cetron, P. H. Caulfield, and R. D. Freshman, "Facts and folklore in R&D management revisited" *Management Sci.*, (to be published).
[3] M. J. Cetron, H. Darracott, and H. Wells, *Report on Technological Forecasting*. Sponsored by the Joint Commanders of the Army Materiel Command, Navy Materiel Command, and Air Force Systems Command (AD 664108); CFSTI, Springfield, Va., May 1967.
[4] M. J. Cetron, R. Isenson, J. Johnson, A. B. Nutt, and H. Wells, *Technological Resource Management: Quantitative Methods*. Cambridge, Mass.: M.I.T. Press, 1969.
[5] M. J. Cetron, J. Martino, and L. Roepke, "The selection of R&D program content—Survey of quantitative methods," *IEEE Trans. Engineering Management*, vol. EM-14, pp. 4–12, March 1967.
[6] M. J. Cetron and T. Monohan, "An evaluation and appraisal of various approaches to technological forecasting," in *Technological Forecasting for Industry and Government*, J. R. Bright, Ed. Englewood Cliffs, N. J.: Prentice-Hall, 1968, pp. 144–179.
[7] M. J. Cetron and A. L. Weiser, "Technological change, technological forecasting and planning R&D—A view from the R&D manager's desk," *George Washington Law Rev.*, vol. 35, July 1968.
[8] K. Ellingsworth, "Technology assessment," M.S. thesis, American University, Washington, D. C., June 1968.
[9] W. D. Guth and R. Tagiuri, "Personal values and corporate strategy," *Harvard Business Rev.*, September–October 1965.
[10] R. S. Isenson and C. W. Sherwin, "Project Hindsight," Office of the Director of Defense Res. and Engrg., Interim Rept. CSTI AD 642 400, June 1966 (revised October 1966).
[11] R. Lenz, "Technological forecasting," CSTI AD 408 085, 1962.
[12] H. Q. North and D. L. Pyke, "Technology, the chicken-corporate goals, the egg," in *Technological Forecasting for Industry and Government*, J. R. Bright, Ed. Englewood Cliffs, N. J.: Prentice-Hall, 1968, pp. 412–425.
[13] A. B. Nutt, "An approach to research and development effectiveness," *IEEE Trans. Engineering Management*, vol. EM-12, pp. 103–112, September 1965.
[14] E. B. Roberts, "Facts and folklore in R&D management," *Industrial Management Rev.*, 1967.
[15] "Sea floor engineering," in *Navy Technological Forecast*, presented at the 1969 Engrg. Foundation Res. Conf., Pacific Grove, Calif.

Cost Effectiveness in R&D Organizational Resource Allocation

BURTON V. DEAN AND LEWIS A. ROEPCKE

Abstract—A method for use in allocating resources to a multilaboratory, multitask research and exploratory program is described. The basic elements of the underlying model are 1) tasks, projects, and laboratories, 2) contributing sciences and technologies (S and T), 3) criticality of such fields to achieving organizational objectives, 4) relative values of objectives, and 5) costs of performing tasks.

Structural models are developed for interrelating tasks, S and T fields, and objectives. A cost-effectiveness model is developed for use in allocating resources to tasks. Research and exploratory development effectiveness is measured in terms of the value of task contribution to organizational objectives.

Results of this study tested by experimentally determined inputs include 1) cost-effectiveness relationships for tasks, projects, laboratories, and S and T fields, 2) log-normal distributions for both project cost and effectiveness, and 3) a systematic procedure for allocating resources to R&D activities.

I. Introduction

A. The Army Materiel Command Multilaboratory Organization

THE U. S. Army Materiel Command's (AMC) research and development accomplishes, on a dollar basis, about 80–85 percent of the Army's applied research and component development. These efforts are

Manuscript received July 1969; revised August 1969. This report was prepared as part of the activities of the Department of Operations Research, School of Management, Case–Western Reserve University, under Contract DA-ARO-D-31-124-G-1034 with Army Materiel Command.

Burton V. Dean is with the Operations Research Department, Case–Western Reserve University, Cleveland, Ohio.

Lewis A. Roepcke is with the Technical Planning Branch, U. S. Army Materiel Command, Washington, D. C.

characterized by the Department of Defense (DOD) as research and exploratory development.

Two kinds of organizations are assigned specific missions to perform the necessary work to provide vastly improved materiel to future armies. The first kind is commodity oriented, i.e., aircraft (Aviation Command), missiles (Missile Command), etc. These commodity commands have as a mission all research and exploratory development peculiar to their commodity area. The other kind of organization is assigned missions in research and exploratory development that do not pertain to a specific commodity, i.e., Ballistics Research Laboratory, Terrestrial Sciences Laboratory, etc. AMC desires to optimize its allocation of technical efforts to accomplish its overall goals to improve the future Field Army's fighting capability on a future battlefield, if the nation determines at that future time the action is necessary.

B. The Technical Planning Branch, Science and Technology Division, Directorate of Developments and Engineering, USAMC

The Planning Branch has, as its primary function, the provision of analytical aids to the AMC Director of Development and Engineering to assist him in realizing an optimum allocation of resources. The branch provides planning support to assist in securing the most suitable R&D program direction and optimum balance between the elements of research and development for the short-, mid-, and long-range time frames[1] (5, 10–12, and 20 years, respectively).

Prior effort at Case–Western Reserve University to provide the Planning Branch with these analytical aids has been concerned with mid-range time frames.

This paper provides the results of a laboratory resource-allocation model and experimental testing that was developed to assist AMC in its laboratory management in those efforts where the detail planning for achieving a specific end item of materiel is not yet possible to structure for use with the mid-range time analytical aids. The experiment included all elements of the problem and was used to test the effectiveness, sensitivity, and ease of use of the developed model that is being reported.

C. Resource Allocation: Cost-Effectiveness System

The purpose of this paper is to describe a method for use in allocating funds to laboratory projects to accomplish specific Army long-range time-frame objectives. The underlying model may be described as a resource-allocation type, with a cost-effectiveness relationship developed to evaluate alternative results of allocating such resources.

D. Planning, Systems Analysis, and Cost Effectiveness

Planning is the process of preparing for the commitment of resources in the most effective and economical fashion and, by preparing, allowing this commitment to be made less disruptively on organizational strategies than by a random process.[2] Investment in AMC planning is the consideration of the alternative allocation of resources that would best achieve the Army's long-range objectives in materiel development.

To accomplish planning it is necessary to take a systems approach that considers the organization as a whole, and uses objective analyses in formulating long-range R&D plans. Of course, subjective estimates must be utilized, but it is necessary to develop the framework, as a *model*, to incorporate these estimates into the planning process.

The model: In this model we made use of systems analysis, which includes the following procedures:

1) a systematic examination and comparison of alternative methods of allocating resources to achieve operational-capability objectives;
2) use of costs of resources and military values to evaluate alternatives; and
3) a method of synthesizing the available information on scientific and technological linkages, needs for breakthroughs[3] in specific areas, relative importance of objectives, and the uncertainty in the underlying R&D process.

It should be pointed out that we use systems analysis to complement the experienced judgment and intuition of scientists and engineers, on the one hand and military planners and tacticians, on the other. Such estimates and judgments have been incorporated in the model developed here.

The methods of system analysis have been applied to many Department of Defense decision problems and areas. It is our purpose to apply this method to the AMC R&D long-range planning problem. Below, an illustrative example is considered as the basic model to be developed here.

Consider an Army operational capability objective (OCO) O_1. The objective may be accomplished by breakthroughs in, say, two scientific and technological fields S_1 and S_2. However, let us assume that S_1 is more important than S_2 in achieving O_1. Suppose we consider two objectives O_1 and O_2. The relative weights of the objectives (0.7 and 0.3) and the contribution of the sciences

[1] B. V. Dean, "A research laboratory performance model," *IEEE Trans. Engineering Management*, vol. EM-14, pp. 44–46, March 1967.

[2] E. K. Warren, *Long Range Planning: The Executive Viewpoint.* Englewood Cliffs, N. J.: Prentice-Hall, 1966, p. 21.
[3] Here, the definition of scientific and technological breakthrough does not necessarily mean unexpected solution to a problem, but that in most cases achievement of planned results from scientific activities are accomplishable. The detailed specific activities may be difficult to plan in detail, however it is possible to predict that an answer will come from specific scientific or technological areas.

to the objectives (S_1, $O_1 = 0.8$, etc.) are given in the following matrix.

Science-Objective Matrix

Sciences	0.7 O_1	0.3 O_2	Weighted Relative Military Value
S_1	0.8	0.2	0.62
S_2	0.4	0.6	0.46

We can calculate the weighted relative military value of each field by multiplying the contributions of the fields to achieving the objectives by the relative importance of the objectives, and summing across objectives.

$$E(S_1) = W_1 b_{11} + W_2 b_{12}$$
$$= (0.7)(0.8) + (0.3)(0.2)$$
$$= 0.56 + 0.06$$
$$= 0.62$$

$$E(S_2) = W_1 b_{21} + W_2 b_{22}$$
$$= (0.7)(0.4) + (0.3)(0.6)$$
$$= 0.28 + 0.18$$
$$= 0.46.$$

It appears on this basis that S_1 is more important than S_2. However, we need to consider the underlying laboratory tasks that contribute to the pertinent fields.

Suppose that two tasks T_1 and T_2 are being considered, where T_2 contributes to S_2 only, and T_1 contributes to both S_1 and S_2. We may express this relationship in the linkage matrix below.

Task-Science Matrix

Task	Science S_1	S_2
T_1	1	1
T_2	0	1

We may now calculate the weighted relative military values of the tasks as follows:

$$E(T_1) = a_{11} E(S_1) + a_{12} E(S_2)$$
$$= (1)(0.62) + (1)(0.46)$$
$$= 1.08$$

$$E(T_2) = a_{21} E(S_1) + a_{22} E(S_2)$$
$$= (0)(0.63) + (1)(0.46)$$
$$= 0.46.$$

We see that the weighted relative military value of task

T_1 is significantly greater than that of task T_2 in the ratio of 1.08:0.46.

We can introduce cost-effectiveness (CE) analysis into the task evaluation and selection procedure by considering the cost of the task, as well as the weighted relative military value above. If C_1 and C_2 are the costs of tasks T_1 and T_2, respectively, and suppose that $C_1 = \$2\,000\,000$ and $C_2 = \$1\,000\,000$, we have

$$G_1 = \frac{E(T_1)}{C_1} = \frac{1.08}{2} = 0.54 \times 10^6$$

$$G_2 = \frac{E(T_2)}{C_2} = \frac{0.46}{1} = 0.46 \times 10^6.$$

Although T_1 is twice as costly as T_2 to perform, the increased CE value in T_1 over T_2 is such that T_1 is preferred to T_2.

E. Structure of the Resource-Allocation Model

The basic structure of the model consists of the following elements.

Operational capability objectives (OCO) O_k.
Numerical military values of the OCO V_k.
Sciences and technologies S_i.
Laboratory tasks (and projects or program elements) T_i.
Needed S_i to achieve OCO a_{ij}.
Criticality of S_i in achieving OCO b_{ijk}.
Weighted criticality of S_i in achieving OCO $a_{ij} b_{ijk}$.
Weighted military value of T_i in achieving $O_k a_{ij} b_{ijk} V_k$.
Weighted military value of $T_i e_i = \sum_{i,k} a_{ij} b_{ijk} V_k$.
Total weighted military value $E_m = \sum_i e_i$.[4]
Total weighted military value $E = \sum E_m$.[5]
Costs of laboratory tasks C_i.
Total available resources $C = \sum_i C_i$ or $C < \sum_i C_i$ or $C > \sum_i C_i$.

The elements and structure are illustrated in Fig. 1.

The interrelationships are illustrated in Fig. 2. Consider the upper right-hand corner. A list of OCO is tabulated, followed by rank ordering and weighting over a numerical scale of values V_k.

A list of groups of sciences and technologies are prepared, using the COSATI (Committee on Scientific and Technical Information) list as an example S_i. For a set of laboratory (or commodity office) tasks T_i, the individual S_i from these groups that are needed to achieve the individual tasks are listed a_{ij}, and for each individual S_i the set of OCO that would benefit from such development along with the degree of criticality is obtained b_{ijk}. Combining these weighted criticalities with the value of the OCO yields the weighted military values of a task in achieving the OCO $a_{ij} b_{ijk} V_k$. Then by summing the weighted military value of a task $e_i = \sum_{ik} a_{ij} b_{ijk} V_k$, the weighted military value of a project $E(P) = \sum_i e_i$ and the total weighted military $E = \sum E_m$ are obtained.

---

[4] Of a laboratory project.
[5] Of the set of laboratory projects or program elements composing the laboratory total program.

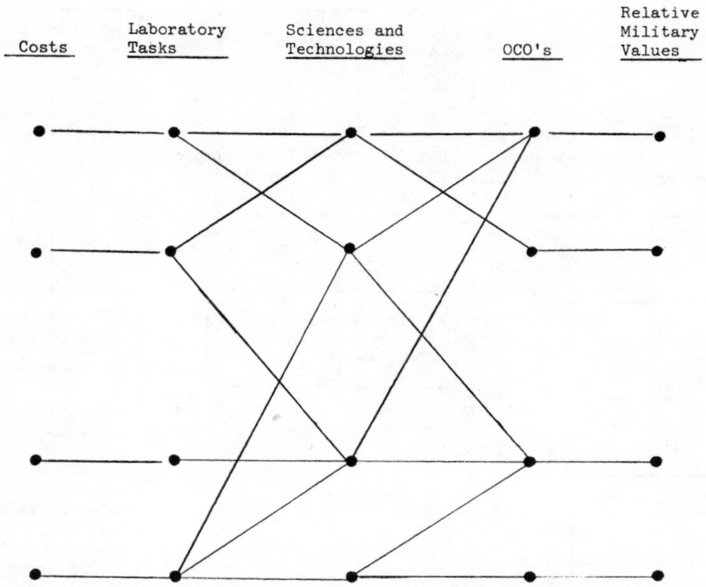

Costs	Laboratory Tasks	Sciences and Technologies	OCO's	Relative Military Values

Fig. 1.   Basic elements and structure of the resource-allocation model.

The total available resources

$$C = \sum_i C_i \quad \text{or} \quad C < \sum_i C_i \quad \text{or} \quad C > \sum_i C_i$$

are allocated to laboratory tasks T_i.

Finally, the cost-effectiveness relationship may be obtained by varying the available funds and calculating effectiveness (total weighted military value) $E = \sum E_m$.

II. ORGANIZATIONAL OUTPUT

A. Introduction

The direct output of an R&D laboratory may be measured in terms of the value of laboratory reports and the laboratory's inputs to system-development activity. Although the number and frequency of such reports may be measured, and an indication of the utility or usefulness of such reports developed, these measurements would have to be related to the overall present and future objectives of R&D activities. In general, there is difficulty in estimating the value of such scientific and technological information for management decision-making purposes. More importantly, no useful measures have been derived for evaluating progress towards future objective goals.

Since laboratory activity must, in fact, essentially be related to the long-range objectives, this study takes as the basic indicator of the value of the output of a laboratory the extent to which ultimate objectives are satisfied. In this way, the difficult problems associated with identifying and measuring intermediate outputs are avoided.

B. Operational Capability Objectives (OCO)

The Army has specified a set of 23 OCO that are to be achieved.[6] The format used for defining operational capa-

[6] Currently, attention is being given to a set of 56 objectives.

bility objectives is given in Table I. This set may be considered to be the defining objectives for an Army mission-oriented R&D laboratory. The degree to which a laboratory contributes to the achievement of these objectives is one indication of the value of that laboratory to the Army achieving its goals. In this study, laboratory performance is measured in terms of the contributions of the laboratory's tasks and projects to advancement in science and technology in furthering the achievement of Army objectives.

Three examples of OCO statements used in this study are Intelligence, Acquisition, and Dissemination (O_1), Automatic Data Processing (O_{12}), and Advanced Energy Sources (O_{16}). Explicit statements of the objectives may be found in Army planning documents.

C. Goals as Time-Dependent Objectives

The operational capability objectives as stated are considered to be independent of a specific time reference. However, in practice, the Army is concerned with achieving the objectives in each of specified five-year time frames. Each laboratory task activity in various portions of its efforts is oriented towards the development of materiel for specific time frames such as Army 80 and Army 85. Accordingly, a portion of the task's goal is to achieve a contribution of the advancement of knowledge necessary to accomplish a specific time-oriented Army objective for materiel development.

D. Rank Ordering and the Measurement of Values of Objectives

The objectives, as time-stated requirements for Army materiel development, were subjectively rank ordered in terms of relative degrees of importance. Although there is some overlap between objectives as described below, the subjective estimation of relative importance is based

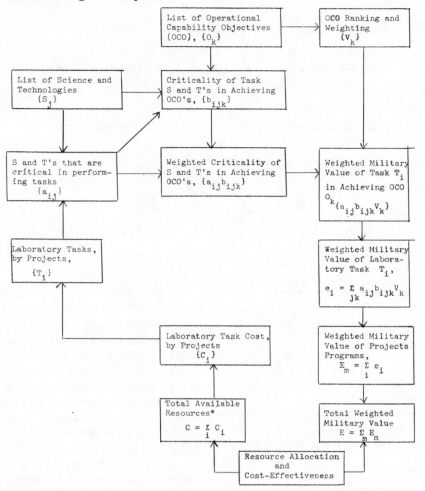

Fig. 2. Flow diagram of the resource-allocation model. Asterisk indicates alternatives $C < \sum_i C_i$ or $C > \sum_i C_i$.

on the essential and critical differences in values to accomplish the Army's many missions on potential future battlefields and to achieving these objectives for the specific time frame.

The OCO have military worth evaluated on an interval scale. Such a scale assigns a numerical value to each OCO and in this study the intervals between OCO are considered to be equal.

The values were consistent with opinions. However, no attempt was made to obtain a consensus of viewpoints, or even a widespread evaluation, or to obtain absolute worth, since what is really needed is relative military worth. Furthermore, it is impossible to forecast the type of environment in which the systems under development will be utilized.

The assumption is made that a linear scale of additive utilities is valid; however, the real world is subject to nonlinearities and significant probabilistic and dynamic factors. Although some sensitivity analysis is performed in this study on the effect of errors in estimating military worth, the fact remains that periodic annual runs of the data and model would obviate the need for a refined non-linear stochastic model at this time.

In order to perform the rank ordering of objectives,

the objectives were classified into two directly comparable categories on the basis of foreseeable directions for scientific and technological efforts and on relatively unforeseeable directions that science and technology can take to achieve the objectives. This classification corresponds to differences in the difficulty in achieving the objective, but not in the corresponding desirability of achievement. Each category was considered separately, and the value-measurement process was carried out for each class. Following the value-measurement process, the objectives in each category were combined into a single class, which incorporates the assumption that objectives selected at random from each set would have equal expected military values.

Subjective estimates of the relative values of the objectives were obtained using the rank ordering and constant differences over a 3:1 scale. The size of the scale is not important since relative values were utilized. A constant-difference assumption, as is used in this paper, is realistic on the basis of the following discussion. The method used for rank ordering and equal intervals develops an interval scale that is a specific case of the direct-rating method ([7], p. 444).

Suppose that the set of m objectives have values given

TABLE I
Format Used for Defining Operational Capability Objectives

Title
Operational Requirement
  Background discussion
  Statement of capability desired
  Impact of capability on operations

Specific Operational Applications
  Level of conflict applicable
    (counter-insurgency, low intensity, high intensity, etc.)
  Environments
    (jungle, mountain, sea, high or low altitude, space, arctic, etc.)
  Functional areas
    (Air and Missile Defense, Anti-armor Warfare, Strategic Offense, etc.)

  Equipment applications
    (aircraft, tanks, missiles, rockets, etc.)

Technological Elements of the Solution
  Likelihood of achievement
  Courses being pursued
  Areas needing support

by the following

$$V_1, V_1 + d_2 = V_2,$$
$$V_1 + d_3 = V_3, \cdots, V_1 + d_m = V_m.$$

Then the differences between successive values are given by the values $d_2, d_3, \cdots, d_m$ and the average difference is given by

$$\bar{d} = \frac{1}{m-1}\left(\sum_{i=2}^{m} d_i\right).$$

Since we are considering a sufficiently large set of objectives, the substitution of $\bar{d}$ for the individual differences will not result in significant error or bias in evaluating laboratory tasks relative to errors in estimating other parameter values in this model. The constant-difference assumption is valid as long as the objectives were rank ordered carefully. The rank ordering of the set of 23 OCO was carefully accomplished.

E. Interdependent Objectives

Since the objectives were not structured to preclude overlap in capabilities sought, an important consideration is the effect of this overlap in objectives on estimating values. If O_1 and O_2 are two objectives, then we may write the value function for achieving the combined objectives as

$$V(O_1 \oplus O_2) = V(O_1) + V(O_2) - (V(O_1 \cap O_2))$$

Estimates of the following values were prepared:

$$V(O_i) \qquad i = 1, 2, \cdots, 23,$$

$$V(O_i \oplus O_j) \quad \text{and} \quad V(O_i \cap O_j)$$

$$i, j = 1, 2, \cdots, 23; \quad i \neq j.$$

It was observed that in only eight of the 252 cases was

$V(O_i \cap O_j)$ more than 25 percent of $V(O_i \oplus O_j)$. In fact, in only 43 of the 252 cases (or less than 20 percent) a nonzero value of $V(O_i \cap O_j)$ occurred. Although the list of objectives was not generated on the basis of independent objectives, an analysis of these objectives in a pairwise comparison indicates that

$$V(O_1 \cap O_2) \ll V(O_1) + V(O_2),$$

and therefore, for analytic purposes, we may assume that

$$V(O_1 \oplus O_2) = V(O_1) + V(O_2).$$

It should be pointed out that although there is an overlap in the OCO as interpreted from their statement, the individual projects and tasks that contribute to achieving the OCO in general do not involve the overlapping elements to any appreciable extent.

Fig. 3(a)–(d) provides an illustrative example of the preceding discussion on the hierarchial relations in the R&D model employed in this study. In Fig. 3(a), operational capability objective O_1 comprises a set of $\{O_{11}, O_{12}, \cdots, O_{1n}\}$ distinct items all of which are needed if O_1 capability is to be realized. O_2, O_3, and O_n each have their own set of items.

As shown by Fig. 3(b), the overlap of O_1 and O_2 results in item (O_{12}, O_{31}) being the same item needed in both O_1 and O_3. O_2 does not overlap either O_1 or O_3.

The projects $\{P_1, P_2, \cdots, P_n\}$ comprise the set of R&D activities that support the set of objectives $\{O_1, O_2, \cdots, O_n\}$. Illustrated in Fig. 3(c) are two projects (projects do not overlap) P_1 and P_2. Each project has a number of tasks T_i. Project P_1 has the set of tasks $\{T_{11}, T_{12}, \cdots, T_{1m}\}$.

Overlaying these sets, Fig. 3(d) shows the basis of the analytical method used in this study. Science and technology S_2 could be overevaluated in terms of weighted military value (O_1 and O_3), but as shown in calculations the effect is small. Task T_{12} supporting both O_1 and O_3 involves different sciences and technologies S_2 and S_3 as the items (O_{12}, O_{31}) and (O_{32}) are different.

III. Laboratories, Projects, and Tasks

A. Multilaboratory Organizations

Some 56 laboratories are organized under the command structure of the Army Materiel Command (AMC). AMC is concerned with providing systems and components to meet Army materiel objectives (future needs) and requirements (needed now). A listing of some AMC laboratories is presented in Table II.

Materiel systems require the effort of a number of AMC laboratories working together to achieve necessary knowledge levels for system development to be profitably undertaken [3]. Both critical problems and supporting development work must be undertaken by the laboratories. Consequently, the laboratory's performance must be measured in terms of 1) the magnitude of the *contributions* of its projects and tasks to sciences and technologies, 2) the *criticality* of the sciences and technologies

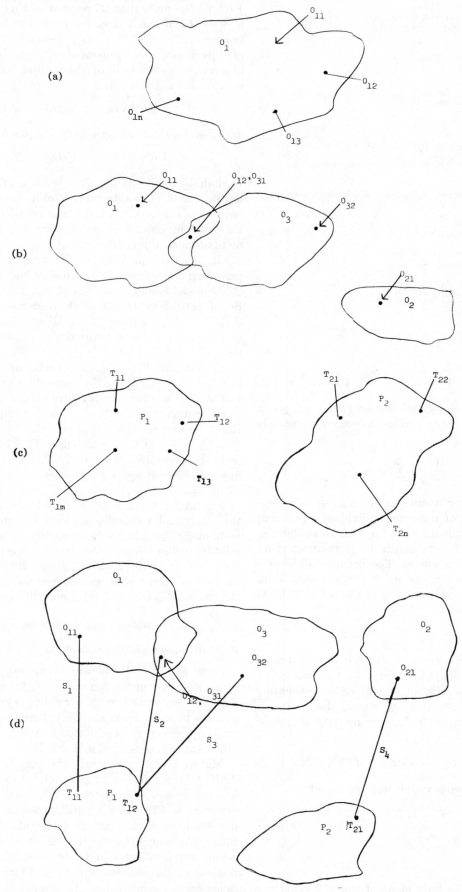

Fig. 3.

TABLE II
ARMY MATERIEL COMMAND LABORATORIES

Commodity Command Laboratories (7)
  Aviation Command (AVCOM)
  Electronic Command (ECOM)
  Missile Command (MICOM)
  Mobility Equipment Command (MECOM)
  Munitions Command (MUCOM)
  Tank-Automotive Command (TACOM)
  Weapons Command (WECOM)

Noncommodity Command Laboratories (9)
  Aeronautical Research Laboratory
  Ballistic Research Laboratory
  Coating and Chemical Laboratory
  Harry Diamond Laboratory
  Human Engineering Laboratories
  Materials and Mechanics Research Center
  Natick Laboratories
  Nuclear Defense Laboratory
  Terrestrial Sciences Laboratory

TABLE III
EXAMPLE OF A MULTILABORATORY PROJECT

Project—Metals Research for Army Materiel

Tasks	Laboratory/Center
Ammunition	Munition Command (Frankford Arsenal) and Materials and Mechanics Research Center
Armor	Munition Command (Frankford Arsenal) and Materials and Mechanics Research Center
Cast metals	Munition Command (Frankford Arsenal) and Materials and Mechanics Research Center
Corrosion and protection	Munition Command (Frankford Arsenal) and Materials and Mechanics Research Center plus Weapons Command (Rock Island Arsenal), Missile Command, Weapons Command (Watervliet Arsenal)
Fracture	Munition Command (Frankford Arsenal) and Materials and Mechanics Research Center, plus Weapons Command, (Watervliet Arsenal)
Joining	Munition Command (Frankford Arsenal) and Materials and Mechanics Research Center plus MECOM (Mobility Equipment Center)
Power metallurgy	Munition Command (Frankford Arsenal) and Materials and Mechanics Research Center
Wrought metals	Munition Command (Frankford Arsenal) and Materials and Mechanics Research Center plus Weapons Command (Rock Island Arsenal), Missile Command, Weapons Command (Watervliet Arsenal), MECOM (Mobility Equipment R&D Center)

in achieving organizational objectives, and 3) the relative military *values* of the objectives.

The overall performance of the AMC laboratories may be measured as the sum of the performance of the individual laboratories.

B. Projects and Tasks

An AMC laboratory plans and programs its activities around projects and/or tasks where a set of tasks might be accomplished across several laboratories (see Table III), or as more frequently occurs, within its laboratory complex. In general, these aggregated tasks are usually broad materiel or technology areas. Specific tasks are uniquely associated with specific projects, without any significant science or technology area overlaps across projects.

Although the goal of the project is oriented towards the accomplishment of a specific technical mission, each laboratory task has assigned responsibility to advance the state of knowledge in one or more specific scientific or technology areas. In some cases, additional areas where contributions occur are discovered after the task has been initiated and work performed.

C. Programmed Tasks of a Laboratory

To illustrate the programmed tasks of a laboratory, a sample for the experiment was selected where the assumption is made that a laboratory is a commodity office. This was necessary as the experiment was conducted in the commodity offices. Consider the segment of a laboratory program presented in Table IV where 6 tasks are involved, leading to advances in the knowledge state of 4 projects. Fifteen sciences and technologies are being advanced by the tasks and these correspond to those S_j critical to 6 operational objectives. In this way a major portion of each laboratory task may be identified with an objective function.

D. Costs

The annual costs of laboratory (or commodity office) work may be identified as follows. Suppose a laboratory is engaged in n tasks. Let C_i = the total amount of annual effort being expended on task i, where $i = 1, 2, \cdots, n$. The laboratory's total annual R&D task cost is found by summing the costs of individual tasks over all tasks undertaken by the laboratory. Projects costs may be calculated by summing the costs of individual tasks over the set of tasks associated with the specific project.

IV. SCIENCES AND TECHNOLOGIES

A. Classification System

Sciences and technologies of interest to AMC are classified according to the COSATI subject category list of the 188 groups in 22 subject fields. AMC is concerned with 119 groups in 21 fields.[7] The complete list is provided below. The reference COSATI list contains a definition for each S_j, thus consistency between assessors, within a reasonable degree, was possible in the experiment.

[7] See COSATI AD624000.

TABLE IV
LABORATORY (COMMODITY OFFICE) PROGRAM

Task	Project	Sciences and Technologies	Operational Objectives Number
Fire Control Parameters	Investigation of Aerial Fire Control	Fire Control	4, 6, 7, 18
Improved Target Acquisition	Investigation of Aerial Fire Control	Fire Control	1, 2, 4, 6, 7, 18
Mounting and Recoil Studies	Investigation of Gun-Type Aerial Weapons	Guns and Aeronautics	6, 7, 18
Passive Homing	Investigation of Missile/Rocket Aerial Weapon System	Navigation and Guidance Missiles	6, 7, 18 6, 7, 18
		Optical Detection	6, 7, 18
		Optics	6, 7, 18
		Radar Detection	6, 7, 18
		Lasers	6, 7, 18
		Communication	6, 7, 18
Input Data Acquisition	Investigation of Aerial Weapon System Effectiveness	Guns	6, 7
		Combat Vehicles	6, 7
		Rockets	6, 7
		Weapons Effects	6, 7
		Missiles	6, 7
Flight Tests	Investigation of Aerial Weapon System Effectiveness	Combat Vehicles	6, 7
		Aircraft Instrumentation	6, 7
		Man–Machine Relationship	6, 7

Scientific Disciplines and Technologies[8]

Scientific Disciplines

Fields	Groups
Aeronautics	Aerodynamics
	Aeronautics
Atmospheric Sciences	Atmospheric Physics
	Meteorology
Behavioral and Social Sciences	Economics
	Humanities
	Linguistics
	Psychology
	Sociology
Biological and Medical Sciences	Biochemistry
	Biology
	Bionics
	Clinical Medicine
	Environmental Medicine
	Microbiology
	Pharmacology
	Physiology
	Radiobiology
	Stress Physiology
	Toxicology
	Weapons Effects
Chemistry	Inorganic Chemistry
	Organic Chemistry
	Physical Chemistry
	Radio and Radiation Chemistry
Earth Science	Cartography
	Dynamic Oceanography
	Geochemisty
	Geodesy
	Geography
	Geology and Mineralogy
	Limnology
	Physical Oceanography
	Terrestrial Magnetism

Scientific Disciplines

Fields	Groups
Materials	Metallurgy and Metallography
Math Science	Mathematics and Statistics
Nuclear Science	Radioactivity
Physics	Acoustics
	Crystallography
	Electricity and Magnetism
	Fluid Mechanics
	Particle Physics
	Plasma Physics
	Quantum Theory
	Solid Mechanics
	Solid-State Physics
	Thermodynamics
	Wave Propagation
Space Science	Astronautics

[8] This listing is an adaptation of the list in Table I, AR 70–9, which is also contained in "DOD-Mondfied COSATI Subject Category List," October 1965, AD624000, Defense Documentation Center. The COSATI list also contains definitions (in the form of "scope notes") for the fields and groups shown in the list.

	Technologies			Technologies	
Fields		*Groups*	*Fields*		*Groups*

Aeronautics — Aircraft / Aircraft Fleet Control / Air Facilities

Behavioral and Social Sciences — Human Factors Engineering / Information Technology / Man–Machine Relations

Biological and Medical Sciences — Bioengineering / Life Support / Medical and Hospital Equipment / Protective Equipment

Chemistry — Chemical Engineering

Earth Science — Snow, Ice, and Permanent Frost / Soil Mechanics

Electronics — Components

Engineering — Computers / Electronic and Electrical Engineering / Information Theory / Telemetry

Energy Conversion — Conversion Techniques / Energy Storage / Power Sources

Materials — Adhesives and Seals / Ceramics, Refractors, and Glass / Coating, Colorants, and Finishes / Composite Materials / Fibers and Textiles / Oils, Lubricants, Hydraulic Fluids / Plastics / Rubber / Special Materials

Mathematics — Operations Research

Ordnance — Ammunitions, Explosives, and Pyrotechnics / Combat Vehicles / Explosions, Ballistics and Armor / Fire Control and Bombing Systems / Guns / Rockets / Underwater Ordnance

Physics — Masers and Lasers / Optics / Particle Accelerators

Mechanical, Industrial, Civil Engineering — Air Conditioning, Heating, Lighting, and Ventilating / Ground Transportation Equipment

Methods and Equipment — Cost Effectiveness / Recording Devices / Reliability / Reprography

Military Sciences — CBR-Warfare / Defense / Intelligence / Logistics / Nuclear Warfare

Missile Technology — Missile Launching and Ground Support / Missile Warheads and Fuses / Missiles

Navigation Communications, Detection, and Countermeasures — Acoustic Detection / Communications / Direction Finding / Electromagnetic and Acoustic Countermeasures / IR and UV Detection / Magnetic Detection / Navigation Guidance / Optical Detection / Radar Detection / Seismic Detection

Nuclear Technology — Nuclear Explosions / Nuclear Instruments / Nuclear Power Plants / Nuclear Propulsion / Nuclear Reactors / Nuclear Weapons Effects / Radiation Shielding and Protection

Propulsion and Fuels — Air Breathing Engines / Combustion and Ignition / Electric Propulsion / Fuels / Jet and Gas Turbine Engines / Reciprocating Engines / Rocket Motors and Engines / Rocket Propellants

Space Technology — Spacecraft

B. Association of Tasks With Sciences and Technologies

Consider a task T_i in a laboratory. With this task may be associated a number of sciences and technologies $T_i \rightarrow \{S_j\}$, where each S_j may be considered to be an output of the task T_i.

At this point, we are not concerned with the relative contributions (see Section V) but with the fact that linkages between programmed activity and output contribution may be identified. This identification occurs prior to the initiation of work started, when authorization is requested, and during the performance when progress is reported or subsequent funding is requested.[9]

C. Criticality of Sciences and Technologies

Consider the set of sciences and technologies associated with a given task $\{S_j\}$. For this task and set we may

---

[9] See document DD1498, program data sheets

---

estimate the *criticality* of the contribution of the individual element S_j to the achievement of an OCO. An example of the linkages is given in Fig. 4.

The numbers appearing in the science and technology and operational capability objectives linkages indicate the relative importance criticality of these linkages, as described in Table V.

Estimates of their relative importance were provided in the experiment by the Army Materiel Command program managers for each of approximately 700 tasks. This matrix, consisting of 700 rows and 29 columns is developed in worksheet form. An example of this matrix is illustrated in Table VI.

V. VALUE OF R&D TASKS

A. Basic Formula for Evaluating Tasks

As we have indicated, the value of a task T_i is dependent on

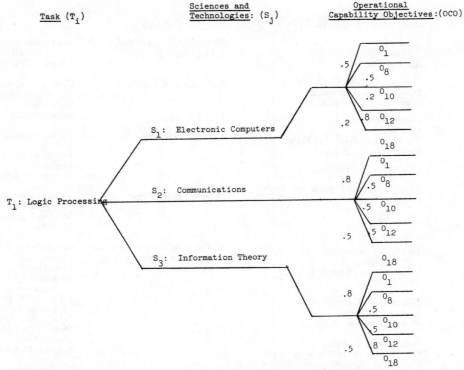

Fig. 4. Illustrative example of the task–science/technology–operational capability objective network.

1) the sciences and technologies $\{S_j\}$ utilized in the performance of task T_i,
2) the criticality of these specific elements $\{S_j\}$ in achieving or contributing to a set of OCO $\{O_k\}$, and
3) the relative military values of the particular set of OCO.

These elements may be incorporated into a single expression as follows [3]. Consider a specific laboratory task T_i. Let

$$a_{ij} = \begin{cases} 1 & \text{if science/technology } S_j \text{ is required} \\ 0 & \text{otherwise} \end{cases}$$

b_{ijk} = the criticality value of the science/technology S_j in contributing to objective, O_k = a value in the set $\{1, 0.8, 0.5, 0.3, 0.2, 0.1, 0\}$

V_k = relative military value in achieving the particular objectives O_k.

Then a_{ij}, b_{ijk}, V_k is the weighted military value of the *linkage* between the task T_i and objective O_k, through the underlying science/technology S_j. The sum

$$\sum_k a_{ij} b_{ijk} V_k$$

measures the value of the linkage $T_i \rightarrow S_j$ expressed over the set of *all* objectives $\{O_k\}$.

Finally, the weighted relative military value of laboratory task T_i may be given by e_i, where

$$e_i = \sum_i \sum_k a_{ij} b_{ijk} V_k$$

expresses the total value taken over all relevant sciences and technologies and objectives.

Similarly, the military value/criticality of a science/technology S_j may be given by f_j, where

$$f_j = \sum_i \sum_k a_{ij} b_{ijk} V_k.$$

The set of laboratory tasks $\{T_i\}$ may be compared on the basis of the values in the corresponding set $\{e_i\}$. Similarly, the sciences and technologies $\{S_j\}$ may be assessed for importance by comparing the values in the corresponding set $\{f_j\}$.

B. Assumptions

We have made several assumptions in carrying out the calculations in Section V-A, as follows.

Additivity of Objective Values: We have assumed that for the objectives O_1 and O_2, the value of achieving both is given by the sum of values for the individual objectives. This would be valid in case of *independent* objectives. However, the set of objectives that have been developed are not independent. In general,

$$V(O_1 \oplus O_2) = V(O_1) + V(O_2)$$

somewhat overestimates the military value of achieving the combined objectives.

Table VII presents the effect of performing the exact calculation in evaluating projects, and illustrates the effects of using both approximate and exact methods in rank-ordering projects. The approximate method over-

TABLE V
CRITICALITY OF SCIENCE/TECHNOLOGY TO THE ATTAINMENT OF OPERATIONAL CAPABILITY OBJECTIVES

	Weight
Absolutely essential Failure of this science/technology will absolutely prevent the attainment of the capability desired.	1.0
Major contribution Failure of this science/technology will result in a significant decrease in one or more of the major performance parameters needed to attain the capability desired. Such degradation probably would not prevent receiving a favorable decision for development of equipment for the inventory.	0.8
Substantial contribution Failure of this science/technology will result in the loss of a highly desirable but not essential capability. Such degradation, while important, probably would not prevent a favorable decision on the development of equipment for the inventory to attain the capability desired.	0.5
Refinement of capability Success of this science/technology will result in some refinement of the present capability. The desired capability, however, could be achieved without this effort.	0.3
Indirect contributions Success of this science/technology will only be an indirect contribution to the capability desired.	0.2
Remote association This effort has only a remote association with the capability desired.	0.1
No contribution	0

TABLE VII
COMPARISON OF METHODS FOR EVALUATING PROJECTS IN OFFICE NU

Project Number	Weighted Military Value (approximate method)	Rank Order	Weighted Military Value (exact method)	Rank Order
A207	50.6	1	41.1	1
A087	18.3	3	15.4	4
A208	19.8	2	17.6	2
A092	17.1	5	11.2	5
A301	17.2	4	15.8	3
A300	11.0	6	10.2	6
A088	10.1	7	10.1	7
A089	8.4	8	8.4	8
A480	6.2	9	6.2	9
A085	5.5	10	5.0	10
A086	3.1	11	3.1	11

estimates values, in general. However, in only 2 of the 11 projects were the values overestimated by more than 15 percent (projects A207 and A092). More importantly, the only change in the rank orders of project values was the interchange of the third- and fourth-ranking projects (A087 and A301).

A second office was selected to evaluate the difference between the approximate and exact methods for evaluating projects. In this case, 20 projects were evaluated and rank ordered using both methods. As may be observed from the data presented in Table VIII, the maximum overestimation in project values is 25 percent. However, only 7 of the 20 projects had ranks that changed, where the maximum change in rank order was 1. The

TABLE VI
ILLUSTRATIVE SAMPLE OF THE CRITICALITY OF SCIENCE/ TECHNOLOGY TO OPERATIONAL CAPABILITY OBJECTIVES

Science/Technology	Operational Capability Objective			
	O_1	O_5	O_7	O_{19}
Missiles	0.3	0.8	1.0	0.2
Communications	1.0	0.5	0.3	0.5
Navigation and guidance	0.5	0.2	0.8	0.1

TABLE VIII
COMPARISON OF APPROXIMATE AND EXACT METHODS FOR EVALUATING PROJECT CRITICALITY IN OFFICE WE

Project Number	Weighted Military Value (approximate method)	Rank Order	Weighted Military Value (exact method)	Rank Order
A295	36.8	1	31.7	1
A558	18.8	2	15.6	2
A291	17.1	3	13.2	3
A293	13.8	4	11.2	4
A559	12.4	5	11.2	4
A304	10.4	6	8.7	7
A302	9.1	7	9.1	6
A353	8.7	8	7.3	8
A290	8.6	9	6.9	9
A314	8.1	10	6.5	10
A296	8.0	11	6.4	11
A288	8.0	11	6.4	11
A289	7.6	13	6.1	14
D583	6.3	14	6.3	13
A316	4.8	15	4.5	15
A294	4.0	16	3.2	16
A312	3.6	17	3.2	16
A299	3.0	18	3.0	18
A354	2.4	19	2.4	19
A310	1.0	20	1.0	20

rank-order correlation in both cases was greater than 0.95.

An analysis was performed of the effect of considering the overlapping of objectives in evaluating the military value/criticality of sciences and technologies in the achievement of the objectives.

Eleven offices were considered in this evaluation where 119 sciences and technologies were evaluated. The evaluations using exact and approximate methods are given in Table IX for 23 of the 119 S_j. These 23 were the 23 most valued S_j on the basis of weighted military value. Rank orders are provided in both cases. It may be observed that of the 23 sciences and technologies considered, there were only 8 rank-order changes caused by the overlapping of operational objectives, where the maximum change of rank value was 1. The rank-order correlation coefficient is 0.98.

While the foregoing sensitivity analysis of the effect of overlapping operational objectives is small and would appear to cause no serious judgment errors to be made, within an office or across the top 23 S_j further testing should be done for other offices where the kind of S_j is more important to more O_k than the S_j of the NU and WE Offices.

TABLE IX

COMPARISON OF APPROXIMATE AND EXACT METHODS FOR EVALUATING CRITICALITIES OF 23 SCIENCES AND TECHNOLOGIES FOR 2 OFFICES (NU AND WE)

COSATI Field/Group	Science/Technology	Weighted Military Value (approximate method)	Rank Order	Weighted Military Value (exact method)	Rank Order
09/03	Electronic Engineering	74.2	1	71.0	1
09/01	Electronic Components	53.3	2	51.7	2
19/01	Ammunition, Explosives, and Pyrotechnics	47.5	3	40.2	3
16/04	Missiles	37.3	4	34.8	4
19/05	Fire Control	28.1	5	24.2	5
19/06	Guns	26.3	6	22.2	6
19/04	Explosions, Ballistics, and Armor	25.8	7	22.0	7
09/02	Electronic Computers	19.4	8	18.6	8
07/03	Organic Chemistry	19.4	8	18.0	9
09/05	Electronic Subsystems	16.7	10	13.8	11
11/04	Composite Materials	15.2	11	14.4	10
15/06	Nuclear Warfare	14.6	12	12.1	13
17/04	Electromagnetic and Acoustic Countermeasures	13.3	13	12.2	12
10/02	Power Sources	10.6	14	10.1	14
20/04	Fluid Mechanics	10.6	14	9.3	15
16/03	Missile Warheads and Fuses	10.0	16	7.0	17
07/04	Physical Chemistry	8.8	17	7.9	16
12/01	Mathematics and Statistics	8.5	18	6.9	18
21/04	Fuels	6.9	19	6.4	19
09/06	Telemetry	6.5	20	6.1	20
14/02	Labs, Test Facilities and Equipment	6.2	21	5.9	21
/03	Rocket Propellants	5.1	22	4.6	22
19/03	Electricity and Magnetism	3.6	23	2.5	23

Additivity of Criticalities: We have assumed that the values of a task having two critical scientific/technological areas S_1 and S_2 is given by the sum of the individual criticalities.

This assumption is equivalent to the following assumptions.

1) The criticality of values for the S_j in terms of their contribution to achieving an objective O_k is *additive.*

2) S_1 is *independent* of S_2 in the sense that the desired accomplishment in S_1 does not greatly depend upon the desired accomplishment in S_2.

To substantiate the validity of assumption 1), some evidence exists that the scale selected in this study is additive. A study conducted at the Air Force Flight Dynamics Laboratory developed a confidence-level scale (Table X). This scale was used as an additive measure in a linear programming model for resource allocation [11]. An additive scale, which measures the contribution of tasks to the accomplishment of technical-development objectives, was utilized in the Air Force linear programming formulation as given in Table XI. The scale used in our study (presented in Table VI) involves a combination of scales involved in task contribution to technical-development objectives (Table XI) and system development (Table XII). The analysis of the individual sciences and technologies that contribute to a sample of tasks indicates that assumption 2) is not seriously violated.

VI. PROJECT-WEIGHTED MILITARY VALUES

A. Estimation of Project-Weighted Military Values

As indicated in Section V-A, the weighted military value of a task e_i is given by

$$e_i = \sum_i \sum_k a_{ij} b_{ijk} V_k$$

This evaluation was carried out for approximately 700 tasks.

Since the tasks are associated with specific projects and are grouped according to offices (or laboratories), the weighted military value of a project E_m is given by the following

$$E_m = \sum_i e_i,$$

where the summation is taken over the tasks that comprise the particular project. This approximation in estimating project-weighted military value is valid, in general, in that the tasks are only loosely coupled. Task interdependencies introduce terms of higher order that would not affect project rank ordering significantly. Equivalently, the success or failure of accomplishing a task's technical objective is not significantly related to that of another task. In many cases, project tasks are accomplished at different laboratories.

B. Office Project-Weighted Military Values

As in the case of the task-project amalgamation, commodity offices consisting of a specified set of projects may be compared.

TABLE X
Engineering Task Confidence-Level Scale Definitions*

	Weight
The current technology is adequate in all respects; detailed design criteria are established	1.0
The current technology is adequate but minor refinements are desirable	0.9
Feasibility has been demonstrated and the current technology is adequate to solve major problems, but improvements in such areas as service life, reliability, and efficiency are needed	0.8
Basic design criteria are available, but extensive testing is required to demonstrate actual feasibility (an ADO might be required at this point)	0.7
Preliminary design criteria are available, but a design at this point would be shaky using only the current information	0.6
A complete exploratory development program, which has a high possibility of successful completion using the most promising approach, is defined	0.5
The most promising approach to solution is indicated through exploratory experimentation, analytical effort, and/or simulation	0.4
Preliminary analysis indicates the potential usefulness of the idea and feasible approaches to the problem	0.3
The problem can be defined and basic idea(s) formulated, but only general approaches to solution are definable	0.2

* Project RDE-FY67 Program, Air Force Flight Dynamics Laboratory, Research and Technology Division, Wright-Patterson Air Force Base, October 18, 1965, p. 2.

TABLE XI
Evaluating the Contributions of Tasks to the Accomplishment of the Technical Development Objectives*

	Weight
Potential breakthrough	1.0
Major advancement	0.8
Average evolutionary advancement (steady progress)	0.6
Refinement or improvement	0.4
Minor contribution	0.2

* Project RDE-FY67 Program, Air Force Flight Dynamics Laboratory, Research and Technology Division, Wright-Patterson Air Force Base, October 18, 1965, Attach. 9.

Table XIII presents summary data on project weighted military values for 127 exploratory-development projects in the 8 R&D offices. There is a significant variability across the projects within an office. The averages and standard deviations of the logarithms of project weighted military values are given. The medians for the 8 offices range from 45.4 to 7.7 or a range of 6:1. A t test was applied to determine whether the offices were significantly different and at what level. For example, ST and GM give a t value of 8.3, which for 49 degrees of freedom $(n_1 + n_2 - 2)$ is significant at the 1.0 level.

Although the sample sizes are too small to test the

TABLE XII
Evaluating the Contribution of a Task to a System

	Weight
Absolutely essential Failure to have this technology available will prevent initiation of the system-acquisition phase.	1.0
Major contribution This technology makes such a major contribution to a system that if it is not funded by the laboratory, the system office will probably fund it to ensure its availability.	0.9
Significant contribution Failure to acquire this technology will result in a significant decrease in one or more of the performance parameters of the system.	0.8
Substantial contribution Refinement of system capability	0.7 0.5
Indirect contribution	0.3
Remote association	0.1

* Project RDE-FY67 Program, Air Force Flight Dynamics Laboratory, Research and Technology Division, Wright-Patterson Air Force Base, October 18, 1965, Attach. 10.

log-normal hypothesis for individual offices, the parameters for each office are given in Table XIII. For each office, the fitted frequency distribution of project values is given by

$$N(E) = N_0 \left[(1\sqrt{2\pi}\ \sigma) \exp - \left(\frac{(y - \mu)}{\sigma} \right)^2 \right]$$

N_0 = number of projects in the office

$y = \ln E$.

μ, σ are given in Table XIII.

VII. Military Value Criticality of Sciences and Technologies f_j

A. Evaluation and Distribution

As indicated in Section V-A, the military value critically of a science/technolology S_i is given by f_i, where

$$f_i = \sum_i \sum_k a_{ij} b_{ijk} V_k.$$

The military value criticalities of the sciences and technologies were calculated, using the method described in Section V-A.

The total range of values is 250:1, or over a range of 74.2 down to 0.3. Within this interval, the distribution is positively skewed, as the median value is 5.7, and the average value is 10.0.

The sciences and technologies were graphed in a frequency distribution. A log-normal distribution was fitted and was found to give good agreement. A t test was applied and the log-normal hypothesis was found to be valid at the 0.025 level. The criticality-value function is given by

TABLE XIII
CHARACTERISTICS OF PROJECT WEIGHTED MILITARY VALUES, BY OFFICE

Office	Number of Projects	Range in Project Weighted Military Value (maximum)	(minimum)	Parameters (average*)	(standard deviation†)	(median)	Weighted Military Value Rank Order
AD	15	72.0	5.2	2.47	0.74	9.5	5
AW	5	28.9	6.2	2.84	0.80	26.2	3
CE	16	140.7	7.4	3.70	0.80	45.4	1
CS	9	32.4	4.8	2.48	0.60	11.7	4
GM	25	21.2	2.9	2.02	0.46	7.7	7
NU	11	50.6	3.1	2.46	0.76	11.0	6
ST	26	81.0	5.0	3.36	0.75	34.0	2
WE	20	36.8	1.0	1.99	0.80	8.0	0
	127						

* $x_i = \ln E_i$, $\mu = \sum_i x_i / n$.
† $\sigma = [\sum_i (x_i - \mu)^2 / (n - 1)]^{1/2}$.

$$N(f) = N_0 \left[\left(\frac{1}{\sqrt{2\pi}\,\sigma} \right) \exp \left(\frac{(x - \mu)}{\sigma} \right)^2 \right]$$

where

$N(f)$ = the number of sciences/technologies that have a criticality value greater than f

$N_0 = 119$

$x = \ln f$

$\mu = \bar{x} = 1.66$

$\sigma = 1.40$.

The parameters of the log-normal distribution were evaluated as follows:

$$\mu = \frac{1}{119} \sum_{i=1}^{119} x_i$$

$$\sigma = \left[\frac{1}{118} \sum_{i=1}^{119} (x_i - \mu)^2 \right]^{1/2}.$$

The cumulative distribution of military value criticalities for the 119 sciences and technologies is plotted in Fig. 5. It may be observed that the relatively large standard deviation ($\sigma/\mu = 0.85$) is reflected in the sharp increase in military value criticalities for the high-ranked sciences and technologies. For example, 50 percent of the total value is accounted for by the top 15 percent of the sciences and technologies. Also, the bottom 50 percent of the sciences and technologies account for only 15 percent of the total value.

B. Relationship Between Science/Technology and OCO

An important measure of performance is the criticality-value relationship between science/technology and the OCO. The relationship is expressed in schematic form in Table XIV.

The military value criticality score is given by summing the values given by weighting each OCO by the corresponding military value. The specific formulas used in calculating criticalities are given in Table XIV. An illustrative science/technology part of the 122 × 23 table is in Table XV.

C. Field Evaluation of Science/Technology Contributions

Table XVI presents the contributions of the 21 subject fields (see COSATI) to the OCO for weighted and unweighted OCO and for the sets of foreseeable and unforeseeable OCO. The purpose of the analysis presented in this section is to answer the following questions.

1) What are the major sciences and technologies and what are their relative contribution to military value?
2) What is the effect of uncertainties in estimating the importance of the OCO?
3) How does the relative importance of the individual sciences and technologies change in considering the foreseeable and unforeseeable Army objectives?

Major Sciences and Technologies: Table XVII and Fig. 6 present the individual and cumulative percentages of the sciences and technologies. The 4 fields of Electronics, Communications and Detection, Ordnance and Physics account for more than one-half of the total criticality score, or 52.1 percent. It may be observed that Electronics always remains the most important area, regardless of OCO weighting and foreseeable/unforeseeable OCO categories, whereas the other 3 fields are always second, third, and fourth, respectively.

Uncertainty in Estimating Relative Importance of OCO: It may be observed that the maximum change in rank orderings of columns 1 and 4 of Table XVI is two. Only Chemistry changes it rank order by two, and 8 other fields change in rank order by one. The 3:1 weighting used in column 1 and uniform weighting used in column 4 does not result in significant differences in relative importance of science/technology fields. Although there is confidence in the relative importance of these fields within this range of uncertainty, it should be pointed out that greater uncertainty, as would be expressed by 5:1 or 10:1 ranges in OCO weights, might produce significant differences in the relative importance of the fields.

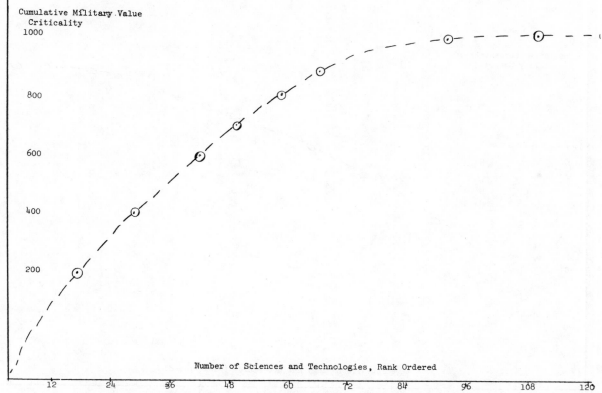

Fig. 5. Cumulative military value criticality of the sciences and technologies.

TABLE XIV
SCIENCE/TECHNOLOGY–OCO MATRIX

S_i	O_k O_1 O_2 $\cdots$ O_n V_k V_1 V_2 $\cdots$ V_n	Military Value Score
S_1		f_1
S_2		f_2
.		.
.	$d_{jkm}*$	.
.		.
S_m		f_n†

* $d_{jk} = \sum_i a_{ij}b_{ijk}$ (sum taken over all laboratory tasks).
† $f_i = \sum_k d_{jk}V_k$ (sum taken over all OCO).

TABLE XV
ILLUSTRATIVE SCIENCE/TECHNOLOGY–OCO MATRIX: CALCULATION OF MILITARY VALUE CRITICALITY SCORES

| Science/Technology | Fore-seeable | | Unforeseeable | | | | Military Value Criticality Score |
	OCO Weight A 3	B 2.8	L 1.0	M 3	N 2.8	W 1.0	
1 Aerodynamics	0	0.5	0	0	0	0	7.9
30 Electronic components	6	2.6	6.0	1.0	2.1	0	149.2
90 Operations research	1.2	0.3	0.8	1.0	0.5	0	50.8
122 Weapons effects	0.2	0	0	0.2	0.5	0	40.4

VIII. ORGANIZATIONAL CONTRIBUTIONS TO OCO ACHIEVEMENTS

The contribution of each organizational unit to a specific OCO may be measured as follows. The criticality value of a task T_i to an OCO O_k is given by

$$E(T_i, O_k) = \sum_i a_{ij}b_{ijk}$$

where the sum is taken over all relevant sciences and technologies.

If we sum this value over all tasks in an organization, we have the performance of the laboratory L with regard to objective O_k that may be evaluated as

$$E(L, O_k) = \sum_i E(T_i, O_k).$$

The values of $E(L, O_k)$ may be provided in matrix form, as in Table XVIII where the rows correspond to individual organizational elements (laboratory, office, and division) and the 23 columns are given by the OCO. The matrix indicates the specific contribution of the individual laboratories to the specific OCO.

The final 2 columns would be given as the measure of the organization's performance E and costs $C(L)$. The measure of performance E is given by

$$E = \sum_k V_k E(L, O_k),$$

where the weighted sum is taken over all OCO and the weights are given by relative military values $\{V_k\}$. The total cost of the laboratory's tasks are given by

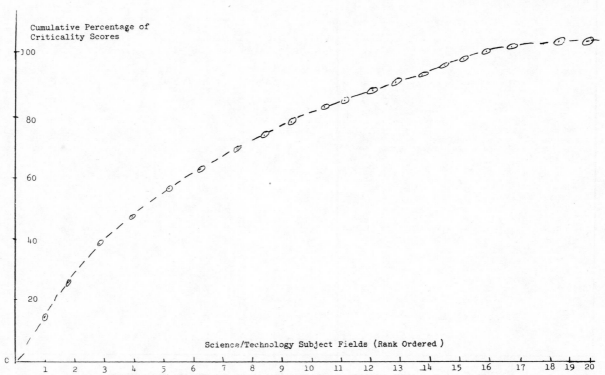

Fig. 6.   Contribution of science/technology subject fields (cumulative percentage versus rank ordered). See Table XVII for ranks.

TABLE XVI
CONTRIBUTIONS OF SCIENCE/TECHNOLOGY FIELDS TO THE ATTAINMENT OF OPERATIONAL CAPABILITY OBJECTIVES

Field	Military Value Criticality Score						Unweighted Criticality Score					
	1		2		3		4		5		6	
Aeronautics	(12)	88.06	(9)	78.26	(16)	9.80	(13)	38.8	(12)	33.6	(16)	5.2
Agriculture	(20)	6.98	(20)	5.92	(20)	1.06	(20)	3.9	(20)	3.5	(20)	0.4
Atmosphere Sciences	(9)	123.55	(11)	74.77	(6)	48.58	(9)	63.1	(9)	37.9	(6)	25.2
Behavioral Sciences	(18)	31.39	(18)	25.87	(18)	5.52	(19)	14.6	(19)	12.1	(18)	2.5
Biologic Medical Sciences	(7)	146.17	(7)	132.25	(15)	13.92	(7)	91.2	(5)	84.6	(13)	6.6
Chemistry	(16)	68.61	(12)	62.47	(17)	6.14	(14)	37.0	(11)	33.9	(17)	3.1
Earth Sciences	(17)	56.07	(17)	39.79	(12)	16.28	(17)	23.5	(17)	17.1	(14)	6.4
Electronics	(1)	503.27	(1)	381.43	(1)	121.84	(1)	248.7	(1)	191.5	(1)	57.2
Energy Conversion	(10)	95.62	(15)	52.86	(8)	42.76	(10)	46.4	(15)	27.7	(8)	18.7
Materials	(6)	196.06	(5)	150.18	(7)	45.88	(6)	93.1	(7)	72.8	(7)	20.3
Mathematical Sciences	(15)	70.72	(16)	50.82	(11)	19.90	(16)	33.9	(16)	25.3	(11)	8.6
Mechanical (etc.) Engineering	(11)	89.16	(10)	74.96	(14)	14.20	(11)	41.6	(10)	35.8	(15)	5.8
Methods and Equipment	(13)	82.26	(14)	59.96	(10)	22.30	(12)	39.8	(13)	29.4	(10)	10.4
Military Sciences	(5)	209.58	(6)	150.06	(5)	59.52	(5)	107.0	(6)	79.0	(5)	28.0
Missiles	(8)	145.05	(8)	112.21	(9)	32.84	(8)	69.5	(8)	54.4	(9)	15.1
Navigation, Communication, Detection, and Civil and Marine	(2)	410.32	(2)	338.72	(3)	71.60	(3)	181.3	(3)	146.1	(3)	35.2
Nuclear Sciences	(19)	22.19	(19)	18.35	(19)	3.84	(18)	15.2	(18)	13.6	(19)	1.6
Ordnance	(3)	401.52	(3)	338.04	(4)	63.48	(2)	197.1	(2)	166.0	(4)	31.1
Physics	(4)	331.12	(4)	222.45	(2)	108.67	(4)	145.2	(4)	104.4	(2)	40.8
Propellant and Fuels	(14)	76.36	(13)	60.38	(13)	15.98	(15)	35.7	(14)	28.3	(12)	7.4
Space Technology	(21)	3.68	(21)	3.68	(21)	· · ·	(21)	2.1	(21)	2.1	(21)	· · ·
Totals		3157.54		2433.43		724.11		1528.7		1199.1		329.6

Columns 1 and 4: Objectives O_1 through O_{23}.
Columns 2 and 5: Objectives O_1 through O_{12} (foreseeable).

Columns 3 and 6: Objectives O_{13} through O_{23} (unforeseeable).
( ) Rank ordering of scientific fields using the specified criteria.

TABLE XVII
Contributions of Science/Technology to OCO's

Rank Order	Field	Percentage	Cumulative Percentage
1	Electronics	15.9	15.9
2	Communications and Detections	13.0	28.9
3	Ordnance	12.7	41.6
4	Physics	10.5	52.1
5	Military Sciences	6.6	58.7
6	Materials	6.2	64.9
7	Biological/Medical Sciences	4.6	69.6
8	Missiles	4.6	74.2
9	Atmospheric Sciences	3.9	78.1
10	Energy Conversion	3.0	81.1
11	Engineering (Mechanical, Industrial, Civil, and Marine)	2.8	83.9
12	Aeronautics	2.8	86.7
13	Methods and Equipment	2.6	89.3
14	Propulsion and Fuels	2.4	91.7
15	Mathematical Sciences	2.2	93.9
16	Chemistry	2.2	96.1
17	Earth Sciences	1.8	97.9
18	Behavioral Sciences	1.0	98.9
19	Nuclear Science and Technology	0.7	99.6
20	Agriculture	0.2	99.9
21	Space Technology	0.1	100.0

$$C(L) = \sum_i C(T_i),$$

where the summation of costs is taken over all tasks T_i in the laboratory. The final columns express a cost-effectiveness relationship across laboratories.

The row sums would be given in the bottom row as

$$E(O_k) = \sum_L E(L, O_k)$$

where the sum is taken over all laboratories. These values indicate the overall contribution of organizations to achieving each OCO.

IX. Cost Effectiveness for Projects

A. Project Costs

Project costs were calculated by summing the annual costs of the tasks associated with each project. Project costs are presented in Table XIX, by office. The total annual costs of $120 million are allocated to 127 projects in the 8 offices for an average annual project cost of $940 000. Annual project costs range from $110 000 to $4.8 million.

B. Project-Cost Distribution

The project-cost distribution is positively skewed, where the median is less than the mean for all offices. A log-normal distribution was fitted to the project-cost distribution. It was found that project-cost distribution is given by

$$N(C) = N_0 \left(\frac{1}{\sqrt{2\pi}\,\sigma} \right) \exp - \left(\frac{y-\mu}{\sigma} \right)^2$$

TABLE XVIII
Organizational Contribution to OCO Achievement

Organization	OCO O_1	O_2	$\cdots$	O_{23}	Organizational Performance	Organizational Costs ($ millions)
AD	.	.	....	.	635.5	$24.85
AW	.	.	$\cdots$	.	97.4	1.80
CE	139	64	$\cdots$	1	834.1	21.60
CS	2	5	$\cdots$	0	125.8	9.59
GM	.	.	$\cdots$	.	193.1	12.48
NU	35	10	$\cdots$	5	167.3	9.94
ST	.	.	$\cdots$	.	976.0	28.10
WE	.	.	$\cdots$	.	192.5	11.51
Totals $E(O_k)$	371	165	$\cdots$	14	3221.7	$119.87

TABLE XIX
Distribution Characteristics of Project Costs, by Office

Office	Number of Projects	Total Costs ($ million)	Range in Project Costs maximum	minimum ($ million)	average
AD	15	$24.85	$4.8	$0.30	$1.66
AW	5	1.80	0.8	0.15	0.36
CE	16	21.60	3.6	0.40	1.35
CS	9	9.59	2.5	0.30	1.07
GM	25	12.48	2.7	0.10	0.50
NU	11	9.94	1.8	0.20	0.90
ST	26	28.10	4.0	0.20	1.08
WE	20	11.51	2.6	0.11	1.74
	127	$119.87			$0.94

where $N(C)dc$ = number of projects that cost between C and $C + dc$.

C. Comparison of Project Costs Across Offices

It may be observed that there is a significant difference in average project costs across offices, ranging from $360 000 (for AW) to $1.74 million (for WE). This range in average costs of almost 5:1 reflects the range of intensity and scope of effort in the projects.

Although insufficient data exist for testing the distribution of project costs by office, as the overall distribution is log normal, it is reasonable to expect that the individual cost distributions are also log normal. Other studies have demonstrated the validity of log-normal distributions of R&D project costs.[10] A sum of independent log-normal distributions is log normal. The cost-distribution parameters are given for each office.

D. Cost Effectiveness for Projects

The cost and effectiveness of each project were calculated. The cost-effectiveness value for a project $K(P)$ is calculated by taking the ratio of project costs $C(P)$ and project effectiveness $E(P)$ where

[10] B. V. Dean, S. J. Mantel, L. Roepcke, *et al.*, "Research project cost distributions and budget forecasting," Case–Western Reserve University, Cleveland, Ohio, TM 107, May 1968; also this issue pp. 176–189.

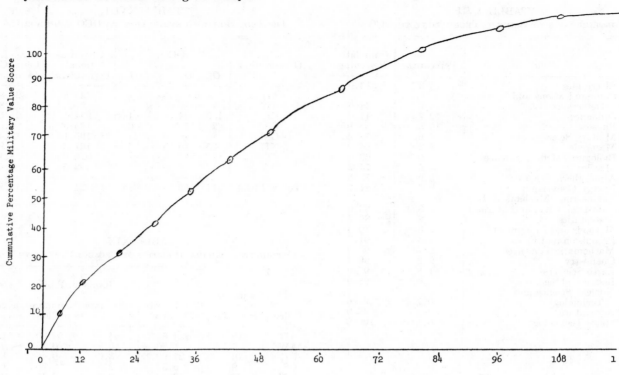

Cumulative Project Costs, $Million

Fig. 7.   Cost-effectiveness relationship for projects.

$$K(P) = \frac{C(P)}{E(P)}$$

and P is a specific project.

A project cost-effectiveness distribution is presented in Fig. 7. Cumulative percentages of total value are plotted against cumulative costs. Twenty percent of the project costs yield approximately one-half of the total military value. On the other hand, the bottom 60 percent of the projects yield only 20 percent of the total value.

X. Cost Effectiveness and Resource Allocation for Offices

A. Cost Effectiveness

Table XX presents the cost and effectiveness for each office. The cost-effectiveness value for the office is calculated by taking the ratio of office costs and office effectiveness E_m where

$$K_m = \frac{C_m}{E_m}$$

and m is a specific office.

It may be observed that the cost-effectiveness ratio K_m ranges over values of 101:18 or 6:1 for the 8 offices, which indicates that major differences in relative payoffs of offices are likely in future periods.

The cost-effectiveness function is presented in Fig. 8,

TABLE XX
Cost Effectiveness for Offices

Office	Number of Projects	Total Value (E)	Total Cost (C) ($ millions)	Cost Effectiveness, C/E (thousands)	Rank Order
AD	15	635.5	$24.85	39	4
AW	5	97.4	1.80	18	1
CE	16	834.1	21.60	26	2
CS	9	125.8	9.59	76	8
GM	25	193.1	12.48	59	6
NU	11	167.3	9.94	59	5
ST	26	976.0	28.10	29	3
WE	20	192.5	11.51	60	7
Totals	127	3221.7	$119.87		

where cumulative percentages of total value are plotted against cumulative costs. Approximately one-half of the available budget, or $61.4 million, provides 73.3 percent of the total value.

B. A Resource-Allocation Model for Tasks and Projects

We now construct a resource-allocation model for a large number of tasks. We may use this approximate model since we are considering a large number of resource categories (or tasks).

The weighted military value of the ith task, if it is funded, is given by

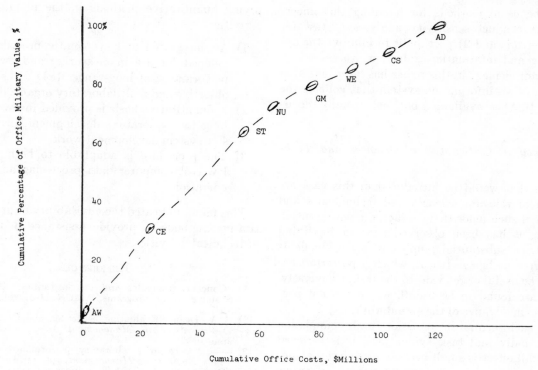

Fig. 8. Cost-effectiveness relationship for offices.

$$e_i = \sum_{j,k} a_{ij} b_{ijk} V_k \tag{1}$$

If the task is selected, the cost is given by c_i.

The resource-allocation (or task-selection) problem is to find the values of x_i corresponding to the tasks to be selected, which maximize the sum of elements in (1) given by

$$\max \left(E(C) = \sum_{i=1}^{n} x_i e_i \right) \tag{2}$$

subject to

$$\sum_{i=1}^{n} x_i c_i \leq C \tag{3}$$

and

$$x_i = 0 \quad \text{or} \quad 1. \tag{4}$$

This model may be solved using dynamic programming to find the optimum values for (2)–(4).

However, a simple rank-ordering procedure will usually be satisfactory. The method consists of the following steps.

1) Rank order the tasks on the basis of cost effectiveness

$$c_1/e_1 < c_2/e_2 < \cdots < c_n/e_n.$$

2) Allocate the $\$C$ to the first m projects such that

$$\sum_{i=1}^{m} c_i \leq C, \qquad \sum_{i=1}^{m+1} c_i > C.$$

3) For use in setting budgets, develop a cost-effectiveness relationship by graphing the n points

$$(c_1, e_1), (c_1 + c_2, e_1 + e_2), \cdots ,$$

$$(c_1 + c_2 + \cdots + c_n, e_1 + e_2 + \cdots + e_n).$$

The constrained laboratory cost-task selection problems may be solved in two steps. Apply rank ordering for each laboratory minimum fund level, applying 1 and 2 to the minimum funding value for each laboratory. Allocate the funds in excess of the minimum level to tasks in each laboratory using cross-laboratory comparisons, up to the maximum allowable for each laboratory. Cost-effectiveness relations may be established for each set of laboratory-funding parameter values. A dynamic programming formulation of the constrained laboratory optimization has been developed and will be reported in a subsequent paper.

XI. Data Problems: Estimation, Uncertainty, and Bias

A. Subjective Estimates

The relative military values of the OCO and the linkages and criticalities of the sciences and technologies have been subjectively estimated in this paper. Uncertainty exists in such estimates, where the degree of uncertainty cannot be estimated since statistical samples of the data cannot be collected and tested. This is a characteristic problem in R&D management decision problems. The usual methods for handling this uncertainty are 1) conduct sensitivity analyses to test for the effect of errors, and 2) post audit to improve the decision-making and information-collection process.

An important element in this paper has been indicated as the design of an information system that collects the information that is available, but not usually documented.

B. Uncertainty in Criticalities of Sciences and Technologies

The errors that would be introduced in this case are the omission of relevant sciences and technologies and the inclusion of such fields that, in fact, are not essential. For example, it has been observed that in justifying fund requests, a substantial number of scientific fields will be reported as being critical, which a posteriori are found not to be useful or relevant to the task. Conversely, other fields are found to be useful, which are not predicted to be so in advance of the actual work.

Although such errors in omission and commission would affect individual task evaluations, it is believed that the overall effect is small because of counterbalancing and the opportunities for annual reviews of tasks, projects, and laboratories.

Another error that may be introduced is the underrepresentation of the contribution of critical sciences and technologies to the set of unforeseeable (or more difficult to achieve) operational objectives. It was observed that three-fourths of the total military-value criticality score is accounted for by the foreseeable objectives, in spite of the fact that equal weights were given to both sets of objectives. It is believed that the effect of this uncertainty is also not significant because of the reasons given previously.

C. Uncertainty in Relative Military Value of Objectives

Considerable uncertainty exists in estimating the relative value of achieving long-range objectives, which is characteristic of long-term military planning.

A sensitivity test has indicated that no significant difference in results exists between 3:1 and uniform scales for evaluating objectives. It is believed that annual reviews would reduce any effect of much greater uncertainties.

XII. SUMMARY

This paper presents the results of an experiment conducted in the Army Materiel Command. The purpose of this experiment was to investigate the adequacy of applying quantitative methods in the planning of R&D activities.

1) An integrated and systematic procedure was developed for use in measuring and evaluating the performance of long-range R&D tasks in a multiobjective and multilaboratory organization.
2) A quantitative basis is provided for technical planning for exploratory development, prior to extensive system development work.
3) The procedure is adaptable to both manual and low-cost computer data processing and tabulating operations.

This paper indicated the advisability of utilizing quantitative methods to provide assistance in the planning of technical activities.

REFERENCES

[1] "Concept, principles and responsibilities," AMC Program Systems Army Programs, AMCR 11-4, vol. 1, p. 7, May 1967.
[2] B. V. Dean, "Evaluating, Selecting, and Controlling R and D Projects," *Am. Management Assoc.*, research study 89, June 1968.
[3] ——, "A research laboratory performance model," *IEEE Trans. Engineering Management*, vol. pp. 44–46, March 1967.
[4] "DOD-modified COSATI subject category list," Defense Documentation Center, Defense Supply Agency, AD 624000, October 1965.
[5] R. T. Eckenrode, "Weighting multiple criteria," *Management Sci.*, vol. 12, pp. 180–192, November 1965.
[6] Example QMDO Plan, Truck-90, Line Haul Heavy Logistical Carrier, Headquarters, Army Materiel Command, Washington, D. C. May 1968.
[7] P. C. Fishburn, "Methods of estimating additive utilities," *Management Sci.*, vol. 13, pp. 435–453, March 1967.
[8] "Additive utilities with finite sets: Application in the management sciences," *Naval Res. Logistics Quart.*, vol. 14, p. 2, March 1967.
[9] I. Fisher, *Mathematical Investigation in the Theory of Values and Prices.* New Haven, Conn.: Yale University Press, 1925.
[10] T. Marschak, T. K. Glennon, Jr., and R. Summers, *Strategy for R and D.* New York: Springer, 1967.
[11] A. B. Nutt, "An approach to research and development effectiveness," *IEEE Trans. Engineering Management*, vol. EM-12, pp. 103–112, September 1965.
[12] ——, "Ancillary benefits of an automated R and D resources allocation system," presented at the 1966 ASME Annual Meeting and Energy Systems Exposition (New York, N. Y.).
[13] "Organization and Functions, Organization, Mission and Functions of Headquarters," AMC, AMCR 10-2, July 1, 1966, pp. 4.19–4.21.
[14] "Qualitative Materiel Development Objective (QMDO) Management," Draft Headquarters, U. S. Army Materiel Command, Washington, D. C., May 16, 1963.
[15] R. H. Rea and T. Synnott, III, *A Framework for the Comprehension and Analysis of Applied Research Effectiveness*, FDP-TM-63-22, Air Force Flight Dynamics Laboratory, Wright-Patterson Air Force Base, Ohio, 1963.
[16] Review and Analysis of AMC Scientific and Technological Activities," Development Directorate, Science and Technology Division, June 5, 1968.
[17] C. K. Robbins, "A Management System for Exploratory Development," Air Force Flight Dynamics Laboratory, Wright-Patterson Air Force Base, Ohio, AD 648 699.

Testing TORQUE—A Quantitative R&D Resource-Allocation System

AMBROSE BEN NUTT

Abstract—This paper discusses the Air Force experiment in testing the resource-allocation model called Technology or Research Quantitative Utility Evaluation (TORQUE). This model, which was developed by an interservice team for the Department of Defense (DOD), provides for a closer coupling between future desired military capabilities and laboratory efforts. Specifically, it addresses the area of exploratory development projects and tasks and attempts to provide a balanced allocation of resources within the laboratory. This paper gives the background of TORQUE, the methodology utilized, and some of the findings. A complete appraisal of TORQUE has not yet been made by the Air Force and, therefore, the final evaluation of the technique has not yet been determined.

TORQUE is an acronym meaning Technology or Research Quantitative Utility Evaluation. In this paper, the genesis of the TORQUE system will be briefly reviewed and the system and its operation will be described. The test of the system recently performed by the Air Force will be covered, along with the results and some of the implications of the test as they may affect the R&D community.

The search for rational methods of allocating and justifying the allocation of resources in an organization is one pursued by every manager. Nowhere has this search been pursued under more difficult conditions than in the field of research and development. The Department of Defense (DOD) Project "Hindsight" [1] and, more recently, Project "TRACES," [2], as well as the literature surrounding attempts to design such methods [3], [4], all testify to the effort to quantify and/or predict research payoffs.

This problem is particularly acute in the Department of Defense where an R&D budget must be defended each year in a Congressional atmosphere increasingly critical of vague statements of future relevance of R&D to the future force structure. In addition, funding for research and exploratory development must compete at each echelon of departmental review with the immediate and pressing needs of systems under development and acquisitions, with their often attendant cost increases, to say nothing of South East Asian (SEA) demands. Obviously then, the need is vital for developing and using methods and techniques that more clearly show the relevance and contribution of dollars spent on research and exploratory developments to future operational forces. Unless this is done, it is clear that funds allotted to this kind of effort

Manuscript received July, 1969; revised August, 1969. This paper was presented at the 21st Annual National Aerospace Electronics Conference (Dayton, Ohio, May 1969).

The author is with the Technical Staff, Air Force Flight Dynamics Laboratory, Wright-Patterson Air Force Base, Ohio.

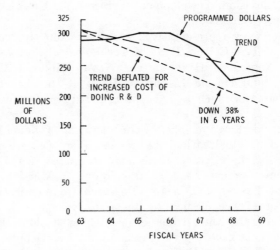

Fig. 1.   United States Air Force exploratory development.

will therefore continue to decrease.

An indication of the nature of the problem is given in Fig. 1, which shows the gradual decline of the Air Force exploratory development budget from 1963 to the present. That this decline took place in an environment of inflation and increased costs for solving more and more difficult technical problems, focuses sharply on the apparent inability of the R&D managers concerned to reverse such a trend in such an environment. (As a matter of interest, in a recent RAND report, this dual impact on expenditures in support of weapon-systems development is referred to as the "modernization/inflation" effect. Using the 1965 dollar as a base, a cost increase in 1971 of 21.1 percent is estimated for inflation, and an additional cost increase due to increased complexity of development is estimated to be 30.8 percent, for an overall total of 51.9 percent.)

Two years ago the Secretary of Defense was quoted as saying that "it is difficult to get a cohesive grasp on the relative worth of exploratory development effort in relation to the Services' objectives." In an attempt to get a handle on this problem, Dr. John S. Foster, Jr., Director of Defense Research and Engineering (DDR&E) in 1967 set up an ad hoc tri-service committee to address the problem of 1) finding a credible method of showing the relationship of the resources expended for exploratory development to future objectives of the Military Services, and 2) achieving balance in the allocation of exploratory development funds.

Under the guidance of Dr. Donald M. MacArthur, Deputy Director of Defense Research and Engineering

(Research and Technology), the ad hoc committee that developed TORQUE consisted of two representatives each of the Army, Navy, and Air Force, and several expert advisers.

The Army representatives were Harold Davidson, a physical scientist in the Office of the Special Scientific Adviser, U. S. Army Research Office, and Lewis Roepcke, Chief, Technical Planning Branch, Scientific and Technical Division, Development Directorate, U. S. Army Materiel Command.

The Navy representatives were the committee chairman Marvin Cetron, Head of Technological Forecasting and Appraisal, Headquarters Naval Materiel Command, and Harold Liebowitz, Head of the Structural Mechanics Branch and engineering adviser for the office of Naval Research.

The Air Force members were Lieutenant Colonel Patrick H. Caulfield, Chief, Laboratory Plans Office, Directorate of Laboratory Plans and Programs, Air Force Systems Command, and Major Joseph P. Martino, Assistant Executive Director, Research Communications, Air Force Office of Scientific Research.

Advisers to the ad hoc group included Colonel Raymond S. Isenson, Special Assistant to the Deputy Director of Defense Research and Engineering (Research and Technology); Peter Fishburn, Research Analysis Corp., an Army contract agency; Robert F. Lockman, Center for Naval Analyses; Lyle V. Jones, University of North Carolina; Frederick S. Pardee, RAND Corp.; Harry Kaplan, Behavioral Sciences Research Laboratory, U. S. Army; and Herbert Solomon, Stanford University.

The basic rationale underlying the objectives of the committee were these.

1) The products of the exploratory development resources expended should lead to increased future operational capabilities of the Services.

2) The R&D resources available will never be sufficient to fund all the alternate approaches to the solutions of R&D problems confronting the Services where such solutions are likely to lead to improved operating capabilities.

3) A method or system devised to aid the Services in preparing an R&D budget with optimal future payoff should answer the following questions. What R&D achievements are desired? When will they be needed? What is their worth? What will they cost?

The resource-allocation system, known as TORQUE, developed by the Tri-Service Committee, supplies answers to these questions by:

1) providing weighted time-phased broad statements of future desired Service operational capability objectives (OCO);

2) providing alternative application options to satisfy these objectives;

3) defining the technological advances required to make these options possible on a timely basis and the importance of these technologies relative to providing the options;

4) determining the resources required to provide these advances on a timely basis; and

5) defining a simulation model that structures the foregoing data to achieve a balanced exploratory development program within any given level of resources made available to the Services.

Fig. 2 shows the operational diagram for the TORQUE system. This diagram illustrates one of the basic tenets of TORQUE, namely that inputs to the system are provided by those who have the most expertise relative to a given input.

Looking at Block 1 of the diagram, the first input and topmost level of TORQUE consists of the set of OCO based on the roles and missions of each Service. These objectives are ranked in order of relative importance, are time and technologically independent (i.e., valid over a long period of time), are statements of things to be done rather than statements of *how* things are to be done, and are based on future world and threat scenarios. These data are provided by the long-range planning organizations of each Service.

Once the OCO are determined and ranked, a set of links between them and the exploratory development program is delineated. (See Fig. 2, Block 2.) This is done by an interdisciplinary (ID) team composed of analysts of advanced systems and subsystems in the Service concerned. (At this point some assistance is provided by laboratory personnel in the TORQUE system, as will be described.) These analysts use the OCO as a frame of reference for conceptualizing the system/subsystem options. In this process, the description, performance, and operating environments of each option are described in enough detail so that the technological needs of each can be defined at a later point in the TORQUE program. The basic ground rules are that options must be provided for each OCO and that the current and projected force structure must be considered, as well as threat data for the mission area under analysis.

Each of the options or alternative approaches for satisfying each OCO must be time phased, i.e., a determination must be made as to when the current system or subsystem in the inventory, if any, will cease to adequately support the capability objective in question. Similarly, an estimate must be made of when the new option will cease to support the capability, i.e., when the enemy will have achieved a countermeasure. For each system, these two times, defined as the year of initial operational capability, are known as the "earliest" and "latest" dates for these options. Where certain subsystem expertise is found only in a laboratory, personnel from that laboratory are called upon to be members

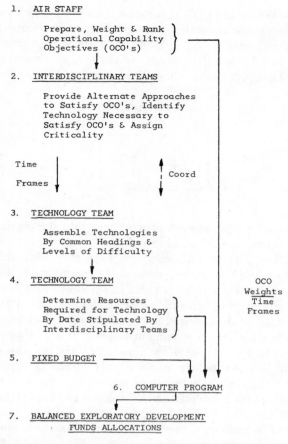

1. AIR STAFF

   Prepare, Weight & Rank
   Operational Capability
   Objectives (OCO's)

2. INTERDISCIPLINARY TEAMS

   Provide Alternate Approaches
   to Satisfy OCO's, Identify
   Technology Necessary to
   Satisfy OCO's & Assign
   Criticality

Time Frames   Coord

3. TECHNOLOGY TEAM

   Assemble Technologies
   By Common Headings &
   Levels of Difficulty

4. TECHNOLOGY TEAM

   Determine Resources
   Required for Technology
   By Date Stipulated By
   Interdisciplinary Teams

OCO Weights Time Frames

5. FIXED BUDGET

6. COMPUTER PROGRAM

7. BALANCED EXPLORATORY DEVELOPMENT FUNDS ALLOCATIONS

Fig. 2. TORQUE data-flow diagram.

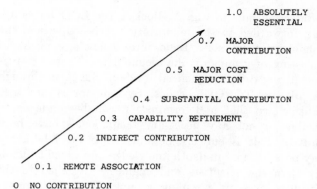

1.0 ABSOLUTELY ESSENTIAL
0.7 MAJOR CONTRIBUTION
0.5 MAJOR COST REDUCTION
0.4 SUBSTANTIAL CONTRIBUTION
0.3 CAPABILITY REFINEMENT
0.2 INDIRECT CONTRIBUTION
0.1 REMOTE ASSOCIATION
0 NO CONTRIBUTION

Fig. 3. Scale for criticality of technology to system/subsystem option.

of the ID team to assist in delineating thhe subsystem options.

The next responsibility of the ID team is the identification of the various technology advancements beyond the current state of the art required to bring each of the system/subsystem options into being, thus permitting achievement of the operational capabilities defined by the Service Headquarters' long-range planning staff. In TORQUE, these technologies are referred to as levels of difficulty (LOD).

These technologies are stated quantitatively as discrete advancements in technology, e.g., the reliability and accuracy of a guidance system, the capability of an external flight-vehicle structure to resist a given temperature for a stated period of time, or the capability to completely analyze the flow field around a vehicle flying at a specified Mach number and altitude. At the same time, the criticality of this technology to the system or subsystem it supports is stated. This is done with reference to a predefined scale going from a minimal contribution to a level that states that the achievement of this technology is absolutely essential to the building of the system or subsystem. (See Fig. 3 for an abbreviated version of this scale.) Now in associating each technology with a system or subsystem, the earliest ini-

tial operational capability (IOC) dates of the system dictate that the technology must be available when the system-fabrication phase begins, i.e., up to seven years prior to the IOC date, depending on the complexity of the system or subsystem.

It should be noted here that a coding system and a series of input data forms and output data formats were designed for the handling and processing of data in the TORQUE system. The codes identified the Service, the operational capability objective, the system or subsystem, and the associated technology. The technology codes divided exploratory development into the following functional areas: 1) intelligence, surveillance, and countermeasures; 2) firepower; 3) mobility; 4) command and control; 5) logistics; and 6) multipurpose (i.e., not exclusively associated with any of the other five functional areas). These functional areas were subcoded and divided into technical domains, projects, and tasks; the latter two being highly correlated with the current Services' technology identification codes. Some of the input forms and their data content were the following.

Operational Capability Objective (OCO) Form
   Code number
   Description
   Relative value

System/Subsystem Form
   Code number
   Description
   OCO supported
   Earliest and latest IOC dates
   Analyst's name and organization

Technology (LOD) Form
   Code
   Description
   System/subsystem supported
   Criticality
   Earliest and latest dates
   Corresponding service, project, and task
   Scientist or engineer and organization.

Referring now to Fig. 2, Block 3, the LOD forms are then forwarded to the laboratory concerned, where the technology team sorts them into technology packages consisting of groups of like technologies. These are further arranged into sequential levels of difficulty through use of the TORQUE codes. System forms are also furnished so that a determination can be made as to whether or not any necessary technologies have been omitted. This is entirely possible since the laboratory may possess more in depth knowledge of a given technology than the scientists and engineers attached to the advanced systems planning groups. Where additional technologies are uncovered, the necessary forms are prepared, sent to the ID team for assignment of criticality, and then returned to the laboratory for packaging.

The next task for the technology team in the laboratory (Fig. 2, Block 4) is to determine the resources required to obtain the stipulated technologies by the time required. This task, referred to as "costing out" is done on the TORQUE Resources Input Form for each LOD. This form shows the LOD code number, the latest year required, system/subsystem supported, cost required by year, and the total cost for achievement.

The resources are determined by deciding whether the work will be done in-house or contracted and thus include contract costs (if any), the cost of laboratory manpower required, and any special laboratory equipment required.

All of the coded time and cost data on the foregoing forms is then transferred to the TORQUE Computer Punch Transcript Form (one for each LOD) for converting to punch cards for processing by the computer in the utility, computation, and resource allocation phase of the TORQUE system (Fig. 2, Blocks 5, 6, and 7). In TORQUE, the budget is "optimized" by obtaining the maximum utility from the efforts funded for a given amount of dollars, or, more exactly, for the total exploratory development of funds allocated to a given Service.

The utility of an LOD in TORQUE is computed using the following simulation model or objective function.

$$U = \sum_{j=1}^{N} C_j W_j Cf t_j$$

where

U = utility of the LOD,
N = number of systems supported by the LOD,
C_j = criticality of the LOD to the jth system supported,
W_j = relative normalized weight or importance of the OCO supported by the jth system,
Cf = the ratio of first-year funds allocated to the technology package to which this LOD belongs to the total funds required to completely achieve the technology,
t_j = timeliness function.

t_j is equal to 1.0 where the LOD is completed between the earliest and latest dates the jth system can use the

LOD. Where the LOD is completed more than two years before the earliest date E and later than two years after the latest date L, $t_j = 0$. Intermediate values between zero and 1.0 are determined by the symmetrical trapezoidal shape of the timeliness function, e.g.,

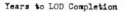
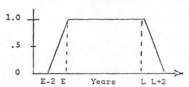

The allocation process programmed into the computer can be summarized as follows.

1) For a given technology package consisting of one or more LOD, a funds-versus-utility computation is carried out for each LOD (funded in the first year) for the first year of program funding (considered by TORQUE) by tenths of the required first-year funding. The funding associated with the maximum slope of this curve is the preferred funding level for that LOD and for the corresponding technology package. (If an LOD supports more than one system, it is costed out so that it is scheduled for completion on the earliest required system's latest date.)

2) The computer, using the budget allocation, selects, from the combination of allocation levels for the various technologies, that set which provides the maximum utility for the funds available.

The results or outputs are then formatted by organization, project, and task showing funds allocated. Other output formats can be designed showing the data in various forms, e.g., priority lists, OCO/system matrix, system/technology matrix, etc., depending on the requirements of the users.

TORQUE is designed to supplement the intuition of managers at all levels by combining expert subjective judgments in a structured fashion to serve as a tool or aid in the decision-making process. It is almost superfluous to add that the system is in no way intended to supplant the manager.

Essentially, TORQUE is a framework for quantitatively converting statements about desired future military operational capabilities into system descriptions, which then can be translated into technological criteria. The methodology is based on the premise that the relative amounts of money spent in various areas of science and technology should reflect the varying degrees of interest in those areas. Because total resources are limited, some project proposals must be denied. Therefore, the problem of allocating funds or achieving balance becomes a matter of determining how much an additional advance in one field is worth to the Department of Defense or the individual agency concerned, as opposed to an advance of equal cost in some other field.

TORQUE offers no panacea or final solution, however, to the problem of balanced exploratory development fund allocation. For instance, it does not explicitly take into account the effects of non-DOD research and development efforts. Other factors not accounted for are technical risks and the inability to work in a technical area due to lack of qualified personnel or manpower-ceiling limitations. Additional considerations for which TORQUE offers no formula include the need of allowing some proportion of the total funds for use in high-risk high-payoff efforts of apparently low systems relevance, which may lead to significantly improved military capability in ways not even now thought of.

The Air Force conducted a test of the TORQUE system during 1968 involving the following organizations and their respective responsibilities.

1) Headquarters, United States Air Force—test direction and definition and ranking of OCO.
2) Headquarters, Air Force Systems Command (Director of Laboratories)—field test coordination.
3) Aeronautical Systems Division (ASD), Space and Missile Systems Organization (SAMSO)—system /subsystem definition and time assessment, technology delineation, criticality, and time assessment.
4) Air Force Flight Dynamics Laboratory—assist ASD, SAMSO, and computer group, further technology definition, and technology costing and packaging.
5) Aeronautical Systems Division (Computer Group)—computer programming and data processing and sensitivity analyses.

The primary purposes of the test were 1) to check the conceptual soundness of the TORQUE system, 2) to determine the operational feasibility of the system, 3) to measure the cost effectiveness of the system, and 4) to evaluate the potential of the system as an aid to resource allocation. Concurrently, personnel involved in the test were directed to recommend changes to the system during the test, which would enhance the effectiveness of the system. All changes made were subject to the prior approval of the Test Director at Headquarters, United States Air Force (USAF).

The test included a trial of the TORQUE system, consisting of the complete system at the OCO level and a limited test at the system/subsystem and technology levels. The test was conducted using a full set of OCO and a partial set of systems/subsystems and technologies. The test at the systems/subsystems and technology levels was constrained by limitation to the technology areas of only one Air Force Laboratory, Flight Dynamics, located at Wright-Patterson Air Force Base, Ohio. This laboratory's technologies covered the entire spectrum of aerospace vehicle technologies, excluding propulsion and avionics (except for the flight control interface); namely, structures, vehicle dynamics, flight control, aerodynamics and aerothermodynamics, internal environmental control, crew escape and crew station, decelerators, landing gear, mechanical subsystems, and simulation.

The chronology and manhours involved at all organizational levels in the test were as follows.

Activity	Dates	Manhours (estimated)
OCO definition	September 1967–January 1968	400
Systems definition	February–June 1968	6500
Technology definition	July–November 1968	3500
Algorithm and data processing	continuous	1300
Administration and evaluation	continuous	2000
		~7 "man years"

A total of 1317 LOD/system combinations were validated for the test; 898 from ASD and 419 from SAMSO. Also validated were 19 OCO, 40 ASD, and 20 SAMSO systems.

Some of the procedural refinements that appeared or were indicated as desired changes during conduction of the test were

1) simplification of terminology (change of technology to task and change of LOD to subtask),
2) utility computation and allocation (change from technology to LOD),
3) rank order (weight) of those systems under each OCO (requires a change in the simulation model),
4) decrease in numbers of criticality definitions,
5) provision of some quantification in OCO definitions,
6) provision for combined ID and technology team effort in definition of LOD,
7) further simplification of LOD input form to allow for multiple-system support identification,
8) decrease in number of systems options,
9) definition of work corresponding to the technology costs delineated for each LOD/year by the technology team.

The concept of sequential levels of difficulty within a technology package was found to be unfeasible during the test, insofar as flight dynamics technologies were concerned. The primary reason was that as one made quantum improvements in a technology area, entirely different technical approaches to the solution of problems encountered were taken, to the extent that the lowest level of solution was of no help in reaching the solution at the next problem level. One example is in the field of airframe bearings where for temperatures up to 1000°F, metals are well within the state of the art; while at 2000°F, ceramic bearings are required whose development does not depend on the technology of the metals.

Some advantages to the systems divisions (ASD and SAMSO) found as a result of implementing TORQUE were closer association with the Air Staff (with an unimproved opportunity to get a better perspective on future systems concepts), and more intimate association with laboratory scientists and engineers for improved communication.

Some advantages to the laboratory resulting from implementing TORQUE were aid to resource allocation, improved communication with systems divisions, improved program credibility, information retrieval on program characteristics and parameters, and a common planning guidance baseline.

With respect to the basic purposes of the test, some preliminary conclusions were made by the author.

1) Procedural soundness—the basic rationale appears reasonable. Consultants outside government with expertise in this area have concurred on this. The absence of a probability of success term in the TORQUE simulation model was questioned. It should be noted that sensitivity analyses conducted on the simulation model did not indicate a need for deletion of any term.

2) Cost effectiveness—as far as the Flight Dynamics Laboratory was concerned, TORQUE could be modified (without substantive changes in the algorithm) to provide an effectiveness equal to a system previously used by the laboratory as an allocation aid and program-data retrieval system. (This assumes that the changes to the TORQUE system discovered during the test as described above are implemented.) Insofar as other or-

ganization levels are concerned, this question is currently being considered by Headquarters, USAF.

The future implications of the TORQUE test are almost solely a function of the evaluation of the test results now being conducted by the Air Force. Suffice it to say that the questions originally raised by DDR&E relative to a means of justifying exploratory development expenditures and achieving a balanced allocation of exploratory development funds will remain, regardless of the TORQUE system evaluation. It would appear that if TORQUE is not adopted, some procedure with similar ends will have to be developed to satisfy the need originally raised by the Secretary of Defense; namely, that of getting a cohesive grasp on the relative worth of the expenditure of exploratory development resources in relation to the Services' objectives, in a way that will make possible a balanced allocation of these resources.

References

[1] C. W. Sherwin and R. S. Isenson, "First interim report on project hindsight (summary)," Office of the Director of Defense Research and Engineering, June 30, 1966.
[2] "Technology in retrospect and critical events in science," Illinois Inst. of Tech., Chicago, Ill., December 15, 1968.
[3] N. R. Baker and W. H. Pound, "R&D project selection: Where we stand," *IEEE Trans. Engineering Management*, vol. EM-11, pp. 124–134, December 1964.
[4] M. J. Cetron, J. Martino, and L. Roepcke, "The selection of R&D program content—Survey of quantitative methods," *IEEE Trans. Engineering Management*, vol. EM-14, pp. 4–13, March 1967.

Madness, Mediocrity, or Mastery. A Threat Analysis for a New Era

HAROLD A. LINSTONE

PREFACE

The American defense community—government and industry—has entered upon a period of flux not encountered since World War II. This study concentrates on the world environment of the 1970-85 period. It is an attempt to set the stage for more detailed corporate long range planning exercises in this area.

Interviewer:	Are you optimistic or pessimistic about the future?
Forecaster:	I am basically optimistic.
Interviewer:	Then why do you look so sad?
Forecaster:	I don't think my optimism is justified.

Most environmental forecasts extrapolate familiar parameters describing familiar trends from the recent past into the future. Never has this practice been more dangerous than it is today.

The two views presented in this discussion underscore the hazards and their significance.

A. A 'Traditional' Look into the Future

1. The Era of the Two Superpowers

For the past quarter century, the United States and the Soviet Union have been the undisputed number 1 and 2 powers. They alone have the ability to effectively destroy any nation on earth, including each other. For example, the McNamara posture statements from 1964 to 1969 indicate that in all but one of the 16 cases he analyzed, the United States can inflict 70 to over 120 million fatalities on the Soviet Union after absorbing an enemy first strike.[1]

Economically, the ratio of strength (in terms of GNP) between the first and second power is of the order of 2:1. If this trend continues, the gap will, of course, widen. A 1965 gap in GNP per capita of $2,300 can easily become a 1985 gap of $3,900

Both have used their power to gain or hold influence in Eastern Europe, Western Europe, Latin America, Africa, the Middle East, and Asia.[2] Currently, over one million American troops are stationed abroad. There are 2,270 U.S. military bases overseas (343 major ones) in 29 foreign countries as well as in U.S. possessions.[3] They range from Greenland to Africa, from Spain to Japan.

The extensive conventional military aid provided by the two superpowers to other countries has occasionally resulted in strange bedfellows:

> Support by one superpower to two opposing nations (e.g., United States to Greece and Turkey, to Israel and Jordan, to Pakistan and India).

> Support by both superpowers to one nation (e.g., Pakistan and Iran each supplied by both superpowers).

The aims of the two superpowers brought them into both cooperation and conflict beginning with World War II in Europe. They cooperated to rescue Europe from Hitler and they divided Germany. Then conflict began. Following the 1948 Berlin crisis, instigated by the Soviet Union, the formation of the U.S. dominated NATO pact in 1949 provided stability. This, in turn, permitted spectacular recovery of the shattered European economy on both sides of the Iron Curtain. Most importantly, the policy of 'conquer and divide' has effectively prevented the rise of a single dominant country (i.e., Germany) in Europe which could once more threaten its neighbors.

Similarly, in the poor world the two superpowers have a history of both cooperation and conflict. Since the demise of European colonialism, a power vacuum has made this area much more the center of superpower activity than the advanced countries. Of more than 50 internationally significant local wars since World War II, only one—the Hungarian revolt—has been fought between advanced industrial states or on the territory of an advanced state.[4] Superpower cooperation is evidenced by the stand against nuclear proliferation and attempts to settle the India-Pakistan conflict.

Conflict has arisen from Soviet efforts to replace U.S. dominance in Cuba (in the U.S. sphere from 1823 to 1959), to replace British and U.S. influence in the Arab world (beginning in 1946 with the Soviet actions in Iran), and to vie with the United States for influence in the former French and Japanese areas in Southeast Asia (Indochina, Korea).[5]

---

[1] W. W. Kaufmann, *The Strategic Nuclear Forces*, 1969, p. 31. The exception is the case where the Soviet Union develops a greater than expected offensive and defensive threat and even then the number of Soviet casualties is about 50 million.

[2] Until 1950, the United States enjoyed a unique image in Europe as the only major country without the 'normal' power aims. Evidence: aid to England, France, and Russia in two world wars, the Hoover and Marshall postwar aid programs.

The author is with the Department of Industrial and Systems Engineering, University of Southern California

---

[3] *L.A. Times*, June 22, 1969, p. A-27. *U.S. News and World Report*, August 4, 1969, p. 47. These figures represent the results of a cutback in bases begun in 1966-67.

[4] R. E. Osgood, 'The Reappraisal of Limited War," *Adelphi Papers* No. 54, February 1969, p. 42.

[5] The American interest in the Pacific actually started with the opening up of Japan. It may almost be viewed as a continuation of the 19th century drive to conquer the Western frontier on this continent. Has it reached its zenith with Korea and Vietnam?

Finally, cooperation is apparent in the initiation of strategic arms limitations talks in 1969.[6]

We can readily extrapolate this era of the superpowers into the next quarter century. But there are signs that the era is drawing to a close. The U.S. difficulties in Vietnam, the Soviet difficulties in Czechoslovakia, as well as the impotence of the United States and Soviet Union in the Middle East, are obvious indications of change. Growing internal difficulties in both nations are also casting their shadows ahead.[7] Thus the limits of power are coming into focus and the 'Age of the Cold War' may well fade into the history books.

2. The Challengers

Extrapolating current trends, a ranking of nations in terms of productivity yields the following table for 1985:

> GNP Ranking (medium estimates)
>
> United States
> Soviet Union
> Japan
> West Germany
> France

Japan and Germany, the two principal instigators and losers of World War II, are the foremost challengers in terms of total productivity. Both have had a very favorable government-business relationship and diverted only minor resources to the military establishment. They exercise economic rather than political power in international affairs.

The 2:1 ratio for the United States-Soviet Union in total GNP is also reasonable for the Soviet Union-Japan. Neither challenger represents a real military threat to the Soviet Union or to the United States in the next 15 years. However, the Land of the Rising GNP may try an economic version of its 'Greater Southeast Asia Co-prosperity Sphere.' Herman Kahn has even suggested that the 21st century may become known as the Japanese century. One wonders how long Japan can maintain its current phenomenal growth rate.[8]

Germany may encourage one of several European options: a fragmented Europe dominated economically by Germany, a loosely federated Europe with no dominating country but a considerable number of common functional institutions, or a strongly integrated Europe which becomes an independent 'Third Force.' A Western European Union can match the Soviet Union in economic strength, i.e., GNP. Medium growth estimates

for 1985 give the Soviet Union a GNP of $788 billion and the combination of West Germany, France, United Kingdom, and Italy $851 billion. So far, Europe has been hampered by inadequate education of its manpower, weak management and marketing capabilities, and inefficient joint ventures. The small and rigid advanced education systems and the apprenticeship concepts are obsolete. There have been numerous instances of European leadership in technology nullified by poor exploitation due to marketing and management (examples: commercial jet aircraft, computers, steel processing). Cooperative international projects such as Euratom, the Coal and Steel Community, and ELDO have not been truly integrated operations. The vacuum has been filled by American companies operating mostly with European financial and manpower resources.[9] A strong European economy will require:

a) Formation of large industrial units with strong management in technologically advanced areas.

b) More surrender of national sovereignty than has been exhibited heretofore.

c) Major revision of the educational system.

d) Drastically changed social structures to provide organizational flexibility.

In recent years, GNP per capita has come into wide use for evaluating and comparing the status of nations. Sawyer[10] considered 236 variables for 82 nations and concludes that 'if one were to know but three characteristics of a nation, their population, GNP per capita, and political orientation would seem to be a good choice.'

Figures A-1 to A-4 (Appendix A) show the dynamics of population and GNP per capita growth for most nations to 1985 on a regional basis. The 1985 GNP per capita ranking differs notably from that shown earlier for GNP.

> Ranking of Countries Moving Beyond
> 'Mass Consumption' Stage
> (medium estimates)
>
> United States
> Sweden
> Canada
> West Germany
> East Germany

Here also we find a clue to the question of continuation of the era of the superpowers. The challengers reaching for the highest level include a different breed of nation. They, rather than the United States, may take the lead in creating a new society.

3. The Poor World

Two-thirds of the nations, with 70% of the world population, have a GNP per capita of less than $500. Figure A-4 (Appendix A) shows the last decade of growth and

---

[6] It is also notable that Soviet trade with capitalist countries has increased 25% between 1958 and 1967.

[7] Soviet writer Andrei Amalrik views his nation in these words: 'Too authoritarian to permit everything, too weak to repress everything, the regime is tottering toward death.' (*Atlas,* February 1970, p. 21.)

[8] There are some interesting contrasts between the United States and Japan. Example: In Japan young industries are supported by the government; later they move to full private control. In the United States, on the other hand, old industries are supported by the government (e.g., shipbuilding, railroads).

[9] According to Servan-Schreiber ('The American Challenge,' p. 14), 90% of the American investment in Europe is financed with European funds.

[10] J. Sawyer, 'Dimensions of Nations: Size, Wealth, and Politics,' *American Journal of Sociology,* **73**, No. 2, September 1967, p. 159.

Figures A-1 to A-3 (Appendix A) indicate their relation to the rest of the world in the next 15 years. The widening gap is evident by the directions of the arrows. Compare, for example, Israel and UAR, Japan and Indonesia.

The most severe problem is in the proper management of human resources (i.e., education) and capital, the key ingredients for development. We usually find one of the following situations:

a) Dictatorship of the right

The establishment is status quo oriented, usually corrupt and incompetent. Often the military establishment is the governing body.

Examples: Portugal, Haiti, Paraguay, Brazil

b) Dictatorship of the left

There is a wide populist power base and engagement of the masses is emphasized. Extravagant promises and ideological trappings accompany socio-economic changes. Often these changes are based on unsound theories and actually retard development. Here, too, the military establishment frequently provides the leadership. Corruption and incompetence also mark many of these regimes.

Examples: China, Cuba, Syria, UAR, Algeria

These dictatorships are often 'supported' by one of the two superpowers with its own aims (and sometimes by both). Usually the United States 'supports' the right, while the Soviet Union 'supports' the left.

c) Moderate or compromise

In this group we see the liberal or reform leadership seeking change by evolution and widening the power base progressively. Again corruption, incompetence, and external 'support' plague the government.

Examples: Chile, Thailand, India

Failure of (c) creates a shift to either (a) or (b). However, we also observe other shifts: from (b) to (c), e.g., Yugoslavia; and (a) to (b), e.g., Cuba.

The need is for highly capable, dedicated, and far-sighted leadership which can mobilize capital effectively, educate and train people rapidly, and manage balanced growth of the nation while preventing domination by other powers—a combination of requirements that is formidable indeed. Today's advanced nations themselves could not solve the problem successfully during their transformation from an agricultural to an industrial society. Violence and revolution accompanied modernization in the United States, Soviet Union, England, Germany, and other nations.

In 1968 the rich nations spent about $6.9 billion in aid to the poor countries.[11] In terms of GNP fraction the U.S. aid program ranked seventh with 0.38% (France led the donors with 0.72%).

---

[11] For comparison, it is noted that the world was spending over $180 billion on arms that year.

It is often said that the advanced nations should increase their technical and financial aid to the poor countries. But it is debatable whether present know-how in the advanced countries is able to provide adequate guidance for balanced growth in the poor nations even if talent and money are liberally applied.

Economically, the desirability of groupings of nations to strengthen their capital-human resource position is as valid for the poor as it is for Europe. Technology has already reduced the dependence of the wealthy on single crops or natural resources of the poor. Synthetic rubber, new foods, electric cars, and materials of the future will further lessen the leverage of the poor countries. The question is whether nationalistic (or tribalistic) prejudices and traditions can be submerged.

Finally, an intriguing question has been raised: can an underdeveloped country skip the industrial stage and move directly to a post-industrial society (see below)?

4. Alliances and Conflict

In a world of two superpowers, alliances are not groupings of equals but instruments placing the weak under the protection or control of the strong. The major post-World War II alliances—NATO-1949, SEATO-1954, OAS-1956, the Warsaw Pact-1955—are all in this 'umbrella' category. While still effective in relations between the two superpowers, the changing environment can only reduce their significance in the next 15 years.

The appearance of challengers who can gain status and influence by strictly nonmilitary means and the worsening plight of the poor world tend to alter the alliance needs considerably. For one thing, 'balance of power' alignments, a hallmark of 19th century Europe, again become possible. However, the two aging superpowers will find it most difficult to recognize and accept change. The key institutions in both countries (e.g., defense, foreign affairs) undoubtedly will press for maintenance of these umbrella alliances. Their principal argument will be that any change will alter the relative positions of the United States and the Soviet Union.

B. A 'New' Look into the Future

The family and the nation have made up the most important social units in the world for many years. Now both are undergoing technology-induced stresses which may dramatically alter their future and invalidate the customary trend extrapolations exemplified by the Traditional Look.

Let us first very briefly consider the family. The impact of technology is deep as two examples will show:

a) The difference in education between old and young reduces the authority of the former and hence loosens family ties.[12]

---

[12] An illustration is afforded by mathematics. Earlier generations were taught Euclidean geometry and the decimal system as 'eternal truths.' Today students learn that many other geometries with opposing axioms are equally correct and that any number greater than 1 can serve as a basis for a number system. The students soon begin to question other ideas accepted by their elders and their social institutions.

b) Communications and transportation have a similar effect. Mobility separates family clans and even separates parents from children. Communications tie in the young to the outside world early in a direct manner without the parents acting as filters.

In short, the family today finds itself weakened in a rapidly changing environment.

The reader may wonder why a defense planning study should even mention the 'family' problem. The explanation will become evident after we discuss the nation in more detail.

During the past 50 years, about 100 new nations have been created. At the same time, supranational concepts have had an ephemeral existence. The League of Nations failed; the United Nations organization is barely alive. The seemingly most successful example—Communism—has been bowing to nationalistic pressures. The COMINTERN failed and conflict in the communist world is also between nations (e.g., Soviet Union-Czechoslovakia, Soviet Union-China).

Success as a nation (like success as a corporation) has required a combination of capable leadership and objectives which motivate and unify its members. Common goals and values, together with competent and adaptive management or administration, create the self-discipline and synergistic group activities which characterize great achievements. Japan and Israel in the last decades are examples of such success.

These two countries also illustrate two essential points:

a) A motivation which serves admirably is fear of survival, represented by threat of military attack against the nation. In the case of Israel, the Arab threat of driving the Israelis into the sea unifies and drives forward a very heterogeneous society.

b) Unless a war results in annihilation, the outcome does not appear particularly significant for national success. Japan and Germany, the losers in World War II, are progressing far better than some of the victors (e.g., England) if measured in terms of productivity or GNP per capita growth.

The meaningfulness of this measure of national success in the next quarter century is open to question:

a) A country which moves beyond the mass-consumption stage into the post-industrial stage where industry becomes a secondary activity can hardly consider productivity as a suitable measure of national status. New measures of individual and group achievement will be needed.

b) The famine-ridden poor nations will not consider industrial productivity central to their success. India has already recognized that in its current stage agricultural improvement is more crucial than industrialization (as recognized by Gandhi). Success of the 'green revolution' cannot be measured adequately by GNP per capita.

c) Problems are mounting in both rich and poor nations which imply that 'success' can no longer be couched in purely economic terms for any country. Money loses its significance for an individual who is incurably ill.

Can the government of the wealthiest nation in history be considered capable if it is unable to (1) protect its citizens against destruction (in the event of nuclear attack), (2) protect its citizens from attack in the streets, (3) efficiently wage combat against a fourth-rate nation, (4) fight a successful 'War on Poverty' at home, (5) assure clean air and water for its citizens, and (6) lead the world in health (e.g., infant mortality rate, expected life span of its men), and (7) plan the evolution of its society beyond the industrial stage?

The time available to solve this nation's problems and avoid crises is clearly limited; one overview of the situation is depicted in Table I.

The source of the global problems facing nations is the exponential growth of technology.[13] In the last 50 years, technology has drastically cut the death rate, thereby causing a population explosion (Figure 1). It has developed high speed global transportation, unleashed vast energy resources, and—most important of all—created near-instantaneous audiovisual communications. Person to person data flow is increasing far faster than GNP, population, energy consumption, or transportation. The speed of human transportation has increased by a factor of 10 in 50 years and only one more such change can be envisioned. But computer speed has been rising (and cost declining) by the same factor every 4 years and the pace is likely to continue for a while.[14] Data are not knowledge, of course, and we are faced with the threat that 'data' may turn into one of the most serious pollutants.

As a result of such technological growth on many fronts the rather old spaceship earth is suddenly becoming an overcrowded global village. As with two people in a telephone booth, every action by one affects the other and cooperation as well as careful planning is essential if any useful objective is to be achieved.

How can national leaders manage homeostatic or balanced development when we possess insufficient understanding of the global 'system,' its subsystems, and their interactions?

Let us look at some of the difficulties:

1. Population Imbalance

Currently, there is a net increase of 69 million people a year. A world which accommodated 3.5 billion souls in 1968 may house 7.5 billion by the year 2000. Asia alone is likely to have a population equal to that of the

---

[13] T. J. Gordon combines annual per capita power use, steel production, intercity passenger travel miles, working force of engineers and scientists, and communications (newspaper circulation, radio and TV receivers) to obtain a technology index. This index is doubling every 20 years.

[14] P. Armer, 'The Individual, His Privacy, Self-Image, and Obsolescence,' Panel on Science and Technology, Eleventh Meeting, Committee on Science and Astronautics, House of Representatives, January 28, 1970.

TABLE I
Classification of Problems and Crises by Estimated Time and Intensity (United States).

Grade	Estimated Crises Intensity (Number Affected X Degree of Effect)		Estimated Time to Crises*		
			1 to 5 Years	5 to 20 Years	20 to 50 Years
1.		Total Annihilation	Nuclear or RCBW Escalation	Nuclear or RCBW Escalation	(Solved or Dead)
2.	10^5	Great Destruction or Change (Physical, Biological, or Political)	(too soon)	Participatory Democracy Ecological Balance	Political Theory and Economic Structure Population Planning Patterns or Living Education Communications Integrative Philosophy
3.	10^7	Widespread almost Unbearable Tension	Administrative Management Slums Participatory Democracy Racial Conflict	Pollution Poverty Law and Justice	?
4.	10^4	Large-Scale Distress	Transportation Neighborhood Ugliness Crime	Communications Gap	?
5.	10^5	Tension Producing Responsive Change	Cancer and Heart Smoking and Drugs Artificial Organs Accidents Sonic Boom Water Supply Marine Resources Privacy on Computers	Educational Inadequacy	
6.		Other Problems— Important, but Adequately Re- searched	Military R & D New Educational Methods Mental Illness Fusion Power	Military R & D	
7.		Exaggerated Dangers and Hopes	Mind Control Heart Transplants Definition of Death	Sperm Banks Freezing Bodies Unemployment from Automation	Eugenics
8.		Noncrisis Problems being 'Overstudied.'	Man in Space Most Basic Science		

*If no Major Effort is Made at Anticipatory Solution.   Source: J. Platt, 'What we must do'. *Science*, 28 November 1969. P. 1118.

entire world today. While 70% of today's population is poor and inadequately nourished, that fraction may rise to 80% by 2000. It is concentrated in Latin America, Asia, and Africa.

It is hoped that agricultural technology will prevent the great famines forecast for the next 25 years. Farm machinery, irrigation, pesticides, fertilizers, and 'transplants' of high yield grains have combined to create the 'green revolution.'

In 1967-68 the wheat harvest in Pakistan reached 7 million metric tons, compared to the previous all-time high of 4.6 million harvested in 1964-65.[15]

World meat production has grown by 75% from 1950 to 1965, fish by 140%.[16] Even today, however, 25% of the

world population uses 75% of its fertilizers. And the poor world has a physical environment which places it at a great disadvantage in food production.

A fourfold increase in food production is required by the year 2000. Technology can:

a) Reduce waste and spoilage (currently esti- mated to cost 20% to 50% of the food produced).

b) Provide storage.

c) Increase yield per acre by production of more and lower cost fertilizers in poor areas.

d) Use salt water irrigation.

e) Produce more high yield varieties of plants (rice, wheat) and create new plants by genetic manipulation.

f) Produce food by direct chemical means (e.g., synthetic foods, proteins from petroleum, and plant protein mixes).

[15] N. E. Borlaug, O. Aresvik, I. Narvaez, and R. G. Anderson, 'A Green Revolution Yields a Golden Har- vest,' *Columbia Journal of World Business*, September- October 1969, p. 12.
[16] G. Borgstrom, 'The World Food Crisis,' *Futures*, June 1969, p. 342.

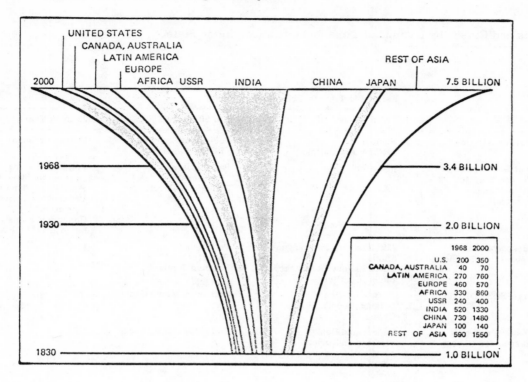

Such changes require effective large-scale government implementation as well as new policies in the area of distribution and pricing of agricultural output.

Reduction of the birthrate is another approach. Contraceptives for fertility control are available but government-sponsored programs have not proven effective to date. India introduced a birth control program in 1951 when the nation's growth rate was 1.3%. After 16 years, the growth rate rose to almost 3%. By 1967, only 2% of India's 95 million couples of reproductive age practised contraception systematically.[17]

Social solutions offer another possible approach. For example, retirement benefits might be geared to the number of children produced by a couple, with income inversely proportional to the number of offspring.[18] The income tax structure can be altered to favor single persons and couples with few children rather than those with many. Foreign aid can be made dependent on effectiveness of population control in the recipient country.

But the net effectiveness of such steps is not at all clear.

2. *Socio-economic Imbalance*

The population problem must be considered integrally with socio-economic development. For example, capital formation increases as the birth rate declines.[19] In other words, reduction of the birth rate is far more critical for the future of the poor world than increase of the food supply. The combination of low fertility and low mortality is desired.

Even the most advanced countries, such as the United States, lack sufficient understanding of socio-economic development.

It has surprised many to learn that the Vietnam War is proving to be the most expensive in American history, if the socio-economic impact on this nation is taken into account. A whole generation will have to pay the cost.[20]

---

[17]   P. Ehrlich, 'Paying the Piper,' *New Scientist*, December 14, 1967.
[18]   J. J. Spengler, 'Population Problem: In Search of a Solution,' *Science*, December 5, 1969, p. 1234.

[19]   H. Frederiksen, 'Feedbacks in Economic and Demographic Transition,'*Science*, November 14, 1969, p. 841.
[20]   For one estimate see J. Clayton, 'Our Mortgaged Future,' *Playboy*, April 1970.

In 1967, Litton Industries set out on a program of 'nation building' in Greece. Over a 12-year period, Litton's system management approach was to attract more than $800 million in investments in the country. Two years later, the investments amounted to only $3. 35 million and the contract was canceled.[21]

In his book, 'Maximum Feasible Misunderstanding: Community Action in the War on Poverty' (sic), Daniel Moynihan observed that the ultimate source of failure was the application of half-baked social science. The poverty warriors assumed they had a scientific answer to poverty when what they really had was merely an interesting hypothesis.

The combination of pressure for change and failure to achieve homeostasis in socio-economic growth leads directly to violence. An analysis of 84 countries for the period 1948 to 1962 substantiates the hypothesis that the faster the rate of change in the modernization process within any given society, the higher the level of political instability in that society.[22] Another study[23] has shown that revolutions, whether French, Russian, or Cuban, tend to follow periods of significant improvement when expectations diverge from aspirations ('the revolutionary gap').[24] This helps to explain the marked increase in riots following the dramatic legislative gains in U.S. civil rights under President Johnson.

To say, then, as Drucker does, that all countries have capital for development and that the claim of a 'lack of capital is euphemism for mismanagement'[25] is to beg the question. We cannot manage very well when we cannot effect balanced growth and this is not possible without an understanding of the 'system.'

The dramatic increase in mobility and instant audio-visual communications throughout the world is likely to have the following result:

The gap between similar levels in most countries will decrease, while the gap between different levels in any one country will widen. In other words, the rich will lead very similar lives in most countries, but the rich and poor in each country will become extremely dissimilar. The dangers inherent in this situation represent one of the most important lessons of history. Consider the Roman Republic.

> 'In an age when all the emphasis is upon wealth, great is the frustration of those forced to remain poor.... No wonder, therefore, that violence and street battles on a scale unheard of before began to disfigure life in Rome.... Was not [Cicero's] plaintive motto <u>concordia ordinum</u> or 'cooperation between the social classes' a plea for the restoration of a vanished social harmony ? No remedy

indeed, but a description of the state of society which a remedy ought to produce, could it have been found.'[26]

3. Ecological Imbalance

Man's impact on the environment was of little concern when his numbers were small and his technological rate of achievement modest. But in recent years the population explosion (Figure 1) and the technological explosion have created a situation where a threat to man's survival on the shrinking spaceship earth is looming. A few examples suggest the seriousness of the threat:

a) Air pollution In the United States, man-made pollutants are currently added to the air at a rate of 160 tons annually. Smog is increasing the incidence of respiratory disease. Chlorinated hydrocarbons, e.g., DDT, are increasingly present in the atmosphere and extrapolation of the present trend may lead to thousands of deaths before 1980. Pollution may significantly alter the weather. Atmospheric temperature changes during the next 50 years are likely to affect the ice caps and the climate over the entire earth. Air pollution changes the rainfall pattern[27] and may also lead to a reduction in absorbed solar radiation.

b) Water pollution Chlorinated hydrocarbons also slow down photosynthesis in marine plant life. Certain phytoplankton types may prove resistant and displace other micro-organisms. Tiny animals which feed on such organisms will in turn be affected by the change and the impact will be felt on higher ocean fish life. Diatoms (sometimes known as 'red tides') may proliferate and destroy vast amounts of marine animal life.[28]

Drinking water in many areas of the United States does not meet Public Health Service standards. A recent sampling indicates that 8 million Americans consume water which exceeds the bacteriological standards set up by the Federal Government.[29] Excessive amounts of iron, manganese, and arsenic have been observed and pesticides have turned up. Cadmium is another dangerous water pollutant.

Another study indicates that the United States may face a fresh water shortage by 1983.

c) Resource management The recent ruination of the Southern California coast as a result of oil drilling operations is well publicized. The cost-benefit evaluation of the Glen Canyon Dam may ultimately prove that project to have been a colossal blunder. Leakage into the reservoir walls may approach 15% of the total average annual flow of the entire Colorado River. Evaporation may cause another 12% annual loss.

In Egypt the waterweeds clogging the shoreline of Lake Nasser behind the Aswan Dam may accelerate evaporation through transpiration to such a degree that there

[21] *Forbes,* December 1, 1969, p. 38.
[22] I. K. and R. L. Feierabend and W. W. Conroe, 'Aggressive Behaviors Within Polities 1948-62: a cross-national study,' *Journal of Conflict Resolution,* September 1966.
[23] R. Tanter and M. Midlarsky, 'A Theory of Revolution,' *Journal of Conflict Resolution,* September 1967.
[24] The Cuban example is illustrated in Fig. A-4. The reversal in GNP per capita is followed by Castro's success.
[25] P. F. Drucker, 'The Age of Discontinuity,' Harper and Row, 1968, p. 128.

[26] F. R. Cowell, 'Cicero and the Roman Republic,' Chanticleer Press, New York, 1948, pp. 276-277.
[27] *Wall Street Journal,* December 31, 1969, p. 1.
[28] P. Ehrlich, 'Eco-Catastrophe!,' *Ramparts,* September 1969.
[29] *Los Angeles Times,* December 21, 1969, p. C-1.

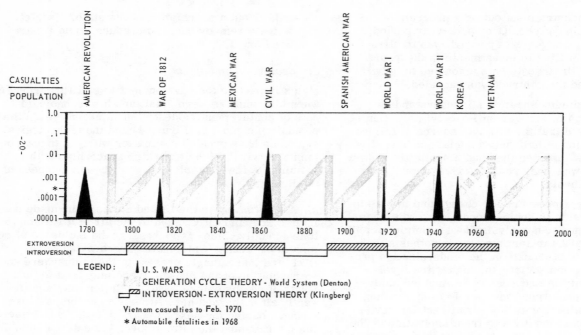

Fig. 2 U.S. Wars

will be insufficient water in the lake to drive the generators. Furthermore, the dam has stopped the flow of silt which in the past offset the natural land erosion. Thus, as much productive farmland may be washed away as is opened up by new irrigation systems around Lake Nasser. As the rich silt has disappeared below the dam, so has the Egyptian sardine catch in the Mediterranean (18, 000 tons in 1965, 500 tons in 1968). Finally, the irrigation area has provided a home for a snail which has infected the local population with schistosomiasis, an agonizing liver and intestinal disease.[30]

The refrain is familiar: we do not adequately understand the system and therefore cannot achieve balanced growth.

4 Military Imbalance

Conducting war has constituted a major function of nations.

Recent research has brought to light some interesting results and shattered familiar slogans. In the past, foreign conflict behavior has been related to various national attributes such as domestic instability, level of economic or technological development, totalitarianism, international communications or transactions, psychological motivations of its people, power or military capabilities. For example, we commonly hear that 'a strong military establishment assures peace.' Rummel's analysis of all nations in the 1950's shows that none of these factors correlate significantly to a nation's foreign conflict behavior.[31]

The one critical positive correlation in an individual country's foreign conflict behavior appears to be time.

The generation cycle theory suggests that major, formalized violence surges in a nation approximately every 25 years.[32] Figure 2 shows the striking correlation of this cycle with U.S. conflicts ever since this nation was created (except for Korea).

The generation cycle constitutes a worldwide pattern, as seen in Denton's work. This suggests some degree of validity in the claim that man's basic drives are at work here. The male apparently has an instinctive need for adventure, for exhibiting courage in front of his peers, and for aggression. For many, war seems to satisfy these needs.[33] A generation which has fully experienced war tends to develop a revulsion against it, but slowly tolerance is built up for the next military orgasm. It is interesting to speculate whether the opposition to a large commitment in Vietnam is not the result of the Korean War. Following too quickly upon World War II, it did not leave time for the normal buildup, which would have led to much stronger support for the Vietnam War (see dashed line). Some advanced countries appear to have been successful in sublimating these human needs into alternatives more desirable than war (e.g., Sweden, Switzerland). Have they paid a price?

---

[30] *Time*, February 2, 1970, p. 62.
[31] R. J. Rummel, 'The Relationship Between National Attributes and Foreign Conflict Behavior,' *Quantitative International Politics: Insights and Evidence*, ed. by J. D. Singer.

[32] F. H. Denton and W. R. Phillips, 'Some Patterns in the History of Violence,' *Journal of Conflict Resolution*, Vol. XII, No. 2, June 1968.

[33] These needs also explain the lack of popularity of nuclear and nonlethal biological/chemical weapons. Pushing buttons in a silo and annihilating millions does not offer much opportunity for 'exhibiting courage in front of one's peers.' Neither does the use of nonlethal weapons.

As Dr. P. G. Bourne points out: 'What people don't like to believe is that there is a real thrill in killing people.' ('Men and Stress in Vietnam,' to be published, quoted in Newsweek, December 8, 1969, p. 35.)

If war occurs who are the likely opponents?

In studying nation pairs in the 1950's, Rummel finds that 'the more dissimilar two nations are in economic development and size and the greater their joint technological capability to span geographic distance is, the more overt conflict they have with each other.'[34] Figures A-1 to A-3 measure size (population) as well as economic development (GNP per capita). Superimposing the ability to span geographic distance, some candidate conflict pairs are indicated by shaded double arrows (1965-70 case on original, potential threats for 1980-85 on the overlay).

Israel and its neighbors Jordan and the UAR provide an excellent illustration (Fig. A-3). They are far apart in wealth and size and will be moving still-further apart in the next 15 years. At the same time, they can easily reach each other. The widening gap between rich and poor nations, evident in Figs. A-1 to A-3, therefore portends increasing dangers of internation conflict between nonequals. Since the U.S. and Soviet conventional (general purpose) forces have been, and continue to be, based on the Western European tradition of war between equals, an imbalance in the military thinking of both superpowers becomes apparent. In Colonel W. F. Long's words, 'the thrust of effort in Vietnam has been as countertradition as it has been counterinsurgent.'[35]

Of the $200 billion spent each year on military forces in the world, about two-thirds is expended by the United States and Soviet Union.[36] And they produce 75% of all the world's arms. Since World War II the United States alone has shipped $50 billion worth of conventional[37] weapons to other countries. In Vietnam it has even become the quartermaster for the enemy. Thus conventional forces have been forced to serve backward as well as advanced nations. The equipment provided may have very little relation to needs. The Soviet Union has shipped amphibious armor to Algeria. Most Latin American countries have combat jet aircraft for prestige purposes; the UAR has surface-to-air missiles and tanks which it cannot operate effectively. Our military advisors in Vietnam for years sought to pattern the RVN forces after the Korean forces which had, in turn, been patterned after the U.S. forces. Both superpowers train military personnel from poor as well as advanced countries to fight frontal wars with their conventional weapons. Although this suggests the continuing occurrence of conventional wars between nations, the pointlessness of supplying conventional weapons to poor countries is now widely recognized:

a) They do not assure balance and stability (Israel against UAR)

b) They do not obviate superpower involvement (543, 000 U.S. troops in Vietnam in 1968)

c) They are ineffective against motivated guerrilla forces

The unsuitability of conventional forces in this type of conflict is a glaring fact.[38] Even when military victory by such forces is attained, it is likely to be hollow. The English defeated the Mau Maus in Kenya, the French defeated the FLN in Algeria—in both cases the loser was the ultimate winner.

Violence in the underdeveloped world will be widespread in the next 15 years. U.S. involvement is in no case inevitable but in all cases physically possible. No countries other than Mexico and Canada can reach the United States with significant ground forces. On the other hand, the United States can effect a large physical presence anywhere. A conscious U.S. decision to become militarily involved is less likely in the next decade in view of the Vietnam experience. However, the 1985-95 period is again one of danger if Figure 2 has significance. This suggests the possibility of a buildup in U.S. general purpose forces after 1980.

The primary concern for all nations in the 1970-85 period will be internal upheaval. The reasons are apparent from the imbalances described here.

The following catalog exemplifies the kinds of conflict today's military planner in any country should consider of paramount concern:

a) Coup
   Revolutionary—Iraq 1958
   Reform—Dominican Republic 1963
      (future: Brazil, Venezuela?)

b) Majority uprising
   Passive resistance—India
   Guerrilla war—Cuba 1953-59
                  Angola—present
                  Rhodesia—present
      (future: Union of South Africa?)

c) Minority uprising
   Urban ghetto—Warsaw 1944
                  Watts 1965
                  Detroit 1967
   Tribal region—Biafra 1967-70
      (future: New York, Quebec?)

d) Other types
   Paramilitary persecution of minorities
      (by private organizations)
   Wanton vandalism
      (destruction of wealthy communities by mobs of poor, destruction of foreign property and personnel in poor nations)
   Anti-establishment disobedience
      (student sit-ins, assassination of establishment leaders, physical attack on ecological degradation sources such as industrial plants)

Such conflicts may rock rich and poor nations to their foundations.

In their final report, Dr. Milton S. Eisenhower and the members of the National Commission on the Causes

---

[34] R. J. Rummel, 'Some Empirical Findings on Nations and Their Behavior,' *World Politics*, January 1969, p. 238.

[35] W. F. Long, Jr., 'A Perspective of Counterinsurgency in Three Dimensions—Tradition, Legitimacy, Visibility,' *Naval War College Review*, February 1970.

[36] *Wall Street Journal*, May 5, 1969.

[37] Conventional is used here in the sense of traditional weapons for European nonnuclear warfare.

[38] 'Why We Didn't Win in Vietnam,' *U.S. News and World Report*, February 9, 1970, pp. 44-45.

and Prevention of Violence warn the President that while serious external dangers remain, the graver threats today are internal:

> 'We solemnly declare our conviction that this nation is entering a period in which our people need to be as concerned by the internal dangers to our free society as by any probable combination of external threats.'[39]

5. *The Organizational Imbalance*

Man creates and innovates continually, yet he also resists change. In Hamlet's words, we would 'rather bear those ills we have than fly to others that we know not of.'

While the pace of technology has accelerated dramatically, the governmental framework for creative action has not altered significantly. The result is increasing incompatibility.

In nature, obsolete organisms die; in society they seem to flourish. When new organizations are created the old ones continue and even expand, regardless of need. In the U.S. Federal Government still has the Rural Electrification Administration, created in 1935, and the Subversive Control Board, created in 1950, although their raison d'etre has long since disappeared. Parkinson gives the example of the British Admiralty: between 1914 and 1928 Admiralty officials increased in number by 78%, while capital ships in commission decreased by 67%.[40] The whole organizational apparatus from planning to action becomes rigid in structure and operation rather than rational and creative. Individual security is sought in organizational constancy. The Civil Service in the executive branch of government, the seniority system in the U.S. Congress, the Curia in the Roman Catholic Church, and the Soviet Central Committee (average age of voting members nearly 60) are all examples of this principle. When individuals at the top or bottom want to implement change they are frustrated. Pope John XXIII and the ghetto priest may have agreed on desirable actions but neither could force change through the organizational hierarchy. For President Nixon the ratio of actual to potential power is very much smaller than it was for President Lincoln.

The U.S. military establishment is geared to large-scale conventional operations in the European tradition. The combination of age, size, and success[4] is very apparent and it promotes organizational rigidity. Creative planning for small, unorthodox actions in underdeveloped country situations poses virtually insuperable difficulties. In Vietnam, the novel Combined Action Platoons and 'Sting Ray' patrols were pioneered by the small U.S. Marine Corps and Special Forces rather than the large U.S. Army. Partly as the result of public

attitudes the military academies are staffed by conformists whose task it is to produce more conformists who will preserve the traditional establishment. Conformism in Vietnam meant that 'the best defense is a good offense' and that the South Vietnamese should be trained for a frontal type war.[42] [43]

Calcification of the organizational framework for action is not restricted to government. It is apparent in industry also.[44]

We have seen the rapid and dynamic growth phase of railroads in the last century, automobiles and steel in the first third of this century, aircraft in the middle third of this century, and computers today. We already recognize the innovative failures of the railroad industry and the rigidity of the American steel and automobile industries. Innovation in off-road ground vehicles has come from aerospace companies, innovation in steel processing from small European companies. Often top management and the lowly engineer are both anxious to try new ideas and diversify, but find themselves stymied by middle management.

Labor unions once were vital instruments of change; today they are bastions of conservatism. Automation is resisted and craft unions force industry to operate with deadly inefficiency. The search for security has led to concepts (e.g., seniority, retirement benefits) which assure obsolescence.

The Peter Principle and the Paul Principle[45] plague us everywhere. The first states that capable individuals are promoted until they attain a position which they are incompetent to fill. The second tells us that individuals in a given position become more incompetent in that position as time goes on (since the job changes and the individual does not). The result: incompetence squared!

One of the few bright spots today in the area of organizational change is the university. Spurred by students and young faculty members, it has entered a period of flux to end centuries of organizational rigidity. There are numerous harbingers of change. Interdisciplinary courses, futures seminars, theme-oriented colleges,

---

[39] *Los Angeles Times,* December 13, 1969, p. 1, and December 14, 1969, Sec. A, p. 8.

[40] C. N. Parkinson, *Parkinson's Law,* Houghton-Mifflin, 1957.

[41] The United States gained militarily 3.1 million square miles in the period 1776 to 1935—second only to Great Britain's 3.5 million square mile gain. ('Why an Army?,' *Fortune,* September 1935, p. 48.)

[42] 'Why We Didn't Win in Vietnam,' *U.S. News and World Report,* February 9, 1970.

[43] Col. W. F. Long, Jr., points to a key difficulty: 'U.S. tradition has not encouraged political development of its military officer corps.... Further, there is no coherent link between military behavior which is domestically acceptable and that which may be required for successful participation in a clandestine war. Without a political mandate or relevant psychological inclination, the military man is simply not professionally fitted to make substantive contributions to political, economic, or sociological problems as regards foreign involvements. He must understand these factors within the context of his profession, but an excessive commitment to them will only detract from his primary concern—military capability.' ('A Perspective of Counterinsurgency in Three Dimensions—Tradition, Legitimacy, Visibility,' *Naval War College Review,* February 1970.)

[44] The difference is that a business enterprise may merge, be absorbed, or go bankrupt.

[45] P. Armer, *loc. cit.*

and other new concepts are sweeping through the halls of ivy.[46]

What conclusion do we draw from this 'new' look at the future?

The price tag of technology is becoming visible. The vital social units of our global society—represented by the family and the nation—are moving into a state of extreme crisis in the wake of decades of phenomenal technological change.

> 'Industrial society is not so much being trans-formed into a post-industrial, technological society as it is breaking down—economically, politically, and culturally.'[47]

C. The Challenge: A New Kind of Planning

1. *Words versus Deeds*

In the last few years, much has been written and mouthed about the future. Reports by distinguished establishment members discuss possible new national strategies and their costs. Futurologists paint glowing pictures of a utopia in which technology overcomes poverty, war, environmental degradation, old age—and in the process probably also humanism.

The missing element almost always is a prescription or roadmap outlining with some degree of realism the means to move from here to there.

Government is looked upon for funding which will rapidly lead to answers to the unsolved problems.[48] And somehow catastrophic side effects will be avoided.

On July 13, 1969, President Nixon created a National Goals Research Staff.[49] He noted that:

> 'It is time we addressed ourselves, consciously and systematically, to the question of what kind of a nation we want to be as we begin our third cen-tury. We can no longer afford to approach the longer range future haphazardly.'

The Staff functions include:

> '—forecasting future developments, and assessing the longer range consequences of present social trends,
> —measuring the probable future impact of alter-native courses of action, including measuring the degree to which change in one area would be likely to affect another,
> —estimating the actual range of social choice—that is, what alternative sets of goals might be attain-able, in light of the availability of resources and possible rates of progress,
> —developing and monitoring social indicators that can reflect the present and future quality of American life, and the direction and rate of its change,

> —summarizing, integrating and correlating the results of related research activities being carried on within the various Federal agencies, and by State and local governments and private organizations.'

An annual report is to be issued setting forth the key choices and their consequences.

The most significant passage in the Presidential announcement is the following:

> 'There is an urgent need to establish a more direct link between the increasingly sophisticated forecasting now being done and the decision-making process. The practical importance of esta-blishing such a link is emphasized by the fact that virtually all the critical national problems of to-day could have been anticipated well in advance of their reaching critical proportions. Even though some were, such anticipation was seldom trans-lated into policy decisions which might have per-mitted progress to be made in such a way as to avoid—or at least minimize—undesirable longer range consequences.

> 'We have reached a state of technological and social development at which the future nature of our society can increasingly be shaped by our own conscious choices. At the same time, those choices are not simple. They require us to pick among alternatives which do not yield to easy, quantitative measurement.'

One point is clear: effective links between forecasting, planning, and decision making must be forged at all levels of our society if this effort is not to become another set of reports for the library file.

Donald Michael is less optimistic: he tells us that there is no chance of society adapting quickly and thoroughly enough to cope with the problems it faces in the coming decades:

> 'Our technological ability to change our world will exceed our ability to anticipate whether we are using it wisely.

> 'We are almost certain to face disaster if we don't plan.... But we are also almost certain to be in deep trouble even with planning because our best plans will be developed and fostered by limited human beings picking and choosing among limited knowledge, very often ignorant of the extent of their own ignorance.'[50]

The Bellagio Declaration on Planning warns that 'the pursuance of orthodox planning is quite insufficient in that it seldom does more than touch a system through changes of the variables.[51]

Our options are:

a) Resist change.

b) 'Muddle through' with minimum planning, relying on luck and divine guidance to prevent uncontrolled, violent, and detrimental change.

[46] H. A. Linstone, 'A University for the Postindustrial Society,' *Technological Forecasting*, I, No. 3, 1970.

[47] V. Ferkiss, 'The Technological Man: The Myth and the Reality,' George Braziller, New York, 1969.

[48] Actually the government can effect the content of technology much more than the rate of advance.

[49] R. M. Nixon, 'The Establishment of a National Goals Research Staff,' The White House, July 13, 1969. Re-produced in 'Technological Forecasting,' I, No. 2, Fall 1969.

[50] Donald N. Michael, 'The Unprepared Society: Planning for a Precarious Future,' Basic Books, New York, 1968.

[51] E. Jantsch, 'From Forecasting and Planning to Policy Sciences,' paper presented at AAAS Annual Meeting, Boston, December 26-31, 1969.

PLANNING — PRESENT PRACTICE

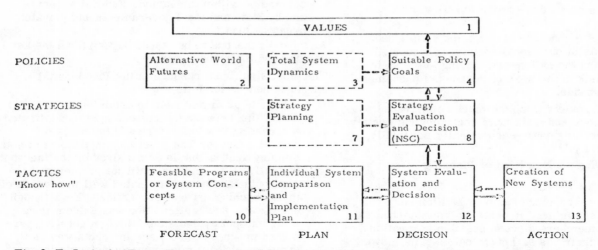

Fig. 3   E. Jantsch, 'From Forecasting and Planning to Policy Sciences,' AAAS Paper, Boston, December 1969.

c)   Accept the challenge to develop our future society through rational creative action, to become <u>magister ludi</u>—master of the game.

The last alternative requires not only a true future orientation and a willingness to embrace change, but a recognition that:[52]

1)   Man is part of nature rather than apart from it.

2)   The whole physical-social environment is a single dynamic system.

3)   This system can be controlled and shaped from within.

4)   Knowledge is the primary strategic resource if such control is to be exercised properly.

5)   Change is not the sole responsibility of the Federal Government. It is the responsibility of all—the individual and the state, the communal group and the corporation.

6)   Change must flow through values, policies, strategies, and tactics, from forecasting to planning, to decision making to action.

2. *Present Practice*

The difference between the flow envisioned here and present practice is fundamental. Consider the current mechanism of change in defense systems. The focal point is the dialog between the technologist and the planner of the using organization (Figure 3, boxes 10 and 11).

At time t_0, when system S_0 with capability C_0 is operational, there is considerable communication between the planner and the technological community (initiated by either side) concerning feasible new capabilities relevant to the missions performed by system S_0.

How accurately can a missile be delivered at a given range by 1980? How fast can submarines move at a given depth?

Now the technological forecaster tends toward pessimism in very long range projections and optimism in shorter range forecasts. This phenomenon has been illustrated by Buschmann[53] (Figure 4a). The curved line (C_1) suggests that no serious technologist anticipated capability C_1 in 1900. By 1920, C_1 was expected to occur after the year 2000 and in 1935 optimism began. The hindsight line shows the actual occurrence date. A recent example, forecasting the fast reactor capability, as also shown. An interesting implication follows from this figure: there is an optimum time to make a forecast—and it is probably in the 15 to 30 year rather than 5 to 10 year span.

Let us assume that our forecaster tells the planner (at time t_0) that a significant advance in technology (C_1) is feasible at time t_1. The planner then includes in his document (box 11) a 'requirement' for a new system S_1 at time t_1 which will take advantage of this anticipated component or subsystem technology. It is noted that we use the term 'capability' and not 'effectiveness.'

At time t_1 it becomes apparent, however, that technology will only reach capability C_1' (Figure 4b). In most cases the planner's decision is to move forward with the new system according to plan rather than delay initiation until capability C_1 is attained at time t_2. The capability gap ($C_1 - C_1'$) is subjected to negotiation and a compromise, C_1'', is reached. The technology forcing function $C_1'' - C_1$ then becomes the source of cost overruns and nonfulfillment of system 'specs.' Thus, system S_1 is acquired and proves to have only marginally superior capability over the existing system S_0. The 'plan' has become the tool for justifying an acquisition previously based on a significant, but unrealizable, technological improvement.

We now return to Figure 3. On the basis of the plan alternative designs are produced and evaluated, a choice is made (box 12), and the system is created (box 13).

---

[52]   V. Ferkiss, ibid.

[53]   R. P. Buschmann, 'A Research Problem: Balanced Grand-Scale Forecasting,' Technological Forecasting, Vol. I, No. 2, Fall 1969.

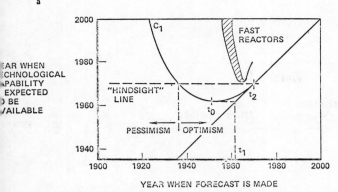

AR WHEN
CHNOLOGICAL
APABILITY
D BE
EXPECTED
AVAILBLE

SOURCE: R. BUSCHMANN "BALANCED GRAND-SCALE FORECASTING"
TECHNOLOGICAL FORECASTING VOL. 1, NO. 2 FALL 1969

Fig. 4b

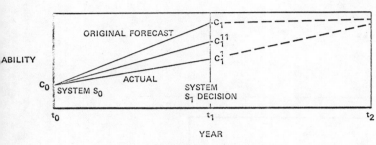

Fig. 4a The Forecasting—Planning Problem

Future environmental forecasts are produced independently (box 2) as are national goals studies (box 4). The National Security Council is the strategic decision-making body (box 8). Henry Kissinger is trying to create a strategic planning staff (box 7), and the National Goals Research Staff may form box 3. Their relation to the other boxes is not yet clear. The driving force of boxes 10 and 11 in the form of new system capabilities and user system replacement planning as well as the dominance of the 'tactical'

level for the entire process are striking. We see a clear reflection of the technological explosion of recent decades. However, the weakness in effecting balanced and controlled change of the total system is also evident. There is no mechanism for reorganization of DOD or for elimination of obsolete forces as a result of changing environments or values. Policy planning does not proceed from forecast to creative action in a rational process nor is there proper interaction between the policy, strategic, and tactical levels.

The desired framework is shown in Figure 5. Boxes 10 and 11 no longer provide the dominant impelling force to the entire process. New institutions and new instrumentalities as well as new systems are created (boxes 5 and 9). There is feedback between all boxes. In other words, innovation flows through the entire network—and this is the challenge of the coming years for every member of our society.

D.   The Impact on Defense Planning

Our stated purpose was to provide a starting point for a defense planning study. We will confine ourselves here to a very brief glimpse at the next steps in relating this background material to defense planning.

We must consider alternative U.S. (and world) futures and develop general defense guidelines for each. We then combine the effects of current force extrapolation and new technology with the implications of the preceding environmental discussion to arrive at alternative force structures for the 1980-85 period. Several iterations of this process are desirable. Finally, a weighting of the likelihood of these alternatives should uncover 'good risk' recommendations for planning.

For example, Table II shows relative emphasis in resource allocation to major areas as a function of four alternative U.S. futures.

Figure 6 shows the result of such an analysis in terms of military expenditures as a function of GNP.

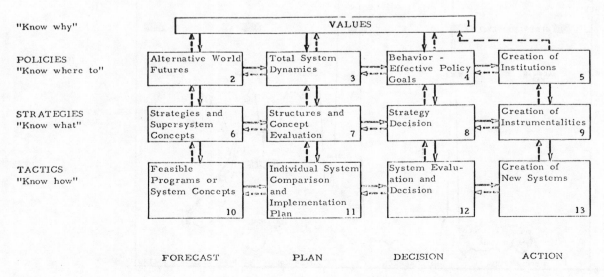

Fig. 5
Adapted from: E. Jantsch, 'From Forecasting and Planning to Policy Sciences', AAAS Paper, Boston, December 1969.

TABLE II
Relative Emphasis in Four U.S. Futures

	U.S. Future			
	A	B	C	D
	Militaristic-Imperialistic	Surprise Free	Nationalistic Inward Oriented	'New Society'
Strategic Offense/Defense	****	**	***	*
General Purpose Forces	****	***	**	*
Manned Space Programs (nonmilitary)		*		*
Other New Programs (nonmilitary)		**	***	*****
Sample Subjective Estimate of Likelihood	20%	40%	25%	15%

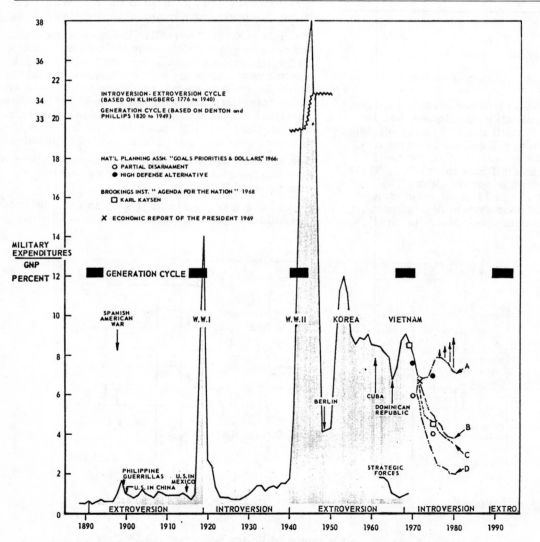

Fig. 6 U.S. Military expenditures as percent of GNP

A simplistic assumption is made in this figure. Real GNP growth and inflation are the same in all four cases (average of 4.4% for the former and 2.3% for the latter). The impact of alternative postures on the total economic growth is not yet well enough understood to permit a meaningful differentiation. One fact is known, however: a high level of defense spending is not a prerequisite for rapid GNP growth. Japan has experienced phenomenal growth while spending only about 1% of its GNP on defense.

For comparison, the figure also shows forecasts prepared by other studies; all of them feature a reduction in the fraction of the GNP given to military expenditures. We note that <u>even the minimum of 2% in 1980 still exceeds the fraction spent in over half the years covered by the data</u>. The budget line of Future A is probably a lower bound for this militaristic environment; as suggested by the vertical arrows, it might rise much higher. In constant dollars Futures B, C, and D lead to a continuing decline in defense budgets.

The figure sets the future into the context of the past and repeats the generation and introversion/extroversion cycles from Figure 2. We observe that U.S. external military activity has not always required vast military expenditures. In the 1890 to 1914 extroversion period this nation was involved with military operations in Latin America and Asia while spending only about 1% of its GNP on military expenditures. Conversely, a large military establishment has not assured peace. The data thus tend to underscore the findings of R. J. Rummel: the military budget does not correlate significantly with foreign conflict involvement (see p. 182)

Any analysis of future forces must take full account of the present planning approach (Figure 3) and the hurdles which impede rational creative planning (Figure 5). Unless there is a dramatic change in modus operandi as well as in the structure of the Department of Defense (doubtful with the expectations of alternative futures used in Table II), the gap between true defense needs and stated requirements will become a chasm in the next 15 years. And this makes 'needs analyses'—when differentiated from market research—as barren an exercise for the defense supplier as it is for the automobile manufacturer.

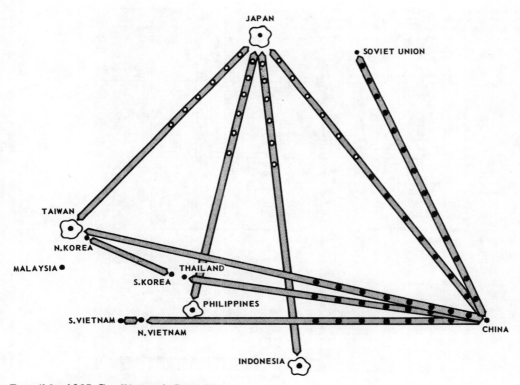

Possible 1985 Conflicts—A Sampling

Appendix A

THE NATIONS OF THE WORLD

Sources:

F. M. Fulton and D. S. Randall
  'Crisis Control Environments 1975-85'
  Stanford Research Institute, Naval Warfare Center
  Memorandum 53, 1969
H. Kahn and A. Wiener
  'The Year 2000,' Macmillan, 1967
H. Linstone et al
  'MIRAGE 80,' Lockheed Aircraft Corporation
  Report DPR/46, 1966

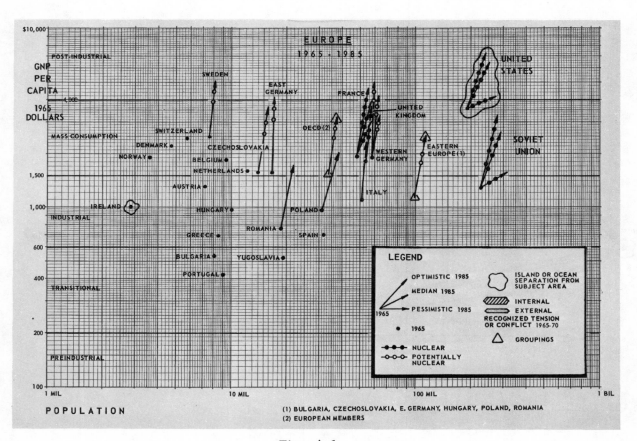

Fig. A-1

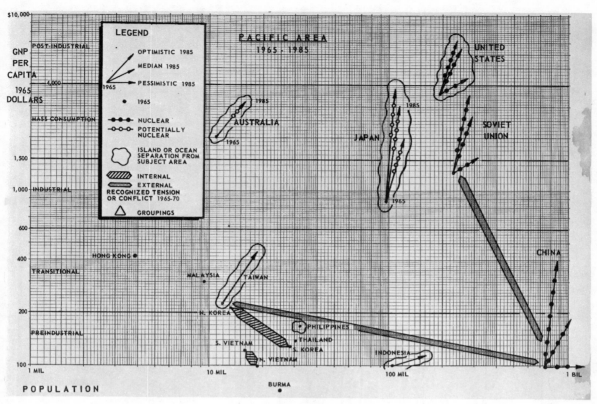

Fig. A-2

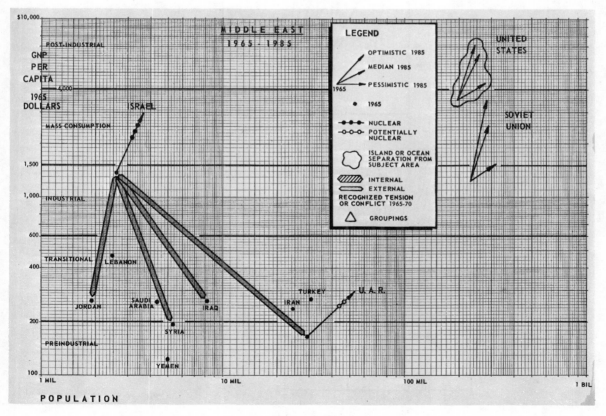

Fig. A-3

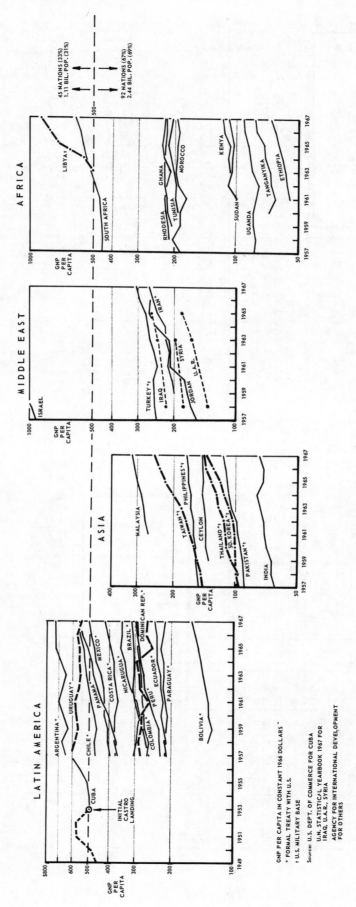

Fig. A4 The Underdeveloped World

Forward Planning: A Pragmatic Approach

J. F. LANGSTON

Events in the future, whether tomorrow, next year, or over a longer period, can best be met by responding to a plan of action rather than reacting to the situation as it develops. A plan is a proposed or agreed to method of action. Planning is then the process of generating a plan. In preparing a plan, various types of data are required as a basis for determining proposed alternatives and/or decisions.

For a realistic application, planning data and the resulting plan are reasonably structured, organized, and written documentation serving as a communications medium. On the other hand, planning is a relatively unstructured, creative process. Lack of structure and organization in planning data and in documentation of the planning leads to poor communications and the possibility that decisions will be made on inadequate or erroneous information. Forcing too much structure in the planning process encourages a continuation of past activities. A balance of structured and unstructured activity is thus necessary in the planning cycle (Figure 1).

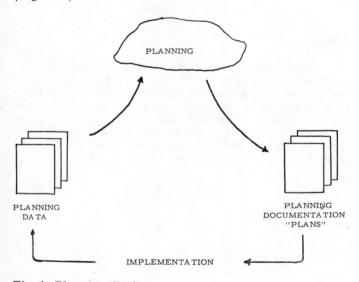

Fig. 1 Planning Cycle

For a small organization, including a small operating unit of a large organization, limited resources dictate a mission oriented R&D effort related heavily to near term business but with provision to support longer term growth. In this situation, planning sometimes tends to be based on assessments of the current situation by key management personnel, with little formal analysis, particularly of the long range effect of decisions. Integrated planning for this environment can start on a pragmatic basis of documenting current decisions, but should be structured so that more quantitative methods can be added as time and resources permit.

The author is with General Dynamics Electronics Division—San Diego Operations

A forward planning activity in the General Dynamics Electronics Divisions' San Diego Operations is in the early stages of implementation (Figure 2). The goal here is to integrate near term and long range planning and to involve all facets of the organization.

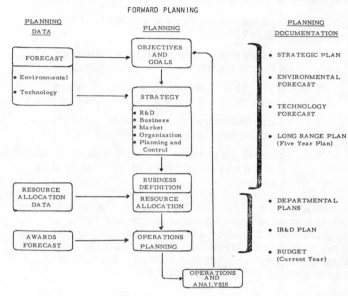

Fig. 2. Forward Planning

Strategic Plan:

A Strategic Plan is being prepared covering a ten year period. This starts with a definition of our broad mission and our business and market spectrum. Utilizing this definition and data from an Environmental Forecast and Technology Forecast, our objectives, goals, and strategy will be formulated. The objectives define our desired future in general, nonquantitative terms. The goals are measurable milestones required to progress toward the stated objectives.

With the overall objectives-goals-strategy documented, the functional departments will then be asked to document strategic plans for their areas in implementing this policy. This data, when reviewed and accepted, becomes a part of the Strategic Plan.

Environmental Forecast:

Viable planning must be based on some concept of the environment in which the organization must function. This forecast documents the best information readily available on future political, economic, sociological, technical and management trends. With limited resources, the attempt here is not to perform a definitive study or even to produce an 'accurate' forecast of the future, but rather to provide information to encourage thinking about the future in a changing environment.

Technology Forecast:

The Technology Forecast will provide a data base covering a ten year period of forecasted technology trends and requirements for future products and systems. Structuring the technologies and future applications to be forecasted is an important factor. For this purpose a matrix of technologies versus products/systems and technologies versus capability was prepared. This defines the technologies to be forecasted and will provide visibility for other uses including:

1   Required technology not available—shall we acquire?

2   Capability not being utilized extensively—eliminate capability or acquire business?

3   Utilization of outside capability—acquire capability or continue to use outside source?

4   Future phase out of a technology—effects on business, personnel and facilities.

5   Business effected by potential loss of technical capability by elimination of R&D or by loss of personnel.

In addition to forecasting the future of the technologies we are using, a forecast of future product/system requirements to meet customer needs will be prepared. This will include identification of technology requirements for these new products for comparison with our projected technology capability.

Long Range Plan:

The Long Range Plan, covering a five year period, is more quantitative than the Strategic Plan and is our official commitment on future business to our Division and Corporate headquarters. This plan includes a detailed financial projection along with a market forecast and analysis, and our R&D program plans for the current year and succeeding four years.

Current Year Plans:

The Strategic and Long Range Plans supply the policy and commitments for preparing our current year budget and IR&D Plan. During the coming year we will start preparation of Departmental Plans for each major functional department.

Resource Allocation:

Resource allocation to date is based primarily on management consensus. Our future plans are to use an allocation model to provide data for management decisions. Initially, this will relate R&D and proposal funding to achievement of organization goals. Since technical personnel are a limiting resource, the inclusion of personnel allocation will also be attempted.

Conclusions:

The forward planning described takes the practical approach of providing a structure that starts where we are and allows incorporation of new areas of planning. Since the planning cycle is an iterative process, continued use is expected to point out the need for changes, particularly in the transition from largely intuitive planning to utilization of more analytical techniques for forecasting and resource allocation.

Coupling of Science to Technological Development

(Review of Concepts and Lessons about R&D Coupling: The Implications for R&D Policies)

ALEXANDER G. HOSHOVSKY, CHIEF, ANALYSIS DIVISION, HQ OAR

and

ERNEST P. LUKE, COL USAF, DEPUTY CHIEF OF STAFF/PROGRAMS, HQ OAR

I. What is Science-Technology Coupling?

As a word, coupling appeared in the R&D vocabulary rather recently. Some think of coupling as a communication process; others as a decision-making process. It concerns the relationships of science, technology, development, production and organizational missions. As used in this paper, the term is understood to mean a multi-directional flow of information which brings social problems, goals and requirements into productive association with the potential of science and technology. Thus it tends to be a communication process among people.

Coupling may be opportunity-oriented, i.e., carried out for the purpose of offering a basis for technological innovations. Coupling may also be problem-oriented i.e., intended to bring current or anticipated problems into productive union with the scientific and technical knowledge. Some coupling occurs naturally where the coupling parties naturally gravitate to each other because it satisfies their mutual interests. Other coupling has to be organized, because there is an apparent absence of common interest, or there may even be antagonism among the involved parties. The coupling between a theoretical scientist and an experimental scientist might be the example of the former. The city planning session on what to do about air pollution falls into the later category.

Science-technology coupling is somewhat analogous to the combination of market research and product marketing in industrial enterprises. The similarity lies in the fact that coupling is a process of uncovering the specific needs for scientific knowledge, as well as a process of selling the potential users on the application of the existing scientific knowledge. Coupling, then, is the way an R&D organization relates itself to the goals of its parent organization and pays back for the capital investments.

II Dimensions of Coupling

Coupling is a popular subject these days, yet it is so poorly defined that the minute it is mentioned it produces vigorous emotions. Some of the disagreements stem from the divergent viewpoints of the discussants. Even within a single person's mind one can often observe a continuous shift of definitions preventing productive discussions. Put another way, each dis-

---

(This paper has been prepared to stimulate discussion about the R & D communications, and represents personal views of the authors. It is not intended to represent the view or the policy of the Office of Aerospace Research or the United States Air Force)

cussant tends to advocate 'his kind of coupling' with the consequence that there are many 'senders' and very few 'receivers'. It is no wonder that the usual top level discussions about science technology coupling, or specific suggestions for coupling improvements, frequently generate more heat than light.

We need to remember that coupling, like other complex concepts, is a multi-dimensional concept, i.e., can be defined in a variety of ways and from multiple points of view.

A variety of elements that can be associated with a given coupling effort are listed in Table A. As can be seen the objectives of coupling can cover a broad spectrum. Depending on the objective, the coupling participants may be 'bench scientists' or military strategists. The nature of the objective and the habits of the participants may dictate the principal communications channels. The coupling events can produce a multiplicity of messages of varying degrees of complexity. Each event can be promoted by a particular combination of incentives, and each coupling effort is resisted by a particular set of barriers inhibiting the achievement of coupling goals.

While it may be desirable to define any given coupling activity by all these dimensions, any intelligent policy consideration requires that there be clear agreement on at least three:

1) What is the specific purpose of coupling (objectives), 2) who are or should be the principal coupling participants and 3) what results will provide evidence that the desired coupling has been achieved. When these factors are known it is possible to pass a more balanced judgement about the organization's present state of coupling activities or to evaluate the appropriateness of the coupling alternatives.

III Lessons from Experience

What do we know about the coupling process? Some scientific knowledge exists, but far too little to draw firm theories. Of course, there is a wealth of experience of those who have performed coupling functions. Unfortunately, most of this knowledge is not documented. In the next paragraphs we would like to share some of this knowledge.

Knowledge about the Adequacy of the Existing Coupling Processes

Experience and observation as well as some evidence from research studies indicates that the scientists in pure sciences and those in applied sciences couple very effectively. The scientists are stimulated by technological and scientific problems (1) and devote

TABLE A

SOME ELEMENTS OF COUPLING

Objectives

Sharing information about phenomena
Solving existing problems in exploratory and advanced
    development
Opening new areas of research
Working on the 'anticipated' problems
Opening new mission opportunities for the parent
    organization
Etc

Participants

Theoretical scientists
Experimental scientists
Technology planners
Managers of non-technological activities
Members of academic community
Military planners and strategists
System analysts
Congress and public
Industrial engineers
Etc

Communication Channels

Documentary Channels
Feasibility studies
Technology application studies
R&D proposals
Concept definition studies
Scientific papers & reports
Annual reviews of technology
Planning documents
State-of-the art reports
Problem definition reports
Technological forecasts
Non-documentary
Visits and personal discussions
Small working study groups
Seminars & courses
Cooperative R&D efforts
Etc

Incentives

Innovative drive of the individuals
Interest at high levels of management
Money, awards, bonuses
R&D projects in jeopardy
Management requirements for the evidence of coupling
The needs of a critical mission
Transfer of technical people
Etc

Results

Message communicated
Innovation introduced into operations
Reallocated resources
Change in strategy and tactics
Consultation provided
Decision to continue or terminate R&D
Improved technological state of art
Etc

Messages

Classified by the contents of the message
Scientific data
Performance of systems & components
The needs of missions/operations
Technological alternatives
People/organizations
Classified by degree of complexity
Simple (concerning the relationship between 2-3
    factors)
Moderate (4-6 factors)
Complex (6 or more factors)
Etc

Barriers

Man-made
Lack of formally approved goals
Organizational message filters
Misdirected incentives
Rigidity of tech-specification
Status quo attitudes
Natural
Diversity & competition of objectives
Complexity of messages
Absence of coupling opportunities
Insufficient resources to prove ideas
Competition of alternative technologies
Unawareness of the existence of potential coupling
    partners
Etc

much time to their identification and solution. Contrary to public opinion, they also seem to devote much of their time to social problems and devise various schemes to deal with such problems.

In the authors' R&D environment the in-house scientists interact frequently with the in-house exploratory development laboratories and participate in many problem-solving exercises. Unfortunately much of this coupling activity is not visible to the R&D mana-

gers who are removed by several hierarchical steps from the laboratory environment.

The coupling between the scientists and engineers has some serious gaps which can be bridged only by time, education, and the services of the intermediaries who can speak the language of both groups. The most serious gaps are in the respective motivations of the participants. As a rule the engineer works from the 'specs'—he has clear objectives, deadlines to meet, standard to achieve. As a result he is less inclined to permit the 'new idea' to upset his schedule.[2] Occasionally he may run into problems for which the solution is not in his 'handbook'. This provides him with incentives to seek new knowledge and this is where the scientists have their chance to introduce innovations. The alternate route is through revision of 'handbooks' and changes of specifications.

Coupling between scientists and managers has many deficiencies. Among the factors that contribute to this condition are the feelings among the scientists that what is good for science is good for society, while the managers emphasize the utility and applicability of research to practical problems of the particular parent organization. The general inability to specify social problems in terms which are meaningful to both the researchers and managers, the inability of scientists to articulate, the time required for scientific findings to be accepted, along with other impediments tend to divide the scientific culture and the management cultures and make communications difficult. Although there are many scientists who maintain a meaningful dialogue with the people who provide them with funds, there are many more who are unable to communicate enough sense of urgency and importance of their projects to convince the management of their value.

The more distant the manager is from the scientific work the more difficult it is for him to rationalize his investment alternatives. When the scientists were few and the money plenty this was not critical. Today serious choices must be made about research priorities. This places both the managers and the scientists in extremely difficult positions, characterized by a mixture of mutual respect and mutual antagonism. Improvements in the way the scientists and managers communicate are clearly needed to solve their mutual problems.

Knowledge about the Barriers and Incentives to Coupling

Many coupling exercises, (such as coupling meetings, travelling 'road shows', etc.) arranged by the management to improve interorganizational coupling have been dismal failures. They have been frequently abhorred by the coupling participants (who attended such events only to show the flag) and mistrusted by managers who saw very little results from the efforts. Wherever productive coupling exercises were found, they were usually distinguished by a high degree of common interest (as in a solution of an identified problem) and a deep involvement of the people who had something to gain from the exercises. The enlightened self interest, where everyone gains and very few lose, seems to be the key to successful coupling.

Optimum organized R&D coupling (as differentiated from natural coupling, where coupling parties naturally gravitate toward each other) is greatly helped by the presence of forecasts of expected future conditions, and clear definition of the expected problems. In the absence of these two elements, coupling at its best seldom amounts to anything more than solving of current problems—clearly not the most profitable area for science-technology interactions.

The exercises dealing with identification of technological problems, translation of scientific knowledge, etc., seem to be rewarding activities for many scientists. Occasionally they act as powerful incentives to coupling[3]. The reason for this appears to be in the evidence that such activities extend the scientists' intellectual horizons, permit exploitation of their unique knowledge and offer opportunities for demonstrating the importance and value of research. They also seem to increase the scientific creativity[1]. The critical element in successful problem-oriented coupling is, however, the scientists' conviction that the problems are worthy of their attention and that somebody really wants to have solutions.

In discussions on R&D coupling one frequently hears that the technology users (or science users) have a responsibility of defining their problems and informing the scientific community about them. A recent study[4], however, has shown that this is seldom possible. The definition of technological problems requires the collaboration of scientists and technologists in which the scientists open the door to opportunities and explain them to the users. Having identified potential applications, it is again the scientists who must understand both the operational and engineering problems and then structure the problems so that they can be solved by better understanding of the underlying physical phenomena.

Where the purpose of coupling is to promote innovations (application of research results) the barriers become formidable. One of such barriers is the unmistakable resistance of 'users' to accept new materials, processes, devices, and theories despite their early laboratory successes. The precise variety of the reasons behind the resistance is not very well known, but some can be specified.

One of the reasons comes from the role played by specifications[2]. The basic problem confronting the new discovery (or technology) is that it is not yet incorporated into the official sets of materials or performance specifications. Thus, unless there is no other alternative, few engineers or designers will run the risk of failure by choosing or specifying a material or device which has not been thoroughly developed and tested. Another reason comes from the engineer's commitment to a given technical approach. An engineer who invests time and effort in the formulation and development of a technical approach, becomes strongly committed to that approach and hence more resistant to new ideas[5].

Knowledge about Management's Role in Coupling

Effective science technology coupling is difficult. This is something that enlightened management recognizes and squarely faces. Most people in R&D have their time fully occupied. Where one expected them to contribute 5 to 10% of their time to science-technology coupling it was necessary to 'liberate' their time from other less productive chores. Moreover, there are usually higher travel budgets and additional requirements for data resources and services. The success usually depends on the top-level support and clearly established policies so that the lower level 'cost accountants' do not inhibit this activity.

Coupling should be everybody's job—not a special activity of selected 'application' or coupling staff. Attempts at specialized offices to couple or transfer new scientific knowledge to practical systems applications have been seldom successful. This occurs because as a rule the coupling staffs lack both the resources (dollars) and the expertise (technical knowledge) to do the job. Where success has been achieved it was caused by bringing the working-level scientists and engineers in a face-to-face confrontation to use their knowledge and resources to mutual advantage. Coupling staffs can help, however, by devising and applying such incentives as special awards or annual progress reviews, by requesting and guiding the conduct of special studies which can offer meaningful coupling opportunities, and by encouraging and supporting the experiments with new coupling techniques.

IV Implications of R&D Management Policies

What are the implications of this knowledge for the R&D management? They fall into three general categories:

a)   Coupling incentives and opportunities.

b)   Coupling machinery and resources.

c)   Coupling visibility and accountability.

1. *Coupling Incentives and Opportunities.*

Despite all the protestation to the contrary, many managers of R&D do not view coupling as a major and significant R&D activity. The rewards for successful coupling are practically non-existent and coupling opportunities are at their best awkward and unsuited to the purpose. What must be done falls into the following areas:

a)   A system of meaningful and tangible rewards must be created to overcome the formidable array of natural and manmade obstacles to coupling.

b)   Management must formally accept the responsibility for creating and nurturing coupling opportunities. These coupling opportunities must be well thought out and offer the prospective participants the psychic and professional benefits to insure their voluntary participation. Management must also forget the idea of 'coupling by proxy', the practice of research managers getting together to tell each other what their working scientists and technologists told them to tell each other.

c)   There must be a clear and widely known management policy that promotes coupling, and protects it from travel restrictions, functional job definitions, and other limitations that bureaucracies are so capable of imposing on the creative people. Top-level interest in coupling results is one way of making such policy a reality.

2. *Coupling Machinery and Resources*

Coupling methods can and should be continually refined and developed to keep up with the changing missions, environments and communication opportunities. They should be examined and those which are found ineffective should be eliminated.

On the other hand repeated efforts to introduce new coupling methods, one on top of another, without a backward look at what it may do to the existing coupling machinery must be avoided. Setting up of small coupling staffs without giving them substantial resources is self-defeating.

To improve coupling, the organization's top management must demand from its staff significant efforts aimed at 'engineering' of a sound and effective coupling machinery. As a minimum, this effort should first look at the dimensions of coupling and decide what kind and level of coupling effort is desirable and required. It should 'discover' what coupling processes are currently in existence, determine which areas of coupling are deficient, and select from the available coupling alternatives those which can be best exploited.

The availability of adequate resources for coupling should be ignored only at a peril to the program. These resources should include the money to pay for the organization of specific coupling events, the conduct of special studies and analyses, and for the provision of effective information support (such as specialized technological problems data banks, directories of points of contact, etc).

3. *Coupling Visibility and Accountability*

The world's most perfect coupling system will be suspected by the management as being inefficient if it is inauditable and invisible. In fact, it appears that the recent flurry of Congressional and Defense management's interests in this topic stem principally from the invisibility of R&D coupling. One solution to make coupling visible is to identify the coupling machinery in a structured way and document it in some form of a guide. Such a guide can show the 'lay' management how coupling is being achieved, as well as aid the newcomers to the organization by indoctrinating them with coupling philosophies and introducing them to coupling practices. In the government departments guides might also prove useful in dealing with the all-too-frequent Congressional criticisms of research relevance and R&D management.

To sum up, the discussion about the adequacy or short-comings of coupling can become more precise by defining what type of coupling is under consideration. Science-technology coupling is a tough game. The successful coupling program requires a strong support of the organization's management, the presence of reasonable coupling incentives, and a committment of adequate resources. When these conditions are met coupling can and will be improved.

References

1)   Donald C. Pelz and Frank M. Andres, *Scientists in Organizations*, John Wiley and Sons, Inc. New York, 1966.

2)   Arthur A. Ezra, *Overcoming Barriers in R&D Coupling, Office of Aerospace Research,* 14 March 1969 (AD 686430)

3) Melvin B. Zisfein et al., *Thraustics Interim Report*, AFOSR 69-2135 TR, Franklin Institute for Research Laboratories, August 1969.

4) C. A. Stone, et al., *Technology in Retrospect and Critical Events in Science*, Vol I (NSF-C-535) Illinois Institute of Technology Research Institute

5) Thomas J. Allen, *Problem Solving Strategies in Parallel Research and Development Projects*, MIT, Sloan School of Management Working Paper # 126-65, 1965.